CW00829481

THE WORLD OF PRIVATE BANKING

The World of Private Banking

Edited by
YOUSSEF CASSIS and PHILIP COTTRELL

Co-Edited by
MONIKA POHLE FRASER and IAIN L. FRASER

ASHGATE

© The editors and contributors 2009

All rights reserved. No part of this publication may be reproduced, stored in a retrieval system or transmitted in any form or by any means, electronic, mechanical, photocopying, recording or otherwise without the prior permission of the publisher.

Youssef Cassis and Philip Cottrell and have asserted their right under the Copyright, Designs and Patents Act, 1988, to be identified as the editors of this work.

Published by
Ashgate Publishing Limited
Wey Court East
Union Road
Farnham
Surrey, GU9 7PT
England

Ashgate Publishing Company
Suite 420
101 Cherry Street
Burlington
VT 05401-4405
USA

www.ashgate.com

British Library Cataloguing in Publication Data
The world of private banking. – (Studies in banking and financial history)
 1. Private banks—History—19th century. 2. Private banks—History—20th century.
 I. Series II. Cassis, Y., 1952–
 332.1'23'09–dc22

Library of Congress Cataloging-in-Publication Data
The world of private banking / Youssef Cassis ... [et al.].
     p. cm. — (Studies in banking and financial history)
 Includes bibliographical references and index.
 ISBN 978-1-85928-432-2 (hbk. : alk. paper) 1. Private banks—History. I. Cassis, Y.,
1952–

 HG1978.W67 2009
 332.1'23—dc22

                                                                2009010011

ISBN 9781859284322 (hbk)
ISBN 9780754695844 (ebk)

Mixed Sources
Product group from well-managed
forests and other controlled sources
www.fsc.org Cert no. SA-COC-1565
© 1996 Forest Stewardship Council
FSC

Printed and bound in Great Britain by
MPG Books Group, UK

Contents

List of Figures

List of Tables

Notes on Contributors

Melanie Aspey joined the Rothschild Archive as archivist in 1994, succeeding Victor Gray as director in 2004. Aspey edited *The Rothschild archive: Guide to the Collection* (London, 2000) and has written about aspects of the Archive's collection and Rothschild history for a number of journals and publications. Prior to joining Rothschild, she was archivist and records manager at News International plc (publisher of *The Times* and other British daily and weekly newspapers) and worked for the Business Archives Council, subsequently serving as a trustee and chairman of that organization for a number of years.

Youssef Cassis is professor of economic and social history at the University of Geneva and visiting fellow at the London School of Economics. He has published extensively on banking and financial history. His latest book, *Capitals of Capital: A History of International Financial Centres, 1780–2005*, was published in 2006 by Cambridge University Press.

Philip L. Cottrell is professor of economic and social history at Leicester University. He has published widely in the areas of international financial, business, economic and social history.

Niall Ferguson is Laurence A. Tisch Professor of history at Harvard University and William Ziegler Professor of business administration at Harvard Business School. He is also a senior research fellow of Jesus College, Oxford University, and a senior fellow of the Hoover Institution, Stanford University. His book *The World's Banker: the History of the House of Rothschild* (1998) won the Wadsworth Prize for Business History. He is also the author of *The Cash Nexus: Money and Power in the Modern World, 1700–2000* (2001) and numerous other books and articles.

Monika Pohle Fraser is an economic historian (D.Phil., European University Institute) and currently a post-doctorate fellow at the Forum for Contemporary History, University of Oslo. She also teaches political and social science courses at State University New York/FIT, Florence. She is currently working on Cold War development aid and European donor countries. Her field of interest and publications are mainly in international financial history of the nineteenth and twentieth centuries.

Victor Gray has taken a leading role in the development of archives in the UK, acting as Chairman of the National Council on Archives and a founder Board

Member of the Museums Libraries and Archives Council. He is currently President of the Society of Archivists. An archivist throughout his working life, he joined and developed the Rothschild Archive from 1993, becoming the first Director of the Rothschild Archive Trust in 2000. He retired from Rothschild in 2004.

Martin Körner † was professor of early modern history at the University of Bern, where he directed the research project 'Bernese state finance in the early modern period'. His many publications include *Solidarités financiers suisses au XVIème siècle* (Lausanne, Payot, 1980) and 'The Swiss Confederation', in R. Bonney (ed.), *The Rise of the Fiscal State in Europe c.1200–1815* (Oxford, 1999).

Ginette Kurgan-van Hentenryck is professor emeritus of Université Libre de Bruxelles and member of the Royal Academy of Belgium. Former dean of the Faculty of Arts and president of the Institute of European Studies, she promoted the Groupe d'Histoire du Patronat de l'U.L.B. She is the editor of *Dictionnaire des patrons en Belgique: Les hommes, les entreprises, les réseaux* (1996), author of *Léopold II et les groupes financiers belges en Chine* (Brussels, 1972), *Rail, finance et politique: les entreprises Philippart (1865–1890)* (Brussels, 1982), *Gouverner la Générale de Belgique: Essai de biographie collective* (Bruxelles, 1996), and co-author of *The Generale Bank* (Brussels, 1997) and *A History of European Banking* (Antwerp, 2000). Her publications concern Belgian economic and social history as well as international relations of Belgium during the nineteenth and twentieth centuries.

David Kynaston was born in 1951 and read Modern History at New College, Oxford. He has been a professional historian since 1973. His principal work is a four-volume history of the City of London, 1815–2000, published between 1994 and 2001. He has also written histories of the *Financial Times*, Cazenove and LIFFE, as well as co-writing a history of Phillips & Drew. With Richard Roberts he has co-edited a history of the Bank of England and co-written a book on the modern City. His latest publication is *Austerity Britain, 1945–1951* (2007). He is a visiting professor at Kingston University.

Dr John Orbell was formerly Head of Corporate Information Services at ING Bank, London Branch, where, inter alia, he was responsible for The Baring Archive and ING's London art collection. He retired in late 2004. He has published in the areas of business archives and business history and is a fellow of the Royal Historical Society and of the Royal Society of Arts. He is currently updating his earlier publication, *Tracing the History of a Business*, and, with Francis Goodall and Richard Storey, is compiling an updated bibliography of British business histories.

Edwin J. Perkins is emeritus professor of history, University of Southern California. He earned his doctoral degree under Alfred Chandler at Johns Hopkins University in 1972. Previously, he had earned an MBA from the University of

Virginia and worked for the Chase Manhattan Bank in New York City. Among his publications are *Financing Anglo-American Trade: the House of Brown, 1800–1880* (Harvard University Press, 1975), *American Public Finance and Financial Services, 1700–1815* (Ohio State University Press, 1994), and *Charles Merrill and Middle Class Investors* (Cambridge University Press, 1999).

Alain Plessis, *agrégé d'histoire*, *docteur d'État* and alumnus of the École Normale Supérieure, is professor emeritus at the University of Paris X Nanterre. His many publications in the field of financial history include *La Banque de France pendant le Second Empire*, 3 vols (1982–85), *Histoire de la Banque de France* (1998) and, together with Michel Lescure, *Banques locales et banques régionales en France au XIXe siècle* (1999).

Luciano Segreto is professor of economic history at the University of Florence. His main research interests are in post-WW2 international business and financial history. Chairman of the Cultural Memory Council of the ICCA, he is a member of the Scientific Committee of the Maison des Sciences de l'Homme d'Aquitaine and of many international journals. Among his most recent publications are *Giacinto Motta: Un ingegnere alla testa del capitalismo industriale italiano* (Rome Bari, Laterza, 2004), *Produrre per il mondo: L'industria reggiana dalla crisi petrolifera alla globalizzazione*, edited by G.L. Basini, G. Lugli and L. Segreto (Rome Bari, Laterza, 2005), *East–West Trade in Cold War Europe: National Interests and Hypocrisy*, in *Towards a New Europe. Identity, Economics, Institutions: Different Experiences*, edited by A. Tonini (Florence, 2006).

Gabriele Teichmann studied history, English literature and philosophy at Bonn and Edinburgh universities. After taking her exams, she worked at the department for economic and social history of Bonn University as well as for the German Association for Business History. In 1985, she started her career with Sal. Oppenheim jr. & Cie. whose head of archives she became in 1989. She has authored or co-authored several books and articles on the history of the Oppenheim bank and family, among them *Wägen und Wagen: Sal. Oppenheim jr. & Cie.: Geschichte einer Bank und einer Familie*, 3rd edn (Munich, 1994 = English edition: *Striking the Balance: Sal. Oppenheim jr. & Cie. a Family and a Bank*, London 1994) and *Faszination Orient: Max von Oppenheim. Forscher, Sammler, Diplomat* (Cologne, 2nd edn 2002). Within the EABH, she has served on a number of committees like the Academic Advisory Council and the Bureau.

Pat Thane has been professor of contemporary British history, Institute of Historical Research, University of London since October 2002. She was professor of contemporary history at the University of Sussex 1994–2002. Her publications include: *The Foundations of the Welfare State* (Longman, 1982 2nd edn, 1996), *Women and Gender Policies: Women and the Rise of the European Welfare States, 1880s–1950s*, co-ed. with Gisela Bock (Routledge, 1990), *Old Age from Antiquity* *to Post-Modernity*, co-ed. with Paul Johnson (Routledge, 1998), *Old Age in England: Past Experiences, Present Issues* (Oxford University Press, May 2000), *Women and Ageing in Britain since 1500*, co-ed. with Lynne Botelho (Longman, 2001), *The Long History of Old Age*, ed. (Thames and Hudson, 2005).

Dieter Ziegler is professor of economic and business history at Ruhr-University Bochum. He has written extensively on British and German business and social history, especially about banks and bankers. The most recent monographs are *Die Industrielle Revolution* (Darmstadt, 2005) and *Die Dresdner Bank und die deutschen Juden (= Die Dresdner Bank im Dritten Reich*, vol. 2 (Munich, 2006).

Introduction

Youssef Cassis and Monika Pohle Fraser

Continuity and Change

The recent rise of private equity is a timely reminder of the persistence of private – as opposed to corporate – interests within the world of finance. The demise of private banking – understood, as it will be in this book, in the broad sense of the word to include merchant and investment banks, as well as finance houses – has been predicted or retrospectively analysed many times over the past 150 years, and yet it has never really occurred. Of course, private banking has declined – if only because there was a time when all banks, with the exception of central banks and a few other public institutions, were private banks. For a while, during the second third of the nineteenth century, they held their own against the emerging joint stock banks. They then became increasingly marginalized without, however, losing all significance, depending on the country and the financial activity in which they specialized – investment banking and wealth management, for example, have traditionally been better suited to private forms of ownership and control than commercial banking.

The story of private banking could, however, be sketched in a different way. In many respects, private banks have always flourished in fairly narrow segments within the world of banking and finance, even during the golden age of private banks, before the emergence of joint stock banks, even when Rothschilds and Barings were the 'masters of the universe'. For the golden age of private banks, from the late eighteenth to the mid-nineteenth century, was an age when banking was still very much in its infancy. Banks and bank offices were few in number; their level of assets and liabilities was, by any measure, very low; a bank account was the privilege of a tiny elite; and the business of banking was mainly subordinate to the needs of trade and commerce. The rise of banking, as an economic pursuit in its own right and as an engine – as well as a product – of modern economic growth, is concomitant with the rise of the joint stock banks. Private banks, to be sure, played a decisive role in this development, both as forerunners (deposit banking in Britain and universal banking in Germany, for example, having their roots in the two countries' private banks' traditions) and as initiators (many a joint stock bank was established by private bankers). But they were no longer the main players once the game took on a new dimension.

From this perspective, the history of private banking displays far greater continuity than usually assumed and this continuity makes its history all the more relevant to the understanding of recent developments.

Whether in their golden age, in times of decline or in eras of revival, private banks have performed the same type of functions. They have been involved in

rather specialized activities, free from competition from joint stock banks. They
have usually dealt with fairly exclusive customers, for example high net worth
individuals, to use today's terminology, or foreign governments. The volume of
their business has tended to be comparatively low (if measured by the number of
customers or branches), but their profit margins relatively high. And they have
consistently been able to influence, and sometimes lead, the profession, through
their socio-professional status, their networks of relationships, but also their
innovative capacity. There have been some digressions from this pattern: private
country banks in particular, which flourished in the nineteenth century in countries
such as France and Germany, were clearly catering for 'ordinary' customers. And
some of the 'specialized' areas dominated by private bankers could be very large
indeed, for example the international issuing business in the City of London
before the First World War. But they are the exceptions that confirm the rule:
throughout their history, private banks have been specialist, rather than generalist,
financial institutions.

Private banking has also been essentially a matter of networks. First and
foremost family networks, as private banks have tended to be family firms – they
can be defined as banks whose owners are also managers, legally organized as
partnerships or general partnerships, with partners having unlimited responsibility.[1]
As institutions, private banks can still be defined in this way today, and some
of them are still alive and kicking, especially in Geneva, the 'capital of private
banking'. However, the notion of 'private banking' has changed since the last
quarter of the twentieth century and now designates a specific activity – portfolio
management on behalf of very wealthy individuals – rather than a form of business
organization. This activity is nowadays mostly being carried out by large universal
banks, and yet family networks are still part of private banking, for example in
the management of family wealth, as witnessed by the development of the
Family Office. Religious networks have been another major constituent, often
superimposed to family ones, as exemplified by national or international banking
dynasties – the Rothschilds being the most famous though by no means the only
such example. The largest networks were formed by the Protestant and Jewish
religious minorities, the former dominant in the eighteenth century, the latter in
the nineteenth, with other denominations, not least the Quakers, also leaving their
mark. Religious networks have certainly weakened, though they have not entirely
disappeared and still play a role in terms of cultural identity. Moreover, elements
of their *modus operandi* can be found in other types of network relationships –
political, ethnic, 'old boys', and others. Finally, social networks have also been part
of the fabric of private banking, here again often in conjunction with family and
religious factors. The gradual integration of private bankers into the upper classes
from the mid-nineteenth century and their ever closer links with the political elites
have been both a cause and a consequence of their moving their business upmarket

---

[1]   Limited partnerships and even joint stock companies whose directors retained the
major part of the capital should also be considered as 'private banks'.

– a position best described by the notion of *haute banque*, which has kept its resonance to this day.

Networks and specialization thus best characterize the history of private banks over the last 250 years. However, identifying these long-term features should not obscure two facts. First, that changes have taken place in their domains of specialization – from commercial banking to wealth management for some, from trade finance to corporate finance for others, to put it in very broad terms. And second, that their significance, in economic, political and social terms, was at its highest during the 'classical' period going from the late eighteenth century to the First World War. This book explores the history of private banking, in its multifarious aspects, during these years.

The Rothschilds: Archetypal and Exceptional

Rothschild is the first name to spring to mind in connection with private banks – even though Walter Bagehot did not consider the Rothschilds as bankers in the narrow English sense of the word, i.e. deposit takers, but as 'immense capitalists'.[2] As Niall Ferguson clearly shows in chapter 1, the Rothschilds were the world's largest private bank for most of the nineteenth century and recognised as such by their contemporaries. The Rothschilds might appear as the archetypal private bankers because of this immediate association between their name and their trade, yet in almost every other respect they were truly exceptional. In terms of size, they were not only the largest private bank; the group's resources (with banks in Frankfurt, London, Paris, Vienna and Naples) remained larger than those of any joint stock bank well until the 1880s, even though the latter included clients' deposits. In terms of wealth, they were collectively the world's richest family. The links keeping the family together were tighter than for other international banking dynasties, such as the Bischoffsheim, the Speyers, the Seligmans and others, with an exceptionally high rate of intermarriage within the Rothschild family (14 out of 18 at the second generation, and still 13 out of 30 at the third generation).

Most importantly, the Rothschilds were dominant in government finance, the most prestigious preserve of the *haute banque* – an activity bestowing both economic and political influence, at home and abroad. Between 1865 and 1914, they handled, solely or in partnership, nearly three quarters of the foreign public sector issues floated in London, the world's leading international financial centre. The Rothschilds faced increasing competition from the 1870s, from both joint stock and private banks. They maintained their supremacy amongst the latter until the First World War, when they eventually returned to normal without, however, losing their legendary status.

---

[2]   W. Bagehot, *Lombard Street: A Description of the Money Market* (London, 1873), p. 214.

Like that of the banking house that has produced them, the wealth of the Rothschild archives is truly exceptional. As Victor Gray and Melanie Aspey show in chapter 2, despite unavoidable loss and destruction, they are of unrivalled interest not only to banking and financial historians, but also to those concerned with political, social, cultural, art and even natural history. The richest material consists of the letters (some 20,000 in total) that the five brothers wrote to each other between 1814 and 1868; written in Judendeutsch, and thus extremely difficult to understand, they have recently been translated and transcribed. But there also the letters from the Rothschilds' correspondents and agents (hundreds of thousands) as well as a huge non-banking material, related to the very wide range of activities in which the family has been involved. In the last twenty years or so, the collections of the Rothschild Archives have been promoted to a wide audience, not least through the publication of a guide, available on the Archive's website. They are now the responsibility of the Rothschild Archive Trust, a charitable trust created in 1999 to ensure the future of the collection and encourage international research.

Patterns of Business Development

The role of private banks in the new financial and corporate environment created, from the mid-nineteenth century, by the growth of the joint stock banks is of particular interest to their long-term historical development. The question is examined in chapter 3 by Youssef Cassis, who rejects a 'decline and fall' framework of analysis and shows, on the contrary, that the fate of private banks varied considerably depending on the country, region, or banking activity. Private bankers engaged in international finance were far more successful in the City of London, where merchant banks were able to maintain their hold on the huge accepting and issuing businesses, than in Paris and Berlin, where the competition from the joint stock banks was much stiffer. Conversely, private deposit banking declined sharply in Britain, but survived in France and Germany, where hundreds of private country banks provided agricultural credit and industrial finance to small and medium-sized enterprises in the provinces, from which the joint stock banks were mostly absent. In both cases, private banks were able to find a niche where they enjoyed a competitive advantage against the big banks. Private bankers, above all members of the *haute banque* in continental Europe, also played a decisive role in the creation of the new joint stock banks, usually to seize the opportunity to raise vast amounts of capital in order to finance large-scale investment. They were often able to keep a strategic control over these new institutions, at any rate until the First World War – a success primarily attributable to their socio-professional status and their network of relationships. Not surprisingly, international bankers proved more successful than country bankers over the longer term, whether as private bankers or as directors of joint stock banks. While the latter were all but wiped out by the depression of the 1930s, the latter survived well into the 1960s.

In chapter 4, Philip Cottrell provides a thorough analysis of the institutional changes taking place in the centre of world finance, the City of London, during the middle decades of the nineteenth century. Cottrell describes the years 1855–1883 as London's 'First Big Bang', a critical period comparable, in terms of institutional restructuring, to the 'Financial Revolution' of the late seventeenth and early eighteenth centuries and 'Big Bang' in the late twentieth century. The changes were brought about by a combination of economic and political developments – the decline of the inland bill of exchange and Britain's increasing exports of capital and the liberalization of company legislation, with the introduction of limited liability and its later extension to banking. The result was the creation of numerous corporate financial institutions which came to dominate most of the City's activities.

However, as Cottrell clearly shows, the institutional restructuring taking place over the mid-nineteenth century was a long-drawn process, if only because of the period's financial instability, and personal enterprise remained a leading or a significant force in a few areas. In the money market, a couple of corporate discount houses ended up handling most of the business, without eliminating a dozen or so partnerships from the scene; while in domestic commercial banking, the London private banks held their own until 1890. The period witnessed a wave of creation of overseas corporate banks as well as finance companies. The latter, mostly short-lived second-rate affairs, were active in company promotion and railway finance but made no inroads in foreign loans and international acceptances, which remained the preserve of the merchant banks – the only type of bank ultimately managing to remain 'private banks'.

This pattern of business development, leading to the ultimate demise of private banks, is reflected in the banks' archives. Large commercial banks, especially in Britain, have been formed through an amalgamation process involving scores of private banks – well over 100 in the case of the NatWest Group (now incorporated into Royal Bank of Scotland), discussed by Fiona Maccoll in chapter 5. Their records are uneven, the archives of small, short-lived banks having often disappeared. In the case of private banks, the distinction between family and business papers is not always apparent, especially in the early days of private bankers, and the former can often fruitfully complement the latter. However, some family papers, including private account books and correspondence, did find their way into the parent bank's archives, thus shedding further light on the activities of several houses, including the Smith banking partnerships, Jones Loyd, Becketts, Prescotts, or Stuckeys – all well-known names in Victorian Britain.

The International Economy

International finance has traditionally been private bankers' privileged domain of activity. This is vividly illustrated by the activities and organization of the leading Anglo-American houses in the nineteenth century, studied by Edwin Perkins in chapter 6. Perkins takes a long-term view and shows how the Anglo-American market moved from being dominated by trade and trade-financing activities in the late eighteenth and early nineteenth centuries to a strong emphasis on large capital transfers through portfolio investment in the second half of the nineteenth century.

Six leading houses dominated that market: Barings, Browns, Rothschilds, Peabody/Morgan, Seligmans, and Kuhn Loeb. Barings were dominant in the early stage, until the 1830s, combining commercial and financial activities, but failed or were reluctant to commit sufficient resources to the American side of their business. They were followed by Browns, who built powerful organizational capacities on both sides of the Atlantic, but remained exceedingly confined to trade finance. The Rothschilds had the financial means to dominate the American market but never sent members of the family to the United States. In the end, and despite significant differences in business organization, the three leading houses in the later part of the nineteenth century, JP Morgan, Seligmans and Kuhn Loeb, all had their headquarters in New York City, a necessary condition once the provision of investment banking services had become the dominant activity.

These houses undoubtedly belonged to a group known in France as the 'Haute Banque' – the upper echelons, in both professional and social terms, of the private banking world, discussed by Alain Plessis in chapter 7. The group was never very clearly defined, as membership was unofficial and based on prestige and reputation. Nevertheless, Plessis clearly underlines its international dimension, which can be seen as one of its defining characteristics. It is significant, for example, that the banking families making up the 'Haute Banque' were often from foreign origins, especially as far as its Protestant and Jewish components were concerned. Moreover, these families retained links with their friends and relatives in foreign countries, not least through marriages and intermarriages, hence appearing as a cosmopolitan world, not entirely assimilated into the French elite. This internationalism was reinforced by travelling, especially in the form of apprenticeships and work experience with a friendly firm in a foreign country.

Above all, the French 'Haute Banque' was international through its activities. Interestingly, with the exception of the Rothschilds and a couple of other houses, their business appears to have been dominated by French credit and financial transactions during their so-called golden age, until the 1860s. Alain Plessis put their decline in the last quarter of the twentieth century into perspective. Their number might have diminished and they were increasingly sidelined by the large joint stock banks. However, they still played a far from insignificant role in international finance, becoming at the same time far more internationally oriented. Mallet Frères, the oldest though not the largest house in the group, is a case in point. Its total balance sheet increased almost threefold between 1860 and 1913, mostly as a result of its international activities: acceptances, in particular, made up 33 to 40 per cent of liabilities in 1913, as against 9 per cent in 1860; while the proportion of foreign accounts rose from one third to two thirds. Other houses appear to have followed the same pattern, securing not only their survival but their prosperity through their adaptation to the global economy.

   Throughout the nineteenth century, the City of London was the world's leading
financial centre, and Baring Brothers were only second to the Rothschilds in the
field of international banking and finance. In chapter 8, John Orbell provides
a useful overview of the London merchant banks' main activities, focusing on
the case of Baring Brothers. They ranged from merchanting and agency work to
corporate finance advice, private banking, and security management. Two of them,
however, were at the core of their business: finance of international trade and
security issuance, and are rightly paid closer attention. One of the chapter's main
interests is the way John Orbell not only presents the very rich material available
in the ING Baring archives (accounts, correspondence with clients and agents,
information books and so on), with occasional reference to that of other merchant
banks, but also underlines its relevance to the study of all aspects of merchant banks'
activities, and identifies the areas which have remained unexplored and could
benefit from systematic use of the records – the whole amounting to a research
programme on private banks and the international economy.

Industrialization

Dieter Ziegler and Luciano Segreto reassess, in chapters 9 and 10, the role and
importance of private bankers during industrialization and the alleged reasons
for their decline. Both take issue with the widely accepted Gerschenkronian
argument that only joint-stock banks could supply the necessary capital to
leading-sector industries.

   For Germany, Ziegler points out that even earlier, by the 1850s, demand for
capital was outrunning private bankers' resources and that the famous banking
dynasties were not amongst the pioneers in industry finance. Still, by the mid-
1850s, when the first joint-stock banks were founded, the basic railway network
linking the Zollverein regions was already built, its length being second only to
the British system. It was not that universal banks squeezed out private banks
from the second half of the nineteenth century and into the twentieth, but rather
that a division of labour evolved, in which a limited number of private banks
had gained an important position. For example, industry and commerce were
not confined to big concerns, and in particular medium-sized industry in the
provinces relied on local private bankers well into the twentieth century, writes
Ziegler. Private banks supplied services which universal banks were unwilling or
unable to provide. Examples include small- to medium-scale finance, rendered
cumbersome and unprofitable by the universal banks' increased bureaucratization,
centralization and hierarchical management style. During the stabilization crisis
German universal banks were simply unable to obtain foreign credit, a 'niche' that
old-established private bankers filled with ease.

   Lastly, in a Gerschenkronian framework of interpretation the de facto
disappearance of private banks in Germany after 1945 looks like a 'natural' result
of market forces. Ziegler shows convincingly that in the case of Germany, the

decline of private banking has to be postponed until the 1930s, when private banks indeed lost many of their 'niches'. It is instead non-economic factors, like the racist policy of the Third Reich, that explain the decline in private banking towards 1945 and after.

Luciano Segreto addresses the different sequence of events in Italy. While statistical analysis has shown that universal banks had from the 1890s crowded out private banks and other lenders in regard to industry finance, he demonstrates that hardly any business was conducted by universal banks without the involvement of one or more private banks. Segreto offers an intriguing picture of the presence of Italian private banks in joint industry finance between 1890 and 1914, thereby confirming the division-of-labour hypothesis. The fact that private banks had de-specialized, taking up industry and railroad finance, might have been overlooked by financial historians, because those banks did not change their company structures accordingly. Limited liability partnerships remained rare until the early twentieth century and private bankers' partaking in major deals under the wings of bigger joint-stock banks remained undetected. In the Italian case personal banking, based on trust and discretion, and often on family ties, remained important through the late nineteenth century and well into the 20th. The weakness of the emergent new State and its enormous financial needs offered a leading role to several major bankers who were particularly adroit in negotiating between the government, parliament, the central banks and the international financial centres, writes Segreto. Towards the end of the nineteenth century re-specialization may have taken place, as indicated by the repeated appearance of certain private bankers specifically in relation to industry finance undertaken by mixed banks.

The private bankers are thought to have been needed not so much to help joint-stock banks spread risk, as above all to secure the placement of securities with the various urban elites. The importance of this specific type of intermediation would seem to be underscored by the stability in the number of private bankers in the years 1913 to 1924, but perhaps even more so by its growth in the war years, which brought the figures for the country's seven major financial centres back to the levels of 1896. Segreto attributes the dramatic decline in the number of private banks after the mid 1920s mainly to the introduction of banking laws which de facto greatly restricted private banks' traditional ways of doing business.

For both, Italy and Germany, it seems to be the big regional private banks whose role in industry finance has been diminished by looking at industrialization through a Gerschenkronian lens. Gabriele Teichmann's study naturally complements the two preceding chapters by putting the spotlight on one of the most successful early industry financiers in nineteenth-century Germany, the Cologne-based bank Sal. Oppenheim. The Oppenheims occupied the middle ranks of the European *haute banque*. They had strong ties with big and medium-sized entrepreneurs in the industrial regions of Germany, France, Belgium, and Luxembourg (to name the most frequent contacts). They pioneered joint-stock banks and kept in close contact as these grew into big universal banks in the second half of the nineteenth century. Teichmann is the archivist of Sal. Oppenheim and provides a 'user's guide' to the Oppenheim Archive.

She maintains that 'for the scholar of banking history ... the Oppenheim Archive is a must if doing research on the industrialization process in Germany between 1825 and 1870'. The archive, formally established in 1939 as one of the first banking archives in Germany, was not initially supposed to be used by outsiders, but to serve as a quick-and-easy means of information for members of the Oppenheim family, writes Teichmann. The establishment of the archive came at a time when the family was under great pressure from the Nazi regime because of its Jewish ancestry. The archive therefore became a symbol of the family's unbroken sense of tradition and its will to persevere. The archival records pertaining to their activities, mainly in shipping and railways, mining and heavy industry, insurance business and banking, are arranged in files devoted to the various companies. In addition, there is the business and private correspondence of the two Oppenheim brothers who ran the bank through the crucial years 1825–70.

Religion, Culture and Society

Socio-cultural factors, primarily religion, have been an integral part of private banking, possibly more so than in any other economic activity. In chapter 12 Ginette Kurgan-van Hentenryck provides an analytical survey of the economic role, social position and political influence of Jewish private bankers in the nineteenth and twentieth centuries, emphasizing the importance of personal and family networks. Their activities originated in the eighteenth century in trade finance in Britain, in international finance in France, in the securities business in the Netherlands, and in the business activities of the *Hofjuden* in Germany. From then on their financial transactions, and often the families themselves, spread across Europe's main financial centres and, later in the nineteenth century, New York. Government loans, as well as trade finance in Britain, made up an essential part of their business, though railway promotion should not be underestimated, especially in France and Germany. Jewish private bankers were also instrumental in the creation of the early joint stock banks, beginning with the Banque de Belgique in 1835 and including the Crédit Mobilier of the Pereire brothers in France as well as the four 'D' Banks in Germany – Darmstädter, Disconto, Deutsche and Dresdner. Their economic influence waned after the First World War, and they were eliminated by the Nazi regime in Germany. However, throughout the twentieth century, they retained a high degree of creativity, as witnessed by the role of Lazards in the merger and acquisition business or of Warburgs in the birth of the Euromarkets.

The economic achievements of Jewish private bankers were partly the result of the nature of their networks – based on strict endogamy; extending internationally; and with loyalty to Judaism being in many cases less a question of religiosity and more a clannish attitude. On the other hand, the wealth and status provided by these achievements did not lead to the same level of integration in all countries, with Jewish private bankers gaining greater acceptance in England, where anti-Semitism was less virulent than elsewhere, and Belgium and France than Germany.

In all countries, direct political involvement was unusual among Jewish bankers, though they were concerned with politics and did enjoy a degree of influence, especially when their advice or services was sought by governments.

The other major religious network, that of Protestant bankers, is analysed by the late Martin Körner, who rightly points out in chapter 13 that, unlike Jewish bankers, who were part of a religious minority in all the countries where they traded, Protestant bankers became part of the majority in Lutheran and Calvinist countries during the sixteenth century.

Protestant banking came into being as merchants and merchant bankers converted from Catholicism to Protestantism. Its network of relationships became internationally visible as early as the sixteenth century, through the financial solidarity existing between European Protestants, especially Swiss, and the Calvinist party in France – an international network which was older and wider than the more restrictive *Internationale Huguenote*, which was limited to the Calvinist banking world.

In non-Protestant countries, Protestant banking was particularly strong in France, as a result of the French state's growing financial needs and the funds provided by the Huguenot International. In the second half of the seventeenth century, Swiss financiers set up branches in Paris where the Protestant bank became increasingly powerful, reaching its apex with Necker's appointment as general financial controller in 1776. In Germany, by contrast, the most important merchant bankers remained Catholic after the Reformation, though the number of Protestant bankers, such as Metzler and Bethmann in Frankfurt, grew in the later eighteenth century. In Catholic Vienna, the dominant position reached by Protestant bankers and financiers such as Wiesenhütter, Steiner, or Johann Fries might well have been due to the government attempts at escaping Jewish finance. As a minority in Catholic countries, Protestants bankers displayed high rates of intermarriage and relied on their financial expertise and networks of relationships for their socio-economic success. As a group, their significance waned in the nineteenth century.

Social status has been an essential attribute of private bankers – resulting from their wealth, family inheritance and gradual integration into the upper classes. From the late nineteenth century, respectability and connections in the highest social circles still enabled private bankers to deal with the most exclusive customers, not least foreign governments, even though their firms were dwarfed in size by the joint stock banks. Social status entailed responsibilities. As Pat Thane clearly shows in chapter 14, elites were committed to philanthropy in Victorian and Edwardian England, a commitment led by the Royal Family. For the financial elites, especially the newcomers and parvenus, supporting the numerous charities of the Prince of Wales, the future King Edward VII, was the price to pay for gaining social respectability. However, she also shows that philanthropy cannot be entirely explained by the aim of checking the advance of socialism nor the desire for social acceptance. A concern for the sufferings of others was also clearly at work, not least among Jewish financiers who felt compassion for the poverty of their co-religionists who had emigrated to Britain from the early 1880s. While the level of philanthropic aid cannot be measured quantitatively, the works of benefactors such as Baron and Baroness de Hirsch, the Bischoffsheims, and Ernest Cassel shed light on a major aspect of the socio-cultural dimension of private banking.

More than any other group of private bankers, the merchant bankers of the City of London were able to rely on the strength of their social assets. Unlike their counterparts in other major European financial centres, they not only survived as family firms well until the 1960s, but continued to form, both socially and professionally, a banking aristocracy in what remained one of the world's two leading financial centres. Looking at recent memoirs, David Kynaston suggests, in the book's final chapter, that their social profile, based on wealth, family inheritance and social connections persisted into the four to five decades following the First World War. He also analyses the complex process of continuity and change in the leading merchant banks, as the City was gradually transformed by the advent of the Euromarkets, its invasion by American banks, and ultimately the 'Big Bang' of 1986. However, private banking had by then taken a new, different meaning, private wealth management – an activity requiring social assets reminiscent of those of the private banker of old.

CHAPTER 1

The Rise of the Rothschilds: the Family Firm as Multinational[1]

Niall Ferguson

This chapter attempts to explain the rapid rise of the Rothschild bank to a position of supremacy in international finance between around 1810 and 1836. The first section describes the size of the bank, which, for most of the nineteenth century, was the biggest bank in the world in terms of capital. The second section discusses the business the Rothschilds did, in particular their development of the international bond market. The third section discusses the structure of the partnership. The fourth section shows how intermarriage helped ensure that capital remained in the family. Finally, an attempt is made to identify the Rothschilds' distinctive business methods. These, it is suggested, provide the best explanation for the Rothschilds' astonishing success.

Between around 1810 and 1836, the five sons of Mayer Amschel Rothschild rose from the obscurity of the Frankfurt *Judengasse* to attain a position of unequalled power in international finance. Despite numerous economic and political crises and the efforts of their competitors to match them, they still occupied that position when the youngest of them died in 1868; and even after that their dominance was only slowly eroded. So extraordinary did this achievement seem to contemporaries that they often sought to explain it in mystical terms. According to one account dating from the 1830s, the Rothschilds owed their fortune to the possession of a mysterious 'Hebrew talisman'. It was this which enabled Nathan Rothschild, the founder of the London house, to become 'the leviathan of the money markets of Europe'.[2] Similar stories were being told in the Russian Pale as late as the 1890s.[3] They form part of a complex web of fantasy which has been – and continues to be – woven around the name Rothschild.

[1] This chapter draws on my book *The World's Banker: a History of the House of Rothschild* (London, 1998). I would like to express my gratitude to Sir Evelyn de Rothschild for giving me unrestricted access to the firm's pre-1918 archive in London (henceforth RAL), and to Victor Gray, Melanie Aspey and their assistants. I would also like to thank the archivists at the Archives Nationales, Paris (henceforth AN), the Centre for the Preservation of Historical and Documentary Collections, Moscow (henceforth CPHDCM) and the Frankfurt Stadtarchiv, as well as those at the other archives and libraries I have used. I have received invaluable research assistance from Abigail Green, Edward Lipman and Rainer Liedtke, as well as Katherine Astill, Glen O'Hara, Harry Seekings and Andrew Vereker.

[2] Anon., *The Hebrew Talisman* (London, 1840), pp. 28ff.

[3] H. Iliowzi, *'In the Pale': Stories and Legends of the Russian Jews* (Philadelphia, 1897).

This chapter, however, is not concerned with the Rothschild myth but with the reality of their rise as bankers. For reasons of space, it mainly concentrates on the period prior to Nathan Rothschild's death in 1836. This was in fact the period when the Rothschilds made their most important contribution to 'the making of modern capitalism'. In part, their contribution was a matter of scale: as the first section of the chapter shows, there had never been a larger concentration of capital than that accumulated by the Rothschild brothers. The second section discusses the various types of business they did, attaching special importance to their development of the international bond market, but also considering their role in the markets for commercial bills, commodities, bullion and insurance. The third section discusses the structure of the partnership. The fourth section shows how exceptionally frequent intermarriage complemented the partnership system by ensuring that capital remained in the family. In the fifth and final section, an attempt is made to characterize the Rothschilds' distinctive business ethos and to identify a set of Rothschild business rules. These, it is suggested, provide the best explanation for the Rothschilds' astonishing success.

Previous attempts to analyse the surviving accounts of the five 'houses' have been hampered by the inaccessibility of archives in London and Moscow.[4] These have now been opened. Analysis, however, is less easy than might be imagined, for two reasons. First, the Rothschilds did not keep accounts in a modern way; indeed, to begin with they hardly kept them at all. The system of partnership contracts (described below) necessitated the drawing up of balance sheets, but at irregular intervals. Nevertheless, it is possible to reconstruct from these documents a fairly satisfactory series for the capital of the combined Rothschild houses. Table 1.1 summarizes the available figures for the combined capital of the various houses in the period 1818–52:

Table 1.1   Combined Rothschild capital, 1818–1852 (thousands of £)

	1818	1825	1828	1836	1844	1852
Frankfurt	680	1,450	1,534	2,121	2,750	2,746
Paris	350	1,490	1,466	1,774	2,311	3,542
London	742	1,142	1,183	1,733	2,005	2,500
Vienna			25	110	250	83
Naples			130	268	463	661
Total	1,772	4,082	4,338	6,008	7,778	9,532

Sources: CPHDCM, 637/1/3/1–11; 1/6/5; 1/6/7/7–14; 1/6/32; 1/6/44–45; 1/7/48–69; 1/7/115–120; 1/8/1–7; 1/9/1–4; RAL, RFamFD/3, B/1; Archives Nationales, 132 AQ 1, 2, 3, 5, 6, 7, 9, 10, 13, 15, 16, 17, 19; B. Gille, *La Maison Rothschild*, vol. II, pp. 568–72.

---

    [4]   The most scholarly work on the subject is the two volumes by B. Gille, *Histoire de la Maison Rothschild, vol. I: Des origines à 1848* (Geneva, 1965) and *Histoire de la Maison Rothschild, vol. II: 1848–70* (Geneva, 1967), which is almost exclusively based on the archives of the Paris house.

Surviving figures for the individual houses are patchy, especially before 1830. For the London house, no comprehensive accounts have survived before 1828, though there is a complete series of profit-and-loss accounts beginning the following year. The accounts are simple: on one side all the year's sales of commodities, stocks and shares are listed; on the other, all the year's purchases and other costs; the difference is recorded as the annual profit or loss. Table 1.2 gives the 'bottom line' data for the period up until 1844.

Table 1.2   Profits and capital at N.M. Rothschild & Sons, 1829–1844 (£)

	Profit/Loss	Capital at end of year	Profit as percentage of capital
1829		1,123,897	
1830	-56,361	1,067,536	-5.0
1831	56,324	1,123,860	5.3
1832	58,919	1,182,779	5.2
1833	75,294	1,258,073	6.4
1834	303,939	1,562,011	24.2
1835	69,732	1,733,404	4.5
1836	-72,018	1,661,386	-4.2
1837	87,353	1,747,169	5.3
1838	83,124	1,820,706	4.8
1839	52,845	1,773,941	3.1
1840	30,937	1,804,878	1.7
1841	-49,769	1,755,109	-2.8
1842	40,451	1,795,560	2.3
1843	23,766	1,819,326	1.3
1844	170,977	1,990,303	9.4

Source: RAL, RFamFD/13F.

Plainly, there were substantial fluctuations in performance, ranging from the very successful (1834), when profits were close to a quarter of capital, to the disappointing (1830, 1836 and 1841). Averaged out, however, profits were rather unremarkable in relation to capital compared with figures for other banks, though this may reflect the fact that all expenses – including the partners' interest on their capital shares – were deducted before net profits were calculated. Thus the figure for profits (or losses) shown here was simply added to (or deducted from) the previous year's capital.[5]

---

[5]   Other merchant banks seem to have defined profits quite differently, which makes comparison in terms of profitability difficult: see on this point J. Armstrong and S. Jones, *Business Documents: Their Origins, Sources and Use in Historical Research* (London/New York, 1987).

The other house for which detailed accounts survive is the much smaller Naples house. Considering its size, the Naples house was singularly profitable, especially in the first decade of its existence. Its average annual profits were more than £30,000 between 1825 and 1829, at a time when its capital was little more than £130,000; and throughout the 1830s and 1840s its profits averaged around £20,000.[6] Unlike the London Paris house, it appears never to have recorded a loss prior to 1848, despite the financial crises of 1825, 1830 and 1836.

There are, unfortunately, no complete data for the profits of the Paris, Frankfurt or Vienna houses in this period. In the French case, the only surviving figures are for the years 1824–8, and they simply tell us the extent of the damage done to James's position by the crisis of 1825 (when his losses totalled no less than £356,000) and the speed with which he recovered from the setback.[7] However, it is possible to infer average annual profits for all the houses from the combined capital accounts (table 1.3), though the irregular periods which elapsed between agreements make these a rather rough guide to performance. These suggest – rather unexpectedly – that the London house was in fact the least economically successful of the three principal Rothschild houses: average annual profits were significantly higher at both Frankfurt and Paris for the period 1818–44.

Table 1.3   Average annual profits, five Rothschild houses, 1818–1844 (£thousands)

	1818–25	1825–28	1828–36	1836–44	1818–44
Frankfurt	110	28	73	79	80
Paris	163	-8	38	67	75
London	57	14	69	34	49
Vienna			11	17	
Naples			17	24	
Total	330	85	209	221	231

Source: As table 1.1.

The question, of course, is whether it is legitimate to make such comparisons when the houses were regarded by the partners as inseparably linked – as, indeed, a single 'general joint concern'. The balance sheets of the Naples house reveal how inextricable the activities of the five houses were: between 1825 and 1850, the share of its assets which were monies owed to it by the other Rothschild houses was rarely less than 18 per cent and sometimes as much as 30 per cent.[8] This

---

[6]   AN, 132 AQ 13/Bilans 06/1821–06/1842.

[7]   Calculated from the fragmentary evidence (primarily half-yearly figures) in AN, 132 AQ 3/2; CPHDCM, 637/1/6/34–42.

[8]   Gille, *Maison Rothschild*, vol. I, p. 248. Cf. CPHDCM, 637/1/6/20–21, Balance Sheet of Naples House, 31 Dec. 1827.

seems to have been the case for all the houses. In 1828, credits to the other house amounted to 31 per cent of the assets of the Paris house.[9]

The most striking point of all is the sheer size of the Rothschilds' bank. In 1815, the combined capital of the Rothschild houses in Frankfurt and London was at most £500,000. In 1818, the figure was £1,772,000, in 1825 £4,082,000 and in 1828 £4,330,333. The equivalent figures for the Rothschilds' nearest rival, Baring Brothers, were £374,365, £429,318, £452,654 and £309,803.[10] To take a single year – 1825 – their combined resources were nine times greater than the capital of Baring Brothers and eleven times larger than the capital of James's principal rival in Paris, Laffitte. They even exceeded the capital of the Banque de France (around £3 million at this time).[11] Nor did the Rothschilds lose momentum in the succeeding years. In 1836 – the next time the partners met to settle accounts and renew their contractual agreement – the capital had increased again to £6,007,707. Barings' capital in that year was £776,650. Eight years later, the Rothschilds had increased their capital to £7,778,200; Barings' had shrunk to £501,944. The main explanation for this dramatic disparity is not just that the Rothschilds made bigger profits. In relation to its capital, the Barings' bank was significantly more profitable on average than the London house.[12] But the Rothschilds ploughed the bulk of their profits back into the business, whereas the Barings tended to distribute profits to the partners (even in years when the bank made a loss) rather than allow capital to accumulate.

How did the Rothschilds make their money? Primarily, the answer is from government finance. Between 1818 and 1832, it has been estimated that N.M. Rothschild accounted for seven out of 26 loans contracted by foreign governments in London, and roughly 38 per cent (£37.6 million) of their total value. This was more than twice the value of their nearest rival.[13] Moreover, the bank's own figures suggest that this may be an underestimate: according to Ayer, the value of State loans issued by Nathan in this period was in fact £76 million, though £8.6 million was shared with non-Rothschild banks.[14] The equivalent total for loans issued by the Frankfurt house in this period is 28 million gulden (c. £2.5 million).[15] In Paris, James came to exercise a near monopoly over French government finance, issuing seven loans with a nominal capital of 1.5 billion francs (£60 million) between 1823 and 1847.[16] Table 1.4

---

[9] CPHDCM, 637/1/6/34–42, Bilan de MM de Rothschild Frères, 30 June 1828.

[10] P. Ziegler, *The Sixth Great Power: Barings, 1762–1929* (London, 1988), p. 374.

[11] Gille, *Maison Rothschild*, vol. I, pp. 163–6, 450f.

[12] Ziegler, *Sixth Great Power*, appendix.

[13] S. Chapman, *The Rise of Merchant Banking* (London, 1984), p. 20.

[14] J. Ayer, *A Century of Finance, 1804 to 1904: The London House of Rothschild* (London, 1904), pp. 14ff. Ayer included not only bond issues but various short-term loans against treasury bills; this may account for the discrepancy.

[15] C. W. Berghoeffer, *Meyer Amschel Rothschild: Der Gründer des Rothschildschen Bankhauses* (Frankfurt am Main, 1924), appendix.

[16] F. Braudel and E. Labrousse, *Histoire économique et sociale de la France, vol. III: L'avènement de l'ére industrielle, 1789–1880* (Paris, 1976), pp. 364–71.

provides figures for the total nominal value of the loans issued by the London and Frankfurt houses in the period; unfortunately, no comprehensive lists of issues exist for the other houses, but the London figures include a substantial number of loans handled jointly with Paris, Frankfurt, Naples and Vienna. These figures confirm that the Rothschilds were, throughout the period, the dominant force in international bond issues. Between 1815 and 1859, the London House issued altogether 50 loans, primarily for governments, the nominal value of which was around £250 million. In comparison, Barings issued just 14 loans in the same period, to a nominal amount of £66 million.[17]

Table 1.4   The nominal value of loans issued by the London and Frankfurt houses, 1820–1859 (by decade) (£)

	NMR	MAR
1820–29	58,715,366	4,892,947
1830–39	43,194,150	3,599,512
1840–49	35,169,611	2,930,800
1850–59	88,485,900	7,373,825

Source: Ayer, *Century of Finance*, pp. 16–81; Berghoeffer, *Meyer Amschel*, pp. 29–42, 206–28.

Table 1.5 breaks down the London figures to show the regional distribution of Rothschild loans (including a small number of quite large private sector issues). These figures show that the contemporary view of the Rothschilds as 'bankers to the Holy Alliance' was exaggerated; the London house's biggest clients were France and Britain, with Prussia, Russia and Austria some way behind.

It is relatively easy to show the importance of government bonds in the balance sheets of the various houses. The earliest surviving balance sheet of the London house (that of 1828) reveals that a very large proportion of the bank's assets – more than a quarter – were invested in British government bonds. The proportion rises to 37 per cent if its holdings of Danish government stock are added.[18] In the same year, 35 per cent of the French house's assets took the form of French 3 per cent *rentes*.[19] The 'State securities account' comprised exactly the same proportion of the Vienna house's assets, suggesting some sort of general Rothschild policy.[20] However, it is much harder to compute the profits made from such issues. Commissions and other charges varied considerably, and some major issues actually lost large sums (the French loan of 1830, for example). If bonds were taken firm ('*à forfait*' in contemporary parlance, that is, bought outright by

[17]   Chapman, *Merchant Banking*, p. 16.
[18]   CPHDCM, 637/1/6/52–57, N.M. Rothschild, balance sheet, 31 July 1828.
[19]   CPHDCM, 637/1/6/34–42, Bilan de MM de Rothschild Frères, 30 June 1828.
[20]   CPHDCM, 637/1/6/22, 25, Abschluss des Wiener-Filial-Etablissements, 30 June 1828; see also AN 132 AQ 3/2 No 5.

the Rothschilds from a government), the commission charged was significantly higher, or the gap between the price paid and the price at which they were sold to brokers was larger. If they were merely sold on commission for a government, with the option to return any which could not be placed, less could be expected. There were also a host of smaller short-term advances to governments which were often very lucrative but do not appear in the figures cited above. Nor do the numerous inter-state transfer payments which the Rothschilds arranged, for example the subsidies paid by Britain to her allies in the final phase of the Napoleonic wars and the 'contributions' from France to the members of the coalition which defeated Napoleon in 1814–15. Few European wars were fought in the nineteenth century without business of this sort being generated for the Rothschilds in their aftermath, though the most celebrated example (the French indemnity to Germany of 1871–3) lies outside the scope of this paper.

Table 1.5   Loans issued by the London house, 1818–1846 (by recipient)

Borrower	Total (£)	% of total
Britain	44,938,547	29.2
France	27,700,000	18.0
Prussia	12,300,400	8.0
Russia	6,629,166	4.3
Austria	3,100,000	2.0
Naples	7,000,000	4.5
'Holy Alliance'*	29,029,566	18.8)
Portugal	5,500,000	3.6
Brazil	4,486,200	2.9
Belgium	11,681,064	7.6
Other States**	5,843,750	3.8
Private sector	24,900,000	16.2
Total	*154,079,127*	*100.0*

* Including Naples.
** Holland, Greece and Denmark.
Source: Ayer, *Century*, pp. 14–42.

The development of the international bond market was the Rothschilds' principal contribution to nineteenth century capitalism. Of course, there had been large-scale international lending before: Neal's work has shown the importance of Dutch investment in the British national debt in the eighteenth century, for example.[21] The Bethmann Brothers had also developed a system of 'partial obligations' to help market the Austrian public debt in Frankfurt and Amsterdam.[22] But the Rothschilds introduced a number of innovations which greatly facilitated capital export, especially from London to the continental powers and to overseas States. The watershed in this respect was the 1818 loan to Prussia which was issued not only in London but in Frankfurt, Berlin, Hamburg and Amsterdam, and featured a number of striking conditions designed to attract investors. First, the loan was to be not in *thaler*, but in sterling, with the interest payable not in Berlin but in London. Second, some of the proceeds of the loan (£150,000) were to be immediately reinvested in English funds, to accumulate interest with a view to the loan's ultimate redemption. Third, the loan was to be secured on Prussian State revenues and certain royal domains.[23] In themselves the sinking fund and the mortgaging of revenues were not novel, of course; but the fact that the loan was denominated in sterling and the interest paid in London marked a new departure for the international capital market. Now it was much easier to invest in foreign funds; and the fact that throughout the century all foreign government bonds paid higher yields than British consols meant that people did. *The Times* did not exaggerate when it later described Nathan as 'the first introducer of foreign loans into Britain':

> for, though such securities did at all times circulate here, the payment of dividends abroad, which was the universal practice before his time, made them too inconvenient an investment for the great majority of persons of property to deal with. He not only formed arrangements for the payment of dividends on his foreign loan in London, but made them still more attractive by fixing the rate in sterling money, and doing away with all the effects of fluctuation in exchanges.[24]

The next step – which the Rothschilds were uniquely placed to take – was to create a completely international market. In his *The Traffic in State Bonds* of 1830, the German jurist Bender identified this as one of the Rothschilds' principal contributions to modern economic development:

---

[21]   L. Neal, *The Rise of Financial Capitalism: International Capital Markets in the Age of Reason* (Cambridge, 1990).

[22]   M. Jurk, 'The other Rothschilds: Frankfurt private bankers in the 18th and 19th centuries', in G. Heuberger (ed.), *The Rothschilds: Essays on the History of a European Family* (Sigmaringen, 1994), pp. 37–50.

[23]   *The Times*, 4 Aug. 1836; F.G. Dawson, *The First Latin American Debt Crisis* (London, 1990), p. 20; D. Kynaston, *The City of London*, vol. I: *A World of its Own, 1815–90* (London, 1994), p. 45f.; W.O. Henderson, *The Zollverein* (London, 1939), p. 31; B. Gille, *La banque et le crédit en France de 1815 à 1848* (Vendôme, 1959), p. 225.

[24]   *The Times*, 4 Aug. 1836, p. 3.

Any owner of government bonds . . . can collect the interest at his convenience in several different places without any effort. As its customers wish, the House of Rothschild in Frankfurt pays the interest of the Austrian metalliques, the Neapolitan rentes [or] the interest of the Anglo-Neapolitan obligations in London, Naples or Paris.[25]

Even more novel was the formal justification for these conditions included in the Prussian loan contract:

[T]o induce British Capitalists to invest their money in a loan to a foreign government upon reasonable terms, it will be of the first importance that the plan of such a loan should as much as possible be assimilated to the established system of borrowing for the public service in England, and above all things that some security, beyond the mere good faith of the government ... should be held out to the lenders .... Without some security of this description any attempt to raise a considerable sum in England for a foreign Power would be hopeless[;] the late investments by British subjects in the French Funds have proceeded upon the general belief that in consequence of the representative system now established in that Country, the sanction of the Chamber to the National debt incurred by the Government affords a guarantee to the Public Creditor which could not be found in a Contract with any Sovereign uncontrolled in the exercise of the executive powers.[26]

Clause 2 of the 'Decree for the Future Management of the State Debt' of 17 January 1819 duly specified that 'If the state should in future for its maintenance or for the advancement of the common good require to issue a new loan, this can only be done with in consultation with and with the guarantee of the future imperial estates assembly.'[27] In other words, a constitutional monarchy, with some kind of representative parliament, was seen in London as a better credit risk than a neo-absolutist regime. Was this a subtle form of political pressure – a kind of financial liberalism, lending its weight at a critical time to the efforts of the Prussian reformers who had been pressing Frederick William III to accept some kind of system of representation?[28] Perhaps, though, Nathan may merely have been

---

[25] R.M. Heilbrunn, 'Das Haus Rothschild: Wahrheit und Dichtung', Vortrag gehalten am 6. März 1963 im Frankfurter Verein für Geschichte und Landeskunde (1963), p. 24.

[26] RAL, XI/109/10/2/4, undated documents relating to Prussian loan proposal, c. Sept. 1817. See also RAL, XI/109/10/3, copy of letter probably from Nathan, London, to 'Sir' [Rother or Hardenberg], 30 Dec.

[27] P.G. Thielen, *Karl August von Hardenberg, 1750–1822* (Cologne/Berlin, 1967), p. 358.

[28] H. Obenaus, 'Finanzkrise und Verfassungsgebung zu den sozialen Bedingungen des frühen deutschen Konstitutionalismus', in G.A. Ritter (ed.), *Gesellschaft, Parlament und Regierung* (Düsseldorf, 1984).

justifying the differential between his terms and those obtained by France from
Baring. What is beyond dispute is that, in stipulating these conditions, Nathan not
only succeeded in making the Prussian loan attractive to British and continental
investors; he also established a model for such international bond issues which
would swiftly become standard.

The export of capital from London and later from Paris was one of the
most remarkable features of nineteenth-century economic development; the
contribution made by the Rothschilds to this globalization of the capital market
has not always been adequately emphasized in the literature. Although some of the
capital channelled abroad by the Rothschilds was undoubtedly used for military
purposes of minimal developmental benefit, much of it was used in a way which
did promote economic growth. This was especially true in the case of those States
(such as Belgium and some German States in the 1830s and 1840s) which raised
money in London in order to finance railway construction. Loans which served to
stabilize fiscal and monetary systems also had positive macroeconomic effects.

In addition to issuing and underwriting commissions, much of the money
which the brothers made on the bond market came not from new issues, but from
speculating in existing bonds. Another way the Rothschilds routinely made money
was by arbitrage, as the price of a given bond varied between London and Paris.
Here the fact that they had branches in five different financial centres gave them a
distinct advantage over their rivals.

Of comparable importance in terms of the volume of business involved,
though not in terms of profits, were dealings in commercial bills. The buying
(accepting) and selling of bills of exchange were among Nathan Rothschild's
principal activities as he stood by his pillar on the Royal Exchange: in 1828, 'bills
receivable' accounted for a quarter of the London house's assets; 'bills payable'
for 5 per cent of its liabilities.[29] Such business was probably less important to
the continental Rothschilds, reflecting the far greater importance of the bill of
exchange as a financial instrument in Britain. It is worth noting the Rothschilds did
not seek to make their money from the commissions they charged for accepting
bills (indeed, Nathan was well known for charging half a per cent less than other
firms);[30] rather, the aim was to profit from exchange-rate differentials between the
various European markets.[31]

The Rothschilds were not as dominant in the market for bills as they were
in the market for bonds, however. In his influential survey of the City, *Lombard
Street*, Walter Bagehot called them 'the greatest . . . of the foreign bill-brokers';[32]

[29]   CPHDCM, 637/1/6/52–57, N.M. Rothschild, balance sheet, 31 July 1828.
[30]   S. Chapman, *The Foundation of the English Rothschilds: N.M. Rothschild as a
Textile Merchant, 1799–1811* (London, 1977), p. 22.
[31]   See e.g., RAL, XI/109J/J/32, James and Anselm, Paris, to Nathan and Nat, London,
5 Nov. 1832.
[32]   W. Bagehot, *Lombard Street: A Description of the Money Market* (London, 1873),
p. 213.

but this accolade properly belonged to Barings.[33] In 1825, Nathan's acceptances totalled £300,000, compared with £520,000 for Barings. Twenty-five years later, acceptances at New Court had risen to £540,000, but the figure for Barings was £1.9 million; and the gap widened still further in the second half of the century, when newcomers like Kleinworts also overtook Rothschilds.[34] Apart from the obvious fact that the Rothschilds put government finance first, this reflected the fact that the greater part of the bills business was generated by transatlantic trade, rather than by trade between Britain and continental Europe, which the Rothschilds were better placed to finance.

Another related field of activity was direct involvement in commodity trade itself.[35] Buying and selling goods rather than paper had been an integral part of Mayer Amschel's original business in Frankfurt, and Nathan himself had begun his career in Britain as a textile merchant, later branching out into 'colonial goods'. However, the Rothschilds' interest in such business appears to have dwindled in the 1820s, and it was not until after 1830 that they took it up again. Unlike Barings, who took an interest in a wide range of traded goods, the Rothschilds preferred to specialize, aiming to establish a dominant role in a select number of markets. The commodities which attracted their attention were cotton, tobacco, sugar (primarily from America and the Caribbean), copper (from Russia), and, most importantly, mercury (from Spain).[36]

Of more importance was bullion broking. This was presumably what Nathan alluded to when he loftily told a Hamburg house in 1817: 'My business . . . consists entirely in Government transactions & Bank operations'.[37] In practice, that generally meant doing business with major note-issuing banks like the Bank of England and the Banque de France. Transfers of gold from England to the continent had been a vital stepping stone towards direct involvement in English war finance before 1815, and the brothers never lost their interest in the bullion business. Here, too, complex calculations were involved, especially when coins were being melted down into bars to be reminted in another market.[38] 'The van loaded with silver ingots' which blocked Prince Pückler-Muskau's access to New Court in 1826 was no rare sight: to judge by the brothers' letters, consignments of bullion worth tens of thousands of pounds regularly passed between Paris and London. There is an old anecdote which describes Nathan threatening to exhaust the Bank of England's reserve by bringing an immense number of small-denomination notes to its counter and demanding gold.[39] Few Rothschild myths

---

[33]   Ziegler, *Sixth Great Power*, pp. 127ff.

[34]   Chapman, *Merchant Banking*, p. 17; Kynaston, *City*, vol. I, pp. 308f.

[35]   Gille, *Maison Rothschild*, vol. I, pp. 401ff., 415–18, 420; vol. II, pp. 546–55.

[36]   Count E. Corti, *The Rise of the House of Rothschild* (London, 1928), p. 75f.

[37]   New York, Leo Baeck Institute, Nathan to Behrend Brothers, 14 March 1817.

[38]   See e.g., RAL, XI/109J/J/33, James, Paris, to Nathan, London, 10 March 1833.

[39]   See e.g., J. Reeves, *The Rothschilds: The Financial Rulers of Nations* (London, 1887), pp. 181ff.

are so diametrically opposed to the truth. In fact, Nathan's relations with the Bank of England were close and mutually beneficial. In December 1825, for example, the Rothschilds supplied the Bank with enough specie from the Continent to avert a suspension of cash payments. Looking back in 1839, the Duke of Wellington had no doubt who had averted disaster: 'Had it not been for the most extraordinary exertions – above all on the part of old Rothschild – the Bank must have stopped payment'.[40]

Interest in money led naturally to an interest in the extraction and refining of precious metals. The Rothschilds' first step in this direction was their involvement in the mining of Spanish mercury (primarily for use in the refining of silver). For over three centuries the mines of Almadén had played a pivotal role in the international monetary system because of the use of mercury in the refining of silver. Traditionally, the Spanish government leased the Almadén mines to private companies, most famously to the great banking dynasty of the sixteenth century, the Fuggers.[41] It was a precedent the Rothschilds followed when Nathan's son Lionel went to Madrid to try to retrieve 15 million francs his father had advanced to the Spanish government.[42] Although he failed to recover the money, he outbid four other companies to secure the new contract to control the mines.[43] This was the beginning of a long and lucrative involvement. Henceforth, when the Spanish government asked for money, the Rothschilds could simply make advances of the sums they had contracted to pay on account of Almadén. Their experience with mercury mining proved useful in the second half of the century when the Rothschilds followed the international shift from silver to gold, acquiring their own gold refinery in London in 1852, establishing agents in California and Australia, and later playing a leading role in South African gold mining.

The final area of business which the Rothschilds entered in this period was insurance. Nathan's involvement in the founding of the Alliance Assurance Company in 1824 has been variously explained. According to the company's official history, it was the result of a casual meeting with his brother-in-law Moses Montefiore; others have suggested that the aim was partly to provide employment as an actuary for their relative Benjamin Gompertz, an accomplished mathematician. A third hypothesis advanced is that the existing insurance companies had been

---

[40]   R. Davis, *The English Rothschilds* (London, 1983), p. 45.

[41]   C.P. Kindleberger, *A Financial History of Western Europe* (London, 1984), p. 26; Corti, *reign*, pp. 120f.

[42]   RAL, XI/109/31a/1/31, Lionel, Paris, to his parents, 11 March 1834.

[43]   RAL, XI/109/32/4/50, Lionel, Madrid, to his uncles and parents, 13 Dec. 1834; RAL, T22/678, XI/109/33/1/2, Lionel, Madrid, to Anthony, Paris, 15 Feb. 1835; RAL, T22/678, XI/109/33/1/2, Lionel to his uncles and parents, 25 May; RAL, XI/109J/J/35, James to Nathan and Nat, 28 Feb.; same to same, 9 March; RAL, XI/109/33/1/9, Lionel to his uncles and parents, 25 March; RAL, XI/109/33/1/20, same to same, 6 June. Cf. J. Fontana, *La revolucion liberal* (Madrid, 1977), pp. 59f. See in general V.M. Martin, *Los Rothschild y las Minas de Almadén* (Madrid, 1980).

discriminating against the Jewish business community.[44] In fact, the Rothschilds had been interested in insurance for some years, not surprisingly in view of the high premiums they themselves had been obliged to pay to insure shipments to the Continent before 1815. By founding the Alliance, Nathan seems to have wanted to break the cartel of three firms – Lloyd's, the London Assurance and the Royal Exchange – which monopolized marine insurance in London.

The significance of their involvement in insurance was partly that it acquainted the Rothschilds with the rudiments of company formation. When they began to involve themselves in continental railways – a subject not dealt with here – they therefore had some experience of the benefits of joint-stock structures. It is worth noting, however, that the nineteenth-century Rothschilds never regarded the joint-stock form as suitable for banking – especially investment banking of the sort undertaken by the Crédit Mobilier and its imitators in the 1850s and 1860s – and remained committed to the private-partnership model until well into the twentieth century.

Finally, it should be said that they only offered current-account and deposit banking services in special cases where they wished to do a favour for an individual (see below) or State. By and large, they disliked holding long-term deposits (like the so-called 'fortress money' left with them by the German Confederation after 1815), fearing the effect of sudden withdrawals on their liquidity. The Rothschilds favoured a high ratio of reserves to liabilities.

If there was a single 'secret' of Rothschild success it was the system of co-operation between the five 'houses' which made them, when considered as a whole, the largest bank in the world, while at the same time dispersing their financial influence in five major financial centres spread across Europe. Essentially, the Rothschild bank was a family firm crossed with a multinational, with three notionally equal 'houses' in Frankfurt, Paris and London and two subsidiary branches (of the Frankfurt house) in Vienna and Naples. This system was regulated by the partnership agreements which were drawn up and revised every few years and which were, in effect, the constitution of a financial federation. These agreements have never been studied properly; yet they were the very foundation of Rothschild success.

In the Hollywood version, Mayer Amschel bids his sons to fan out across Europe as he lies on his deathbed. In fact, the partnership evolved gradually and it was not until the 1820s that his brothers began to consider themselves permanently settled in, respectively, Frankfurt (Amschel), Vienna (Salomon), Naples (Carl) and Paris (James). When members of the family were interrogated by the French police in 1809, Mayer Amschel was still calling himself the sole proprietor (*Inhaber*) of the firm, while his sons were merely his 'assistants' (*Gehülfen*).[45]

---

[44]   Sir W. Schooling, *Alliance Assurance, 1824–1924* (London, 1924), pp. 1f.; E.V. Morgan and W.A. Thomas, *The Stock Exchange* (London, 1962), p. 129; P.L. Cottrell, 'The Business Man and Financier', in S. and V.D. Lipman (eds), *The Century of Moses Montefiore* (Oxford, 1985), pp. 29ff.; Kynaston, *City*, vol. I, p. 62.

[45]   CPHDCM, 637/1/4, Transcript of interrogation of Mayer Amschel and his family, 10 and 11 May 1809.

However, when a formal legal partnership contract was drawn up in September 1810, its preamble explicitly stated that 'a trading company already existed' in which Mayer Amschel, Amschel and Salomon were the 'associates' (*Associés*). The principal function of the 1810 agreement was to make Carl a partner, giving him a 30,000 gulden share of the total capital of 800,000 compared with Mayer Amschel's 370,000, Amschel's 185,000 and Salomon's 185,000; and to guarantee that James would become a partner (also with a share worth 30,000 gulden) when he attained his majority. Nathan had to be left out as he was in 'enemy' territory. In this, and in other respects, Mayer Amschel remained in charge: he alone had the right to withdraw his capital from the firm during the period of the agreement, he alone had the right to hire and fire employees of the firm, and his unmarried sons could only marry with his permission.

In other respects, however, the agreement would act as a model for future agreements between the brothers and their descendants for most of the nineteenth century. Profits were divided in proportion to capital shares, no partner was to engage in business independently of the others and the agreement was to run for a fixed period of years (in this case, ten). The most striking clause in the agreement stated what would happen were one of the partners to die. Each solemnly renounced the rights of his wife, children or their guardians to contest in any way the amount of money agreed by the surviving partners to be the deceased partner's share of the capital. Specifically, his widow and heirs were to be denied any access to the firm's books and correspondence.[46] This was the first formal statement of that distinctive and enduring rule which effectively excluded Rothschild women – born Rothschilds as well as those who married into the family – from the core of the business: the hallowed ledgers and letters. Mayer Amschel's revised will, drawn up as he lay dying in 1812, reinforced this principle.[47] In practice, Rothschild women were never entirely excluded from business affairs. Caroline, Salomon's wife, became so involved in Nathan's massive speculative purchases of British stock in 1816 that she began having dreams about consol prices.[48] Nathan's wife Hannah always took a keen interest in the business. Certain in-laws – Moses Montefiore, for example – also played an important role in Rothschild operations as clerks (managers), brokers or agents. However, the formal exclusion of women and in-laws from the partnership and its accounts was always maintained: they literally had to sit outside while the partners deliberated at the occasional 'summits' which regulated the collective affairs of the various houses.

There was never strict equality between the partners or the houses. According to the preamble of the 1815 agreement, the brothers' 'partnership property in London, at Paris and at Frankfurt on the Main consists of the sum of £500,000 or

[46]   RAL, RFamFD/3, Gesellschaftsvertrag [between] Mayer Amschel Rothschild, Amschel, Salomon and Carl, 27 Sept. 1810. Cf. Berghoeffer, *Meyer Amschel*, pp. 165ff.

[47]   Berghoeffer, *Meyer Amschel*, pp. 201ff.

[48]   RAL, T32/125/2, XI/109/5A, Salomon and his wife, Brighton, to Nathan, Hannah and Davidson, 16 Aug. 1816.

thereabouts', but most of this (around two-thirds) was Nathan's.[49] In order to adjust for this preponderance, the contract sought to redefine the brothers' collective assets by excluding certain items (presumably real estate), and redistributing some £200,000 in the form of promissory notes of £50,000 each from Nathan to his four brothers. The resulting shares of a total notional capital of £336,000 were Nathan, 27 per cent; Amschel and Salomon, 20 per cent each; Carl and James, 16 per cent each. Moreover, it was agreed to defray all expenses from the London house's revenues and to share net profits at the end of each year equally.[50] In the three years during which this contract ran, the brothers' capital grew at a phenomenal rate, as we have seen. So much of this increase was due to Nathan's speculations in consols that, although the proportions of the total capital were more or less unchanged, his brothers now agreed to weight the distribution of profits in his favour. There were now technically 'three joint mercantile establishments [conducted] under their the . . . five partners' mutual responsibility': N.M. Rothschild in London, M.A. von Rothschild & Söhne in Frankfurt, and James's new house in Paris, de Rothschild Frères. Henceforth, half of all the profits of the London house would go to Nathan, while his brothers would receive an eighth each; he would also receive four-sixteenths of the profits of the other two houses, while his brothers received three-sixteenths apiece. The 1818 agreement also introduced a new system whereby each of the partners received four per cent of their individual capital share per annum by way of an income (there were no dividends or any other kind of profit-distribution); while any lump sums spent on legacies for children, houses or landed estates were to be deducted from the individual's capital. In addition, 'to preserve regularity in the books and accounts' it was agreed 'that in the running transactions of the three joint establishments *although they form but one general joint concern* each respectively is to charge exchange, brokerage, postages, stamps and interest pro and contra at the rate of 5 per cent'.[51] To reinforce the sense of collective identity it was now specified that each House had to inform the others of the transactions it carried out on a weekly basis.

Although initially intended to run for just three years, this agreement was in fact renewed until 1825.[52] Significantly, the agreement of that year restored the 1815 system whereby profits were shared equally, reflecting the fact that the capital of

---

[49]   CPHDCM, 637/1/6/5, Articles of Partnership between Messrs Rothschild, 21 March 1815. Cf. Gille, *Maison Rothschild*, vol. I, p. 447f. It is not entirely clear from this document what the total value of the firm's capital was. The preamble states it to be around £500,000, but the stated shares amount to just £136,000. From comments made in correspondence in late 1815, the former figure seems more probable, though it may include valuations of real estate as well as more liquid capital. See RAL, XI/109/2/2/124, James, Paris, to Nathan, London, 2 Oct.; RAL, XI/109/2/2/126, Carl, Amsterdam, to Nathan, London, 3 Oct.

[50]   CPHDCM, 637/1/6/5, Articles of Partnership between Messrs Rothschild, 21 March 1815.

[51]   CPHDCM, 637/1/6/7/7–14, Articles of Partnership, 2 June 1818. Emphasis added.

[52]   CPHDCM, 637/1/6/27–28, Indenture, 25 Aug. 1824.

both the Frankfurt and Paris houses had grown so rapidly as to outstrip that of the London house. On the other hand, Nathan's personal share continued to be counted as more than a quarter of the joint capital, which now stood at more than £4 million. Moreover, although Salomon and Carl had by now effectively settled in Vienna and Naples, their houses were not given equal status with the original three, and continued to be treated as mere 'branch establishments' of the Frankfurt house. This was probably intended to check the fissiparous tendencies which developed as the brothers saw less of one another. Revealingly, the partners now bound themselves 'mutually [to] inform each other . . . of all the transactions of whatever nature they may be which have occurred' on a monthly rather than weekly basis.[53]

The next accounts drawn up in 1828 revealed that, though the partners' personal shares remained formally unchanged, the relative importance of the London house had continued to decline. Its share of the total capital was now just over 27 per cent, compared with 42 per cent in 1818.[54] This share increased only very slightly in the eight years which intervened before the next such meeting in Frankfurt. As a result, the continental partners were able to request new and potentially more favourable terms for the distribution of profits. The final agreement was that Nathan should receive 60 per cent of the profits of the London house but just 10 per cent of the profits from Frankfurt, Naples and Vienna, while his brothers would each get 10 per cent from the London house and 22.5 per cent from the continental houses.[55] This rule clearly increased the relative autonomy of the London house.

The fact that, despite numerous conflicts of interest and profound centrifugal forces, this system continued with only minor modifications until the 1870s and was still formally in operation until 1904 was a triumph of collective familial consciousness. Of all Mayer Amschel's achievements, this was the greatest; for it was his last commandment – to maintain family unity – which provided the inspiration for later generations to transcend their personal or political differences. Salomon once attributed 'all our luck to the benediction which our father gave us an hour before he passed away'.[56] Amschel remembered his father telling him on his deathbed: 'Amschel, keep your brothers together and you will become the

---

[53]   CPHDCM, 637/1/8/1–7; also RAL, RFamFD, B/1, Articles of Agreement between Messrs de Rothschild [Amschel, Nathan, Salomon, Carl, Jacob and Anselm], 31 Aug. 1825. See also AN 132 AQ 1, Unsigned, unheaded document, apparently the draft 'Testament', 31 Aug.

[54]   CPHDCM, 637/1/6/44, 45, No. 4 General Capital, 26 Sept. 1828; CPHDCM, 637/1/6/17, General Inventarium . . . des gesamten Handelsvermögens, 26 Sept. 1828; CPHDCM, 637/1/6/31, [untitled deed signed by Anselm and the five brothers], 26 Sept.; CPHDCM, 637/1/7/48–52, Abscrift [Partnership agreement], 26 Sept.; AN, 132 AQ 3/2/No 5, General Inventarium, 26 Sept.

[55]   A clause was added, however, which stated that if the profits of the Paris, Frankfurt, Naples and Vienna houses exceeded those of the London house to the point that 22.5 per cent of their total profits exceeded 60 per cent of the London house's, then the division of the profits would revert to the old system of equal shares of the whole.

[56]   RAL, T64/158/2, Salomon, Berlin, to Amschel, Nathan and James, 24 Feb. 1818.

richest people in Germany.'[57] More than twenty years later, this principle was enshrined in a new partnership agreement, drawn up following the death of Nathan himself:

> [W]hen, almost forty years ago, [our father] took his sons into partnership with him in his business, he told them that acting in unison would be a sure means of achieving success in their work, and always recommended fraternal concord to them as a source of divine blessing. In accordance with his venerable wishes, and following the promptings of our own hearts, we therefore wish today, through this renewed agreement, to reinforce our mutual dependence and hope, in this new league of brotherly love, to guarantee the success of the future activities of our House.[58]

The same theme of paternally-ordained brotherly unity was developed still further in a separate annex to the agreement.[59] Nearly thirty years after Mayer Amschel's death, his eldest son was still reminding the other partners of the same, all-important nexus between unity and success.[60]

In practice, of course, it was easier to make such pious affirmations than to practise brotherly love. For most of the period under discussion here, the brothers were not equals at all; in effect, Nathan inherited his father's role as *primus inter pares*. This was made clear in 1814, when Nathan's desire to dictate his brothers' movements precipitated a violent quarrel. A distraught Carl took to his bed, warning that 'if he carried on in this way', Nathan would 'soon have a partner in the other world'. Salomon also complained of 'severe pains in my back and legs' and accused Nathan of 'regard[ing] the other four brothers as stupid schoolboys'. James was more cool, sarcastically accusing Nathan of 'dictat[ing] about millions as if they were apples and pears'.[61] But all their protests merely elicited from Nathan a stark threat to dissolve the business.[62] This had the desired effect. Henceforth, Nathan gave the orders more or less unchallenged, as Salomon acknowledged in August 1814. He now clearly saw himself in a subordinate, advisory role: '[W]e regard

[57] RAL, XI/109/2/3, Amschel, Frankfurt, to Nathan, London, 12 Jan. 1815.

[58] CPHDCM, 637/1/7/53–69, Vollständige Abschrift des Societäts-Vertrags … Übereinkunft 30, July 1836.

[59] CPHDCM, 637/1/7/70–72, Anhang to Agreement, 30 July 1836.

[60] CPHDCM, 637/1/309, Amschel, Frankfurt, to his brothers and nephews, 11 Nov. 1841.

[61] RAL, T28/5, Davidson to Nathan, London, 24 June 1814; RAL, XI/109/0/2/7, Davidson, Amsterdam, to Nathan, London, 21 June; RAL, XI/109/0/2/13, Carl, Frankfurt, to James, 24 June; RAL, XI/109/0/2/15, James and Salomon, Amsterdam, to Nathan and Salomon Cohen, London, 27 June; RAL, XI/109/0/2/14, Carl, Frankfurt, to James, 28 June; RAL, XI/109/0/3/2, Salomon and James, Amsterdam, to Nathan, 28 June.

[62] RAL, T29/73, XI/109/0/3/16, Nathan, London, to Salomon, Carl, James and Amschel, 3 July 1814.

you as general-in-chief, with ourselves as lieutenants-general.'[63] There continued
to be occasional rows; but for all their differences, the brothers did stick together,
albeit under Nathan's self-consciously Napoleonic leadership rather than on the
basis of an idealized fraternal harmony.

Perhaps the greatest challenge for any family firm is to 'bring on' the next
generation. Fortunately, most of the second generation inherited their parents'
fertility: although Amschel failed to produce any children whatsoever, his brothers
produced no fewer than 13 male heirs. Yet it is striking that Nathan and his brothers
did not follow their father's example by establishing at least some of their sons in
new financial centres. The plan for a 'sixth house' on the other side of the Atlantic
remained no more than a pipe-dream; probably the biggest mistake the Rothschilds
made. The best explanation for this is that the five brothers trusted five of their
sons enough to groom them as their successors, but the others insufficiently to give
them the major responsibility of setting up a new house.

The integration of the next generation required fairly regular revision of the
partnership contract. In 1825, Salomon's son Anselm was admitted as a sleeping
partner and in 1828 he became a 'real Associé'. By 1836, Nathan felt his eldest son
Lionel was ready to become a partner on the same footing as Anselm, and it was
as much to agree the terms of Lionel's elevation as to celebrate his marriage that
the brothers met in Frankfurt that year. However, before the new contract could be
signed, Nathan became ill with a rectal abscess and, after a few weeks of wretched
medical treatment, died. It was a fraught and uncertain moment in the history of
the firm; but 'the commanding general' had just enough energy left for a final
exercise of his domineering will. Salomon described how 'three days before his
death he told me all his thoughts and wishes with regard to the will which he then
drew up, and which I then had written out in accordance with his intentions'.[64] In
effect, his three sons were to inherit his share in the partnership and to manage it
collectively. Above all, they were to maintain 'unity, true love and firm unity' – a
conscious echo of his own father's last words.[65]

It has often been assumed that James, who had many things in common with
his deceased brother, simply stepped into Nathan's shoes as senior partner. The
reality is rather different. As in the past, the older Rothschilds sought to counteract
the firm's centrifugal tendencies by appealing to the hallowed principle of fraternal
'concordia': 'In what has our strength been until now?' remonstrated James in
a letter to his nephews of 1839. 'Only in that people knew that one place will
support the other. . . [A]s you well know, the well-being of our family is closer to
my heart than anything else.'[66] 'Let us do business again in peace and in harmony

63   RAL, T29/159, XI/109/0/6/11, Salomon, Paris, to Nathan and Salomon Cohen, 17
Aug. 1814; RAL, T29/181, XI/109/0/8/7, Salomon to Nathan, London, undated, c. end of Aug.;
RAL, XI/109/9/4/6, XI/109/10/1/6, Salomon to Nathan, London, undated, c. early 1818.
64   Corti, *Reign*, pp. 150–2.
65   CPHDCM, 637/1/7/70–72, Anhang, 30 July 1836.
66   RAL, X1/109J/J/39, James, Nice, to his brothers and nephews, 16 March 1839.

and not quarrel with each other', he pleaded the following year. 'If peace reigns between us this will only bring us good fortune and blessings and both you and we should not lack anything.'[67] Perhaps not surprisingly, it was decided when the partners met at Paris that same year to leave the 1836 agreement unaltered, as – in the words of Nathan's widow – 'the Elder Brothers appear to be content with things as they are and require no change'.

However, as Hannah herself noted, 'The counting house of each having their [i.e., its] own capital should be independent, and they must regulate the income of each party to make all those concerned equally so, the Elder Members' capital being so much greater they have more to say'.[68] Two years later, Lionel was able to modify the partnership agreement in precisely that way. By formally withdrawing £340,250 from their personal share of the combined capital, he and his brothers brought their proportion – and therefore the amount of annual interest they received – into line with those of their uncles, ending the situation whereby Nathan (and his heirs jointly) had been the biggest 'shareholder'.[69] In doing so, it might be thought, Lionel was surrendering an advantage. Indeed, he surrendered even more by leaving the 1836 system intact for the distribution of the combined profits, which had specified that just 10 per cent of the continental houses' profits went to the London house. However, Lionel's objective was primarily to retain the relative autonomy of the London house. His real victory was to defeat James's proposal – first put forward nearly thirty years before – that the partnership between the five houses should be made public.[70] Thanks to Lionel, the precise nature of the relationship between the five houses remained shrouded in mystery, a secret between the partners and their lawyers. Such secrecy was a Rothschild tradition, but it is tempting to conclude that Lionel already preferred not be bound too tightly to the other four houses. On the other hand, when the supreme crisis of 1848 came – the moment when the Rothschilds came closest to ruin – it became clear that complete autonomy was not really an option for the London house. It stood to lose too much if the Paris and Vienna houses collapsed, as they would have done without assistance from London. In fact, the 1850s saw a new tightening of the links between the houses, especially between London and Paris; and the Rothschild system was strong enough to survive the profoundly disruptive wars of the period 1859–71, when the houses more than once found themselves on opposing political sides.

If the secret contractual ties between the five houses were asymmetrical and often strained, this was to a large extent counterbalanced by the marital ties which acted as a secondary source of family unity. After 1824, to a quite remarkable

[67] RAL, X1/109J/J42, James, Paris, to his nephews, 14 Nov. 1842.

[68] RAL, RFamC/1/20, Hannah, Paris, to Mayer, London, 22 Aug. 1842.

[69] CPHDCM, 637/1/7/88–92, Uebereinkunft, 30 Aug. 1844; also CPHDCM, 637/1/9/1–4.

[70] RAL, XI/109/48/2/6, Lionel, Frankfurt, to Nat, Paris, 28 Aug. 1844; RAL, XI/109/48/2/8, same to same, 29 Aug.

extent, Rothschilds tended to marry Rothschilds. Of 21 marriages involving descendants of Mayer Amschel between 1824 and 1877, no fewer than 15 were *between* his direct descendants. Although marriage between cousins was far from uncommon in the nineteenth century – especially amongst German-Jewish business dynasties – this was an extraordinary degree of intermarriage. 'These Rothschilds harmonize with one another in the most remarkable fashion', noted Heinrich Heine. 'Strangely enough, they even choose marriage partners from among themselves and the strands of relationship between them form complicated knots which future historians will find difficult to unravel.'[71] Not even the royal families of Europe were as closely in-bred, though self-conscious references to 'our royal family' suggest that the Rothschilds regarded them as a kind of model.[72]

Of closely related significance was the family's attitude towards religion. The fact that the Rothschilds were Jews is at once hugely important and profoundly difficult to interpret. Mayer Amschel once recalled that 'in my youth I was ... a very active merchant, but I was disorganized, because I had been a student [of the Talmud] and learnt nothing [about business]': this casts doubt on any simple notion of the relationship between religion and financial aptitude.[73] Probably, membership of a tightly knit 'outsider' group helped when it came to constructing credit networks, and perhaps there was a kind of work ethic derived from Judaism. But, obviously, these points can be made with equal force about the various Protestant sects, as indeed they were by Max Weber. In fact, it may be that being Jewish was less important to the Rothschilds than *staying* Jewish. As Ludwig Börne noted with grudging admiration, they had 'chosen the surest means of avoiding the ridicule that attaches to so many baronized millionaire families of the Old Testament: they have declined the holy water of Christianity'.[74] It was a fact which also impressed Benjamin Disraeli, himself (like Börne) born a Jew but baptized. It should be stressed that the degree of the Rothschilds' religiosity varied greatly: James was notoriously lax about observance, did not keep kosher and often worked on the Sabbath. His nephew Wilhelm Carl, at the other extreme, became a firm supporter of the Orthodox revival in Frankfurt, to the bemusement of his Anglicized cousins. However, what most members of the family shared was a belief that remaining Jewish was in some way integral to their good fortune; and that to deviate from Judaism would be to jeopardize this.

Nothing illustrates this more clearly than the family's reaction when Hannah Mayer, Nathan's second daughter, converted in order to marry a Gentile (Henry Fitzroy, a younger son of the Earl of Southampton) in 1839. When her uncle James first heard of the relationship, he was appalled. 'Nothing,' he thundered

[71] S.S. Prawer, *Heine's Jewish Comedy: A Study of his Portraits of Jews and Judaism* (Oxford, 1983), pp. 331–5.

[72] RAL, T20/34, XI/109/48/2/42, Nat, Paris, to his brothers, 4 Sept., probably 1844.

[73] RAL, RFamAD/2, Mayer Amschel, Frankfurt, to Nathan, undated, c. June 1805.

[74] Prawer, *Heine's Jewish Comedy*, p. 359f.

could possibly be more disastrous for our family, for our continued well-being, for our good name and for our honour than such a decision, God forbid. I hardly even dare mention it. To renounce our religion, the religion of our [father] Rabbi Mayer [Amschel] Rothschild of blessed memory, the religion which, thank God, made us so great.[75]

By converting, James felt Hannah Mayer had 'robbed our whole family of its pride and caused us such harm that it can unfortunately not be redressed any more':

> I believe that [religion] means everything. Our good fortune and our blessings depend upon it. We shall therefore wipe her from our memory and never again during my lifetime will I, or any other member of our family, see or receive her . . . as if she had never existed.[76]

Even her own mother echoed these sentiments.[77] Only her brother Nat supported her decision.

On closer inspection, James's response had more to do with the structure of authority within the family, and the obedience the younger generation owed to their elders, than with religion per se:

> I and the rest of our family have not only always had the wish, but indeed have always brought our children up from their early childhood with the sense that their love is to be confined to members of the family, that their attachment for one another would prevent them from getting any ideas of marrying anyone other than one of the family so that the fortune would stay inside the family. Who will give me any assurance that my own children will do what I tell them if they see that there is no punishment forthcoming? Should my own daughter, after she has married, say, 'I am miserable because I didn't marry a Duke although I had enough money to do so, and I see that, despite the fact that this woman renounced her religion, and despite the fact that [she] married against the wishes of her family, she is nevertheless accepted [by the family]. It would have been the same with me.' Do you really think that all the nicely conceived projects [will come to fruition] – i.e., that Mayer will marry Anselm's daughter, that Lionel's daughter will marry the child of another member of the family so that the great fortune and the Rothschild name will continue to be honoured and transmitted [to future generations] – if one doesn't put a stop to this?[78]

---

75   RAL, X1/109J/J/38, James, Paris, to Lionel and Nat, London, 11 Nov. 1838.

76   RAL, X1/109J/J/39, James, Heinrichsbad, to Nat, Paris, 29 June 1839.

77   RAL, RFamC/1/83, Hannah to Nat, 19 May 1839.

78   RAL, X1/109J/J/39, James, Heinrichsbad, to Nat, Paris, 16 July 1839. See also Davis, *English Rothschilds*, p. 60.

The most striking point about James's outpouring is the way he equated 'religion' with endogamy: 'pride in religion' meant, in practice, intermarriage within the Rothschild family 'so that the fortune would stay inside the family'.

It is not enough to explain the Rothschilds' success purely in terms of their over-developed sense of familial solidarity, of course. Other Jewish banking families established themselves in multiple locations; but none came close to enjoying the Rothschilds' financial success. One further explanation is that the Rothschilds evolved a peculiarly effective set of business 'rules' and practices; the essence of the familial structure of the firm was that these were then passed from generation to generation. Indeed, it is possible to find examples of Mayer Amschel's great-grandchildren repeating his precepts in their correspondence with one another.

Conspicuous by its absence, it should be noted right away, was any regard for systematic accounting, despite Mayer Amschel's repeated admonitions on this subject. For example, in August 1814 – a critical moment in the firm's history – Salomon and Amschel had to confess that they were 'completely confused and do not know where the money is'. 'Together we are all rich and if all the five of us are taken into consideration we are worth quite a lot', wrote Salomon anxiously to Nathan. 'But where is the money?'[79] 'The payments we have to make are big, far too big', lamented Salomon the following year. 'Dear Nathan, you write that you have one million or two million over there. Well you really must have, because our brother Amschel is bust. We are bust. Carl is bust. So one of us must have the money.' In fact, the continental Rothschilds only averted 'bankruptcy' at this time by means of short-term borrowing.[80] As Salomon said, too much of their accounting was being done 'in the head' instead of on paper.[81] In fact, it was not until February 1816 that Nathan remitted sufficient funds to Frankfurt 'to pay all our debts'.[82]

Matters only improved gradually. Double-entry book-keeping was introduced in Paris and Frankfurt between 1816 and 1818.[83] Profit-and-loss accounts apparently began to be kept in London in 1828, and prior to 1873 balance sheets

---

[79]   RAL, T29/173, XI/109/0/7/13, Amschel to James, 22 Aug. 1814; RAL, T29/181, XI/109/0/8/7, Salomon to Nathan, London, 31 Aug.

[80]   RAL, XI/109/2/2/97, Amschel to his brothers, 21 Sept. 1815; RAL, XI/109/2/2/115, Amschel to his brothers, 28 Sept.; RAL, XI/109/2/2/116, Amschel to Carl and Nathan, 28 Sept.; RAL, XI/109/2/2/120, James and Salomon to Nathan, London, Sept.; RAL, XI/109/2/2/119, Salomon, Paris, to Nathan, London, 30 Sept.; RAL, XI/109/2/1/58, Salomon to Nathan, undated fragment, c. Oct.

[81]   RAL, XI/109/2/2/129, Salomon, Paris, to Nathan, London, 4 Oct. 1815; RAL, T30, XI/109/2/2/167, Salomon and James, Paris, to Nathan, London, 11 Nov.; RAL, XI/109/2/2/175, Carl, Amsterdam, to Nathan, London, 20 Nov.

[82]   RAL, T31, XI/109/4/1/7, Amschel, Frankfurt, to Nathan, London, 5 Jan. 1816; RAL, T31/87/2, XI/109/4, Amschel, Frankfurt, to James, Paris, 1 Feb.

[83]   RAL, T32/49/1, XI/109/5A, Amschel, Berlin, to Carl, 19 July 1816; RAL, T33/22, XI/109/5B, James, Paris, to Nathan, London, 14 Oct.; RAL, T33/283/1, XI/109/5B, same to same, 18 Oct.; RAL, T64 /212/3, Carl, Frankfurt, to Salomon, April 1818.

were drawn up only when the partnership agreement had to be revised. Incredibly, parts of the London bank were still not using the double-entry system as late as 1915.[84] It would appear that each transaction was simply assessed on its own merits and that, in the case of New Court, separate departments developed on a distinctly haphazard basis. There was no regular scrutiny of overall performance and the partners were often surprised by the results when they were drawn up. Nor were the various offices run on especially rational lines. Staff continued to be recruited from a relatively narrow pool – birth in the Frankfurt Judengasse was always an advantage in James's eyes – and were treated with paternalistic generosity while being wholly excluded from executive decision-making. By the standards of modern management consultancy, the London house was a nightmare, though it was only after the First World War that contemporaries began to identify organizational backwardness as a possible cause of relative decline.[85]

Yet propelling the Rothschilds forward, despite these apparent handicaps, was a set of simple but effective business 'rules'. The first and most elementary was that they worked extremely hard and put business first. In a revealing letter to a recalcitrant French customer in 1802, Nathan asked: 'Do you think that my Father will sell . . . Goods upon his own bills . . . without Profit? You are quite mistaken, my father's Chimney will not smoke without Profit'.[86] Of all the five brothers, Nathan inherited this trait in its most pronounced form. 'All you ever write', complained Salomon wearily in 1815, 'is pay this, pay that, send this, send that.'[87] But Nathan gloried in his ascetic materialism:

> I am writing to you giving my opinion, as it is my damned duty to write to you . . . I am reading through your letters not just once but maybe a hundred times. You can well imagine that yourself. After dinner I usually have nothing to do. I do not read books, I do not play cards, I do not go to the theatre, my only pleasure is my business and in this way I read Amschel's, Salomon's, James's and Carl's letters.[88]

Even when he was in his seventies, Amschel's working hours in Frankfurt were from 8 am to 7 pm, six days a week.[89] Their youngest brother James had the same approach. 'I think of nothing else but business', he assured Nathan. 'If I attend a society party, I go there to become acquainted with people who might be useful for

84   RAL, RFamFD/7A, Memorandum by Charles, 1915.
85   See R. Palin, *Rothschild Relish* (London, 1970).
86   RAL, I/218/36, Nathan to M.G. Gaudoit, Paris, 18 Aug. 1802; RAL, 1/218/36, Nathan to M.G. Trenelle, 5 September.
87   RAL, XI/109/2/2/156, Salomon, Paris, to Nathan, London, 29 Oct. 1815.
88   RAL, T31/1/5, Nathan, London, to Amschel, Carl and James, 2 Jan. 1816. See also RAL, T34/1, NMR 288, Nathan to Amschel, Frankfurt, 3 Jan. 1816.
89   RAL, T25/104/1/4/77, Anselm, Frankfurt, to Nat, Paris, 9 July 1841; RAL, T23/243, XI/109/42/3/22, same to same, undated, 1842; RAL, T18/338, XI/109/47/1/70, Hannah, Frankfurt, to Lionel, London, undated, 1844.

the business.'[90] Throughout his life – until his final illness in 1868, when he was 76 – James worked indefatigably, writing and dictating letters almost every day, even when supposedly 'taking the waters' or observing the Sabbath.

Second, client relationships – which invariably meant relations with governments – were assiduously cultivated. 'Father of blessed memory used to say', recalled Salomon, '"Any Court appointment means [business] advantages".'[91] Equally, once a 'court' had been secured, it had to be kept. As Mayer Carl recalled, 'Uncle [Amschel] used to say that Governments are like teeth: if you lose them, you never get them back again'.[92] But which governments? An important Rothschild insight (again originating with Mayer Amschel) was that it was 'better to deal with a government in difficulties than with one that has luck on its side'.[93] The Rothschilds took great care to assess the bargaining power and creditworthiness of governments before doing business with them. Some countries were dismissed as too risky, for example the former Spanish states of Latin America; conversely, others (e.g., Prussia and Russia) were regarded as too strong to concede profitable terms. It was the countries in between – politically weak enough to have to pay generous commissions, but not so weak that they were likely to default – which the Rothschilds preferred.

How could attractive clients be won? From the very earliest days, the Rothschilds firmly believed in winning market share by undercutting their rivals. This principle was still being cited by James in the 1830s. In 1836, for example, James gave his nephews some revealing advice about how to sell French bonds on the Paris stock exchange:

> When you are buying or selling rentes, try not to look at making a profit, but rather, your aim should be to get the brokers used to the idea that they need to come to you. . . . [O]ne has, initially, to make some sacrifices so that the people then get used to the idea to come to you, my dear nephews, and as such one first has to spread the sugar about in order to catch the birds later on.[94]

A related principle was that many small deals were as good as a few big deals: the Rothschilds never turned up their noses at trifling transactions, and James was fond of telling his nephews to 'do business' even when only the tiniest sums were to be made. This might seem so obvious as to be a truism. But when Alexander Baring sought to exclude the Rothschilds from the French reparations loan in 1817, he

---

[90]   RAL, T63/5/1, XI/109/8, Salomon and James, Paris, to Nathan, London, 6 Nov. 1817; RAL, T5/171, IX/85/1, James to Nathan, 24 Jan. 1818.

[91]   RAL, XI/109/9/4/6 109/10/1/6, Salomon to Nathan, Jan. 1818.

[92]   RAL XI/109/101/2, Mayer Carl, Berlin, to his cousins and nephews, London, 19 March 1870.

[93]   RAL, T30; XI/109/2/2/170, Amschel, Frankfurt, to Salomon and James, Paris, 15 Nov. 1815.

[94]   RAL, XI/109J/J/36, James, Paris, to his nephews, London, 15 Nov. 1836.

made it clear to James's rival Laffitte that this was because of the Rothschilds' 'Jewish' business methods, which he refused to adopt:[95]

> Baring told him: 'These gentlemen are working like Jews. How could we cooperate? Their principles are different. They are working on 20 transactions at the same time . . . with the only aim to do business. It is like stock-jobbing. . . He added that we are right in what we did because we succeeded and made money. However, he does not want – so he said – to do business in this manner. Now we try – so he said – to bring down the English stocks, after having sold ours, in order to buy them back.[96]

It was not their religion per se, in other words, so much as their business methods which Baring found objectionable, though he instinctively thought of these as 'Jewish' in character.

Equally important was the careful cultivation of 'friends in high places'. Of all Mayer Amschel's pieces of business advice, this was the one most frequently cited by his sons. 'You know, dear Nathan', wrote Salomon in October 1815, 'what father used to say about sticking to a man in government.'[97] And again: '[Y]ou remember father's principle that you have to be ready to try everything to get in with such a great government figure'.[98] Nor had Mayer Amschel left them in doubt as to how such politicians could best be wooed: 'Our late father taught us that if a high-placed person enters into a [financial] partnership with a Jew, he belongs to the Jew (*gehört er dem Juden*)'.[99] Among the most important Rothschild 'clients' in this period were Karl Buderus, the Elector of Hesse-Cassel's senior finance official; Karl Theodor Anton von Dalberg, Prince-Primate of the Rheinish Confederation from 1806 to 1814; Leopold of Saxe-Coburg, consort to Princess Charlotte, only child of George IV, and later (1830) King Leopold I of the Belgians; John Charles Herries, British Commissary-in-Chief in October 1811, later (briefly) Chancellor of the Exchequer and President of the Board of Trade; Charles William Stewart, third marquis of Londonderry, Lord Castlereagh's half-brother, British delegate at the Congresses of Vienna, Troppau, Laybach and Verona; the duc d'Orléans, later Louis Philippe, King of France; the Austrian Chancellor Prince Metternich; and Prince Esterházy, the imperial ambassador in London.

If the Rothschilds were generous to those whose political influence they valued, they treated their banking rivals very differently. In the early years, a pattern of fierce hostility to all competitors was established. The brothers habitually talked of 'putting spokes in wheels' of rival 'scoundrels' and 'sharpshooters', or dealing

---

95   J. Laffitte, *Mémoires de Laffitte* (Paris, 1932), pp. 114f.

96   RAL, T64/179/2, XI/109/9, James, Paris, to his brothers, 14 Feb. 1818.

97   RAL, XI/109/2/2/149, Salomon, Paris, to Nathan, London, 21 Oct. 1815.

98   RAL, XI/109/2/2/153, Salomon and James, Paris, to Nathan, London, 25 Oct. 1815.

99   RAL, T63 138/2, Salomon and James, Paris, to Nathan, London, 22 Oct. 1817.

them 'blows where it hurts'.[100] Their father's classic advice on this subject – much repeated down the generations – was 'If you can't make yourself loved, make yourself feared'.[101] James in particular never lost his competitive edge. '[M]y heart breaks when I see how everyone is trying to push us out of the business deal.' he wrote to his nephews in 1844. 'The stone on the wall is envious and is an enemy of us.'[102] His campaign against the Pereire brothers after they broke with him and set up the Crédit Mobilier was relentless, and ultimately successful.

One of the crucial ways in which the Rothschilds consistently outdid their rivals was by having superior political and financial intelligence. In this period, postal services were slow and insecure: letters sent from Paris to Frankfurt usually took just 48 hours in 1814; but mail from London could take up to a week to reach Frankfurt, and the service from Paris to Berlin took nine days in 1817.[103] Compulsive correspondents as they were, the brothers were always trying to find ways of speeding the postal service up. So anxious was Amschel to have up to date exchange rates from London in June 1814 that he asked Nathan to send his letters by more than one route – via Paris and Amsterdam as well as Dunkirk – and to use colour-coded envelopes so that his contact at the post office could tell at a glance whether the exchange rate was rising (blue) or falling (red).[104] Increasingly, however, they dispensed with the post, relying instead on their own private couriers, including agents at Dover who were authorized to charter boats for Rothschild business.[105] In 1815, Nathan famously got the news of Napoleon's defeat first, thanks to the speed with which a Rothschild courier was able to relay the fifth and conclusive extraordinary bulletin (issued in Brussels during the night of 18/19 June) via Dunkirk and Deal to reach New Court roughly 24 hours later. This was at least thirty-six hours before Major Henry Percy delivered Wellington's official despatch to the Cabinet.[106] By the mid-1820s, such couriers were being sent regularly: in December 1825 alone, the Paris house sent 18 couriers to Calais (and hence to London), three to Saarbrücken, one to Brussels and one to

[100]   RAL, XI/109/0/3/4, Carl, Frankfurt, to Salomon, 29 June 1814; RAL, T29/63, XI/109/0/3/5, Amschel, Frankfurt, to Salomon, 29 June; RAL, XI/109/0/3/7, Carl, Frankfurt, to Salomon, 30 June; RAL, T30, XI/109/2/3/26/1, Amschel to James, Paris, 26 Jan.; RAL, T30, XI/109/2/3/49, Amschel, Frankfurt, to Carl and Nathan, 31 Aug.

[101]   RAL, T27/216, James, Paris, to Salomon and Nathan, 8 March 1817.

[102]   RAL, X1/109J/J/45, James, Paris, to his nephews, London, 18 March 1844.

[103]   RAL, T29/181; XI/109/0/7/21, Carl, Frankfurt, to Salomon, 23 Aug. 1814; RAL, T63/28/1, XI/109/8, Carl, Berlin, to his brothers, 4 Nov. 1817.

[104]   RAL, XI/109/0/2/1, Amschel, Frankfurt, to Nathan, London, 19 June 1814; RAL, XI/109/0/2/5, Amschel to Salomon, 29 June.

[105]   RAL, T5/29, Braun, [James's clerk in] Paris, to James, London, 13 Sept. 1813. Cf. L. Wolf, 'Rothschildiana', in idem, Essays in Jewish History, ed. by C. Roth (London, 1934), pp. 266f.

[106]   Wolf, 'Rothschildiana', pp. 281ff.; Corti, Rise, p. 137; Lord [Victor] Rothschild, The Shadow of a Great Man (London, 1982), pp. 135–7.

Naples.[107] From 1824, carrier pigeons were also used, though the brothers do not seem to have relied on these as much as has sometimes been assumed.[108] This system retained its edge until well into the 1830s, when the development of the railway, the telegraph and the steamship opened a new era in more public forms of communication. In one of his first references to 'telegraphic communication', James complained revealingly to Nathan: 'Over here people are too well informed and there is therefore little opportunity to do anything'.[109]

Closely connected with their enthusiasm for swift communication was a penchant for secrecy. The five brothers almost always corresponded with one another in *Judendeutsch* (German transliterated into Hebrew characters) partly to make life difficult for the prying eyes of Metternich's spies. When more security was needed, they used simple codes. The first of these was used when Mayer Amschel was looking after the finances of the exiled Elector of Hesse-Kassel, in defiance of the French authorities in the Rhineland. Later, when gold was being shipped semi-legally across the Channel to France in 1812–13, letters referred to Nathan as 'Langbein', London became 'Jerusalem', and the transfers of bullion across the Channel were codenamed 'Rabbi Moses' or 'Rabbi Mosche'.[110] This culture of secrecy was inculcated early. At the age of just eleven Salomon's son Anselm refused to let his teacher correct a letter he was writing to his father. 'My dear mother', the boy explained, 'how can I possibly divulge the secrets which I share with my father to Mr Sachs?'[111]

The development of this network of swift and secure communication had a number of 'spin-off' benefits. First, it allowed the Rothschilds to offer a first-class postal service to the European elite. While in London in 1822, Chateaubriand received 'an important despatch' from the Duchess of Duras through her 'protegé Rothschild'.[112] The idea soon caught on. By 1823, 'receiving news from Rothschild' was an integral part of the Countess Nesselrode's routine.[113] Perhaps the most distinguished – if not the most powerful – enthusiasts for the Rothschild postal

[107] Gille, *Maison Rothschild*, vol. I, pp.187f.

[108] See e.g., RAL, XI/109J/J/36, James, Paris, to Nathan and his sons, London, 20 April 1836; RAL, T25/104/0/86, Isaac Cohen, Boulogne, to Lionel, 8 Sept. 1840. Cf. Rothschild, *Shadow*, pp. 135–7.

[109] RAL, XI/109J/J/36, James, Paris, to Nathan and Nat, London, 19 May 1836.

[110] RAL, T27/63, Amschel, Frankfurt, to James, Paris, 17 June 1811; RAL, T27/60, Amschel, Frankfurt, to James, 23 June; RAL, T27/15, XI/82/10/8, unidentified author to Nathan, 15 Oct.; RAL, T27/73, XI/38/81a/6, 28 Jan. 1814.

[111] RAL, T29/13, Gelche, Frankfurt, to Salomon, 23 March 1814.

[112] F.R. Chateaubriand, *Correspondance générale de Chateaubriand* (Paris, 1913), vol. III, pp. 663f.

[113] D. Lieven, *The Private Letters of Princess Lieven to Prince Metternich, 1820–1826* (London, 1948), p. 237.

service after 1840 were the young British Queen Victoria and her consort Prince Albert.[114]

Their courier service also meant that the Rothschilds were in a position to provide a unique news service. Major political events as well as confidential information could be relayed from one city to another well ahead of official channels. In 1817, James offered to relay details of French diplomatic despatches from Paris to London – made available by a 'friend' in government circles – so that they reached Nathan before the despatches themselves reached the French ambassador.[115] In 1818, a British diplomat bound for the Aix Congress was 'struck very much' by Nathan's 'correct information as to the details of our party and his knowledge of the persons likely to compose it, some of whose names I believe had not even transpired at the Foreign Office'.[116] When the Duc de Berry was assassinated in February 1820, it was the Rothschilds who broke the story in Frankfurt and Vienna.[117] Likewise, when Princess Charlotte died in 1821, it was again the Rothschilds who spread the news to Paris.[118] Canning disliked the fact that the Rothschilds constantly scooped British ambassadorial reports; but he could hardly afford to ignore news like the Turkish capitulation at Ackerman.[119] The Rothschilds also broke the news of the French revolution of July 1830 to Lord Aberdeen in London and Metternich in Bohemia.[120]

It was not long before statesmen and diplomats began themselves to make use of the Rothschilds' network of communication, partly because it was quicker than the official courier systems used for relaying diplomatic correspondence, but also because messages of a non-binding nature could be sent from government to government indirectly via the brothers' own private correspondence. By the early 1830s, the Rothschilds were providing a vital channel of semi-official communication between Paris, London and Vienna at a time of acute international tension. It is not hard to see why they were willing to provide this service. Clearly,

---

[114]   RAL, T23/157, Stockmar to Lionel, 20 July 1840; RAL, T18/270, XI/109/46/1/31, Anselm, Frankfurt, to Lionel and Billy [Anthony], London, 2 March 1844; RAL, T51/28, XI/113/2B/2, Anson, Osborne House, to NMR, 23 July 1845; Cf. Davis, *English Rothschilds*, p. 132f.

[115]   RAL, T27/280, XI/109/7 (also T62/ 85/4), James, Paris, to Salomon and Nathan, 18 June 1817.

[116]   Kynaston, *City*, vol. I, p. 54f.

[117]   Corti, *Rise*, p. 242; Gille, *Banque et crédit*, p. 262.

[118]   P.F.H. de Serre, *Correspondance du comte de Serre 1796–1824, annotée et publiée par son fils* (Paris, 1876), vol. IV, p. 249.

[119]   A. Aspinall (ed.), *The Letters of King George IV, 1812–30* (Cambridge, 1938), vol. III, p. 175.

[120]   Corti, *Rise*, pp. 424f., 427f.; F. Balfour, *The Life of George, 4th Earl of Aberdeen* (Paris, 1922), vol. I, pp. 254f.; N. Gash, *Mr Secretary Peel* (London, 1961), p. 638; F. von Gentz, *Briefe von Friedrich von Gentz an Pilat: Ein Beitrag zur Geschichte Deutschlands im XIX. Jahrhundert*, ed. by K. von Mendelssohn-Bartholdy (Leipzig, 1868), vol. II, pp. 288f.

it gave them advance knowledge of great power foreign policy as it was being formed, and this in turn allowed them to make better-informed investment decisions. It also gave them a chance to pursue their own political agenda (which generally aimed at averting war between the great powers because of its negative financial consequences). Given that they dominated the international bond market and therefore had substantial leverage over most of the major European states – none of whom could contemplate war without resorting to borrowing – the Rothschilds were plainly more than mere messengers.

Of course, if the Rothschilds had relied solely on their own five houses for intelligence, the system would have been very limited. But they soon developed a 'reach' which extended far beyond their original European bases. As none of Mayer Amschel's grandsons wished or was allowed to establish a new foreign 'house', this was done by building up a select group of salaried agents employed to take care of the bank's interests in other markets: principally Madrid, St Petersburg, Brussels and later New York, New Orleans, Havana, Mexico and San Francisco. The lines of communication with these agents formed a complex new intelligence and business network. Men like August Belmont in New York or Daniel Weisweiller in Madrid inevitably enjoyed considerable autonomy because of their remoteness and their greater local knowledge; but although permitted to trade on their own account they always remained Rothschild agents and were not allowed to forget it. Nor was this network of formal influence all; of comparable importance was the larger but looser network of links to other banks, as well as to stockbrokers, central banks and financial newspapers.

In 1826, the liberal Fournier-Verneuil made the first of many claims that the French government – in this case Villèle's – was the corrupt puppet of 'the aristocracy of finance, the most arid and least noble of all aristocracies' at whose head stood none other than 'M. le baron R...'. [121] Two years later, the Radical MP Thomas Duncombe complained in the British House of Commons about 'a new, and formidable power, till these days unknown in Europe':

> master of unbounded wealth, he boasts that he is the arbiter of peace and war, and that the credit of nations depends upon his nod; his correspondents are innumerable; his couriers outrun those of sovereign princes, and absolute sovereigns; ministers of state are in his pay. Paramount in the cabinets of continental Europe, he aspires to the domination of our own.[122]

In the mid-1830s, an American magazine gave a similar assessment, though in less pejorative terms: 'The Rothschilds are the wonders of modern banking . . . holding a whole continent in the hollow of their hands. . . . Not a cabinet moves without

---

[121]   M. Fournier-Verneuil, *Paris: Tableau moral et philosophique* (Paris, 1826), pp. 51–2, 64f.

[122]   *Hansard*, New Series, vol. XVIII, pp. 540–43.

their advice'.[123] The English diarist Thomas Raikes noted at around the same time: 'The Rothschilds have become the metallic sovereigns of Europe. From their different establishments in Paris, London, Vienna, Frankfurt and Naples, they have obtained a control over the European exchange which no party ever before could accomplish, and they now seem to hold the strings of the public purse. No sovereign without their assistance now could raise a loan'.[124] An anonymous German cartoonist made essentially the same point (though more vividly) when he portrayed a grotesquely caricatured Jew – clearly a composite Rothschild – as 'Die Generalpumpe' (a play on the double meaning of the German *pumpen*, to pump or to lend). Rothschild, the cartoon suggests, is a monstrous engine, pumping money around the world.[125] By the end of this period, many observers had begun to see the Rothschilds as more than merely allies of the European States: they now appeared to have acquired a unique power of their own which was independent of the great powers and near universal. In his essay 'Rothschild and the European States' (1841), Alexandre Weill made the point succinctly: while 'Rothschild had need of the States to become Rothschild', he now 'no longer needs the State, but the State still has want of him'.[126] A year later, the liberal historian Jules Michelet noted in his journal: 'M. Rothschild knows Europe prince by prince, and the bourse courtier by courtier. He has all their accounts in his head, that of the courtiers and that of the kings; he talks to them without even consulting his books. To one such he says: "Your account will go into the red if you appoint such a minister"'.[127]

The economic historian is often tempted to juxtapose myth and reality. However, although some qualification is clearly needed, such views were, though exaggerated and often gratuitously hostile, not very far wide of the mark. In the way it expanded and dominated the international capital market, the Rothschild bank was in many ways 'the World Pump' of the *Vormärz* era. The remarkable thing is that, despite its enormous wealth and its multinational character, the firm remained at heart a family concern, albeit with a very distinctive ethos and set of business methods. These, rather than any mystical aid, constituted the real Rothschild talisman.

---

[123]   Quoted in R. Glanz, 'The Rothschild Legend in America', in *Jewish Social Studies* (1957), p. 20.

[124]   Kynaston, *City*, vol. I, p. 90f.

[125]   V. Cowles, *The Rothschilds: A Family of Fortune* (London, 1973), p. 71.

[126]   Reeves, *Rothschilds*, p. 101.

[127]   Gille, *Maison Rothschild*, vol. I, p. 487.

CHAPTER 2

The Rothschild Archive

Victor Gray with Melanie Aspey

In order to explain the history of the body of material which today makes up the Rothschild Archive, I must begin with an elementary early history of the Rothschild family. Mayer Amschel Rothschild, a member of the Frankfurt Jewish community, was a merchant dealing in general goods, including textiles but with a specialism in historical coins sold by mail order, which brought him to the attention of a number of important collectors. In 1798, his third son, Nathan Mayer, as part of a strategy for expansion, moved to England to buy much sought-after English textiles at the best terms for supply into mainland Europe. He stayed in Manchester until 1809 when he made a final move to London and concentrated on an aspect of trading activity which he had been gradually developing – that of mercantile credit.

Meanwhile, back at home, his four brothers had been playing a full part in their father's business, both in the Frankfurt office and by travelling in increasingly wide circles on the firm's business, developing and feeding a broadening range of contacts and agents. This circle was put to a corporate test in 1814 when Nathan was commissioned by the British government to assemble substantial quantities of gold from around Europe to feed Wellington's army and to pay the subsidies due to Britain's allies. The conspicuous success of their corporate activity meant that they were well poised after the war to take up an important and eventually central role in the field of bond issues on behalf of European and other governments.

As a result of this development, by the early 1820s, not only was Nathan a key figure in London banking, but James had established himself in Paris as de Rothschild Frères, Salomon was spending much time in Vienna, where his presence developed into the firm of S.M. Rothschild, Carl took off for Naples, setting up C.M. de Rothschild e figli, and Amschel developed his father's home business in Frankfurt, M.A. Rothschild und Söhne. Of these branches, the Naples bank closed in 1863 after Carl's death and the fall of the monarchy, the Frankfurt bank closed in 1901 for want of a male Rothschild heir, its business being transferred to the Disconto-Gesellschaft. The Viennese bank was seized by the Nazis in 1938 and aryanized. The Paris bank persisted, until it was nationalized in 1981 and then, eventually, allowed to recreate itself as Rothschild & Cie Banque. The London bank still flourishes.

The archival history of these five institutions is chequered, to say the least. Nothing survives – to the best of our knowledge – from the Naples bank, which was always, like Vienna, regarded as a branch office to Frankfurt. It is known that on its closure, whatever survived of interest went back to Frankfurt, to suffer in time the fate which was to await the corpus of archives of M.A. Rothschild und Söhne. Five railway-carriage loads of documents were pulped on its closure in 1901. A significant number of important earlier documents were set aside for transfer to Paris but even much of this fell victim to over-caution or neglect and was burned. The papers of the Viennese bank were assumed to have been destroyed by the Nazis on their seizure of the Bank.[1] In 1994, we became aware of the survival of some papers in the Special State Trophies Archive in Moscow, which contains huge quantities of material seized by the Russians on their advance at the end of the war. Several scholars, not least Niall Ferguson, have had the chance to examine them since. They clearly do not represent a full body – what remains indeed has the air more of a mixed bag of papers grabbed hastily from desks and cupboards, rather than a systemic assembling of a full bank archive – but they contain an interesting and important clutch of papers from the early years of the Frankfurt bank, apparently put together as a proto-family archive by Salomon in Vienna in the 1840s. The brothers' sense of their own lifetime achievement can be seen not only, therefore, in the iconographic paintings of the semi-mythical stories of their beginnings which they commissioned in these years, but in this very practical desire to see a historical record retained.

Prior to the nationalization of the French bank in 1981, the archives of de Rothschild Frères had been transferred to the custody of the Archives Nationales and are now stored in the Centre des Archives du Monde du Travail at Roubaix, in northern France. These are far more comprehensive, covering the whole period from as early as 1811, immediately upon James's arrival in France, through to the Second World War. Extensive series of copies of outgoing letters survive as well as the routine incoming correspondence from the other Rothschild banks and their agents. There is a great deal of material on the French family's involvement in commercial activities, including railways in France, Lombardy, Austria and beyond, and involvement in oil, minerals and mining. Access to these archives is given with the written permission of the French family.[2]

In comparison with all these vicissitudes in mainland Europe, the archives of the London bank have enjoyed comparative stability from external upsets and disasters. From very soon after Nathan's arrival in England, and before Nathan began to involve himself in the business of banking, records survive – somewhat miraculously, given Nathan's own complete disorganization as a record keeper, the subject of more than one rebuke from his father. Indeed, the body of books and papers which survive from his years as a textile merchant in Manchester are in themselves regarded by historians of commercial and industrial development as among the most significant bodies of evidence surviving for the textile industry from this time and place. They include ledgers and journals, correspondence and accounts with small cutters, dyers and printers, together with one of the family's

---

[1]   More is now known about these papers. See the concluding paragraph by Melanie Aspey.

[2]   Applications for access to these papers (Fond AQ132) should be made to the CAMT who will forward a request for access to The Rothschild Archive.

most prized survivals, the so-called Cotton Book, a sample book used by Nathan Mayer when travelling, to display textile samples to his clients and take orders, from which he commissioned suppliers in and around Manchester.

From the beginning of the banking years in London, there is a very wide-ranging archive which continues through to the present day. I cannot say comprehensive – I wish I could – because the process of steady and efficient storage of papers for evidential purposes within the business has, across two centuries, been tempered by periodic and deliberate phases of destruction. Both the second and third heads of N.M. Rothschild & Sons (NMR), Baron Lionel and Natty, the first Lord Rothschild, required their executors to destroy all personal papers from their years of office that were held on the bank's premises, setting a family tradition which has been honoured all too frequently for an archivist's taste. These purges have not, it has to be said, affected the routine correspondence and files of the Bank; only those clutches of documents which arrived on and emanated from their own personal desks. Nevertheless, as you will recognize, these are precisely the sources which historians would most have wished to survive. It is a matter of daily regret to us – though tempered by the sheer volume and quantity of what remains. This last point indicates the peculiar quality of the Rothschild banking archive – its intermixture of personal and business papers. This of course is far from unique, but given the widespread involvements of the Rothschild family across two centuries, it gives to the archive its particular richness and diversity. For the members of the Rothschild family in London, the Bank was an extension of their study at home as well as a place of banking business. When the cause was right, the offices at New Court were put to use without hesitation. So, for example, there survives, from the 1930s, a valuable body of paperwork relating to the Central British Fund for German Jewry, a body set up by Lionel and Anthony de Rothschild in the early 1930s and functioning from New Court in order to find employment for Jewish refugees from the Nazi regime. In a totally different vein, from earlier on, there survive, from the Estates Department of the Bank, housed in New Court and handling property management and private accounts on behalf of the partners, papers relating, for example, to the purchase of plants and seeds for the gardens of the Rothschilds' first substantial country house, Gunnersbury; building accounts for more than one of the later great houses; and records of purchases of jewellery and paintings. All of these are sought after by social historians of many shapes and persuasions.

Most importantly, this mixture of business and social is embodied in the letters which each of the brothers wrote to the others (and to their nephews) in the years between 1814 and the death of the last of them in 1868. It is these letters which form the richest material for historians – or rather, will form the most fertile seedbed in years to come. The letters have a quality all of their own. There are some 20,000 letters surviving in this series. Written mostly in Judaeo-German (or Judendeutsch), they have largely hitherto defied attempts to prise open their meaning (of this I shall say more). The Hebrew script when deciphered reveals not Hebrew words but German beneath. In itself then, a knowledge of Hebrew script and German, might, one would have thought, have opened them up. Added to these two complications however is the particular problem of the handwriting of each of the brothers, each highly individualistic and unrelenting in its individuality. Amschel, in particular, in Frankfurt, had devised a way of joining up separated Hebrew characters which is almost unique to himself. Once this barrier is passed, there remain the problems of a fairly idiosyncratic German – often ungrammatical and ambiguous, with a sprinkling of Hebrew words within the text. Finally – and ironically, perhaps, least impenetrable of all – there remain the use of code words for key places, players and commodities in their transactions – Jerusalem for London, Pheasants for Gold, etc.

The complications which have hitherto kept historians away from this material were sufficiently clear to the brothers themselves in writing the letters for them to feel confident of the medium as a safe haven from prying external eyes. The letters are therefore extremely frank, open, uncompromising, and often earthy in their comments on contemporary personalities and situations. From the campaign to fund Wellington, through the years of revolution, 1830 and 1848, and beyond, a succession of the major financial, economic and political events of the nineteenth century are described from the extremely well-informed perspective of the Rothschild brothers, by then major players on the world financial scene. All this alongside the humdrum and the everyday. Alongside the *haute politique*, you will find the news of a child's health or a request to send some small, favourite item of confectionery or a fashionable piece of clothing, for example. There can be no doubt that these letters, in their own right, constitute the core of the richness of The Rothschild Archive.

The only disappointment is that we have only a handful of Nathan's own letters. Given their essentially private nature, copies of his letters were not systematically kept or stored by him in the Bank and sadly, among the French bank's archives – the only other of the banks to have a substantial series of records from the time – the private correspondence between the brothers was not retained. We can only guess, therefore, from the brothers' responses and the few items that survive, at the tone he adopted in his letters, and imagine the dyspeptic outbursts which produced squeals of outrage and hurt from the others.

Around and beyond this series are letters from the Rothschilds' correspondents and agents around the world. As with other merchant banks of the period, it was upon this increasingly developed body of informants that the Rothschilds depended for up-to-date information. The network stretched from Manchester to Macao, from St Petersburg to Valparaíso. Among the letters arriving at New Court are, for example, items from Benjamin Davidson in San Francisco giving a graphic description of the town in the gold-rush years of the 1840s or from J.B. Montefiore describing Australia in its own first flush of gold fever. These letters, of which there are not tens but hundreds of thousands (not all of them, of course, equally riveting), remain largely unexplored, though it is clear that an increasing body of scholars are becoming aware of them and there are promising signs of their developing use. In recent years, the value to national economic and financial history of the detailed accounts of conditions, supplied by local agents, has been reflected in the work of scholars using the Rothschild agents' letters in such places as Spain, Hungary, Cuba and Mexico.

It is also important to grasp the fact that the London banking archive is as much a history of the other sister banks – for at least part of their history – as it is of itself. The most informative and best-preserved material is that received from those banks – the in-letters – both private and general. Given the detail packed into the pages of these letters on local markets, politics and society, they constitute by far the best source anywhere for an understanding of the local positioning of the Rothschilds and their banks and the level and type of access they had to local news.

Much more could be said about the range of business papers surviving from NMR. I could talk of mining, bullion, sovereign loans and private clients. But this task has already been well achieved by Simone Mace, a former archivist, in an article in 1992 in *Business Archives: Sources and History*.[3]

It is important to add to any description of The Rothschild Archive as it stands an indication of the non-banking material which is included in the collection. I have already drawn attention to the fact that business and personal affairs are often inextricably mixed among the papers. But the vault of the family bank has, from the earliest days, been recognized as an obvious repository for material arising from personal activity and relating to the family's history. Over recent years, with a growing commitment by the Rothschild family to the development and maintenance of the Archive in London as a centre for research in many aspects of Rothschild history, this trend has increased and members of the family, both in the UK and beyond, have chosen to place papers in the custody of the archivists in London. Given the range of activities in which the family has been involved across two centuries this predictably brings to our doors a diversity of researchers, many of whom might not normally be expected to find their way into a bank archive. Principal among them are art historians, who find, concealed among the personal accounts and letters, many records of the acquisition of fine furniture and Old Masters during the heyday of collecting; for example, from Baron Ferdinand, whose collections now survive – in part at least – at Waddesdon Manor. Among the family papers are the diaries – in German – of Charlotte, wife of Baron Lionel, head of the Bank from 1836 to 1878, full of comments on social and political events, and throwing much light on the key issues of the day, viewed from the perspective of an intelligent and centrally placed observer – ideal hunting ground for the social historian.

Two significant bodies of papers which have arrived are the so-called Laffitte Papers – confusingly called, not after the rue Laffitte in Paris where de Rothschild Frères' offices were located, but after the château and vineyard where they were later stored. These, deposited by a member of the French branch of the family, contain miscellaneous but substantial files extending back in some cases to the earliest decades of Baron James' activity in Paris. Alongside papers relating to

---

[3]   S. Mace, 'The Archives of the London Merchant Bank of N.M. Rothschild & Sons', in *Business Archives: Sources and History*, vol. 64, 1992, pp. 1–14.

the acquisition and stocking of the estate and mansion at Ferrières and of many other French houses, and papers relating, to take an example, to the will of Victor Hugo, an account holder with the Bank, there are many useful and interesting files demonstrating the distinctive approach of the Paris house – distinctive, that is, from the London bank – with its considerable involvement, through the family, in a wide range of industrial companies, including Le Nickel, Rio Tinto, the Chemin de Fer du Nord and the oil fields of Baku and Batum. There are also one or two surprises, like the files of letters sent regularly to the Bank by an unidentified informer, giving reflections on and details of contemporary political issues, both internal and external, from the heart of French government and society in the 1880s and 1890s.

Supplementing these are the body of papers of the French family, formerly, like the Austrian papers I mentioned earlier, in the Special State Trophies Archive in Moscow and released by the Russian Government in 1994. These contain a random collection of papers relating to the activities of the French family in the late nineteenth and early twentieth centuries, including the drafts of a number of plays by Henri de Rothschild, political correspondence of Maurice de Rothschild, Député for the Hautes Alpes in the 1920s and 1930s, and the correspondence with artists and art dealers of Baron Edmond at the turn of the century.

The complex of subjects within the Archive – indeed, within individual documents – places particular demands on the archivist, demands which can only ultimately be met by the completion of detailed item-by-item cataloguing. In an archive the strength of which is based upon correspondence, and in correspondence which regularly touches upon a range of subjects, nothing less than this detailed treatment can ensure that the researcher is directed to all relevant letters on a particular theme and has explored every avenue before he can be sure his search is complete. We are light-years away from achieving this. The archive contains millions of letters, and the cataloguing is complicated by the fact that they are written in a range of half a dozen or more languages. The availability of a spectrum of language skills among our staff is vital.

Nevertheless, we have determined not to be daunted by the size of the task and have embarked on the first stage of a multi-level plan to open up the archive. The initial stage is to produce a guide to the contents of the Archive which will indicate the broad content and significance of every individual group of letters, volumes or other documents. That challenge, spearheaded by Melanie Aspey, has come to fruition with the publication of the Guide in 2000.[4] The Guide serves to indicate to us, within the Archive, the relative importance of individual groups of papers, so that a structured programme of cataloguing down to the next level – which in many cases will be the level of the individual document – can be undertaken. In this, we shall make full use of database and text-retrieval software to ensure the most rapid access to individual subjects and persons.

---

[4]   M. Aspey, *The Rothschild Archive: a Guide to the Collection* (London, 2000).

In a sense, we already know which are the most important series for historians. They are, as I have indicated, the Judendeutsch letters between the brothers. Since 1989 a scheme of translation and transcription has been under way, using the services and skills of Mordechai Zucker. Nine years later, something like 15 per cent of the total has been completed. The publication of Niall Ferguson's history,[5] together with the publication of the Guide, will, we can confidently predict, increase the level of demand among historians for access to these letters, and already thought is being given to the possibility of accelerating the programme and possibly publishing, in one form or another, the results thereof. In the course of this exercise it is a very real option to pursue the route of storing the scanned images of the original Judendeutsch alongside, possibly, a transcription of the underlying German text, and certainly an English translation, opening up the possibilities of word-search and of critical assessment of the translations.

These goals are obviously the targets for development towards which we work. In the meantime, like any other banking archive, we respond to the needs of researchers, both external and internal to the Bank. I have already mentioned the unusually broad range of academic researchers who come to us, and part of our goal in publishing the forthcoming Guide will be to ensure that this volume of use increases. It is also a goal to roll back the admittedly, by today's standards, fairly conservative date of closure after which material has not until now been accessible to researchers. This has stood, for many years, at 1918. Already we are countenancing requests for material to be made available for the period up to 1930, restricting access only where proper schedules of the records have not yet been made. The next target will be 1939, and so on, that movement forward limited almost wholly and solely by the speed at which catalogues of material can be compiled.

In all of this development we enjoy the active support of the members of the Rothschild family still connected to the Bank, of those who form part of the Archive Panel which oversees the work of the professional team and of those who have deposited material with us. The substantial investment made in the preservation of the archive begs some sort of return, and the fullest exploration of it by historians constitutes that perceptible and measurable benefit to the outside world, acknowledged by the family.

While there is a firm commitment to welcoming and attracting the academic community to the Archive, there is another equally important aspect of our work which has, quite properly, to be accommodated alongside. It has been a central aim of the current staff of the Archive to ensure that the Archive works effectively and promptly to meet the needs of the N.M. Rothschild Group throughout its offices in some forty countries around the world. In this, we have sought to be more than reactive. Of course, like other archives, we respond to historical enquiries when presented to us by staff, but we have sought to go beyond this, presenting

---

[5]   N. Ferguson, *The World's Banker: a History of the House of Rothschild* (London, 1998).

information in a readily available format before the question is ever asked. Our range of leaflets, covering the history of Rothschild involvement in countries all around the world, best typifies this approach.[6]

Most ambitious of all has been the compilation of 'Rothschild Interactive', a CD-ROM containing some 2000 screens of information on the history of the Rothschild family and its commercial activities. The CD-ROM is the result of some two years of research by the staff of the Archive. Viewers will be able to roam around the family tree, explore biographies of individual members of the Rothschild family, learn about their interests and artistic collections, their houses and gardens, investigate their charitable work in many countries and see a range of cartoons, portraits and literary extracts relating to the family. On the business front they will be able, by touching a globe, to go to any country with which the family has been involved and explore the history of that involvement. Alternatively, they can choose a business sector – be it gold refining, asset management or wine growing – and view an account of that involvement. The CD-ROM is seen as a valuable business tool for those who wish rapid access to a body of detailed knowledge past and present and an attractive corporate gift for clients. It will demonstrate very effectively the degree to which the Archive has been able to make a positive contribution to the current life and marketing activities of the Bank.

What the CD-ROM will prove to those who are sceptical of the value of retaining a substantial archive is the fascination of the history of the Rothschild family and bank. Even for those bankers who profess no interest whatever in the past and regard it as an unjustifiable nostalgia trip – and believe it or not there are such – the realization that clients are far from uninterested – indeed thirst for knowledge of that history – comes as a powerful correction.

This has been amply demonstrated by the exhibition which the Archive has researched and produced for display, during our bicentenary year, in the Museum of London, which has also provided effective backdrop for the entertaining of clients.

I make no apology for finishing with an account of these intra-institutional, even commercial, aspects of the work of the Archive. I remain firmly of the view that, on the day when an archive ceases to be seen as having a living value to its originating organization, a kind of atrophying begins, slow perhaps, but nevertheless unremitting and ultimately detrimental – if not fatal – to its long-term well-being. I am pleased to report that, in this case, the patient is not only healthy, but positively bursting with life.

---

[6]   More ambitiously some of these leaflets have been transformed into booklets of varying size and format. For example R. Schofield, *Along Rothschild Lines: the Story of Rothschild and Railways across the World* (London, 2002); C. Shaw, *The Necessary Security: an illustrated History of Rothschild Bonds* (London, 2006).

The Rothschild Archive at the beginning of the 21st century

Melanie Aspey

The fact that there are two names associated with this article now that it appears in print is perhaps an early indication that changes have taken place at The Rothschild Archive since this paper was delivered in 1998, changes which, it must be said, we could not have envisaged at the time, not the least of which is the impact of the Internet.

The Rothschild Archive: a Guide to the Collection finally appeared in 2000, its route to press impeded slightly by increased demands placed on the archivists: from the business, in support of current projects, including the transformation of the Museum of London exhibition into a travelling display; and from the academic community, in pursuit of the sources highlighted in Niall Ferguson's commissioned history, which he acknowledged to be 'something of a research agenda'.[7] The guide was distributed to archives and libraries, users and donors to promote the collection and to suggest the myriad subjects that might be fruitfully pursued in the Archive's London reading room. Accompanying the guide was a card, asking recipients to register for printed updates that would be produced as new material became available either through deposit or as the closure period was relaxed. While more material has become available, not a single printed update has been produced, for the simple reason that the guide appeared in the same year as the Archive's website was launched, and it is through this medium that information about the collection has been disseminated.

In 1999 N.M. Rothschild & Sons transferred the Archive's collections to The Rothschild Archive Trust, an educational charity whose board consists of members of the Rothschild family and outside advisers. The founding chairman of the board was Emma Rothschild, daughter of Victor, third Lord Rothschild, who first opened up the collection to the research community in 1978. As an independent body, the Trust is well placed to attract deposits of records from every branch of the Rothschild family, and has been successful in this part of its mission. The records of the Viennese house were finally retrieved from the Moscow archives in 2001, and in 2004 ownership of the records of de Rothschild Frères, on deposit with the French Archives nationales since the 1970s, was handed to the Trust, thus uniting in a legal if not a physical sense all known surviving records of the Rothschild businesses.[8] The fate of the business records of S.M. von Rothschild of Vienna,

[7]   N. Ferguson, *The World's Banker: the History of the House of Rothschild* (London, 1998).

[8]   For an account of the records transferred from Moscow, see V. Gray, 'The return of the Austrian Rothschild archive', in The Rothschild Archive's *Review of the Year 2001–2000* (2002). For a description of the archives in the Archives nationales' Centre des archives du monde du travail, see A. Sablon du Corail, J. Comble and M. Aspey, 'Rothschild Reunited:

those retained by the Nazi-appointed administrator, has been described in the final report of the Austrian Historical Commission.[9]

The Archive's website has enabled the work that was described earlier in this paper as 'in progress' to be disseminated to the widest possible range of users. The impact on the project to transcribe and translate the Judendeutsch letters has been the most profound, allowing the publication of the documents as digitized images, German transcripts and English translations and, perhaps more importantly, permitting interaction with users so that the most comprehensive analysis of each letter might be achieved. The Archive's focus has always been on the content of the letters, rather than the style in which they are written, but recently the archivists have begun to explore possible research opportunities in partnership with academic institutions that will focus on the linguistic importance of the collection.

There is already a model for a partnership of this kind: *Jewish Community and Social Development in Europe 1800–1940: the case of the Rothschilds* was initiated in 2004 with a generous research award, and has since developed with the assistance of two further grants so that the project, hosted at the Archive and overseen by an Academic Advisory Committee, consists of a director, a project co-ordinator and a team of researchers working in archives across Europe and in Israel.[10]

The Rothschild Research Forum,[11] a password-protected area within the Archive's website, is the result of another partnership, this time with curatorial colleagues from Waddesdon Manor, a former Rothschild home now owned by the National Trust. The aim of the Forum, launched in 2003, is to promote the existence of Rothschild collections and sources, and to enable remote users to gain access to the collections in advance, or instead, of a personal visit. In 2005 the archivists published on the site a guide to sources relating to the history of the Credit Anstalt, material for which there has always been a great demand from researchers, the first of the finding aids that have been prepared for material beyond the Archive's original closure date of 1918.

News of the Forum appeared in The Rothschild Archive's *Review of the Year 2002–2003*, another manifestation of the Trust's commitment to promoting the collections to the widest possible audience. The *Review*, published annually since 2000, contains a report of the Archive's activities and major acquisitions as well as featuring articles by researchers based on their use of the Archive's resources. Copies are placed prominently in the public spaces of the business, which continues to house the Archive, providing a welcome link with the creators of the archives of the future.

the Records of de Rothschild Frères', in The Rothschild Archive's *Review of the Year 2004–2005* (2005).

[9]   http://www.historikerkommission.gv.at/

[10]   http://www.rothschildarchive.org/ib/?doc=/ib/articles/project1. Hanadiv, the Fritz-Thyssen-Stiftung (Cologne) and the Arts and Humanities Research Council have supported the project at various stages.

[11]   http://www.rothschildarchive.org/ta/

At the time of writing the archivists are in the process of planning another publication, this one based on papers that were presented in November 2006 at a colloquium in Roubaix jointly organized with the Centre des archives du monde du travail, with the theme 'The Rothschilds and Eastern Europe'. The occasion at which this paper was first delivered, a conference organized in London by the EABH in conjunction with N.M. Rothschild & Sons on the occasion of the bank's twohundreth anniversary, and the recent Roubaix event have much in common, and demonstrate the fact that in spite of all the changes in The Rothschild Archive in the intervening period and regardless of the changes that may occur in the future, the mission of the Archive remains the same: to preserve the record of the past, to make the material available to researchers, and to enable the sharing of information for the common good.

The Baring Archive, which passed into the ownership of ING following the collapse of Barings in 1995, was in 2008 placed by them on permanent loan in a charitable trust, The Baring Archive Ltd. This is in order to ensure the Archives's long term preservation. It continues to be located at ING Bank's offices at 60 London Wall, London EC2M 5TQ, where it is administered by the Trust's Archivist, Moira Lovegrove. tel 0044 2077 67 1000; baring.archive@ing.com; www.baringarchive.org.uk

CHAPTER 3

Private Banks and the Onset of the Corporate Economy

Youssef Cassis

The emergence of a 'new bank' in the second third of the nineteenth century represented a decisive turning point in the long-term development of banking, whether seen from an institutional or an economic perspective. This bank was new in three respects: first, it was a joint-stock bank; second, it was a deposit bank – more precisely, a bank that collected its deposits through a network of branches; and third, it was an investment bank.[1]

Admittedly, these characteristics were not entirely new – private bankers had been collecting deposits and dealing in securities while forerunners of joint-stock banks had appeared in Scotland in the eighteenth century. Yet the change was momentous. From an institutional perspective, private banks progressively gave way to large joint banks. And from an economic perspective, this change corresponded to a massive surge in banking and financial affairs, with bank deposits increasing by a factor of seven to ten in the major European countries in the half century preceding the First World War.[2] Banking concentration intensified likewise,[3] while the big banks became giant firms, ranking among Europe's largest companies by the turn of the twentieth century.[4]

The causes and, especially, the consequences of this 'banking revolution' have raised major issues revolving around the many facets of the contribution of banking to economic growth and industrial development. What was the role of private banks in this age of concentration of capital, which gathered pace in the last quarter of the nineteenth century? As early as 1864, the *Daily Telegraph* commented that the sale of the famous English private bank Loyd, Jones & Co. to the London and

---

[1]   These three characteristics did not always coincide in these new institutions. While the first was common to all of them, a degree of specialization in the second (especially in Britain, to a lesser extent France) or the third (especially in Germany and Central Europe) can usually be observed.

[2]   See, for example, F. Capie and A. Webber, *A Monetary History of the United Kingdom, 1870–1982* (London, 1985); J. Bouvier, *Un siècle de banque française* (Paris, 1973); R. Tilly, 'An Overview of the Role of the Large German Banks up to 1914', in Y. Cassis (ed.), *Finance and Financiers in European History, 1880–1960* (Cambridge, 1992).

[3]   See M. Pohl, T. Tortella and H. Van der Wee (eds), *A Century of Banking Consolidation in Europe* (Aldershot, 2001).

[4]   See Y. Cassis, *Big Business: the European Experience in the Twentieth Century* (Oxford, 1997).

Westminster Bank was 'a big confession that the era of private firms has passed and that the day of joint-stock banking is fully and finally acknowledged. It is an avowal that one kind of banking must give way to the other, which is the better'.[5]

The prediction did, of course, in the end materialize, though the process greatly varied, whether in speed, extent or significance, depending on the country, region or type of bank involved. The history of private banks during the onset of the corporate economy, from around 1870 to 1914, does not fit easily into a simple 'decline and fall' framework of analysis. It is more complex, and therefore more interesting, raising the question of the conditions of their survival, their lasting economic significance, and their complex relationships with the joint-stock banks. These questions are examined in this chapter. The main argument is that the lasting significance of private banks can be explained both by the competitive advantage which they enjoyed in some areas, and by the economic, political, and socio-cultural context of late-nineteenth-century banking development. This context, however, differed between countries, with the competitiveness of private bankers varying accordingly. The comparative approach adopted here attempts to account for these differences. The chapter is divided into five parts. After a brief definition of private banks, the world of the *haute banque* is analysed in some detail, followed by a shorter discussion of provincial private banks. A fourth part considers the contribution of private bankers to banking development, and some conclusions are proposed in a fifth and final part.

What is a Private Bank?

For the purpose of this study, private banks have been defined in terms of ownership rather than activity. In the nineteenth century and during most of the twentieth century, a bank was considered as a private bank if its owners were also its managers. Such banks were usually family firms. Their legal form was generally that of partnerships, or a general partnership, with partners having unlimited responsibility; but there were also private limited companies and even joint-stock banks whose directors retained the major part of the capital. The current functional definition of private banking – portfolio management on behalf of very wealthy individuals – only took shape in the last quarter of the twentieth century. Beforehand, private banks were engaged in all types of activities: commercial banking, investment banking, merchant banking, indeed universal banking, as well as wealth management. Specialization in one or another activity depended on strategic choices or on the constraints deriving from a specific banking system.

These various activities were performed at two different levels. The first level was the world of the *haute banque*, the old established private banks mostly involved in the financing of international trade and the issue of foreign loans – what

---

[5]   Quoted in T.E. Gregory, *The Westminster Bank Through a Century*, 2 vols (London, 1936), vol. 1, p. 283.

is known in Britain as merchant banking. The second level was the less glamorous world of country banking: the local and regional banks which provided banking and financial facilities to small and medium-sized businesses in the regions.

The World of the *Haute Banque*

The decline of private banks was nowhere steeper than in Britain – with less than forty still in existence at the turn of the twentieth century, as against several thousands in countries such as France and Germany. Yet nowhere did private bankers flourish more than in the City of London. This paradox reflects the peculiarities of the English banking system: its extreme specialization and the divorce between domestic and international banking, still prevailing in the late nineteenth century.[6] In Britain, the decline of private banks was the decline of private *deposit banks*, which had continuously lost ground ever since the appearance of the first joint-stock banks in the late 1820s. However, the largest, richest and best connected houses were able to resist until the last decade of the nineteenth century. This group mainly consisted of the major London private bankers, whether in the City (Glyns, Barclays, Smiths) or the West End (Coutts), who formed an integral part of the banking aristocracy – another name for the *haute banque*.

The private banks' problem was that they were losing much of their significance as one of the wheels of the English banking system: their functions were almost identical to those of the joint-stock banks, competition was stiffening and size was increasingly becoming a matter of concern as a result of the amalgamation movement which gathered pace in the 1880s and, especially, the 1890s. In addition, as the small provincial banks were absorbed by the big joint-stock banks, London private bankers were progressively deprived of one of their basic activities, which was to act as London agents for the country banks. In the end, they had to give way: the number of private banks that were members of the London Clearing House decreased only slightly between 1870 and 1890, from 13 to 10; it then fell sharply to five in 1891, and to one in 1914.[7]

However, for private bankers engaged in international finance, the 1870s were the dawn of a golden age, which was to last until the First World War. Far from declining or simply resisting the trend towards consolidation, merchant bankers – the other component of the English *haute banque* – expanded enormously the scale of their activities, taking advantage of the pivotal role played by the City of London in the growth and globalization of the world economy. London's position as the financial centre of the world meant, first, that the bulk of world trade was financed through the medium of bills of exchange drawn on London; and second,

---

[6]   P.L. Cottrell, 'The Domestic Commercial Banks and the City of London, 1870–1939', in Y. Cassis (ed.), *Finance and Financiers in European History, 1880–1960* (Cambridge, 1992).

[7]   See Y. Cassis, *City Bankers, 1890–1914* (Cambridge, 1994), pp. 15–18.

that London was the leading centre for the issue of foreign loans and equity.[8] The development of the acceptance and issuing activities, which were the two pillars of merchant banking, offered tremendous opportunities, both to existing firms and to newcomers.

Consider first acceptances, the 'bread and butter' of merchant bankers' income. Estimates of their total volume show an increase from between £50 to £60 million in 1875–6 to about £140 million in 1913 – though they recorded a sharp fall in the early 1890s (from £90 to £50 million) following the Baring Crisis. The merchant bankers were probably responsible for some 70 per cent of this total – that is, around £100 million.[9] Foreign issues also increased dramatically in the second half of the nineteenth century. British portfolio foreign investment has been estimated at about £195 to £230 million in 1854.[10] By 1913, it had jumped to some £3.5 to 4 billion, with major booms of capital export taking place in the early 1870s, the 1880s and the decade preceding the First World War. Private banking houses, above all merchant banks, were able to maintain their hold on the huge London issuing business, being responsible for 37.2 per cent of all new issues between 1870 and 1914. Admittedly, they lost market share – from 53 per cent between 1870 and 1874 to 35 per cent in the years 1910–1914 – mostly to the joint-stock banks, whether British or overseas.[11] Nevertheless, they remained by a significant margin the largest single intermediary in the London market.

As a result, the number of merchant banks and other private banks involved in international financial operations increased substantially during this period. Estimates vary, as such banks were engaged in a great variety of activities, including trade, brokerage, foreign exchange, arbitrage, company promotion and others. Their total number increased from 45 in 1885 to 105 in 1914 according to some estimates,[12] from 39 in 1990 to 63 in 1910 according to more conservative ones.[13] As for the select group of top-ranking accepting houses – those invited to the first meeting of the Accepting House Committee in August 1914 – it comprised a mere 21 names.[14]

---

[8]   See R. Michie, *The City of London: Continuity and Change, 1850–1990* (Basingstoke and London, 1992); D. Kynaston, *The City of London*, vol. 2: *Golden Age, 1890–1914* (London, 1995); Y. Cassis, *Capitals of Capital: A History of International Financial Centres, 1780–2005* (Cambridge, 2006).

[9]   S. Chapman, *The Rise of Merchant Banking* (London, 1984), pp. 105–7, 209.

[10]   P.L. Cottrell, *British Overseas Investment in the Nineteenth Century, 1870–1914* (London, 1975), p. 13.

[11]   A.R. Hall, *The London Capital Market and Australia, 1870–1914* (Canberra, 1963), p. 72.

[12]   Chapman, *Merchant Banking*, p.58.

[13]   R. Roberts, 'What's in a Name? Merchants, Merchant bankers, Accepting Houses, Issuing Houses, Industrial Bankers and Investment Bankers', in *Business History*, vol. 35, 3, 1993.

[14]   See Cassis, *City Bankers*, pp. 30–31.

However, a comparable increase, largely due to the arrival of new talent, could also be observed in other major financial centres, especially Paris and Berlin. What characterized the City of London was the unique position enjoyed by the top merchant banks. Despite a comparatively modest size,[15] a small group of private firms continued to keep the upper hand in the most important financial operations conducted in the world's leading financial centre, keeping at bay competition from joint-stock banks, overseas banks and foreign banks.[16] In an increasingly competitive market, most of the old established houses (N.M. Rothschild, Sons & Co., Baring Brothers & Co., J.S. Morgan & Co., J.H. Schröder & Co., C.J. Hambro & Son), all founded before 1840, managed to retain their competitive advantage.[17] Latecomers were relatively few: Kleinwort, Sons & Co. in the 1850s, Lazard Brothers & Co. in the 1870s,[18] while steep decline and extinction proved rare, Stern Brothers being the most notable case.[19]

How to account for this success? The main reason is that, however fierce, competition was nonetheless constrained in international banking.[20] In the accepting business, there was undoubtedly some restraint on the part of the clearing banks. The reasons for their relative passivity have to do with the English banking system's specialization and a division of labour, at both a business and a socio-professional level, within the City of London. The inroads made by the joint-stock banks in the accepting business were not considered tolerable by the City establishment, in other words, the leading merchant banks. 'Considerable pressure' was apparently put on the clearers during the early 1900s in order to reduce their involvement, [21] though their market share continued to grow, to reach 24 per cent in 1913. The domestic market also benefited from a degree of protection since foreign banks' acceptances were not eligible at the Bank of England, whether for

[15]   In terms of total assets, N.M. Rothschild, Sons & Co., still the City's largest merchant bank in 1913 with £25 million, was less than a quarter the size of the top three clearing banks: London City and Midland Bank, Lloyds Bank, and London County and Westminster Bank, with respectively 109, 107 and 104 million.

[16]   See Y. Cassis, 'London Banks and International Finance, 1890–1914', in Y. Cassis and E. Bussière (eds), *London and Paris as International Financial Centres in the Twentieth Century* (Oxford, 2005), pp. 107–18.

[17]   See N. Ferguson, *The World's Banker: the History of the House of Rothschild* (London, 1998); P. Ziegler, *The Sixth Great Power: Barings, 1762–1929* (London, 1988); K. Burk, *Morgan Grenfell 1838–1988: the Biography of a Merchant Bank* (Oxford, 1989); R. Roberts, *Schroders: Merchants & Bankers* (Basingstoke and London, 1992); B. Bramsen and K. Wain, *The Hambros 1779–1979* (London, 1979).

[18]   J. Wake, *Kleinwort Benson: the History of Two Families in Banking* (Oxford, 1997); A. Sabouret, *MM Lazard Frères et Cie: une Saga de la fortune* (Paris, 1987).

[19]   P. Emden, *Jews of Britain* (London, 1944), pp. 542–3.

[20]   See Cassis, 'London Banks', p. 113.

[21]   According to J.S. Morgan & Co, in December 2006, quoted in Kynaston, *City of London*, vol. 2, p. 293.

discount or as security for a loan, unless endorsed by two English signatures.[22] As for the issue of loans and equities on the London capital market, it was restricted by custom and practice to British firms. Foreign banks were involved in those issues simultaneously floated across several centres, but they did not compete with British firms on their home turf. The leading clearing banks only timidly entered the issuing business in the early twentieth century, a domain where the influence of the overseas banks remained limited, despite their special links with the countries that regularly called on the London capital market. Merchant banks were far better placed, on account of their expertise and contacts, to see foreign issues through to a successful conclusion.[23]

Private international bankers were in a different position in continental Europe. For one thing, the scope for international financial operations was far more restricted than in Britain, and for another joint-stock banks were able to secure a larger share of this business. However, conditions were far from being identical across Europe. The *haute banque* remained stronger in France than in Germany and was also able to prosper in smaller countries with old banking traditions, such as Switzerland.

The dominance of the Parisian *haute banque* over French international finance reached its peak in 1871–2, with the issue of the two war indemnity loans, amounting to 5.2 billion francs – the levy required by Bismarck to pay for France's defeat by Prussia in the 1870 war. The French *haute banque*, led by the Rothschilds, was able to keep control over these issues, with the new joint-stock banks very much in the position of junior partners, though their influence was to increase in the process. Rothschild and the *haute banque* kept their hold over the first loan, securing the bulk of the lucrative commissions. In order to play a more active role and get a larger share of the second loan, the newly formed joint-stock banks decided to join forces and form a coalition, the so-called 'syndicat des établissements de crédit'. The move proved successful, though for the time being the Rothschild group remained in control. However, with its 35.7 per cent share, the syndicate, led by the Banque de Paris et des Pays-Bas, founded in 1872, had gained a foothold. From then on, an ever-increasing share of the foreign loans issued in Paris was handled by the 'établissements de crédit'.[24]

---

[22]   In 1913, three of the ten largest accepting houses were foreign banks – Dresdner Bank, Disconto-Gesellschaft, and Crédit Lyonnais. Their acceptances were mostly used to finance the trade of their home country through employing sterling-denominated bills and the London discount market.

[23]   The exception here was the Hong Kong and Shanghai Banking Corporation, which played a pioneering role in Chinese government loans between 1895 and 1914. The bank had a unique competitive advantage thanks to its knowledge of Far Eastern business, the support of the Foreign Office, owing to the political nature of a number of these loans, and finally its relationships in the City, especially, and significantly, with the Rothschilds. See G. Jones, *British Multinational Banking 1830–1990* (Oxford, 1993), pp. 119–30.

[24]   See J. Bouvier, *Les Rothschild* (Paris, 1967); E. Bussière, *Paribas 1872–1992: L'Europe et le monde* (Antwerp, 1992).

Of course, the opposition between 'private' and 'joint-stock' banks should not be overemphasized. Private banks continued to be included in the various groupings which presided over French international finance before the First World War and many a private banker remained highly influential. However, as distinct, independent firms, private banks had to surrender control over international financial operations during the last quarter of the nineteenth century. In that respect, they differed markedly from their English counterparts. As a consequence, the members of the Parisian *haute banque* formed a smaller group than the London merchant banks, in terms of both the number of banks making up the group and – with the exception of the Rothschilds – the size of these banks. By the end of the nineteenth century, it was generally considered to have comprised eight banking houses: de Rothschild Frères, Hottinguer & Cie, Mallet Frères & Cie, Vernes & Cie, de Neuflize & Cie, Heine & Cie, and Demanchy et F. Seillière.[25] These banks still held some important assets which enabled them to play a role in the financial sphere out of proportion to the actual size of their firms. One was their prestige and network of relationships. They partly remained bankers to foreign governments, paying the coupons of the loans they had issued in the past – Hottinguer, for example, held the large deposits of the Russian and Ottoman governments. They were also entrusted with the funds of very wealthy customers, whether private or corporate, and at the beginning of the twentieth century, wealth management started to become their main activity. Their other asset was their massive presence on the boards of the major railway companies, insurance companies, *banques d'affaires* and, of course, the Banque de France.[26]

In addition, like London, Paris was packed with private banking and finance houses, which were more or less large and more or less recent.[27] Some of them were of foreign origin and formed part of international family networks present at the same time in several financial centres, firstly London and New York. This was, in particular, the case for Lazard Frères, E.N. Raphaël, Seligmann Frères and A.J. Stern. Those that were closest to the *haute banque* mainly took an interest in wealth management, whereas others were involved in activities of a more financial nature (company promotion, investment, arbitrage and others), usually in relation to a particular part of the world. Traditional banking business, like collecting deposits (by offering attractive rates) and granting short-term credit, had not completely disappeared. Some banking houses specialized in discounting bills of exchange and others in acceptances. These varied activities at once reflected and contributed to Paris's cosmopolitanism and vitality before 1914.

---

[25]   E. Kaufmann, *La banque en France* (Paris, 1914), pp. 166–74.

[26]   A. Plessis, 'Bankers in French Society, 1880s–1960s', in Y. Cassis (ed.), *Finance and Financiers in European History, 1880–1960* (Cambridge, 1992).

[27]   In his survey on French banking at the beginning of the twentieth century, Eugen Kaufmann estimated the number of private banks in Paris at some 150, in addition to the banking houses of the *haute banque*. Kaufmann, *La banque en France*, p. 175.

The notion of *haute banque* does not easily fit the world of German banking – even though several members of the London and Paris *haute banque* were of German origin. The reasons have to be sought in the socio-economic context as much as in the economics of German banking. The concept of *haute banque* accurately describes a social status which, by the late nineteenth century, had become characterized by great wealth, an aristocratic lifestyle and connections with the world of high politics. German private bankers were unquestionably very wealthy,[28] but the lack of a capital city, as well as a financial centre, of the calibre of London or Paris was a hindrance to their reaching a truly global influence.[29] In any case, no more than a dozen banking houses could be considered as belonging to the *haute banque*, but they were scattered around a number of financial centres: Bleichröder, Mendelssohn, Warschauer in Berlin; Bethmann, Rothschild and Speyer in Frankfurt; Oppenheim in Cologne; Behrens and Warburg in Hamburg. This was the core of a group whose frontiers inevitably shifted between 1870 and 1914, with the decline and the occasional disappearance of some, the mergers and takeovers of others, the rise of a few newcomers. By the eve of the First World War, only Mendelssohn in Berlin and Oppenheim in Cologne had retained a top position; Frankfurt's decline continued with the close of the Rothschild house; while the most notable newcomers were Warburg, who were to become Germany's leading private bankers in the interwar years.[30] However, as in other financial centres, numerous private houses, usually involved in banking as well as other financial activities (stockbrokerage, arbitrage and others) were active in Germany, especially in Berlin.

The problem faced by German private bankers was that the new universal banks were competing in all fields of banking activity, from the provision of credit to industrial customers and the financing of foreign trade to the issue of securities on behalf of foreign companies and governments. Private bankers were able to maintain a relative prominence in the 1870s and early 1880s. Thereafter, the credit banks took the leading role in international finance. The issuing syndicates became

---

[28]   See W.E. Mosse, *Jews in the German Economy: the German-Jewish Economic Elite 1820–1935* (Oxford, 1987); D. Augustine, *Patricians and Parvenus: Wealth and High Society in Wilhelmine Germany* (Oxford/Providence, 1994); M. Reitmayer, *Bankiers im Kaiserreich: Sozialprofil und Habitus der deutschen Hochfinanz* (Göttingen, 1999).

[29]   See Cassis, *Capitals of Capital*, ch. 3.

[30]   See W. Treue, 'Der Privatbankier am Wende der 19. zum 20. Jahrhundert, in *Tradition*, vol. 5, 1970; M. Pohl, 'Festigung und Ausdehnung des deutschen Bankwesens zwischen 1870 und 1914', in Institut für bankhistorische Forschung e.V. (ed.), *Deutsche Bankengeschichte*, vol. 2 (Frankfurt, 1982), p. 263; Reitmayer, *Bankiers*; F. Stern, *Gold and Iron: Bismarck, Bleichröder and the Building of the German Empire* (London, 1977); M. Stürmer, G. Teichmann, W. Treue, *Striking the Balance: Sal. Oppenheim jr. & Cie. a Family and a Bank* (London, 1994); R.R. Rosenbaum and A.J. Sherman, *M.M. Warburg & Co. 1798–1938: Merchant Bankers of Hamburg* (London, 1979); R. Chernow, *The Warburgs: The Twentieth-century Odyssey of a Remarkable Jewish Family* (London, 1993).

dominated by the Deutsche Bank and the Disconto-Gesellschaft rather than by Mendelssohn and Bleichröder, especially in the new areas of capital exports such as Latin America, China and the Ottoman Empire; the more personal relations of the private banking networks continued to play an important role in financial transactions with the United States and Russia. Private bankers were usually offered a share of the business and could occasionally take the lead, like Mendelssohn in Russia. But for a typical Argentinean loan to be issued in London, Paris and Berlin, Baring Brothers had as partners the Banque de Paris et des Pays-Bas and the Disconto-Gesellschaft rather than a private bank.

In industrial finance, private bankers could no longer, by the 1880s, contemplate an intervention on a scale comparable to that of the credit banks. They managed, however, to retain a high degree of influence, visible through their presence on the supervisory boards of the country's major companies. In 1900, according to a recent survey, half of the directorships of German leading industrial companies were held by private bankers, as against 42.5 per cent for the directors of the 'great banks' and 7.5 per cent for representatives of provincial banks. Private bankers were still ahead, by one per cent, in 1913 and did not lose ground in any dramatic way before the mid-1930s. They were able to offer a more personalized service, highly valued by industrial companies, thus exploiting a niche and turning their limited resources into an advantage.[31] In all European countries, an aristocracy of private bankers survived until the First World War, though they did not necessarily belong to the international *haute banque*. Such a membership depended either on family links or on the global importance of the financial centre from which a banker operated.

After London, Paris and Berlin, Brussels probably ranked fourth in the European hierarchy and was the most international of the second tier financial centres, mainly as a result of the strong presence of a cosmopolitan *haute banque*. The Belgian *haute banque* reached its apogee in the third quarter of the nineteenth century, with families such as the Bischoffsheim (a name tied to the Banque de Belgique, founded in 1835, and the Banque de Paris et des Pays-Bas), Lambert (the Rothschilds' representative in Brussels), Oppenheim and their networks of relationships both in Belgium and across Europe.[32] Like most of their counterparts in continental Europe, Belgian private bankers lost ground to the universal banks, in the first place the Société Générale de Belgique,[33] in the course of the nineteenth century, though a few of them remained highly influential. The most successful

---

[31]   D. Ziegler and H. Wixforth, 'The Niche in the Universal Banking System: the Role and Significance of Private Bankers within German Industry, 1900–1933', in *Financial History Review*, vol. 1, 2, 1994, pp. 99–119.

[32]   See S. Tilman, *Les grands banquiers belges (1830–1935): Portrait collectif d'une élite* (Bruxelles, 2006).

[33]   See G. Kurgan-van Hentenrynk, *Gouverner la Générale de Belgique: Essai de biographie collective* (Bruxelles, 1996); H. Van der Wee (ed.), *The Generale Bank 1822– 1897* (Tielt, 1997).

was the Banque Lambert, to which Léon Lambert (who had married Lucie de Rothschild) gave a new impetus, not least through his support for King Leopold II's infamous exploits in Congo. Other prominent private bankers included Josse Allard, particularly active in founding Belgian and foreign companies; and Edouard Empain, a self-made man who made his fortune setting up transport companies and power firms and who founded his own bank, the Banque Empain, in 1881.

In terms of overall influence within their banking system, the leading Dutch private bankers enjoyed a very favourable position until the very end of the nineteenth century. This was due to the comparatively weak development of the large commercial banks and the inordinate role played by the call-money advanced to the Amsterdam Stock Exchange (the so-called *prolongatie*) in the money market, whose amount was more than twice the country's aggregate fixed deposits by the eve of the First World War.[34] As late as 1890, the private banks could still compete *in terms of size* with the joint-stock banks, with total balance sheets reaching about 20 million guilders for houses such as Hope & Cie or R. Mees & Zoonen, and about 30 million for the Twentsche Bank, then the country's largest. It was not before 1910 that the gap really widened.[35]

Private international bankers remained a far more significant force in Switzerland than in any other European country bar Britain. The country was imbued with banking, especially private banking, traditions. This partly explains the longstanding success of the Swiss *haute banque*. Its survival was also the result of a regional specialization: the new credit banks (Crédit Suisse) in Zurich, the old private banks in Geneva.[36] Geneva abounded in private banking dynasties, some dating back to the Huguenot diasporas of the sixteenth and seventeenth centuries. There were still some fifteen houses belonging to the Geneva Protestant *haute banque* in the late nineteenth century, led by Hentsch & Cie (established 1796), Lombard Odier & Cie (1798) and Pictet & Cie (1805), all linked by a dense network of family relationships. They managed vast amounts of capital on behalf of a wealthy cosmopolitan clientele. They were thus able to preserve a niche market where they enjoyed a unique competitive advantage based on their old-established reputation for financial expertise; their international network of relationships, especially with the Parisian *haute banque*; and the emerging role

---

[34]   J. Jonker, 'Spoilt for Choice? Banking Concentration and the Structure of the Dutch Capital Market, 1900–1940', in Y. Cassis, G.D. Feldman and U. Olsson (eds), *The Evolution of Financial Institutions and Markets in Twentieth Century Europe* (Aldershot, 1995).

[35]   J. Jonker, *Mees Pierson. The Link Between Past and Future: 275 Years of Tradition and Innovation in Dutch Banking* (Amsterdam, 1997), pp. 17–19.

[36]   Switzerland's third financial centre, Basel, hosted the Swiss Bankverein, the country's largest bank at the turn of the twentieth century, established by the city's old private banking families. See M. Mazbouri, *L'émergence de la place financière Suisse (1890–1913): Itinéraire d'un grand banquier* (Lausanne, 2005).

of Switzerland as a refuge for foreign capital.[37] Their activity, however, was not confined to wealth management. They remained involved in investment banking, in particular through finance companies linked to the nascent power industry,[38] with Guillaume Pictet, senior partner of Pictet & Cie, pioneering investment in US electricity companies.[39]

At the heart of the Habsburg Monarchy, Vienna had grown into a financial centre of no mean standing. Banks could rely on a rich private clientele and served a dynamic regional industrial *Mittelstand*. But above all, Vienna was the turntable of Austria-Hungary's international financial transactions, from foreign exchange and bill discounting to the all-important reception and distribution of foreign capital.[40] However, such financial activity did not benefit private bankers. From the 1880s, their decline was faster than in most other European countries, including Germany. The *haute banque* was not spared, with the disappearance of such names as Sina, Springer, or Wodianer. Schoeller, Austria's second-largest private bank, was able to survive, though its real independence was questioned following the sale in 1910 of its industrial empire to the Credit-Anstalt.[41] The exception was of course the Rothschilds, led by Albert de Rothschild and after his death in 1911 by his son Louis. Not only were the Rothschilds the last surviving major private bank in Austria; they were also a force to be reckoned with alongside the seven large Vienna joint-stock banks. They remained the largest shareholders of the Credit-Anstalt, Austria's largest bank, which they had founded in 1855, though by the late nineteenth century they were no longer in control. The Rothschilds' strength also derived from their role in government finance. They enjoyed a monopoly in the issue of Austrian state loans until 1886; this monopoly was then granted to the so-called Rothschild group until 1910,[42] when the issue of government stock was entrusted to the *Postsparkasse*, the Post Office savings bank. Nevertheless, the Rothschilds remained highly influential in government finance while increasingly turning their attention towards industrial finance.

---

[37]   See Y. Cassis and J. Tanner, 'Finance and Financiers in Switzerland, 1880–1960', in Y. Cassis (ed.), *Finance and Financiers in European History, 1880–1960* (Cambridge, 1992), pp. 49–56, 106–7.

[38]   See S. Paquier, 'Swiss Holding Companies from the Mid-nineteenth Century to the Early 1930s: the Forerunners and Subsequent Waves of Creation', in *Financial History Review*, vol. 8, 2, 2001, pp. 163–82.

[39]   *Pictet & Cie, 1805–1955* (Geneva, 1955), pp. 52–5.

[40]   See B. Michel, *Banques et banquiers en Autriche au début du vingtième siècle* (Paris, 1976), pp. 49–56.

[41]   Ibid., pp. 106–7.

[42]   Besides the Rothschilds, the group included the Credit-Anstalt, the Boden Creditanstalt, together with three Berlin banks: the Disconto-Gesellschaft, Bleichröder and Mendelssohn.

Private Country Banks

Moving from the capital to the regions is moving either to near-complete void or
to the realm of statistics. In some countries, such as Britain, private country banks
had all but disappeared by the last decade of the nineteenth century. In others, such
as the Mediterranean and the Scandinavian countries, provincial country banking
never really took off, the gap being filled by savings banks and other types of cooperative and mutual banks. Provincial private banks survived at the very heart of
continental Europe, above all in France and Germany, where hundreds of small
and mostly anonymous banks remained part of the local economy until the First
World War.

The realm of statistics is, however, fraught with great uncertainty. Estimates of
the number of private banks vary within very broad bands and recent research has led
to drastic revisions. Take France, a country long seen as under-banked during most
of the nineteenth century. According to Rondo Cameron's early estimates, there were
369 banks in France in 1870, totalling 469 outlets, compared with 1,628 outlets in
England and Wales.[43] Recent estimates by Alain Plessis based on the reports of the
branch inspectors of the Banque de France, show that there were no less than 2,000
bankers in France in 1870, possibly as many as 3,000, taking into account all types of
capitalists who carried out discount transactions.[44] These are of course estimates, but
there can be little doubt that banking was plentiful in provincial France in the last third
of the nineteenth century. Competition stiffened from the 1870s onwards, especially
as the big deposit banks (Crédit Lyonnais, Société Générale, Comptoir d'escompte)
started to build their networks of branches. However, local private bankers were far
from being wiped out. There were still thousands of local banks in France on the eve
of the First World War. Some estimates put their number at around 1,000 to 1,200
plus a good 1,200 *escompteurs*;[45] others go as high as 3,162, two thirds of them with
less than six employees.[46] One explanation for such resilience lies in the attitude of
the big banks. Even though they expanded by setting up networks of branches across
the country, they did not cover the entire territory and had but scant interest for local
business. The gap was filled by local private bankers, who concentrated on specific
tasks, especially agricultural credit and industrial finance.[47]

---

[43]   R. Cameron, *Banking in the Early Stages of Industrialization* (Oxford, 1967).

[44]   A. Plessis, 'Le "retard" français: la faute à la banque? Banques locales, succursales
de la Banque de France et financement de l'économie sous le Second Empire', in P. Fridenson
and A. Straus (eds), *Le capitalisme français, 19ᵉ–20ᵉ siècles: Blocages et dynamisme d'une
croissance* (Paris, 1987).

[45]   A. Liesse, *Evolution of Credit and Banking in France* (Washington,1909), quoted
in S. Nishimura, 'The French Provincial Banks, the Banque de France and Bill Finance,
1890–1913', in *Economic History Review*, vol. 48, 3, 1995, p. 538.

[46]   F. Schaum, *Das Französische Bankwesen* (Stuttgart, 1931), quoted in M. Lévy-
Leboyer, 'Préface', *Les banques en Europe de l'Ouest de 1920 à nos jours* (Paris, 1995), p. V.

[47]   L. Bergeron, *Les capitalistes en France (1780–1914)* (Paris, 1978), pp. 109–10.

Local banks had their weaknesses. On the liability side, their resources tended to be meagre. On the assets side, they were almost exclusively tied to the local economy and their risks were insufficiently diversified. Nevertheless, they did contribute positively to France's economic growth. In particular, individual weaknesses should not obscure the overall strength of the regional financial structures which emerged at the end of the Second Empire. Two main factors contributed to the working of the system. One was the relationships linking together local banks of the same region, underpinned by constant credit flows, with the larger among them connected to Parisian banks, to which they could turn if necessary. Another was the spread of the branches of the Banque de France, whose presence in provincial cities provided a steady source of credit and a reduction in the cost of borrowing.[48] And while the bulk of country private banks remained very small firms, some of them, such as Varin-Bernier in Bar-le-Duc (North-East), Henri Delvider & Cie, or Verley, Decroix & Cie, both in Lille, grew into regional banks and adopted modern banking techniques.[49]

Estimates of the number of private banks in Germany reveal a similar order of magnitude. According to the Banking Directory, there might have been as many as 2,180 private bankers in 1892 and 2,564 in 1902. These figures, however, should be considered as the upper limit as they include a fair proportion of very short-lived private banks as well as firms engaged in other, not strictly banking, activities.[50] The figure given by the Central Association of German Bankers, 1,800 for 1913, is probably closer to the number of private bankers proper; while the number of private banks keeping a giro account with the Reichsbank was somewhat smaller: 1,386 in 1902 and 1,221 in 1913.[51] Whichever set of figures is considered, it is obvious that the number of private banks hardly declined before the First World War. Moreover, their combined total assets increased from 2.5 to 4 billion Marks between 1880 and 1913. However, their overall influence, measured by their per centage of German banks' total assets, considerably weakened, from 21 per cent in 1880 to 10 per cent in 1900 and just over 5 per cent in 1913.[52] But their contribution to economic development cannot be doubted: they primarily catered for local small business. Local private banks fitted into the 'division of labour' within the German

---

[48]   A. Plessis, 'Les banques locales, de l'essor du Second Empire à la "crise" de la Belle Epoque', in M. Lescure and A. Plessis (eds), *Banques locales et banques régionales en France au XIXe siècle* (Paris, 1999).

[49]   Bergeron, *Les capitalistes en France*; H. Bonin, *Histoire de banques: Crédit du Nord 1848–1998* (Paris, 1998).

[50]   Treue, 'Der Privatbankier', p. 228. The figures are based on the *Deutsche Bankierbuch.*

[51]   Pohl, 'Festigung und Ausdehnung'; K.A. Donaubauer, *Privatbankiers und Bankenkonzentration in Deutschland von der Mitte des 19. Jahrhundert bis 1932* (Frankfurt am Main, 1988), p. 13.

[52]   Calculated from Wixforth and Ziegler, 'The Niche', p. 103.

universal banking system.[53] The great banks provided 'development assistance to the strong', but they badly neglected small and medium-sized enterprises.[54] The latter, however, could turn to the regional joint-stock banks or to the local private banks, depending on their size and needs.

The Lasting Influence of Private Bankers

One of the main contributions of private bankers in the second half of the nineteenth century was the establishment of the new joint-stock banks, which have dominated the financial world ever since.[55] Such major banks as the Deutsche Bank, the Dresdner Bank and the Commerz-Bank in Germany, the Banque de Paris et des Pays-Bas (now part of BNP Paribas) in France, the Banque de Bruxelles (now integrated into ING) in Belgium, the Swiss Bank Corporation (now part of UBS) in Switzerland, or the Credit-Anstalt (now part of Bank of Austria Creditanstalt, a subsidiary of UniCredit) in Austria – to give but a few well-known names – were all founded by private bankers in the third quarter of the nineteenth century.[56] In Britain, by contrast, the initiative for the foundation of the new joint-stock banks in the 1830s and 1840s had come from merchants and industrialists rather than private bankers, who were at first antagonistic to the 'new bank'. However, the difference between Britain and continental Europe should not be overstated. On the one hand, private bankers were instrumental in the creation of several British overseas banks in the 1850s and 1860s. Glyn, Mills & Co., London's largest private bank, was particularly active in the field with the promotion of six such banks, including the Bank of Australasia, the Imperial Ottoman Bank, the Anglo-Austrian Bank, and the London and Brazilian Bank.[57] On the other hand, the conversion of private banks into joint-stock banks led to the formation of several major clearing banks, Lloyds Bank and Barclays Bank being the most prominent among them.[58]

---

[53]   D.Ziegler, 'Banking and the Rise and Expansion of Industrial Capitalism in Germany', in A. Teichova, G. Kurgan-van Hentenryk and D. Ziegler (eds), *Banking, Trade and Industry: Europe, America and Asia from the Thirteenth to the Twentieth Century* (Cambridge, 1997), pp. 142–4.

[54]   R. Tilly, 'German banking, 1850–1914: Development Assistance to the Strong', in *Journal of European Economic History*, vol. 15, 1986, pp. 113–52.

[55]   The continuity between the 'old' and the 'new' bank was clearly established by David Landes some fifty years ago in his seminal article 'Vieille banque et banque nouvelle: la révolution bancaire du XIXe siècle', in *Revue d'Histoire Moderne et Contemporaine*, vol. 3, 1956.

[56]   See L. Gall et al., *The Deutsche Bank 1870–1975* (London, 1995); Bussière, *Paribas*; H. Bauer, *Société de Banque Suisse, 1872–1972* (Basel, 1972).

[57]   P.L. Cottrell, 'A Cluster of Corporate International Banks, 1855–75', in *Business History*, vol. 33, 3, 1991.

[58]   See R.S. Sayers, *Lloyds Bank in the History of English Banking* (Oxford, 1957); M. Ackrill and L. Hannah, *Barclays: the Business of Banking 1690–1996* (Cambridge, 2001).

In taking such initiatives, private bankers were more pragmatic than visionary. Few imagined the huge development the new institutions would rapidly undergo, or the threat to their own position that they would soon represent. Their main objective was to seize the opportunity of raising vast amounts of capital in order to finance large-scale investment, especially in transport equipment. To what extent were they able to maintain a degree of control over the banks they had created? The answer is, once again, complex. In the first place, expectations varied considerably. Take for example the private bankers who had converted their bank into a joint-stock company: some simply desired to cash in and retire, while others were determined to remain fully in command and expand their business to face up to competition. Private bankers who had taken part in the foundation of a new bank expected, if not complete control, at least close supervision of the conduct of the business and a degree of strategic guidance. The chances of remaining in control in the short to medium term depended on several factors. One was the size of the stake taken in the company: in the last analysis, major shareholders are in the best position to influence policy. Being a major shareholder, however, depended in turn on the ability, or the desirability, to maintain a high stake in an expanding company whose capital was regularly increased. Another factor was the provisions of company law, in particular those concerning the competence of the board of directors. In Germany, real influence over the conduct of business usually required membership of the *Vorstand* (executive board) rather than the *Aufsichtsrat* (supervisory board). In countries such as Britain and France, by contrast, membership of the single board of directors was in principle sufficient.

Remaining in charge of large joint-stock banks proved difficult, though not impossible, for private bankers. In any case, this was not necessarily the most desirable option and there were few attempts at holding on to full *managerial* control. Barclays Bank was the most conspicuous example, with all its directors remaining active bankers.[59] Attempts at maintaining *strategic* control were more common and met with mixed success, ranging from the frustration and disappointment of being excluded from the inner circle to the satisfaction of having a well-oiled machine at one's disposal. Contrast, for example, the Deutsche Bank with the Banque de l'Union Parisienne or the Swiss Bank Corporation. The Deutsche bank was founded in Berlin in March 1870 to finance foreign trade. Its founders, in the first place Adelbert Delbrück, intended to run the bank from the administrative board, taking the major policy decisions and delegating their implementation to managing directors. However, the latter were not prepared to be treated as mere subordinates. A power struggle ensued and turned to the advantage of the executive board, led by Georg von Siemens, who increasingly pushed Adelbert Delbrück to the sidelines.[60]

The Swiss banking Corporation was founded in 1872 by five Basel private banks, in association with a group of German and Austrian joint-stock banks.

---

[59]   Cassis, *City Bankers*; Ackrill and Hannah, *Barclays*.
[60]   Gall et al., *The Deutsche Bank*, p. 118.

However, unlike their counterparts at the Deutsche Bank, the private bankers remained firmly in control: not only were they in a majority on the board of directors, but no managing director was appointed until 1899, after the bank had considerably expanded – and changed its name from Basler Bankverein to Schweizerische Bankverein. Responsibilities were henceforth increasingly delegated to professional managers, although a proper managing board was not set up before 1929.[61] The Parisian *haute banque* remained equally in control of its *banque d'affaires*, the Banque de l'Union Parisienne (BUP), even though it had been founded with the Société Générale de Belgique in 1904, a full generation later than the Swiss Bank Corporation. The board of directors included representatives of the six founding private houses, the Société Générale, and the old Banque Parisienne taken over by the new bank, as well as a few independent people. More importantly, each of the founding private banks was represented on the board's management committee, a body which met twice a week and was responsible for making the decisions concerning all aspects of the bank's activities. Significantly, the general manager was not in regular attendance at these meetings.[62]

Beyond the differences between individual banks, there is the question of the position of private bankers within their country's corporate banking structures. In all European countries, a fair proportion of the joint-stock banks' senior executives continued to be recruited from the world of private banking until well after the First World War. As senior managerial positions became compatible with an upper-class status, they attracted an increasing number of scions of old banking families who brought to their bank a huge network of business relationships. However, English private bankers were able to remain in a particularly strong position. On the one hand, they adapted remarkably well to the new banking structures: over a third of the directors of the country's leading joint-stock banks were former private bankers. Old private banking families were thus able to perpetuate themselves in the big joint-stock banks, especially though by no means exclusively at Barclays bank. On the other hand, the City aristocracy, still firmly entrenched in the world of private banking, was able to retain a collective control over the financial sector of the British economy through its massive presence on the boards of the major joint-stock banks, overseas banks and insurance companies, as well as the Court of Directors of the Bank of England.[63] Though parallels could be found elsewhere, especially in Paris, such a control was deeper and wider than in any other international financial centre.

[61]   Bauer, *Société de Banque Suisse*; Mazbouri, *L'émergence de la place financière suisse*.
[62]   E. Bussière, 'La politique financière de la Banque de l'Union Parisienne de 1919 à 1931', Mémoire de maîtrise (University of Paris IV, 1977), pp. 253–69; H. Bonin, *La Banque de l'union parisienne (1874/1904–1974): Histoire de la deuxième grande banque d'affaires française* (Paris, 2001), pp. 18–43.
[63]   See Cassis, *City Bankers*.

Concluding Remarks

Private banks were not wiped out by the advent of the 'new bank' in the second quarter of the nineteenth century or by the wave of banking consolidation which took place across Europe in the two or three decades preceding the First World War. Their survival was uneven. In the realm of high finance, they remained the dominant force in the City of London, whereas they increasingly played second fiddle in Paris or Berlin. Conversely, private country banks still flourished in France and Germany when they had all but disappeared in Britain. Rather than survival, one should thus talk of the continued success of private banks in some specific banking and financial activities – a success reflected by the fact the number of private banks engaged in these fields actually rose; that they retained and sometimes even increased market share; that several of them grew in size and profitability, not only in the City of London, but also in the French provinces; and that the services they offered were, if not unique, at least not readily available from the big banks.

The reason for these successes are mostly to be found in the capacity of private bankers to find niches where they enjoyed a competitive advantage against the big banks. Nevertheless, a degree of protection from market forces, deriving from economic, social, institutional and cultural factors, also played a part. The combination of these two elements varied both in space and time. Success lasted longer for the *haute banque* than for the country banks. The latter were eventually sidelined during the depression of the 1930s whereas the former retained both their influence and their status as private banks well until the 1960s before increasingly turning themselves into public companies. There is no doubt that City merchant banks were in a strong position on the eve of the First World War. In London, but also New York, investment banking, in the broad sense of the word, remained the preserve of private firms. This has much to do with the banking architecture prevailing in Britain and the United States. It might be anachronistic to talk of market-oriented financial systems before 1914, but there is no doubt that the capital markets played a greater role in London and New York than in Paris or Berlin. Such an orientation left greater room for the development of private and individual initiatives, as witnessed by the development of the City and Wall Street in the last thirty years.

CHAPTER 4

London's First 'Big Bang'? Institutional Change in the City, 1855–83

Philip L. Cottrell

There is a peculiar fascination to some people in making money on the Stock Exchange. I know hundreds who would rather make £50 on the Stock Exchange than £250 by the exercise of their profession; here is a nameless fascination, and in the year 1871 the favourite form of making money on the Stock Exchange was by applying for shares, selling them at whatever premium they were at, and that money was considered made, and was considered – I say considered – honourably made. I reveal no secrets because I am incapable, but you would be amazed to see as applicants the names, the excellent names of most honourable men, and women too, for the ladies were not backward in the year 1871, her grace did not object to write to ask me whether she could have 50 shares in this or that company, my lady dropped me a polite line, sometimes with a card for a conversazione, to ask if she could get 20 shares in such and such a company. Public writers – clergymen – I hope the bar will forgive me for saying so – barristers also were not deficient in applications to me, and not merely to me but to any body connected with public companies, for allotments when shares were at a premium.

> A. Grant, *Twycross v. Grant and Others: Speech of Albert Grant*
> (London, 1876), p. 126.

With its contemporary ring, applying the description 'Big Bang' to mid-nineteenth century organizational changes in the English financial sector, above all to the London markets, might rightly be queried. Furthermore, the depiction itself might be ambiguous. 'Bangers' for many past generations of English schoolboys meant the almost lethal, small fireworks, such as 'Imps', available for Guy Fawkes Night celebrations. Their detonations could be ear-splitting while consuming precious pocket money in a matter of seconds, with nothing to show afterwards. Some particular London institutions, 25 years after 'Big Bang', might draw up somewhat comparable balance sheets for their participations in that financial explosion. Since the phrase was coined during the early 1980s, others could argue that the analogy was being drawn with developments in the science of cosmology – a theory about the origins of the universe. 'Big Bang' has been put forward as the seminal explosion that initiated the expanding universe, yet it has also been hypothesized that expansion will ultimately be exhausted, causing inward collapse. Putting aside the danger of mixing metaphors, possibly more appropriate is not a 'Bang' but a 'Bonfire' which consumed restrictive practices in the 1980s. This further 'Great Fire' of London enabled an institutional restructuring of the City during the late twentieth century to maintain its long-established, leading position in world finance.

The London markets' formal origins date from the 'Financial Revolution' of the late seventeenth and early eighteenth centuries. A critical period in their further development was the mid-nineteenth century when much of their pre-'Big Bang' institutional structures fully emerged. Primarily, the shaping of the mid-Victorian City was the result of contextual factors: Britain's prime position as *the* industrialized nation and the overwhelming role that its economy thereby played in the developing world economy. Nonetheless, domestic decontrol and further liberalization had a significant bearing. The general company code was radically reformed in 1855 and 1856 to allow limited liability companies to be readily established. Promoters of corporate, non-banking financial intermediaries responded almost immediately to this new freedom and, likewise, founders of joint-stock banks when such institutions were brought under the new permissive company law through specific legislation passed between 1857 and 1862. Corporate discount houses, limited joint-stock banks, both domestic and overseas, and finance companies then rapidly rose to dominate most of the City's financial markets.

Yet there were areas of successful resistance, and personal enterprise continued to be the force on the Stock Exchange's floor, within metropolitan private banking and amongst the City's merchant banks. Although the 'square mile's' private banks were to wane from the 1890s, the merchant banks withstood the new corporate finance companies' short-lived challenge during the mid-1860s, thereafter largely holding their ground until the 'Big Bang' of the late twentieth century. The City's mid-nineteenth century organizational transformation was therefore incomplete in terms of joint-stock institutions' rapidly achieving total supremacy.

The organizational restructuring of London financial institutions over the mid-century is the more remarkable since the period was financially tempestuous. Major crises erupted in 1857 and 1866, and the City was also affected to some degree by the American and Central European financial collapses of 1873. Furthermore, English banking was shaken by the City of Glasgow Bank's failure in 1878. As well as the shocks of these major events, the mid-century was punctuated by a series of minor upheavals of some consequence, such as the 1860/1 'leather crisis'. All strained the liquidity of the English financial sector to varying degrees and consumed financial capital, something that may have borne hardest upon practitioners of personal as opposed to corporate financial enterprise.

I

The financial and monetary context for the City's mid-nineteenth century organizational transformation can be illustrated. Figure 4.1 portrays the volume of bills of exchange, which reached a historic maximum during the early 1870s' cyclical upswing, although with foreign bills declining less markedly thereafter

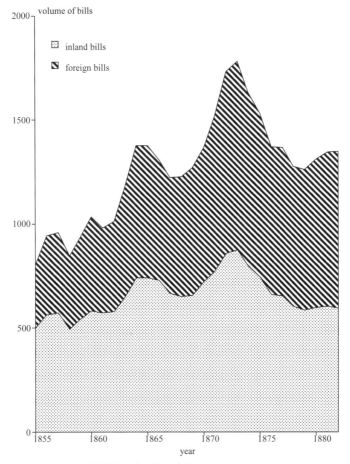

Figure 4.1   Volume of bills, inland and foreign, £m

than inland bills.[1] Nishimura has cogently argued that the inland bill's increasing disuse was primarily due to reductions in inventories and the chain of commercial middlemen that serviced them. These developments were a consequence of the further growth of the national railway system during the 1860s.[2] They had a marked impact upon the composition of banking assets, to such an extent as to provoke comment from the 1880s about the shortage of 'good bills'.[3] The impact

[1]   Data drawn from S. Nishimura, *The Decline of Inland Bills of Exchange in the London Money Market 1855–1913* (Cambridge, 1971), Table 15, p. 93 and Table 17, p. 97.

[2]   Nishimura, *Decline of Inland Bills of Exchange*, pp. 77–9.

[3]   J. Dick, 'Banking Statistics of the U.K. in 1896', in *Journal of the Institute of Bankers*, vol. 17, 1897; 'Business in the United Kingdom – Its Progress and Prospects', *Bankers' Magazine* (1894); and P.L. Cottrell, *Industrial Finance 1830–1914: the Finance*

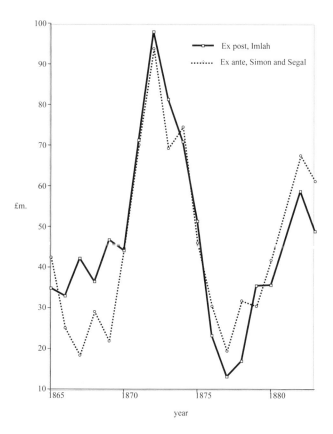

Figure 4.2   Estimates of Capital Exports 1865–83, £m

of new transport technologies – the railway, the improvement of oceanic shipping and the spreading global telegraph networks – also comparably affected drawings of foreign bills, but their use was sustained by the international gold standard's workings, which further developed from the early 1870s.

The greater internationalization of the City's dealings equally arose from Britain's mounting exports of capital from the mid-1850s, displayed in figure 4.2.[4] This shows the 1873 apogee of the first long swing in British overseas investment,

and Organization of English Manufacturing Industry (London/New York, 1980), pp. 200–202. See also, M. Collins, 'Long-term Growth of the English Banking Sector and Money Stock, 1844–80', in *Economic History Review*, 2nd ser., vol. 36, 1983, pp. 383–5.

[4]   Data drawn from A.M. Imlah, *Economic Elements in the Pax Britannica* (Cambridge, Mass., 1958), pp. 72–5; and M. Simon, 'The Pattern of New British Portfolio Foreign Investment, 1865–1914', reprinted in A.R. Hall (ed.), *The Export of Capital from Britain 1870–1914* (London, 1968), pp. 38–9.

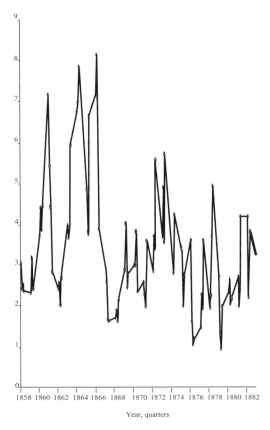

Figure 4.3   Interest rate on 3 month bank bills

the trough of the late 1870s and the initiation during the early 1880s of what proved to be a second long swing that crested in 1890.

The mid-century inception of Britain's becoming *the* world supplier of capital provided new opportunities for merchant banks, both established houses and newcomers to the City. The accumulation of further foreign capital assets also had direct and indirect effects for British overseas and domestic corporate banks.

The decline of the inland bill from 1873 and the onset of the British economy's becoming a 'chronic' exporter of capital are both features of the mid-century financial transition. This occurred against the background of a far-from-benign monetary environment. The tempestuous nature of the mid-Victorian decades, especially the 1860s, is clearly displayed in the available quarterly data. Figure 4.3 displays the interest rate on 3-month bank bills,[5] a time series with a staccato rhythm. Also shown

---

[5]   Calculated from the weekly series compiled in Nishimura, *Decline of Inland Bills*, Table 30, pp. 114–28.

in figure 4.3 is the series' declining trend after the mid-1860s, a notable period of high nominal rates, the fall in nominal interest rates thereafter being apparent whether peaks or troughs are compared. The very pronounced fluctuations in interest rates over the entire period were the product of many forces and, equally, had a diverse range of effects, with Goschen in particular commenting at the time on the consequences for 'John Bull' of 'dear money' and 'cheap money'.[6]

Bankers' balances at the Bank of England's head office, in terms of quarterly averages, are plotted as a bar chart in figure 4.4.[7] As with interest rates, this series provides greater detail on the period's stormy monetary conditions. It should be noted that the weekly data from which figure 4 is derived display pronounced seasonal movements caused by the quarterly collection of taxes and the payment of interest on the National Debt. These very marked fluctuations may not have been totally muted by the transformation of the original weekly series into quarterly averages This is because the third quarters of years (July–September) in the derived quarterly series display no troughs (major or minor) while being the most distinct periods of peaks (major or minor). Indeed, 17 of the 25 peaks in the quarterly data occur during the third quarter. Such an outcome may be related to the dominance of the underlying seasonal pattern of fiscal payments and disbursements (which gave rise to the Bank of England's providing special market facilities during the 'shuttings' of the stock transfer books). Nevertheless, it is possibly not a coincidence that financial and monetary panics, whether major or minor events, occurred during the autumn. The only significant exception is the 1866 crisis, which erupted during the spring.

Bankers' balances with the Bank of England were the domestic commercial banking system's second line of reserves after till money.[8] Figure 4.4 clearly displays their secular expansion over the period – at least until the early 1880s. Their growth points to the almost relentless expansion of commercial banking over the mid-century in terms of increasing deposits and, in turn, their mobilization as credit facilities. However, the series' rising secular trend, albeit only to the early 1880s, indicated in figure 4.4 was also the product of another operative factor. This was the recognition by domestic commercial bankers of the need to hold greater liquid reserves, brought home to them by their experiences of the period's

---

[6]　Viscount Goschen, 'Seven Per Cent', first published in *Edinburgh Review* (Jan. 1865); and 'Two Per Cent', first published in *Edinburgh Review* (Jan. 1868); with both reprinted in *Essays and Addresses on Economic Questions* (London, 1905).

[7]　Calculated from Bank of England, *Bank of England Liabilities and Assets: 1696 to 1966* (London, 1967) [reproduced from *Bank of England Quarterly Bulletin* (Jun. 1967)], Table B, pp. 16–66.

[8]　On the role of bankers' balances, see L.S. Pressnell, 'Gold Reserves, Banking Reserves, and the Baring Crisis of 1890', in C.R. Whittlesey and J.S.G. Wilson (eds), *Essays in Money and Banking in Honour of R.S. Sayers* (Oxford, 1968), pp. 186–7; C.A.E. Goodhart, *The Business of Banking 1891–1914* (London, 1972), pp. 209–11, 218–9; and P.L. Cottrell, *Investment Banking in England 1856–1881: a Case Study of the International Financial Society* (New York/London, 1985), vol. II, pp. 671–6.

bankers' balances

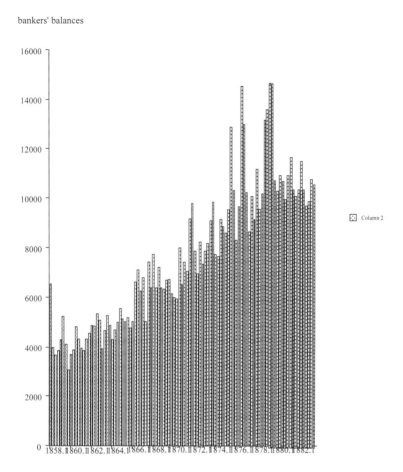

Figure 4.4   Bankers' balances at the head office of the Bank of England,
quarterly averages, 1858–83, £'000s

monetary and financial crises, especially that of 1866. Repeated financial and
monetary disruption constituted one force responsible for figure 4.4's bar chart
having a serrated upper edge, while another was cyclical fluctuations. These wave-
like movements can be more clearly displayed by removing the underlying trend,
as has been done to generate figure 4.5.

The series for bankers' balances has been de-trended pragmatically. This
involved making 'guess estimates' of a rising series of minimum reserve floors, it
having been assumed that there were upward step changes in commercial banks'
reserves, a result of growing liabilities but more particularly of reactions to major
monetary disturbances. The size of these inferred changes was determined from an
inspection of the data's behaviour. The 'detected floors' to bankers' balances have
been set at £4m. from first quarter 1858 (following the 1857 crisis), at £6m. from

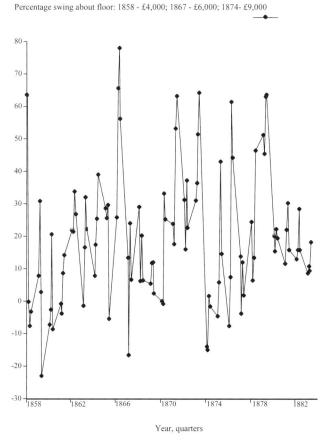

Figure 4.5   Bankers' balances with Bank of England head office, percentage swing around estimated reserve floors

first quarter 1867 (following the 1866 crisis) and at £9m. from first quarter 1874 (following the international events of 1873).[9]

Lagging an inferred floor change to the first quarter of a post-crisis year allows the full (proportional) extent of the increase in reserves in the wake of panic or severe disruption to be displayed. Figure 4.5 portrays the proportional net swings around the presumed sequence of rising reserve floors. For any quarterly average figure of net bankers' balances, the proportional net swing has been calculated in the following, two-stage manner: total balances *minus* the 'guess estimate' of the

---

[9]   The 1878 crisis produced only a short-term shock, with bankers' balances declining thereafter. However, as the banks' public liabilities also fell during the aftermath of the City of Glasgow Bank crash, their cash ratios rose. See M. Collins, 'The Banking Crisis of 1878', in *Economic History Review*, 2nd ser., vol. 42, 1989, p. 521.

appropriate floor level with, second, the arising net sum (positive or negative) shown as a *percentage* of the presumed floor level for the relevant sub-period (£4m. 1858–66; £6m. 1867–73; and £9m. 1874–83). Some confidence in this transformation of the original data is given by negative proportional swings in the calculated series only occurring either immediately after crises (possibly indicating some initial, panic-induced overshooting of reserve requirements) or during cyclical slumps when the accumulation of banking assets and liabilities was adversely affected in the short term.

Clearly evident in figure 4.5 are proportional rises in bankers' balances induced by crisis – in first quarter 1858, during 1866 and 1873 and over 1878/9 following the City of Glasgow Bank crash. Also revealed are the proportional rises in bankers' balances that went with the economy's cyclical expansion over the mid-1860s and the early 1870s, although not during the different, less expansive monetary environment that appears to have prevailed during the weak upswing of the early 1880s following the City of Glasgow Bank crash. What is equally displayed is the far-from-smooth nature of monetary expansion and contraction throughout the entirety of the so-called 'Great Victorian Boom' (which is also marked out in the time path of 3-month bank bills (figure 4.3)). In these terms, the period was not one 'Big Bang' but a series of explosions, some minor, some major, with a possible dampening of fluctuations only setting in by the early 1880s, to suggest the onset of different conditions.

II

A new financial, possibly explosive, factor operative during the mid-Victorian period was a consequence of the general coming of limited liability, in Acts passed in 1855 and 1856. The availability of limited liability through the establishment of limited joint-stock companies by the mere registration of memoranda of association (each signed by a minimum of seven persons, who however individually needed only to acquire just one share, on which no capital was required to be subscribed), greatly changed business organization, at least potentially. However, this new permissiveness came too late to have any significant general shaping effect upon the mid-1850s cyclical upswing.

The possibility of establishing limited joint-stock companies was not a totally radical departure in the case of banking. Promoters had been able to found joint-stock domestic banks, albeit with unlimited liability, since 1826, and by 1843 117 were in existence. However, speculative excesses over the mid-1830s, especially during the first six months of 1836, had provoked the passage of regulating legislation – Peel's Joint Stock Banking Act of 1844. This measure so strictly controlled further corporate bank formations that only 12 new institutions were established over the years to 1857 when the Act remained on the statute book.[10] British-based corporate overseas banks could also be founded before the mid-1850s liberalization of company law, but only by the time-consuming and costly process of gaining a royal charter through approaches to the Board of Trade and the Treasury.

The provisions of the legislation of 1855 and 1856, which so radically changed English company law, did not apply to banking. Banks only began to be assimilated into the new permissive code through Lowe's 1857 Act. This largely repealed the 1844 legislation (although not the requirement of a minimum share denomination of £100), on the grounds that Peel's statute had not addressed the problem of banking mismanagement while having placed significant barriers in the way of establishing new banks. Lowe's Act also allowed private banks to have a maximum of ten partners rather than six, which had been determined by the Bank of England's corporate privileges dating from 1707 and 1711.[11] The continuing question of whether joint-stock banks should equally enjoy the privilege of limited liability was only resolved as a result of Headlam's activities in the Commons during 1858.[12] Yet it was not until the first consolidating Companies Act of 1862 that the last vestiges of Peel's 1844 regulatory bank formation code were repealed.

The responses of promoters of corporate financial enterprises are displayed in figure 4.6.[13] Its trace displays clear cyclical fluctuations, marking out the booms of the mid-1860s, of the early 1870s and of the opening years of the 1880s. However, it is distorted to some extent by post-crisis reconstitutions, especially after 1866, making for something of a false picture of promotional activity waxing and waning almost in symmetry. Furthermore, the numbers of domestic banks are buoyed up to a degree by some existing joint-stock institutions that took advantage of the legislation from 1858 in order to acquire the privilege of limited liability for their shareholders. This motivation particularly came to the fore after the 1878 City of Glasgow Bank crash, which led to a specific statute in 1879 that enabled existing unlimited joint-stock banks to acquire reserve liability. Moreover, although figure 4.6 is of 'effective' registrations, thus omitting abortive and small companies, it aggregates public and private companies. The important difference between these two types of corporate undertakings was not to be recognized legally until 1907, despite private company formation having been evident from the general coming of limited liability in 1855.

The importance of corporate financial enterprises as publicly established companies, especially during the mid-1860s flotation boom, only becomes evident when Spackman's contemporary annual censuses of public company formation are

---

[10]   K.S. Toft, 'A Mid-Nineteenth Century Attempt at Banking Control', in *Revue Internationale d'Histoire de la Banque*, vol. 3, 1970.

[11]   H. Thring, *Joint Stock Companies Acts 1857* (London, 1858).

[12]   *Bankers' Magazine* (1858), pp. 209–13.

[13]   Data drawn from H.A. Shannon, 'The Limited Companies of 1866–1883', in *Economic History Review*, vol. 7, 1933, Table C, pp. 312–13.

Number of 'effective' registrations by type of company

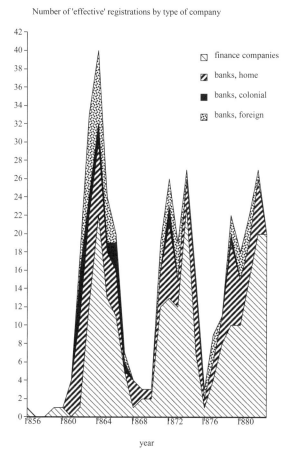

Figure 4.6   'Effective' corporate financial registrations in London, 1856–83

considered. These suggest that, between 1863 and 1866, banks, discount companies and finance companies collectively accounted for 36.4 per cent of capital offered for public subscription and 27.1 per cent of capital publicly subscribed.[14] Public financial promotions, although significant, were not to have the same weight in new issues during the subsequent flotation booms of the early 1870s and the

---

[14]   Calculated from the Spackman composite list published in *The Commercial History and Review of 1866*, p. 35 [supplement to *The Economist* (9 Mar. 1867)]. These annual lists of public companies, compiled by Messrs. Spackman, were published annually in *The Times* on 31 Dec. from 1860. Up to 1862 they provide merely names of public companies and their nominal capitals, only becoming more detailed from 1863. It was maintained that solely public companies were enumerated 'as many never get beyond registration, and others are registered for private purposes'.

opening years of the 1880s. Consequently, if there was a mid-century 'Big Bang', it took place during the mid-1860s boom.

The arrival of corporate financial institutions had a range of significant effects. These included: activity in the new issues market, especially over the mid-1860s, arising from their very promotion; changing the organization of both the domestic banking system and the London money market; augmenting the domestic provision of banking facilities; giving a new basis to British overseas banking; and the founding of corporate institutions that were to challenge briefly the position of private merchant-banking houses. Their impact upon private enterprise in finance will be reviewed by examining each financial market in turn as the presence of corporate institutions came to bear. This gives some order to the following review, but it must be borne in mind that there were also some interconnections. These arose particularly from the finance companies' activities, as some promoted domestic and overseas banks while one – General Credit & Finance (Co. Ltd.) – was reconstituted as a corporate discount house during the aftermath of the 1866 crisis. Furthermore, the International Financial Society (Co. Ltd.) had personal connections with some London merchant banks and Glyn, Mills, a London private bank. Moreover, Albert Gottheimer (subsequently Baron Albert Grant) used the post-1856 permissive company law to enhance his notorious, two-decade career as a financier and promoter, beginning with establishing his own corporate discount house in 1860.[15]

III

In his detailed studies of London registrations of limited companies, Shannon used the term 'finance companies' to assist classification, albeit that he further distinguished among these particular institutions depending on whether they were designed to be colonial, or domestic or foreign concerns. However, 'finance companies' had a particular meaning for mid-Victorians, being the corporate City undertakings set up over the mid-1860s to operate in the money market and undertake new issues. What proved to be their brief impact will be examined later. The discussion here will begin by considering effects of the establishment of corporate discount houses, the first sub-type of significant City 'finance companies' to be founded.

The forces that motivated the creation of corporate discount houses from 1856 appear to have been the London money market's rapid growth over the mid-1850s, cyclical upswing and the substantial profits generated by London joint-stock banks. The first were the National Discount and the London Discount, both of which survived the 1857 crisis, while the General Discount was established amidst that financial upheaval. The need for further principals in the London money market

---

[15]   See P.L. Cottrell, 'Albert Grant', in D. Jeremy (ed.), *Dictionary of Business Biography*, vol. II (London, 1984).

with greater equity capital, potentially available by turning to shareholders, further arose from the impulsive reaction of Bank of England directors to the 1857 crisis.

Led by Governor Neave, the Bank's directors quickly maintained that the 1857 panic had erupted due to the private discount houses' inadequate reserves. However, this was a faulty diagnosis, arising from miscomprehensions about the differences between bill broking and bill dealing. Indeed, the Bank's directors did not understand the workings of the unique, three-layered English banking system, especially during a crisis. When subject to panic-induced monetary stringency, the commercial banks both reduced their call deposits placed with the discount houses and bought fewer bills from Lombard Street. This was in order to augment their reserves, especially their balances with the Bank of England. As a consequence, the discount houses (collectively, the middle-layer 'buffer' in the system) were forced to rediscount bills with the Bank, the only lender of last resort, in order to replenish their own liquidity. The regular holding of higher reserves by the discount houses would have been of little avail since, essentially, they acted to provide liquid assets to the banking system – call deposits (the banks' third line of reserves) – and bills as the banks' short-term investments. The houses substantially generated their own earnings from their respective partners' expertise regarding the quality of bills acquired and the differences between the rate paid on bankers' call deposits on the one hand and their bill buying and selling discount rates on the other. With its 1858 'shutting rule' the Bank broke the vital links in the three-layered banking system between itself, the discount houses and the banks. The rule closed the discount houses' running accounts at the Bank, thereby restricting their general access to the Bank's facilities solely to the quarterly 'shuttings' periods, when illiquidity was caused primarily and artificially by money flows shaped by government tax receipts and the closure of the National Debt transfer books.[16]

The 1858 rule, maintained formally until 1890, provoked two decades of hostility between the Bank and the discount houses, of which the first major episode was Overend, Gurney's attempted run on the 'Old Lady' in 1860. Furthermore, the rule may have further encouraged the establishment of corporate discount houses, such as Albert Gottheimer's seamy Mercantile Discount Company, formed in April 1859.[17] It failed during the 'leather crisis' of 1860/1, as did the General and the London. Furthermore, the London & Provincial Discount appeared and disappeared within three months during 1861, leaving only the National of the recent corporate creations.[18]

---

[16] Evidence of S. Neave, Governor of the Bank of England, to *Select Committee on the Bank Acts* [*B.P.P.*, 1858, XIII], qq. 396, 398–406, 605–18, 627–35, 640–44 and 715–19.

[17] On his questionable business mores at even this early stage of his career, see S. Xenos, *Depredations; or Overend, Gurney & Co., and the Greek & Oriental Steam Navigation Company* (London, 1869), p. 56.

[18] On the 'leather crisis', see *The Economist* (7 July 1860), pp. 726, 739. For general developments, see *Bankers' Magazine* (1860), pp. 150–52; and consult W.T.C. King, *History of the London Discount Market* (London, 1936), pp. 215–33.

The 'leather crisis's' impact appears to have halted further corporate discount house promotions until early 1863, when the announcement of the National's profits for the second half of 1862 may have sparked another founding spree. Only two amongst the seven new companies that were immediately projected had some substance – City Discount and Joint Stock Discount – the latter having acquired the business of James Freeling Wilkinson. Likewise, in 1864 the Discount Corporation bought out two private houses – J. Bruce & H.S. Coulson and Weston & Laurie – and the formation of Consolidated Discount was based upon the conversion of Fraser Sandeman & Co. One other comparable conversion was London Mercantile Discount, which acquired Womersley & Burt. However, the Financial Discount was an untutored foray into the business of the London money market, involving no acquisition of the personal expertise which *The Economist* maintained was vital for success in bill dealing.[19] These new companies failed to dent the established supremacy of the National, the management of which augmented its reserves during 1864 by increasing its subscribed capital. The National's turnover rose by 50 per cent between 1864 and mid-1865, enabling the payment of a 20 per cent dividend from 1864 to 1866.

The rise of the corporate houses, big, small and speculative, led one of the two remaining major private discount houses – Alexander's – to merge with Cunliffes & Co. on 1 January 1864. The other – Overend, Gurney & Co. – was converted into a limited company in mid-1865, something that some hailed as inaugurating 'a new era of limited liability'. Those less sanguine, including *The Economist*, smelt a rat, suspecting that the 'house at the corner' had 'lock-ups', arising from previously having undertaken business beyond normal bill dealing that required financing only obtainable by an appeal to shareholders.[20] This outline review does not permit a detailed analysis of either Overend, Gurney's affairs[21] or the 1866 crisis in which the collapse of Overend, Gurney figured so prominently.[22] Over-reaching management with a speculative trait had led this private discount house to undertake 'exceptional' business during the mid-1850s boom. The lure of greater profits apparently obtainable from medium- and long-term affairs had the same effects over the mid-1860s but was now coupled with some of the new corporate houses' managerial inexperience and overtly speculative nature.

Problems set in from autumn 1864, and became publicly evident with London Mercantile's collapse in 1865. The involvement of the London money market with

[19]   *The Economist* (1860), pp. 1392–3.

[20]   *The Economist* (1865), pp. 845–6.

[21]   Unfortunately, the late Professor F.W. Fetter's researches into Overend, Gurney have never been published.

[22]   See P.L. Cottrell, 'Railway Finance and the Crisis of 1866: Contractors' Bills of Exchange and the Finance Companies', in *Journal of Transport History*, n.s., vol. 3, 1975; and R.A. Batchelor, 'The Avoidance of Catastrophe: Two Nineteenth-Century Banking Crises', in F. Capie and G.E. Wood (eds), *Financial Crises and the World Banking System* (London, 1986).

financing new railway construction, so that Thompson Hankey at the Bank could rightly call some of the arising paper not bills but mortgages, became public from January 1866. Joint Stock Discount went into liquidation shortly afterwards. The reverberating crash of Overend, Gurney on 10 May was followed by ultimately abortive attempts to rescue the businesses of Consolidated Discount and Financial Discount. The Discount Corporation, reconstituted as the United Discount Corporation, survived by concentrating upon short-dated bills despite little free capital which none were prepared to top up.

Among the corporate houses formed between 1856 and 1865, only the National rode out the turmoil of the 1866 crisis largely unscathed, the sole blot upon its assets arising from a connection with Joint Stock Discount. Its board raised further capital between January 1866 and March 1867 on which initially a dividend of 20 per cent was paid. With its robust position, re-buttressed during the crisis period, the National's management seized market opportunities arising from the 1866 crisis's winnowing force. Its sole major corporate competitor was the General Credit & Discount, the post-crisis reconstitution of a finance company – General Credit & Finance. This was the last corporate discount house to be successfully established before the late-twentieth-century restructuring of the London market. Its management embarked upon their new business field with a very sizeable capital – £1.5m – although this may have been required to nurse pre-1866 'lock-ups'.[23]

After the 1866 crisis, Alexander's was the sole major private discount house, although having a business smaller than that of the National. Yet the 1866 crisis had the further effect of inducing the spawning of new private houses out of the ruins of failed partnerships, with Overend, Gurney producing three alone. In addition, a further eight were established between 1866 and 1868.[24] Amongst these was Gillett Brothers, founded by some of the partners in a private Quaker Oxfordshire country bank.

The Gilletts' personal connection with the London money market had begun in 1861 when William Gillett had joined George Brightwen to form a discount house. After seven uneasy years their partnership was dissolved, but a new house was then founded in Lombard Street. Guided by William, it was undertaken by his brothers, Alfred and George, together with Thomas Aggs, a cousin and former shipbroker, and Samuel Seymour Grubb, a fellow Quaker who had worked for William and Brightwen. Alfred managed the business, which within five years had become exceedingly promising, earning about 15 per cent on capital, some of which was inter-family loans.[25]

William returned to Lombard Street in mid-1872 with a plan to convert what was substantially his brothers' business into a limited company. He put forward this

[23] See Cottrell, *Investment Banking* , vol. II, pp. 418–20, 423–6, 428, 462–4, 497–500, 552–3, 643–5.

[24] Much of the preceding paragraphs has been drawn from the still unsurpassed King, *London Discount Market;* see, in particular, pp. 229–61.

[25] R.S. Sayers, *Gilletts in the London Money Market 1867–1967* (Oxford, 1968), pp. 1–16, 30–32.

proposal on various grounds, depending on who was the listener: the National's current difficulties provided a market opportunity; or the firm in any case required greater capital, which his own social connections could supply; or all involved would benefit from the substantial premium likely to be obtained on the shares. William's grandiose plan for incorporation was intricate, involving a partnership acting for his proposed limited company, but miscarried when executed. Few shareholders were attracted, many having been put off by the adverse effects upon principals in the money market of the sudden rise in interest rates during February 1873. Worse still, existing customers closed their accounts with Gillett Brothers because of distrust and distaste of corporate enterprise. The arising imbroglio led to long-lasting legal disputes between William and his brothers, Alfred and George, who continued the old private business. The consequences of the tiered conversion contracts of 1873 were not legally resolved until 1894, only for fresh problems immediately to arise as a result of Alfred's sudden death.[26]

Gilletts' business during both the 1860s and 1870s was largely with provincial banks, private and joint-stock, insurance companies and a few railway companies. Initially, the house primarily dealt in trade bills, endorsed by their banking clientele, which Gilletts screened and monitored for quality on the basis of the creditworthiness of the originating parties. London credit agencies were used but Gilletts developed their own expertise that they shared, probably most often with the banks on their 'special' customer list. At the height of the early 1870s boom, Gilletts handled £2m. in bills, but this thereafter fell away, to average £1.3m. during the decade's latter years. The business had begun on a country banking connection, reflecting Gilletts' own origins, but subsequently the house's staple came increasingly to be Indian bills. These bore the names of the institutions with which exporters of cotton, jute, rice and tea etc. banked, together with those of the British overseas banks that financed international commerce. Such varying types of commercial paper were joined over the 1880s by Treasury Bills, which acted to a degree as a counterweight to give a broad stability to Gilletts' bill case.[27]

Gilletts' experience shows that there was still room for personal enterprise on mid-Victorian Lombard Street and that 'joint-stock-ism' had not been accepted by all. Nevertheless, the London market money's organizational structure was completely changed during the decade after 1856 through the National's becoming the dominant house, until it too was overshadowed by another corporate institution – Union Discount – during the closing decades of the nineteenth century. Furthermore, Gilletts' particular experience points to the general, secular waning of private enterprise within domestic banking, as the bulk of their money-market business shifted from relationships with private country banks to Oriental bills over the 1880s and 1890s. In the case of the London money market, the 'Big Bang' of the 1860s had significant immediate effects, and its subsequent, rippling aftershocks were also potent shaping forces.

---

[26]	Ibid., pp. 17–29.
[27]	Ibid., pp. 35–62.

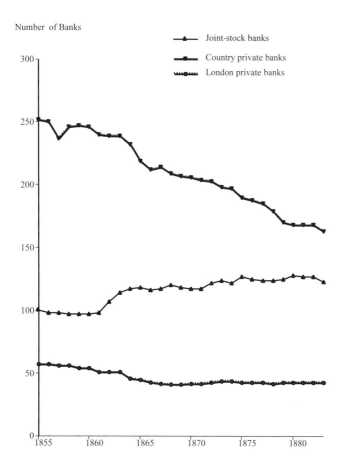

Figure 4.7   Numbers of English and Welsh banks, by type, 1855–83

IV

With respect to domestic commercial banking, there was less scope for the postulated 'Big Bang' of the mid-1860s to have a dramatic impact comparable to the very significant institutional changes that it wrought within the London money market. On the one hand, legislation had allowed banks to be established as joint-stock concerns since 1826 (albeit without limited liability for their shareholders), while, on the other, country private banking had been declining since 1815. In this respect figure 4.7 traces the continuation over the mid-century of established trends in patterns of organizational development.[28] Nevertheless, the piecemeal repeal of Peel's 1844 regulatory code between 1857 and 1862 brought about an

---

[28]   Data drawn from Nishimura, *Decline of Inland Bills*, Table 1, pp. 80–81.

acceleration in the corporate banks' rise to total ascendancy, if only because there was a contemporary consensus that England remained 'underbanked' during the early 1860s.[29] Indeed, eight new limited joint-stock banks were established during 1861 and 1862, that is, before the law specifically regulating the creation of such institutions was totally reformed by the 1862 Companies Act (which only became operative from November 1862). However, there was some surprise within the banking profession at the very number of new corporate institutions put before the investing public during the mid-1860s flotation boom.

It was recognized that, if successful, the limited banks would bear hardest upon the remaining private houses. Indeed, as during the 1830s, many were conversions of private banks. The continuing absorption of private country banking houses by joint-stock banks was joined in 1858 by the availability of limited liability for banks. This soon led investors in established unlimited institutions to consider their positions. They responded negatively, with 2,510 of 'the most substantial men' liquidating their holdings over 1863/4 in 48 unlimited banks established before 1857.[30] Furthermore, as the boom set in, general sentiment began to change, *The Economist* commenting that 'A country is badly off which has too few banks – it is almost as unfortunate if it has too many'.[31]

As pointed out earlier, the mid-1860s boom was marked by 'fits and starts' so that bank investors had a 'bumpy ride' before the crisis of 1866. Bank share prices fell abruptly in December 1863, when Bank rate went to eight per cent, and there was another Stock Exchange convulsion during early May 1864 in which the calling-up of capital by new companies played a part. The monetary stringency of autumn 1864 again had adverse effects, heightened by the collapse of the Leeds Bank in October, which caused investors to doubt the solidity of any banking enterprise. Nonetheless, 'bulls' had sufficient optimism to drive the market up again though only for a few months. Prices of bank shares fell in late January 1865, and they never regained dynamism as the autumnal monetary stringency of 1865 finally extinguished 'bull' speculative interest.

Some of the new institutions were small, local affairs, comparable to their joint-stock predecessors of the 1830s, like, for instance, the Leeds & County Bank Ltd. of 1862, itself a reformation of the Joint Stock Banking Co. of Pontefract, Wakefield & Goole formed a year earlier. Other Yorkshire corporate banks had even humbler beginnings, as with the Exchange & Discount Bank Ltd. of 1866. This had begun in 1860 with a capital of £8,000 as the personal enterprise of John

---

[29]   B.L. Anderson and P.L. Cottrell, 'Another Victorian Capital Market: a Study of Banking and Bank Investors on Merseyside', in *Economic History Review*, 2nd ser., vol. 28, 1975.

[30]   *Bankers' Magazine* (1864), p. 328; and see, in general, P.L. Cottrell, 'Credit, Morals and Sunspots: the Financial Boom of the 1860s and Trade Cycle Theory', in P.L. Cottrell and D.E. Moggridge (eds), *Money and Power: Essays in Honour of L. S. Pressnell* (Houndmills/London, 1988), pp. 45–53.

[31]   *Commercial History and Review of 1863* [supplement to *The Economist* (20 Feb. 1864)], pp. 3–4.

James Cousins and had, initially, an office so small that it could only accommodate one customer at a time. Cousins withstood the consequences of the 1864 failure of the Leeds Bank, and when his own bank was subsequently incorporated, he was its principal shareholder.[32]

The formation of new provincial corporate banks went in parallel with the setting up of London joint-stock limited banks: Alliance of London & Liverpool, East London, Imperial, Metropolitan & Provincial, North London and South London. They had various parents, the Imperial being the product of the efforts of a Scots merchant who gradually recruited a board from among the City's cosmopolitan membership – H.L. Bischoffsheim, A.P. Petrocochino, P. C. Ralli and D. Stern – and their presence as directors greatly assisted in maintaining the bank's share price from 1864 until the 1866 crisis. The East London was the creation of a Mr Sleigh, who was sufficiently able to recruit an MP and a compiler of directories for its board.[33] Another, initially titled the South Eastern Banking Company, was promoted in February 1864 by a finance company, the London Financial Association. It was the conversion of the private West Surrey Bank of C.E. Mangles & Co., and subsequently acquired the Ramsgate Bank of Messrs Burgess & Canham.[34]

The foundation of limited banks accompanied the inception of what proved to be significant trends in the structure of English domestic banking. One was the beginning of a sustained impetus to branch. The number of offices per bank rose from 2.9 in 1855 to 4.3 in 1866, a rise predominantly a feature of joint-stock banking, for which the overall ratio of offices per bank increased from 6.3 to 8.7.[35] Branching took further the declared intention of some of the new banks' managements and promoters to link the metropolis with the provinces. However, more important for the inception of nationwide banking were the decisions of the managements of two established joint-stock banks. During the mid-1860s, the National Provincial's directors decided to forgo the profits of a provincial note issue in order to open a fully-operational London branch. At the same time, the board of the London & County (a joint-stock deposit bank established in 1836 under the declaratory clause in the Bank of England's renewed charter) re-invigorated their bank's branching policy. For the most part, however, this involved the widening of its network solely within the Bank of England's protected metropolitan note-issuing area. Consequently, these two branching strategies were complementary and in 1874 resulted in the London & County and the National Provincial being

---

[32] W.F. Crick and J.E. Wadsworth, *A Hundred Years of Joint Stock Banking* (London, 3rd edn, 1958), pp. 221–3.

[33] Crick and Wadsworth, *Hundred Years*, pp. 297–9. Sleigh may have been involved in the earlier creations of the Bank of Egypt and the Ottoman Bank.

[34] Cottrell, *Investment Banking*, vol. I, pp. 334–5.

[35] Nishimura, *Decline of Inland Bills*, Table 1, pp. 80–81.

the only two English banks that each had more than 100 offices – 149 and 138 respectively.[36]

A further structural change in English domestic banking arose from the acceleration in the rate of banking amalgamations, with eight in 1863 and ten in 1864. These mergers included some of considerable significance, as they caused the disappearance of major private banks. Heywood, Kennard & Co. was acquired by the Bank of Manchester in 1863 and, in the following year, Jones Loyd & Co. was taken over by the London & Westminster.[37] Expectations, arising from investor interest in bank shares during the mid-1860s, no doubt also led to many stillborn schemes. An example is the International Financial Society's banking fusion plan. This City finance company's directors participated, along with members of a 'first-class London house', in an attempt from July 1864 to bring about 'the amalgamation of existing banking interests throughout England'. Within four months, the scheme had got as far as involving specific banks, like Messrs Becketts of Leeds, while other bank managements, such as that of the Birmingham Banking Co., approached the London finance company to be included. Yet the project dragged, and by January 1865 its promoters' continuing discussions had concluded that success required the inclusion of an existing London bank. However, this potentially far-reaching scheme finally ran into the sands during the opening months of 1865. Prices of bank shares had weakened but there were also other particular reasons. Bagehot 'was unable to take part in the Direction' while the North Western Bank, the Commercial Bank of Liverpool and the Birmingham Banking Co. withdrew, formally or informally. By spring 1865, with the collapse of the bull market in bank shares, there were no longer any grounds for the promoters' expectation of a profitable share issue.[38]

As in the London money market, the 1866 crisis cut a swathe through the ranks of the new limited banks and also established institutions. It brought down the Bank of London, the Consolidated and the Metropolitan & Provincial while, in the provinces, the recently converted Barned's Bank failed, as did the Birmingham Banking Co., the Preston Banking Co. and the South East of England. Others, such as the Alliance, the East London and the Liverpool Union were badly shaken. Some – the Consolidated, the East London (as the Central Bank of London), the Metropolitan and the Preston – were either re-established or reconstituted.[39] It was not only, variously, bad business, bad management and lack of reserves due to

---

[36]   Crick and Wadsworth, *Hundred Years*, pp. 36–7; and Nishimura, *Decline of Inland Bills*, Table 2, p. 84.

[37]   J. Sykes, *The Amalgamation Movement in English Banking 1825–1924* (London, 1929), pp. 31–2.

[38]   Cottrell, *Investment Banking*, I, pp. 335–8.

[39]   *Bankers' Magazine* (1866), p. 1325; Crick and Wadsworth, *Hundred Years*, pp. 68, 150, 302–7; T.E. Gregory, *The Westminster Bank Through a Century*, vol. I (London: 1936), pp. 42–7, 51, 54, 57–68; and R.S. Sayers, *Lloyds Bank in the History of English Banking* (Oxford, 1957), pp. 208, 209, 211, 212.

recent creation that had brought these institutions low but also the 'bear' selling of their shares, a feature of 1866's opening months. This led to Leeman's Act, which attempted to prevent speculators from selling shares that they did not possess but it soon became a dead letter, totally disregarded by the London Stock Exchange within a decade.[40]

The memory of some of the new limited banks' relatively brief lives failed to check further promotions of domestic banks, especially during the upswings of the early 1870s and of the opening years of the 1880s. A number were once more the conversions of private banks, such as the Cornwall (Tweedy, Williams), the Craven (Birkbeck, Robinson), Crompton & Evans Union Bank and Manchester Joint Stock (Robertson Fraser & Co.). Some of these were undertaken as responses to the consequences of the City of Glasgow Bank crash for unlimited banks, whether private or joint-stock. Other promotions were mayflies of boom periods and especially of the weak upswing of the early 1880s: Cheshire Banking Co. (1882–4), Hull District (1879–80), and National Mercantile (1878–81). The remaining 18 had business careers of some longevity – on average 17 years – which for at least eight came to an end only because of the amalgamation movement that further accelerated over the 1880s.[41] However, only one of the post-1866 new corporate banks – the Lancashire & Yorkshire (1872–1928) – had any immediate major impact upon the market. In this, it was unusual amongst all new corporate domestic banks established between 1870 and 1920.

Capie has put forward that limited banks formed after 1870 generally failed to rapidly establish significant positions because the market was not wholly contestable. A constraint to their progress arose from the monopolistic position of the London Clearing House, formed by London private banks during the late eighteenth century, which accepted joint-stock institutions as members only from 1854.[42] However, membership was not automatic and some London corporate banks of the mid-1860s – the Imperial and the Metropolitan & Provincial – were initially refused entry. Opposition came from not only the continuing vested interests of metropolitan private bankers but also the London unlimited joint-stock banks founded between 1834 and 1857. The managements of the latter still considered that all the assets of every shareholder were required to back an institution's business. Certainly, one factor at work within the amalgamation movement from the 1880s supporting Capie's interpretation was the acquisition of

---

[40]   *The Economist* (2 Mar. 1867), pp. 231–2, 237–8; and E.V. Morgan and W.A. Thomas, *The Stock Exchange* (London, 1962), pp. 147–8.

[41]   Data drawn from F. Capie and A. Webber, *A Monetary History of the United Kingdom, 1870–1982*, I, *Data, Sources, Methods* (London, 1985), Appendix II, pp. 539–76.

[42]   F. Capie, 'Structure and Performance in British Banking, 1870–1939', in Cottrell and Moggridge, *Money and Power*, pp. 96–100.

London clearing banks by some provincial banks, such as Lloyds and the Midland, in order to secure their direct institutional entry into the clearing.[43]

Nonetheless, when examining why corporate banks founded after 1870 failed to make a mark nationally, it has to be borne in mind that the majority of them were conceived as local institutions, like their predecessors of the 1830s. Their managements had little intention of developing either major regional or national business catchment areas. In these terms, it is not surprising that none became a significant deposit holder. They were not competing in the national deposit market, however defined, but rather at a parochial level. Instead, their main *national* impact arose from their promotions collectively increasing the number of English and Welsh joint-stock banks to a historic maximum of 128 in 1880. As, generally, their objective was providing local banking facilities, the prime competitive edge of the post-1870 corporate banks bore upon the remaining private country banks.[44]

The Lancashire & Yorkshire was different, being nationally successful. This was due in part to its not being an entirely new bank in 1872, having arisen out of the Alliance of London & Liverpool's Manchester branch. Its manager, John Mills, began to free his local domain from 1866, his efforts achieving success from April 1871. As such, the Lancashire & Yorkshire was the product of particular personal enterprise. On its establishment, the bank soon began to branch, opening four offices over the first year of its separate existence and a further two by the close of 1874. Expansion went along with riding out the minor financial crisis of 1875 by the employment of significant reserves, which cushioned the bank against London bill brokers 'rejecting some of the very finest paper'.[45] Except for the conversions of existing private banks, no other post-1870 corporate banking creation began with such a head start, given by customer accounts accumulated over a previous decade.[46]

---

[43]   P.L. Cottrell, 'The Domestic Commercial Banks and the City of London, 1870–1939', in Y. Cassis (ed.), *Finance and Financiers in European History 1880–1960* (Cambridge, 1992), p. 48.

[44]   For one example of their lending business – that of the Swansea Bank (1872–1888) – see Cottrell, *Industrial Finance*, pp. 213, 219–23.

[45]   G. Chandler, *Four Centuries of Banking*, II, *The Northern Constituent Banks* (London, 1968), pp. 516–29; Anon., *The Story of the Lancashire & Yorkshire Bank Limited 1872–1922* (Manchester: n.d. [1922]); and, for John Mills in particular, see L.H. Grindon, *Manchester Banks and Bankers; Historical, Biographical, and Anecdotal* (Manchester, 2nd edn, 1878), pp. 311–12; and Cottrell, 'Credit, Morals and Sunspots', esp. pp. 54–5, 58–61.

[46]   The other bank in Capie's tabulations that enjoyed some initial, rapid deposit growth, albeit relative, was the Birmingham, Dudley & District. However, Capie is mistaken in regarding this as a new institution formed in 1874. Rather, it was the reconstitution of a bank first established during the 1830s. See Capie, 'Structure and Performance', Table 3.5c, p. 98 and, for the Birmingham, Dudley & District, Crick and Wadsworth, *Hundred Years*, pp. 55, 66; and A.R. Holmes and E. Green, *Midland: 150 Years of Banking Business* (London, 1986), pp. 15, 16, 19, 26, 38, 59, 69, 71, 73, 75, 83, 104.

Probably some 13 entirely new private English country banking houses were also set up between 1857 and 1883 and one thereafter.[47] Nonetheless, their foundations in no way offset the long-established declining trend in private country banking. In terms of the total number of banking offices, private country houses were of some importance during the late 1870s only in the agricultural shires, where they numbered 159 with, in aggregate, 400 branches. Even so, in this last retreat, they were in local competition with 43 joint-stock banks which collectively had 380 branches.[48] Many of the private houses that survived to the mid-century were located in the Home Counties, where they had a degree of shelter from joint-stock competition given by the Bank of England's post-1833 corporate monopoly of note-issuing. This had prevented the establishment of competing joint-stock note-issuing banks within a 65-mile radius of London, and meant that the south east, beyond the metropolis's central urban core, lacked adequate banking facilities, a condition still remarked upon until the 1890s. However, the semi-monopolistic position of note-issuing private banks in the area around London was challenged from the mid-1860s by the further expansion of the London & County's branch network. Thereafter, from the mid-1870s, the position of these particular private banks was made more problematic by the decline of cereal prices, which had damaging effects upon south-eastern arable agriculture, especially in Cambridgeshire and Essex.

London private banking did not wane to such an extent over the mid-century. Possibly 17 new houses were established in the metropolis between 1858 and 1883, and a further nine thereafter.[49] They had very divergent natures, including Cockburn's Guaranteed Cheque Bank and the banking arm of William Whiteley's department store in Queensway. As this suggests, some reflected the new banking of the mid-Victorian period generated by the demands of the growing middle classes and, thereby, had little in common with their predecessors in the West End and the City. Others were very personal creatures, such as Grants (1872–94), the last business vehicle of Albert Gottheimer/Baron Grant in association with

[47] Data drawn from Capie and Webber, *Monetary History of the United Kingdom*, vol. I, Appendix II, pp. 539–76. The uncertainty arises from when it is possible to check the entries in the enumeration of Capie and Webber with other sources. For instance, they appear to indicate that Hedge Wells & Co. was established in 1858, whereas Sayers shows that this was a successor house to Wells, Allnatt, Wells & Wells of Wallingford, which opened in 1797. Similarly, Sayers considers Pomfret [Barra] & Co., 1875, to have developed from Jemmett, Whitfield & Jemmett of Ashford, Kent (1791). See Sayers, *Lloyds*, pp. 281, 282.

[48] W. Newmarch, 'The Increase in the Number of Banks and Branches ... 1858–1878', *Bankers' Magazine* (1879), pp. 849–61.

[49] Data drawn from Capie and Webber, *Monetary History of the United Kingdom*, vol. I, Appendix II, pp. 539–76. Again, the uncertainty arises from when it is possible to check the entries in the enumeration of Capie and Webber with other sources. For instance, they appear to indicate that Brooks & Co. was established in 1864, whereas Sayers shows that this was a reconstitution of a house established in 1824. See Sayers, *Lloyds*, p. 281.

Maurice, his brother. Like the Guaranteed Cheque Bank (1880–4), a number had very brief business lives, including Cates & Son (1875–8), A.S. Cochrane (1875–8) and A. Masters & Co. (1880–2).

Whereas the aggregate deposits of provincial joint-stock banks exceeded those held by all private country banks in 1871, the London joint-stock banks only finally gained institutional dominance as deposit holders in the metropolis during the boom of the early 1870s.[50] The relative vibrancy of mid-century London private banking compared with private country banking is difficult to explain, because of its long-established heterogeneity. Indeed, that heterogeneity may be one reason for its overall greater resilience. To go further is almost impossible, as there is only one history of a City private bank, Glyn, Mills, which was in some respects more like a merchant bank,[51] whereas other business histories are of primarily elite West End houses: Childs, Coutts, Drummonds and Hoares, none of which would provide the necessary general pointers.[52] All in all, an overall assessment of London private banking *throughout* the nineteenth century remains a long-standing unconsidered item on the English banking historian's research agenda.

The growth of joint-stock banking, undertaken by new and established institutions, took forward deposit/cheque banking, especially during the early 1860s and early 1870s. The liabilities of private banks, metropolitan and provincial, grew more slowly – at about a third of the rate of their joint-stock competitors over the mid-century period – with the result that their share of total public liabilities declined to about a third by the late 1870s.[53] Overall expansion was checked in the short-term by the 1866 crisis, but only brought to almost a halt by the 1878 crisis caused by the failure of the City of Glasgow Bank. This led to the money supply, primarily bank deposits, growing slower than output, and this, along with falling holdings of monetary and prime banking reserves, contributed to the price deflation of the first phase, 1873–86, of the 'Great Depression' of the last quarter of the nineteenth century.[54]

---

[50]   See Capie and Webber, *Monetary History of the United Kingdom*, vol. I, Table III.(3), p. 432.

[51]   R. Fulford, *Glyn's 1753–1953: Six Generations in Lombard Street* (London, 1953).

[52]   P. Clarke, *Child & Co. 1673–1973: the First House in the City* (London, 1973); E. Healey, *Coutts & Co., 1692–1992. The Portrait of a Private Bank* (London/Sydney/Auckland, 1992); H. Bolitho and D. Peel, *The Drummonds of Charing Cross* (London, 1967); and [C. Hoare & Co.], *Hoare's Bank: a Record 1673–1932* (London, 1932). See also J.A.S.L. Leighton Boyce, *Smiths the Bankers 1658–1958* (London, 1958).

[53]   Collins, 'English Banking Sector', pp. 375–81; and *idem*, 'English Banks and Business Cycles, 1848–80', in Cottrell and Moggridge, *Money and Power*. The estimates of Capie and Webber are in broad agreement, indicating that, over the period 1878–87, joint-stock banks held 69 per cent of all English bank deposits; calculated from Capie and Webber, *Monetary History of the United Kingdom*, vol. I, Table III.(3), p. 432.

[54]   D.E. Moggridge, 'Keynes as a Monetary Historian', in Cottrell and Moggridge, *Money and Power*, pp. 138–43; and Collins, 'The Banking Crisis of 1878': On expectations

Although amongst institutions south of Hadrian's Wall only one bank failed (West of England & South Wales District), and three stopped payment (the Cornish Bank of Tweedy Williams & Co. [subsequently converted], Fentons of Rochdale and the Preston Banking Company), while the Bank of England did not face a cash crisis, the collapse of the City of Glasgow Bank had widespread effects within England and Wales. Branches of both the Yorkshire Banking Co. and the York City & County experienced runs, as did the Queen's Building Society and savings banks in Lancashire. In the north east, Hodgkin & Co., Lambton & Co. and other local banks approached the Bank of England's Agent for assistance. Other banks were badly shaken as the failure of the City of Glasgow reverberated upon their illiquid advances to industrial customers at the trough of a trade depression. This was the experience of both Lloyds and the Midland in Birmingham.

One clear consequence of the 1878 crisis was the greater adoption of limited liability, especially by unlimited banks established before 1857. The failure of the *unlimited* City of Glasgow directly ruined 2,000 families, as their resources were repeatedly drained to satisfy the bank's depositors. This showed that opponents of limited liability for banking were technically correct when they had maintained that depositors in unlimited banks were fully covered. However, that only 254 out of the City of Glasgow's 1,819 shareholders were solvent after this bank's affairs had been wound-up revealed to all the costs involved. The answer was 'reserved liability', with the necessary legislation quickly passed in 1879, largely due to the efforts of George Rae, General Manager of the shaken North & South Wales Bank.[55] During the early 1880s, 27 unlimited joint-stock banks quickly took advantage of this new legislative provision and, by the 1890s, very few joint-stock banks were unlimited concerns.

The further take-up of limited liability, albeit reserved liability, had yet another consequence for private commercial banking in both London and the provinces. The 1879 Act introduced greater publicity requirements, including the publication of half-yearly balance sheets. This placed partners in many of the remaining private banks in a dilemma. If they presented their accounts, then, generally, these would display reserves proportionally smaller than those of their joint-stock competitors. If they did not, the absence of a balance sheet would raise questions over their solvency. The escape from this situation proved to be amalgamation with joint-stock banks. During the 1880s there were 66 amalgamations between private and joint-stock banks, some of which also arose from other operative factors, such as a waning of personal entrepreneurial drive or, simply, a psychological loss of faith.[56]

---

of the occurrence of a crisis in 1878, see Cottrell, 'Credit, Morals and Sunspots', pp. 63–4.
[55]   Crick and Wadsworth, *Hundred Years*, p. 428.
[56]   Sykes, *Amalgamation Movement*, pp. 30–43: see also, Sayers, *Lloyds*, pp. 244–56.

V

The formation of domestic limited joint-stock banks from 1861 was soon accompanied by the founding of overseas corporate banks, both colonial and foreign (see figure 4.8).[57] Their promotion became publicly evident from early 1863. Many initially had 'Anglo-continental-European' titles whilst their foundations were thought, at the time, to have been encouraged by the London money market's 'comparatively favourable aspect'.[58]

British-based overseas banking was a comparatively new development. A few English banks, comparable in nature to domestic private country banks, had been established abroad, primarily in French Channel packet ports and Paris. Otherwise, there was overseas 'trade' banking, largely undertaken by branch houses of London merchants and merchant banks. This private foreign banking, albeit of a restricted kind, built upon Britain's early established position as the linchpin of the world economy. During the late 1840s, according to a contemporary British survey, there were about 1,500 British mercantile houses overseas compared with 500 French, with nearly half of the latter located in the Mediterranean and Levant region. However, that survey overlooked German commerce which, in 1845, had 340 extra-European houses, largely sited in the New World – 170 in the United States and 100 in Latin America.

Alongside English mercantile branch houses from the 1830s were a number of banks, incorporated by royal charter,[59] each operating within a specific area of the British Empire, the only major exception being the Ionian. Together with English private mercantile houses, these institutions financed international trade and operated in the foreign exchange markets, but also developed local deposit branch banking.[60] In 1860, immediately prior to promoters of overseas banks responding to the opportunities of the new permissive company law, there were 15 British incorporated overseas banks with, collectively, 132 branches. The majority of their assets were located in Asia and Australasia.[61]

London-based colonial banking expanded under the new company law, with at least 30 new institutions formed between 1857 and 1866 (13 during the mid-1860s boom). However, many were highly speculative in nature and so unable to withstand the 1866 crisis, of which the most spectacular example was the collapse of Agra & Mastermans. Initially an expatriate Indian private bank founded during the 1830s, it became a London-based corporate concern from 1857, and in 1864

---

[57]   Data drawn from Shannon, 'Limited Companies of 1866–1883', Table C, pp. 312–13.

[58]   *Bankers' Magazine* (1863), p. 53; and A.S.J. Baster, *The International Banks* (London, 1935).

[59]   The exceptions to incorporation by charter were: Bank of Australasia (1835), Union Bank of Australia (1837) and the Australian Joint Stock Bank (1853).

[60]   G. Jones, *British Multinational Banking 1830–1990* (Oxford, 1993), pp. 13–15, 19–21.

[61]   Jones, *Multinational Banking*, p. 23.

Registrations, by type of institution

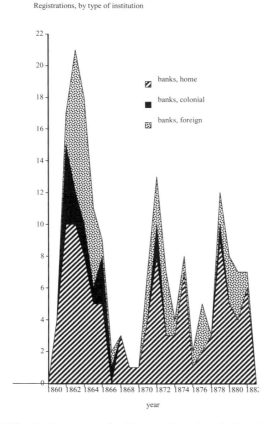

banks, home

banks, colonial

banks, foreign

Figure 4.8   'Effective' corporate banking registrations in London, 1856–83

merged with the private bank of Masterman, Peters, Mildred & Co., thereby extending its range to metropolitan banking. Before 1866, it had also opened branches in Australia, China and continental Europe while developing unwise relationships with the finance companies, in particular General Credit & Finance and the (English) Crédit Foncier.[62]

The Agra, like some domestic banks and other overseas banks, was a victim of 'bear' share selling during the opening months of 1866, with in its case its shares consequently falling from £67 to £5 at its closure. A similar target was the European, originally in 1862 the Union Bank of England & France, which had then merged with the English, Belgian & Netherlands and the London, Birmingham & South Staffordshire. Another 'bear' sell, the London, Bombay & Mediterranean, was, likewise, the product of three boom mergers. The Agra's closure brought down

[62]   A.S.J. Baster, *The Imperial Banks* (London, 1929), pp. 129–30; and Jones, *Multinational Banking*, pp. 23–4.

the British & Californian which, although promoted by the London Financial, had subsequently become involved with the burgeoning 'three continents' bank. Among the new London-based overseas banks only the Agra was reconstituted after the crisis and solely as an 'Anglo-Indian' bank. This was undertaken by the important London and Manchester accountant, David Chadwick, who also put new, post-crisis life into two domestic banks: the Consolidated and the Preston.[63]

From the 1830s, British corporate overseas banks had interconnections arising from interlocking directorships. One responsible but particular factor was the interests that various partners in a London private bank, Glyn, Mills, took in their creation, beginning with the Union Bank of Australia formed in 1837. Thereafter, members of this Lombard Street house were involved in the Bank of Egypt (1855/6), the Ottoman (1856, a progenitor of the Imperial Ottoman Bank of 1862), the London & Brazilian (1862), the Anglo-Austrian (1863) and the Imperial Bank of Persia (1889). City associates of Glyn, Mills, in turn, promoted the Anglo-Italian (1864), the 'private' London & San Francisco (1865), the Bank of Roumania (1866), the German Bank of London (1871), the Mercantile Bank of the River Plate (1872), the Banque de Constantinople (1872) and the English Bank of the River Plate (1881).[64] These instances are indicative of the broader, general interest that private City houses as a whole took in the new overseas corporate banks, which went beyond supplying prestigious and decorative directors for their prospectuses. It was in complete contrast to any involvement with new domestic corporate banks, the only significant exception being the 'City' directorate of the Imperial. Furthermore, in some cases, private banking's interrelationships with British-based corporate overseas banking involved not only City personalities but also European 'Haute Finance'. With respect to the Imperial Ottoman, this arose from the compromise amalgamation of competing syndicates for the concession, leading to the bank's having management bases in Constantinople and Paris as well as London. In other instances, members of the City drew directly upon their respective European networks, resulting in, for instance, the German Bischoffsheim's involvement in the London & Brazilian, the London & San Francisco (plus J. May and R. Sulzbach (Frankfurt) and C. Griswold (Paris)), the Mercantile Bank of the River Plate (along with Paribas, H. Oppenheim, Louis d'Erlanger and Louis Beer), Société Générale

---

[63]   *Bankers' Magazine* (1866), pp. 1324, 1325; Baster, *International Banks*, pp. 42–3, 158, 246; D.S. Landes, *Bankers and Pashas* (London, 1958), pp. 244, 290, 292; and Cottrell, *Investment Banking*, I, pp. 408–9. For Chadwick, see P.L. Cottrell, 'David Chadwick', in D. Jeremy (ed.), *Dictionary of Business Biography*, I (London, 1984).

[64]   A.S.J. Baster, 'The Origins of British Banking Expansion in the Near East', in *Economic History Review*, vol. 5, 1934/5; *idem*, *International Banks*, pp. 95, 99, 112–19, 158; D. Joslin, *A Century of Banking in Latin America* (Oxford, 1963), pp. 64–5; P.L. Cottrell, 'London Financiers and Austria 1863–1875: the Anglo-Austrian Bank', in *Business History*, vol. 11, 1969; and *idem*, 'The Coalescence of a Cluster of Corporate International Banks, 1855–75', in G. Jones (ed.), *Banks and Money: International and Comparative Finance in History* (London, 1991).

de l'Empire ottoman and Banque de Constantinople. In the case of the Mercantile Bank of the River Plate, foreign subscriptions comprised 45 per cent of its initial equity capital, excluding founders' shares.

The 1860s were also marked by a brief flurry of interest in developing Anglo-European banking (often in terms of introducing the cheque), and Anglo-Californian banking. Longer lasting was the development of British overseas corporate banking in Latin America – in Argentina, Brazil, Chile and Uruguay. Some of these particular banks extended their business to support the British building of local railways while financing the subsequent export of crops that their lines brought to the ports. In the case of Latin America, the new corporate British overseas banks largely replaced British branch mercantile houses from the 1860s in the finance of international trade, leading to a number subsequently becoming better known by their commercial speciality than their legal title. For example, the Anglo-South American Bank was usually referred to as the 'nitrate' bank.[65] This affected particular private houses with South American interests, such as A. Gibbs & Sons and F. Huth & Co. However, more broadly, a complementary balance of business interests developed. Private London merchant houses and merchant banks came to be primarily concerned with the finance of Anglo-American trade and European trade where they were long established, while chartered banks predominated in the Orient (along with Anglo-Indian agency houses) and Australasia, and successful mid-century corporate overseas banks operated particularly in South America. Nonetheless, there were always individual exceptions, and all were affected to a degree by the further shift of the London joint-stock banks into the business of foreign trade acceptances from the late 1860s. This development led to some London joint-stock bankers becoming directors of British overseas corporate banks so that at their board meetings representatives of sections of the 'old' and 'new' City sat side by side.[66]

All British overseas banks largely conducted their local foreign business, especially the finance of international trade, on the basis of deposits amassed by their branches. This provided an in-built insurance against any arising exchange risk. Branches that could not be self-financing and so therefore had to call upon London head offices for funds were regarded as being in 'overdraft', the cost of which was set against their profitability and viability. However, from the 1860s, these banks turned to British depositors, often employing the arising funds to finance medium-term overseas assets. British deposits were usually of an extended term and, hence, matched the banks' more illiquid foreign engagements. After the 1866 crisis, they were cheaper and so thereby generated further profits given the 'turn' with local rates overseas.[67] Deposits in overseas banks based in London

---

[65] Jones, *Multinational Banking*, pp. 24–5, 32–3.

[66] Baster, *International Banks*, p. 247; and Crick and Wadsworth, *Hundred Years*, pp. 307–9.

[67] Jones, *Multinational Banking*, pp. 31–2.

had become significant by the late 1870s, being equivalent to about a fifth of the deposits held by *all United Kingdom* domestic banks.[68]

VI

Probably the most explosive element of the mid-nineteenth century 'Big Bang' was the finance companies. Some of their multifarious activities during the hectic boom of the mid-1860s have already been referred to *en passant* in previous sections.[69] Between 1863 and 1865, 35 finance companies were formed publicly in both the City and the provinces, as were seven closely related land-finance companies. Each had a particular origin, but the general, seminal forces that shaped their birth and subsequent nature were the London money market's 'exceptional' business from the 1850s, industrial banking and the marked increase in British capital exports after the mid-1850s. These generalities were mixed with particularities, such as Anglo-European financial co-operation from the 1850s and a strong business emphasis upon the Near East and the Orient. The latter had arisen, first, from Europe's financial penetration of the Ottoman Empire brought about by the Crimean War, second, the Indian Mutiny and, third, the American Civil War and the ensuing 'Cotton Famine'.[70]

Their room for manoeuvre within the City and the English financial sector was constrained in part because of the already well-filled, established specialist niches that comprised the markets. There was little opportunity for the finance companies to penetrate domestic banking, beyond promoting further corporate institutions, although a few raised some loan capital by taking term deposits and issuing short-term debentures, which totalled £0.35m. in mid-1865. Their own record shows that there were few possibilities for their managements and staffs to deal in fine bills, a business which many of the lesser corporate discount houses also found difficult to penetrate. As will be discussed later, the finance companies' bill cases largely arose from facilities provided to railway contractors, paper also taken up by Overend, Gurney along with the corporate discount companies and some of the new limited banks. Being forced to work largely upon the basis of their own equities and creditworthiness, they had no substantial openings for developing as fully fledged investment or universal banks despite outwardly being modelled upon the Crédit Mobilier.

In any case, the Mobilier was rightly distrusted within the City and England during the early 1860s. Even the one finance company that came from within the 'square mile', the International Financial Society, immediately ran up against this opposition, while an invitation to Barings to be one of its founders received the

---

[68]   Capie and Webber, *Monetary History of the United Kingdom*, pp. 253–4.

[69]   For a full account and analysis, see Cottrell, *Investment Banking*, I, pp. 175–417, II, pp. 418–56.

[70]   See Cottrell, *Investment Banking*, vol. I, pp. 86–128.

reply from Bates that 'We consider ourselves a sort of Crédit Mobilier ourselves alone'.[71] Indeed, although the International was created by seven City merchant and merchant banking houses as a result of a proposal from Charles Mallet, it never had a formal connection with the Crédit Mobilier and severed any relationship with it after the Mexican loan debacle of 1864. The other major London-Paris institution, General Credit & Finance, nearly miscarried through the difficulties that arose in the creation of the Société Générale, its putative French partner.[72] Nevertheless, this particular link was thereafter sustained, largely through Edward Blount, despite the post-1866 transformation of the General Credit into a discount house and its 1885 merger with Union Discount Corporation.

With the exceptions of the International and, to a much lesser extent, the General Credit, the finance companies of the mid-1860s were generally not some form of institutionalization of private English banking, whether City or provincial. Members of the London Financial's board provided it with some links to joint-stock banking, both provincial (National Provincial), and London (City Bank) and, possibly, a more tenuous connection with Overend, Gurney. The General Credit's directorate had only one such interlock (Alderman Salomans with the London & Westminster), and likewise, the English & Foreign Credit with the Alliance of London & Liverpool. Rather, most were second-rate affairs or even bucket shops that during the mid-1860s took advantage of the gullible investing public's apparently almost insatiable appetite for banking and financial shares, whatever their provenance. *The* example is the Crédit Foncier and Mobilier of England, the mid-1860's vehicle of Albert Gottheimer/Grant. It first appeared in January 1864 as the Crédit Foncier with a largely Irish directorate, promoted by the Mercantile Credit Association, whose manager, Henry John Barker, had been associated with Gottheimer in the Mercantile Discount of 1859–61. Very quickly, the Crédit Foncier and the Mercantile Credit gave birth to the Crédit Mobilier, a clone of the Foncier through having the same board and manager, who now styled himself as Grant. The identical twins had merged by the close of the year and the resulting institution claimed over the opening months of 1866 to have a relationship with the Paris Crédit Mobilier which assisted neither.[73]

The main activities of the finance companies initially comprised foreign and domestic company promotion, primarily the former, which was almost an entirely new field that had been opened up by the 1855/6 liberalization of company law. Amongst their new creations were financial institutions, home and overseas.[74] Such

---

[71] Guildhall Library, London [henceforth GLL]: papers of A. Gibbs & Sons [henceforth Gibbs Papers], Ms 111036/3, H.H. Gibbs Private Letter Book, to W. Gibbs, 1 May 1863; and see Cottrell, *Investment Banking*, vol. I, pp. 129–58.

[72] See Cottrell, *Investment Banking*, vol. I, pp. 104–7.

[73] See Cottrell, *Investment Banking*, vol. I, pp. 111–12, 118, 120, 127.

[74] Apart from those already mentioned in the text, they comprised during the mid-1860s: Albert Insurance, Anglo-Egyptian Bank (with Agra & Masterman's), British Columbia & Vancouver's Island Investment, International Land Credit, Land Mortgage

activity during 1864 resulted in their managements being collectively responsible for securing more than a fifth of the funds subscribed through the formal new-issue markets to company and railway securities. Despite the scurrilous nature of many of the finance companies, their corporate midwifery had something of a positive effect. Although the particular London-registered companies that they publicly promoted enjoyed no longer lives than all those effectively registered, with half insolvent within five years, the finance companies were primarily involved with the types of companies that experienced the shortest survival rates: home and foreign financing, colonial and foreign banking, shipbuilding and shipping. Concerns in these categories founded by the finance companies subsequently enjoyed greater longevity than their immediate peers, if only a year or two.[75]

In marked contrast, the finance companies made no real impression upon the market for foreign sovereign loans, although the nominal value of such securities quoted on the London Stock Exchange rose substantially from the early 1850s. The public involvements of the General Credit and the International merely comprised: the £1.5m. 6 per cent Venezuelan loan (1863); the £12.365m. 6 per cent Mexican loan (1864); and the £8m. Italian 5 per cent State Domain loan (1865). However, alongside these few public issues were private participations as members of issuing syndicates (London and Anglo-European) and the provision of private short-term finance to 'bridge' a government's treasury from one public issue to another.[76] Consequently, Thomas Baring largely drew the wrong conclusion when he considered that the founding of the International Financial Society would create a 'formidable rival to the Rothschilds'.[77] Instead, London merchant banks continued – to 1914 – to be the principal issuers of overseas securities, meeting competition for this business only from overseas banks and agencies and, in the case of corporate enterprises, these undertakings' bankers.[78]

Instead of foreign loans, the finance companies as a group concentrated on facilitating railway building, specifically, from mid-summer 1864, by supporting contractors as opposed to companies. This was a response to the general subsidence of activity on the London new-issue markets after spring 1864, but their involvement in such affairs was hinted at from the moment of their inception. One of the London Financial's directors, J.E.C. Koch, had previously obtained finance to complete his Welsh railways from Overend, Gurney. The General Credit's board included Blount, Thomas Brassey's partner, while its Paris institutional partner – Société Générale – had a directorate with a strong railway flavour, personified in

Bank of India, Land Securities, Mauritius Land Credit & Agency, Ottoman Financial Association, Queensland Sheep Investment, Société Financière d'Egypte and Société Générale Russe de Crédit Foncier et Industriel.

[75] See Cottrell, *Investment Banking*, vol. I, pp. 414–15.
[76] Ibid., vol. I, pp. 297–318.
[77] GLL: Gibbs Papers; Ms 11036/3, H.H. Gibbs PLB, to W. Gibbs, 1 May 1863.
[78] A.R. Hall, *The London Capital Market and Australia 1870–1914* (Canberra, 1963), p. 72.

Paulin Talabot. Amongst the lesser finance companies, beginning from 1863, there were some specifically designed to support civil engineering projects and their undertakers, led by the Public Works Credit Company of London & Paris. Others, like the Contact Corporation, worked in tandem with the main finance companies, in its case, Mercantile Credit, with which it shared bankers, the navy agents Hallet, Ommanney & Co.

After the 'mania' of the mid-1840s, the new-issue market had lost its appetite for railway shares, especially those of new domestic companies, and consequently their construction was only maintained, to be taken up to boom levels during the 1860s, by contractors becoming financiers. They were paid in stock and shares, securities then mobilized by drawing bills secured upon them. Such contractors' bills were discounted in the money market, a business with which Overend, Gurney had become involved since the mid-1850s. From summer 1864, the finance companies joined Overend, Gurney and some of the corporate discount houses and banks in accepting this paper. Bill finance kept contractors in business but could only be ultimately liquidated once lines were open and profitable to permit the underlying long-term securities, railway company stocks and shares, to be offered to the public. This is why Thompson Hankey was right to call this paper not bills but mortgages.

During the 1860s boom, the necessary liquidation of 'mortgage bills' was ultimately prevented by monetary contraction from autumn 1865 drying up sources of short-term finance for contractors. As a result, railway contractors went bankrupt before the completion of lines, let alone their opening for traffic. Watson, Overend & Co. went in January 1866, followed by Thomas Savin, and these failures quickly brought down the Financial Corporation and the Contract Corporation while causing Joint Stock Discount 'extreme difficulties'. The climax was reached when Peto & Betts, one of the two major railway contracting firms, failed, along with Overend, Gurney and Imperial Mercantile Credit, on 'Black Friday'. The May 1866 crisis not only rendered the finance companies illiquid and unviable but wreaked havoc throughout domestic railway finance, causing a number of operating companies, new and established, to be forced 'into Chancery'.[79]

Five major finance companies survived the 1866 crisis but only one, General Credit, reconstituted as General Discount, continued to be a significant financial institution. The deaths of the others were long drawn out, often involving unsuccessful reconstitutions. The Crédit Foncier continued to 1879, the Imperial Mercantile Credit to 1883 and the London Financial until 1888. From 1892 the International, now under very different management, was effectively an investment trust and, as such, at the turn of the century became a component of the '69 Old Broad Street group'.

The 'finance company era' of the City was brief, merely three years. Similar companies were established later although none ever even cut a meteoric trail across the City's sky like their predecessors of the mid-1860s. Some were by intent

---

[79]   See Cottrell, 'Railway Finance'.

private affairs, such as the Syndicate Union, established by the Anglo-Austrian Bank, the General Discount, the Imperial Ottoman Bank and the International Financial Society in 1870. Another comparable private affair, and more successful for some years, was the London Banking Association of 1872, an institutionalized London-Paris merchant banking alliance, of which the Austro-Egyptische Bank, the Credit-Anstalt and the St. Petersburg International Commercial Bank were also members. This acted as a medium for both the provision of short-term finance to the Spanish government in 1872, 1874 and 1875 and the foundation of the Mercantile Bank of the River Plate in 1872, while issuing American railroad stocks in 1874.[80]

London merchant bankers, with their continental European partners and correspondents, might have occasionally during the mid-nineteenth century availed themselves of the advantages of the corporate form of business organization. Yet they clung to the private partnership for undertaking most of their affairs. In the minds of middle-class investors, they became synonymous with issuing houses, primarily of overseas securities. But only a few regularly undertook this activity, and when they eventually organized themselves professionally, they took the name 'Accepting Houses', reflecting their prime interest in the finance of international trade, which one of their members called 'bread and butter' business, flotations being the 'jam'. Before the self-applied label of 'acceptance house', many, like their continental European peers, had simply styled themselves merchants.

A merchanting background provided the necessary knowledge of the creditworthiness of drawers of bills. The application of that expertise during the mid-century could have startling consequences. Kleinworts began extending acceptance credits immediately after the 1857 crisis and, within three years, had an involvement of £0.8m., a growth in business which had augmented the firm's capital by £80,000. Almost a decade later, the partnership's equity had grown by a further £370,000, nurtured by 600 world-wide accounts, of which American and German were the most important. Within two decades, the house became a first-class London name so that its paper was eligible for rediscount at the Bank of England. Such a rating was based upon acceptances totalling £2.35m. in 1870, backed by a capital of £0.91m., four-and-a-half times the sum invested in 1858. Schroders had taken a further six years, from 1852 to 1870, to enjoy the same expansion of partners' equity.[81] Specialization was a factor that assisted such growth, with Robert Benson & Co., one of the founders of the International Financial Society, concentrating upon trans-Atlantic and Oriental trades. North American commercial associations and past family investment interests also led Bensons to act as the London agent for the Illinois Central Railroad. This went along with involvements

---

[80]   Capie and Webber have mistakenly categorized the London Banking Association as a London joint-stock bank. See Capie and Webber, *Monetary History of the United Kingdom*, p. 541.

[81]   R. Roberts, *Schroders: Merchants and Bankers* (Houndmills/London, 1992), p. 43.

in other American railways, together with Brazilian, Canadian and Indian railway companies, during the mid-century.[82]

Victorians rather pompously decorated panels of the new Royal Exchange Building of 1844 with romanticized paintings of the classical Phoenician Empire, in an obvious allusion. This also reflected that overseas trade was still at the heart of the City despite the edifice's predecessor having housed a segment of the Stock Exchange. Engagement with overseas trade was the learning school for the provision of international credit that then acted as a sheet anchor for the other, various businesses into which London mercantile houses moved and diversified. The finance companies never had that stabilizing element, but instead mostly emerged out of the desperate financial conundrum of mid-century railway contracting, which proved to be their undoing.

VII

The City's mid-century transformation was rounded out by the opening of branches of foreign corporate banks. The first were established by Scottish joint-stock banks, beginning with the National Bank of Scotland in 1864. These were followed by the City offices of continental European banks – the Crédit Lyonnais and the Société Générale in 1871, and the Deutsche Bank in 1873.[83]

The reordering of the City's institutional structures was also accompanied by changes in its built form. New institutions and expanding established enterprises required suitable accommodation. In 1863 Kleinworts had built a new freehold office in Mincing Lane in the favoured 'commercial Italianate' style that cost £42,000. Specific commissions went along with speculative developments, a feature of the City since the mid-1820s. One mid-1860s example is the City Offices Company, promoted jointly by the Crédit Foncier and Mercantile Credit in 1864. This real-estate company had options on sites in the vicinity of the Bank of England 'in places most suitable for offices, the present scarcity of and the extraordinary demand for which are well known'.

Surviving physical evidence in the late 1990s of the City's physical transformation over the 1860s and 1870s include: National Bank (13–17 Old Broad Street – 1861), National Provincial (15 Bishopsgate – 1864–5), both employing Italian Renaissance conventions in their design, and the deliberately less imposing building erected for F. Huth & Co. (11 Tokenhouse Yard – 1869–71). The National Discount's premises combined French and Cinquecento motifs (33–5 Cornhill – 1857–8) and, unusually for the period, were the result of an

---

[82] J. Wake, *Kleinwort Benson: the History of Two Families in Banking* (Oxford, 1997), pp. 91–5, 97–102.

[83] H. Bonin, *Société Générale in the United Kingdom* (Paris, 1996); and L. Gall, 'The Deutsche Bank from its Founding to the Great War 1870–1914', in L. Gall et al., *The Deutsche Bank* (London, 1995), pp. 17–18.

architectural competition. What is considered to be the finest surviving mid-
century bank building was designed by Somers Clarke I in a Venetian Gothic style
at 7 Lothbury for General Credit, built during 1866 as the finance company was
being transformed into a corporate discount house. These commissioned designs
were matched by other, speculative office developments. Surviving examples of
the latter can be found, for instance, at 19–21 Billiter Street, 103 Cannon Street,
59–61 Mark Lane (City of London Real Property Company), 65 Cornhill and 25
Throgmorton Street.[84]

VIII

The excesses of the City's mid-nineteenth century 'Big Bang' were tellingly
lampooned, and no better than by R.M.L. Meason, who, in the guise of 'City
Man', wrote in his 1866 *Profits of Panics* of the affairs of the Arungabad Bank,
the Bamford & Newington Extension Railway, finance companies and the Bank
of Patagonia. This was his second warning as, over 1865, he had compiled a set
of comparably barbed, well-based sketches for Charles Dickens's *All The Year
Round*, subsequently put together as *Bubbles of Finance*.

Meason was part of the long tradition of English financial satire from which
readers winced rather than learnt. The ashes of the mid-century 'Big Bang' were
more formally but briefly raked over after the 1866 crisis by a parliamentary
inquiry not into banking (such as those that had immediately followed the 1847
and 1857 crises and had involved Commons and Lords committees) but limited
liability.[85] The collapse of company promotions but especially of foreign lending
during the mid-1870s led to a much lengthier investigation, involving separate
parliamentary committees that probed company law,[86] foreign sovereign lending[87]
and the Stock Exchange (of which Sir Nathaniel Rothschild was a member).[88]
Past misdemeanours were aired as committee members reviewed two decades
of experience but the results of their probing led to no consequent, positive
legislation. Despite Lowe recanting on the axiom by which he had initiated the
repeal of Peel's 1844 regulatory banking legislation – 'Free Trade in Capital'
– the only warning to depositors and investors continued to be *caveat emptor*! It
was to have little effect.

---

[84]   S. Bradley and N. Pevsner, *The Buildings of England, London* I: *The City of
London* (London, 1997), pp. 110–11, 112, 113; and plates 99, 103. For the General Credit/
Discount building, see also Sir John N. Summerson, *The Architecture of Victorian London*
(Charlottesville VA, 1976).

[85]   *B.P.P.*, 1867, X.

[86]   *B.P.P.*, 1877, VIII.

[87]   *B.P.P.*, 1875, XX.

[88]   Exceptionally, a Royal Commission – *B.P.P.*, 1878, XIX.

The collapse of the City of Glasgow Bank in 1878 brought to an end the 'Big Bang' of the mid-nineteenth century. This was most evident in the resulting less expansive monetary environment that prevailed from autumn 1878 until the mid-1880s. New banks continued to be publicly formed but not in such numbers as had led to cascades of prospectuses during the mid-1860s and early 1870s. Indeed, the creation of domestic limited banks during the 1880s was related more to existing institutions adopting reserved liability than to the founding of entirely new corporate houses. Corporate overseas banking waxed, especially with the apogee of the Australian pastoral boom during the mid-1880s that sucked in medium-term deposits from all over the British Isles but particularly the east coast of Scotland. The finance companies were replaced by more solid and more worthy investment trusts, the first of which, Foreign & Colonial, was established by Glyn, Mills in 1868.

The 'Big Bang' largely sounded the death knell of personal private enterprise within most of London's financial markets. The money market after 1866 was dominated by, first, the National and, then, the Union. Private houses continued, indeed new private discount houses were established, but although many enjoyed considerable longevity, they remained minnows, never expanding to challenge the position of the corporate houses. In provincial commercial banking, joint-stock institutions totally gained the upper hand as a result of the promotional booms of the mid-1860s and early 1870s, followed by the consequences of the 1878 collapse of the City of Glasgow Bank. Even when, in the occasional instance, conversion meant in practice just that – the former partners became the principal shareholders – this only delayed the extinction of the local private banker for a decade or so. After 1878, size became of increasing consequence, and the amalgamation movement from the 1880s led to the sweeping up into bigger units of small joint-stock and private banks alike.

Private banking persisted in the City but its days were numbered after 1878 except for the most specialist house. Although its members continued to refer to themselves as partners, Glyn, Mills was converted into a 'private' joint-stock concern in 1885. They had rejected the idea of constituting a block of private banks as a defensive measure, instead adopting the strategy of specialism, which one partner explained in terms of 'I believe that we shall do best by preserving a characteristic which we alone of all the *large and serious* banks possess namely of having only one door'.[89] Barclays, a decade later, drew precisely the opposite conclusion. At the time, there was no clear guidance. Dimsdales amalgamated with Prescotts in 1891 to form a corporate concern, only to be acquired by the Union of London & Smith's Bank two years later. Fullers was taken over by Parr's Banking Co. Ltd in 1891, paralleled by the Midland's acquisition of Lacy, Hartland, Woodbridge, whereas in 1893 Herries Farquhar amalgamated with Lloyds. Whatever hesitations over how to respond, time was running out, of which

[89] Fulford, *Glyns*, pp. 226–7.

a further reminder was the Baring crisis of 1890, in the wake of which Martins became a joint-stock bank.

The exception to these patterns of business development in which 'joint-stock-ism' triumphed with the 'Big Bang' was City merchant banking. The finance companies of the mid-1860s never made inroads into the kernels of their businesses – acceptances – and only created a very limited and brief indent with regard to the flotation of foreign sovereign loans. All in all, the business worlds of these two outwardly competing groups of institutions hardly overlapped. The consequences of the 1866 crisis removed any possibility of a head-on competitive collision.

Being involved in primarily foreign bills, merchant banks were less affected by the increasing disuse of the inland bill after the early 1870s. Nonetheless, they had competitors for the finance of foreign trade in the form of British-based corporate overseas banks and London joint-stock banks. However, the English feature of what Landes has previously called the 'financial revolution' of the mid-century was the involvement of some members of London's merchant banking community (and their continental counterparts) in the creation of City-based corporate overseas banks. This was no short-term promotional commitment, as these personal links persisted until 1914, and not infrequently into the interwar period. Moreover, such institutions had London joint-stock bankers on their boards by the early 1870s and, thereby, constituted one of the few meeting places that drew members from a number of the City's financial markets. The fundamental importance of the 'bread and butter' acceptance business for the merchant banks has long been recognized, but its precise dimensions and contributions are only beginning to come into focus with the very welcome series of scholarly house histories, published since 1989. These institutions largely represented the continuing world of private banking after the 'Big Bang' of the mid-century.

CHAPTER 5

Banking and Family Archives

Fiona Maccoll

Introduction

The age of private banking has long since passed and the hundreds of local banks which once populated towns across England and Wales have been eclipsed by the development of joint-stock banks. However, these private banks, owned and managed by a small number of partners, played a vital and unique role in the development of both the modern economy and banking.

Initially, banking developed in London, and it is estimated that there were 40 or so private banks operating in the capital by the end of the seventeenth century. The number of banks outside London, however, only began to grow rapidly during the second half of the eighteenth century. It is estimated there were about 12 provincial or 'country banks' in 1750. By 1810 their number had grown to 650.[1] The majority of these banks remained small and locally based, often operating from only one office.

Changes to banking law in 1826, enabling joint-stock banks to be formed, ultimately led to the demise of private banks. The number of private banks declined during the nineteenth century as some failed and others converted to, or were taken over by, joint-stock banks. By 1904, just 35 remained in business.[2] Similarly, private banks in the City of London were finding it increasingly difficult to compete with joint-stock banks. For example two well-established private banks, Prescott's of Cornhill and Smith Payne & Smiths of Lombard Street, became joint-stock concerns in 1891 and 1902 respectively.

NatWest Group, itself formed as a result of the amalgamation of nearly 200 banks, numbers well over 100 private banks amongst its constituents.

Historical Research

In 1956, L.S. Pressnell in his seminal work *Country Banking in the Industrial Revolution* remarked that private country banks had been subject to remarkably little historical investigation. The fact that his book is still the classic text in this field suggests that this remains the case today.

---

[1]   L.S. Pressnell and J. Orbell, *A Guide to the Historical Records of British Banking* (Aldershot, 1985), p. xvi. A revised edition of this work is: J. Orbell and A. Turton, *British Banking: a Guide to Historical Records* (Aldershot, 2001).
[2]   Ibid., p. xvii.

Of the private banks which later became part of NatWest, only the Smith banking partnerships have been thoroughly investigated.[3] By contrast, Beckett and Co., the last large private banking partnership in England, merely warrants an appendix in T.E. Gregory's history of the Westminster Bank.[4] Similarly, private banks in the City of London such as Prescott's and Jones Loyd remain largely unresearched.[5] The study of private banking undoubtedly provides ample opportunities for new research.

Sources for the Study of Private Banks

The primary sources for those undertaking research into private banks are the banks' own corporate records. Typically, these will include partnership agreements, correspondence and accounting records. Unfortunately, there are few equivalents of that major source for joint-stock banks – the board of directors' minutes. With the exception of Prescott's Bank, where partnership minute books exist from 1839, and Beckett & Co., who recorded the partners' meetings from 1904, the decisions of partners were rarely minuted. Indeed, there would be little need to do so in small local partnerships where the partners were actively involved in running the business on a daily basis.

Lost or Destroyed

Regrettably, many records of small private banks have long since disappeared. While this might be expected in the case of those that failed, leaving no successor, it is also true of those that were taken over. In the case of NatWest's private banking constituents, for example, only four small volumes remain from the firm of Hankey & Co., which operated for 150 years in the City of London. Likewise, Shilston Coode & Co. of St. Austell and Thomas Butcher of Tring both traded for over a century. Their only surviving records identified to date, however, comprise those drawn up in connection with forthcoming amalgamations. Indeed, a brief review of *A Guide to the Historical Records of British Banking* by L.S. Pressnell and J. Orbell confirms this is the case for many private banks. The survival of additional papers that throw further light on these banking businesses becomes, therefore, far more significant.

---

[3]   J.A.S.L. Leighton-Boyce, *Smiths the Bankers 1658–1958* (London, 1958). H.T. Easton, *History of a Banking House* (1903).

[4]   T.E. Gregory, *The Westminster Bank Through a Century*, vols 1 and 2 (London, 1936).

[5]   However, D. Kynaston, *The City of London*, vols 1 and 2 (London, 1994, 1995) does include original research on these banks.

The Connection between Families and Private Banks

The reason why family papers may prove of value in this respect is because private banks were often controlled by the same families over long periods of time, with sons, sons-in-law, nephews, cousins and brothers-in-law taking part in the business. The successors of the eighteenth -century banker William Minet were his nephew Hughes Minet and his cousin's son Peter Fector. This family connection was reinforced when Fector married Hughes Minet's sister.[6] This was not an unusual occurrence, as families involved in joint banking partnerships often intermarried. Daughters' marriages could bring new blood into the business. The success of the Manchester banking firm of John Jones, banker and tea merchant, was largely driven by Jones' son-in-law Lewis Loyd, who joined the firm after his marriage. Sometimes the family connection could extend over several centuries: the Beckett family were bankers for over six generations and the Smith family for even longer.

Family businesses also provided employment for members of kin. A letter from Samuel Jones Loyd, Lord Overstone, to Lewis Loyd junior in 1863, following news of the sale of the family firm Loyd Entwisle, amply illustrates this point. Overstone commented that the sale was made 'without any consideration of the future interests of young members of the family. … Your brother Edward's sons – William's sons – Entwisle's sons – Dyce Nicol's sons. And has it been forgotten there are six nephews of Col. Loyd wholly unprovided for … who bear the name of the family and must carry that name about the world in humble poverty?'[7]

Not that all the younger members of the family were enthused by their chosen profession. Rowland Smith writing in 1849 complained: 'I am fixed at the bank on a high stool with nothing to do except look at an occasional customer who comes in about twice an hour (for this is market day and consequently more busy than usual)'.[8]

Family Papers

The private papers of these banking families may throw light on their banking interests which were not otherwise recorded, or that have long since disappeared. Even if the banking records do exist, private papers may reveal additional information not found in the formal record. Private papers may also contain details of personal tensions within the family business, the interplay between banking and other business activities and the private wealth of banking partners. The latter was an important factor in maintaining confidence in private banks, for without the protection of limited liability, partners might be required to call on their private assets to settle banking debts.

[6] L.A.M. Sencicle, *Banking on Dover* (London, 1993).

[7] D.P. O' Brien (ed.), *The Correspondence of Lord Overstone*, vols 1–3 (1971).

[8] Letter to S.G. Smith, NatWest Group Archives, ref. 4615.

The Location of Source Material for Private Banks

Families seem to have made little distinction between their own private papers and banking records. As a result, both exist at a variety of locations – in the archives of banks, in local record offices or other publicly accessible repositories, or in private hands. Fortunately Pressnell's and Orbell's *Guide* provides an invaluable tool for locating them.[9]

For example, although Thomas Barnard & Co. of Bedford became part of NatWest and a researcher might reasonably expect to find their records in the NatWest archives, they were actually retained by the Barnard family. Subsequently, they were deposited, along with the estate and private family papers, with Bedfordshire and Luton Archives Service.

Similarly, partnership agreements and correspondence, relating to both the banking and other business and family interests of the Minet and Fector families, were deposited by a descendant with University College London.

Conversely, some family papers survive among the banking records and now reside in bank archives. When a private bank was taken over, banking often continued to be conducted from the same building. Consigned to the strongroom and cellars, the family papers remained in situ. At NatWest, there are many private papers connected with family matters – especially those of a quasi-legal nature – marriage settlements, wills and probate, as well as papers connected with property, estates and other business interests.

Once bank archives were established, banking archivists also acquired records from banking families by purchase or gift. In the case of the Smith family, the continued involvement in banking, notably by Eric L. Smith as chairman of National Provincial Bank from 1930 to 1950, led to the deposit of many private Smith family papers in the NatWest archives. Westminster Bank added to its holdings of Crompton Newton and Co. records by purchasing some eighteenth-century account books belonging to the Crompton banking family in the 1960s. In addition archivists of both the Westminster Bank and the National Provincial Bank sought to identify and copy archives of private banks still remaining in family hands.[10]

Records in Private Hands

Some banking and family records still remain with family members. Unfortunately records held in private hands often disappear. In the 1950s the archivist of the National Provincial Bank was informed about the existence of a letter book belonging to William Fryer, son of the founder of the Dorset bank, Fryer & Sons. Copied extracts from this letter book are held in the NatWest archives, but the

---

[9]   Pressnell et al., *Guide*.

[10]   Westminster Bank and National Provincial Bank merged in 1968 to form National Westminster Bank.

whereabouts of the original is now unknown. A note about these extracts states that most of the letters were to bill brokers, but none of these was considered sufficiently interesting to summarize. All that survives are some interesting anecdotes, such as the conditions of employment of a nineteenth-century clerk.[11]

Indeed tracing and contacting descendants of banking families may lead to the discovery of additional records. Writing of Samuel Jones Loyd, later Lord Overstone, and formerly a partner in Jones Loyd and Co., T.E. Gregory lamented: 'There are no "Overstone papers" to throw light upon an enigmatic character'.[12] D.P. O'Brien, however, located a large collection of Overstone's correspondence in 1964. The papers were found in the attic of a house of a descendant.[13]

New discoveries are still being made. Recently, a postal historian approached NatWest Group Archives with information that he had acquired two small eighteenth-century volumes recording details of bills of exchange, along with correspondence addressed to both the law firm of Brocklehurst Bagshaw and Brocklehurst the bankers.

The Brocklehursts were lawyers who later turned to banking, and these records appear to have been retained by the law firm Brocklehurst Bagshaw. The volumes containing details of bills of exchange from 1799 are significant because, if they prove to be the records of the Brocklehurst family, they provide evidence for the Brocklehursts' discounting bills well before they were known to be involved in banking.

Business and Private Papers

The distinction between banking and other business interests is least apparent in the records of early bankers. Indeed many of the first country bankers commenced banking as an adjunct to their main business activity. Thomas Smith, founder of the Smiths banking partnerships, was a mercer and the Stuckeys of Langport were general merchants as well as bankers. Surviving account books and letter books often cover all aspects of their business interests. They provide a particularly fruitful source of information about early banking activities.

The Crompton family from Derby were originally wool merchants and commenced their banking activities around the early eighteenth century. An account book belonging to Samuel Crompton (d.1759) contains details of both businesses. From 1707 to 1709 the book was used as a wool merchant's delivery book. A typical entry is: 'Nov the 28 [1707] sent Mr Daws a packe of Good Jarsy [jersey] woole at 6.10.0 at Derby'.[14] These entries cease in 1709 and the book was only used again in 1725 – this time as a cash book. The ensuing entries contain

11   NatWest Group Archives, ref. 3158.
12   Gregory, *Westminster Bank*, vol. 2, pp. 158–9.
13   O'Brien, *Correspondence*, vol. 1, p. 3.
14   NatWest Group Archives ref. 10565.

a mixture of personal and business information. In 1725 Crompton recorded the purchase of a suit for his son, Samuel junior, for 8 shillings.

The cash book also reveals Crompton was engaged in banking activities, as a note of all sums deposited with him along with the name of the depositor and the note issued as a receipt were carefully recorded. From May that year, the entries become less detailed and only the total of deposits received was entered. It has been estimated that an interest rate of 3.5 per cent was payable on such deposits.[15] The cash book also shows that Crompton accepted funds for transfer to London at a charge which earned between 0.5 per cent and 0.75 per cent.

Samuel Crompton junior maintained a private account book from 1739 to 1768.[16] While this largely contains information of a non-banking nature, it does include references to banking. Details of the wages of bank clerks, the transportation of money to London and elsewhere, and dealings with the bankers Messrs Milnes and Wilkinson of Chesterfield, are also recorded.[17]

Moreover, Peter Graham's recent research into the Smith family, who established private banks in Nottingham, London, Hull, Lincoln and Derby between the 1650s and early 1800s, has revealed further evidence of the intermingling of the early bankers' business interests. Graham has found that Thomas Smith's casting-up account stock book dated 1653–1659[18] contains information which suggests that Smith was involved in banking as early as 1655.[19] The stock book lists each type of cloth held and its value. The accounts for 1655 record he had stock total of £370, debts owing to him of £51 and debts owing by him of £65. He also refers to 'lent money' and money 'in house' of £16. Graham tentatively suggests that the inclusion of 'lent money' provides evidence of Smith's diversification into banking activities.

Similarly, the letter books of early bankers reveal a mixture of personal, business and banking affairs. A letter book dated 1760–1784 belonging to Abel Smith II (grandson of Thomas Smith) is a good example.[20] Correspondence in 1760 with Thomas and John Tipping of Manchester show Abel was sending them gold in return for bills of exchange. In September that year he wrote that 'the bills you mention at long dates will be no inconvenience to us. The present scarcity of money everywhere you can be no stranger to, which must still grow worse during the continuance of the war. If money is scarce at Manchester perhaps we could

---

[15]   Unattributed article *Mr Chest and Mr Box*, Westminster Bank Review, Aug. 1952.

[16]   NatWest Group Archives, ref. 11682.

[17]   Ibid., ref. 707.

[18]   Ibid., ref. 2248.

[19]   P. Graham, *Private Banking in the East Midlands: a Study of Samuel Smith Esquire and Co.* paper delivered at Nottingham University, May 1998. I am indebted to Peter Graham of Nottingham University for sharing his discoveries about the Smith banking family while working on the Smith papers in the NatWest archives.

[20]   NatWest Group Archives, ref. 11682.

order cash into your hands to the amount of £1000 at a time if it should be worth our while for you to send us bills payable in London in lieu thereof'.

In November he wrote again, advising the Tippings of the dispatch of a box of over £2000 in gold coin, noting 'last night I sent the box to my friend Mr. Southwell to prevent suspicion, but neither he nor anyone else knows the contents except my clerks, but Mr. Southwell guesses it is cash as I have often employed him on the same occasion.'

Other letters were more personal. In 1762 he wrote to the Reverend Ward about his eldest son: 'I had expected the assistance of my eldest son who is now fit for business, but he has desired to go to Cambridge and I did not choose to deny his request. This will put me under some difficulty till Abel is ready for business which has determined me to send him to Derby … where he will have the opportunity of making further progress with the languages and the same time qualify himself in writing and accounts as I shall soon want him in the counting house'.

Other correspondence included letters to another son, William; letters to the Commissioner of Taxes (as Smith collected taxes for remittance to London); letters to his partner René Payne in London; and correspondence on other matters, such as the purchase of an assembly room in Nottingham and local politics.

NatWest archives also hold a letter book dated 1778–1809 belonging to Samuel Stuckey (1740–1812), general merchant and banker of Langport in Somerset.[21] Initially the letter book contains copies of letters to and from Stuckey's daughter, Elizabeth. Soon afterwards, however, the book is used to record the business correspondence of her father, Samuel. While most letters concern the trade in salt and other goods, others contain references to banking.[22] The survival of this letter book is significant because so few other records document the family's banking activities before the private Stuckey banks merged into a joint-stock bank in 1826.

In addition, the letter books reveal a close business connection with Simon Pretor of Sherborne, who was also a banker. Although most of their correspondence concerns trade in salt, Pretor recommended his London bankers, Langstone, Lockhill Towgood and Amery, to Stuckey. In November 1779, Stuckey wrote to them about opening an account: 'It will be my object to make it as much worth your while as possibly I can, at sometimes I may have a few hundreds in your hands at others be rather shorter; but at no time over draw my amount…. I presume I may pay about seven or eight thousand per annum through your hand'.

In 1807, Samuel's nephew, Vincent, appears as a new signatory in the letter book. Vincent joined Samuel in business following his marriage to Samuel's daughter in 1801. He later took over direction of the banking business. By 1809 his uncle appears to have been withdrawing from active management of the business, for the letter book contains a letter from Vincent to Thomas Farley at Worcester,

---

[21]   NatWest Group Archives, ref. 10257.

[22]   S. Snell, *Stuckey's Bank. The Importance of a Family Banking Concern on the Economy of Langport and Somerset, 1770–1909*, paper delivered at the Langport and District Historical Society, Feb. 1998.

stating that Samuel is 'much the same as he has been for some time past, but troubles himself very little about business'.

Further details of the bank's activities can be gleaned from Vincent Stuckey's letter to Messrs Messiter, bankers of Wincanton: 'By our existing arrangements we are enabled to negotiate the local notes of the banks of Dorset, Wilts, and Hants but we have no objection to take from you the notes of the banks west of Wincanton. Also Wells, Bath and Bristol notes and bills and will pay the amount to your bankers in London in 14 days after receiving them. We also shall be glad to carry on a weekly exchange of the notes of our respective houses and pay the balance through our London bankers, a plan we wish to adopt with all respectable houses'.

The Private Accounts of Banking Partners

The private papers of banking partners can contain information about the profitability of the business which may not be available from other sources. Several private account books surviving among the family papers of the Barnard banking family of Bedford include references to 'partner's share' in the profits of the business. The private account book (1806 to 1840)[23] of Thomas Barnard I (1784–1853), son of the founder of the bank, notes an income of £883 in 1809, of which £845 were the profits from the partnership. There are regular references to partnership profits in the ensuing years, and by 1840 his share had risen to £4,700.[24]

Thomas II, son of Thomas I, maintained a private account book[25] from the time he joined the partnership in 1854. This also contains details of his annual share of the profits and a valuation of property including bank capital and buildings in 1885. The private account books of Thomas Barnard I and II both include information about their personal wealth and investments.

Interestingly, Lord Overstone's papers include a memorandum of his wealth in 1874.[26] Although written many years after his resignation from the banking business, it contains an account of the annual profits of the Jones Loyd partnership from 1817 to 1848. Overstone calculated that the total profits of the bank over that period were £2.2 million and his share amounted to £563,000.

Pressnell noted that considerable emphasis was placed by contemporaries on the personal wealth of private bankers, as these assets might be called upon in the event of the banking firm's suffering financial difficulties. One of the most visible signs of wealth was the ownership of land. Private family papers provide much evidence of this and other personal assets. Lord Overstone's papers, for example, contain the investment ledgers of both Lord Overstone and his father Lewis Loyd.

---

[23] Bedfordshire and Luton Archives and Records Service, ref. DDBD 1205.
[24] Notes on the private account books of the Barnard Family, NatWest Group Archives, ref. 181.
[25] Bedfordshire and Luton Archives and Records Service, ref. DDBD 1238.
[26] O'Brien, *Correspondence*, vol. 3, pp. 1274–5.

Lord Overstone's investments ledgers have enabled Ranald Michie to compile a detailed analysis of his personal wealth from 1823 to 1883.[27] Much of Overstone's investments were in land, as were the investments of the earlier generation of partners in Jones Loyd, his father and two uncles.[28]

Family Correspondence

Although only a small number of letters may still remain, correspondence between family members can provide insights into the development of banking. Several letters to Abel Smith II from his sons during the 1770s survive in the NatWest archives. These include his son Robert's report on the London business in 1775 and references to the difficulties caused to the partnership by Abel Smith's decision to withdraw funds deposited with the bank in London.[29] A letter to Abel Smith from his son Abel III in 1777 describes the opportunities for opening a bank in Hull and the importance of obtaining the remittance of customs revenues for such a business.[30]

Several letters around the 1740s from Peter Fector to the merchant William Minet record Peter's entry into the business run by William and his father Isaac. They also provide evidence that banking had developed from the activities of the Dover side of the business by 1744. In a letter of September that year, Peter notes: 'Scarce one packet arrives [in Dover] but brings half a dozen letters at least with accounts for sundry sums of Money to be distributed among the [French] prisoners. I go two and three times a week in the prison. ... The Commission on these articles is small being but 6d in the Pound, but the number of sums make it answer pretty well'.[31]

Unfortunately, it is fairly rare for long series of family correspondence to survive. One notable exception is a collection of letters written to Samuel George Smith from various members of the family, between 1846 and 1900.[32] As well as private family affairs, their subject matter covers a wide range of topics, including problems at the Derby, Hull, Lincoln and Nottingham Smith Banks and discussions about possible amalgamations. In 1852 a letter from one of the Nottingham partners complains that the partners there had 'let the trade accounts of the town go to other banks by our not keeping pace with the times' and suggests

---

[27]   R.C. Michie, 'Income, Expenditure and Investment of a Victorian Millionaire: Lord Overstone, 1823–1883', in *Bulletin of the Institute for Historical Research*, vol. 58, 137, May 1985, p. 67.

[28]   Ibid., pp. 75–7.

[29]   Leighton-Boyce, *Smiths*, pp. 78–82; NatWest Group Archives, ref. 2637.

[30]   Ibid., pp. 190–91; NatWest Group Archives, ref. 2619.

[31]   Sencicle, *Banking*, p. 10.

[32]   NatWest Group Archives, ref. 4615.

a merger with another private bank in Nottingham, Wright and Co., 'who could by their trade connections employ our surplus money to advantage'.

Peter Graham's recent study of the correspondence indicates the letters are a rich source of information. They reveal, for example, tensions within the partnerships which may not be found in the more formal records. By the end of the nineteenth century, the letters show the concern of the partners about the lack of capital in the business and the consequent difficulty in competing with joint-stock banks. A further series of letters from family members to Herbert Francis Smith from 1889 to 1900 contain discussions concerning amalgamation proposals.[33]

The Use of Family Papers

To trace papers which are held outside banking archives, the researcher is best advised to consult Pressnell's and Orbell's *Guide*[34] and the National Register of Archives.[35] Although the former contains references to papers of banking families, the authors rely on the holding repository to provide details. If the repository is unaware that their collections of family papers contain references to banking, these will not be included.

One should also be aware that even when extensive collections of family papers are held, the references to banking may be slight and not immediately obvious from the finding aids provided. The Derby Local Studies Library holds a large collection of papers relating to the Pares family of Leicestershire, who ran private banks in Leicester and London. Correspondence amongst these papers dating from 1760–1840 is described as dealing with family and business affairs and financial, political and legal matters. However, only a thorough investigation of the material would reveal their value in relation to banking.

While the Overstone papers number in excess of 2,000 letters, only a small number contain any references to the banking business of Jones Loyd. However, amongst these letters there is also a valuable account of the history of Jones Loyd written by Overstone in 1864. This includes references to his father's entrance into the partnership, a dispute with his father concerning the assignment of shares in the profits, and the division of the London and Manchester sides of the business. The papers also include a mid-nineteenth-century account of the life of Overstone's father Lewis Loyd, for whom little source material appears to have survived.

---

[33] NatWest Group Archives, ref. 4616.

[34] Pressnell et al., *Guide*.

[35] National Register of Archives, Quality House, Quality Court, Chancery Lane, London, WC2A 1HP. Web address: http://www.hmc.gov.uk/nra/abtnra.htm

Conclusion

The private papers of banking families can provide important source material for the study of private banks. They become even more valuable in this respect because in many cases the corporate records of private banks are meagre or have not survived. I hope that this chapter will encourage both the further investigation of the role of private banks and the use of this under-appreciated resource.

CHAPTER 6

The Anglo-American Houses in the Nineteenth Century

Edwin J. Perkins

This chapter focuses on the activities of the major Anglo-American merchant banking houses during the nineteenth century. My goals here are twofold. First, I plan to review briefly the most important institutional trends in the Anglo-American trade and capital markets over the course of several centuries to provide the proper background. Second, I will discuss the main accomplishments and shortcomings of the leading firms in this dynamic market, with comparisons and contrasts included where appropriate.[1] Let me warn readers in advance that I will devote a disproportionate amount of time and space to the House of Brown, an important firm in the Anglo-American market with Baltimore origins. I wrote a detailed book on the Brown partnership over two decades ago.[2] I know the Browns best, and I will draw on my prior strengths in this context. I also intend to focus my attention primarily on events on the American side because, again, I am much more familiar with that scholarly literature. With these prejudices and limitations cited, we may now proceed with the discussion.

The Anglo-American financial sector passed through four distinct phases from British colonization in the early seventeenth century through the end of the nineteenth century. These four stages were: 1) an absence of institutional specialization, 1600 to 1790; 2) an institutional emphasis on trade and trade financing, 1790 to 1820; 3) a mixture of trade-related activities and portfolio investments, 1820 to 1860; and 4) an emphasis on large capital transfers through portfolio investments, 1860 to 1900. The overall trend was to downplay the trade sector and to move toward the capital markets. Irrespective of the purpose of the funding, during this entire era the flow of trade credit and long-term capital was invariably from Europe across the ocean to North America.

Throughout most of the colonial era in British North America, a period of over 150 years, the transatlantic institutional linkages between the providers of various financial services were never very strong, and few, if any, linkages were enduring. Indeed, the word atomistic immediately springs to mind in describing the institutional structure of this immature market. The financial services provided

---

[1] The best book on merchant banking in Britain is S. Chapman, *The Rise of Merchant Banking* (London, 1984).

[2] E.J. Perkins, *Financing Anglo-American Trade: The House of Brown, 1800–1880* (Cambridge Mass., 1975).

to American colonial traders involved in international shipments were offered by hundreds of independent British merchants on an ad hoc basis. In the aggregate, the amount of British capital tied up in American trade debt grew increasingly large in the third quarter of the eighteenth century. If the partners in any Anglo-American mercantile firm thought seriously about making an effort to develop a stronger commitment to this rapidly growing market before the middle of the eighteenth century, the effort was not sustained – or, at least, the documentation has not survived. As the volume of trade expanded, the underlying conditions for specialization became more favourable. As far as we know, the Barings, beginning in the second half of the eighteenth century, were the first entrepreneurs on either side of the Atlantic Ocean to act on the idea of creating a transatlantic organizational permanence. We will return to a discussion of the Barings' achievements later in the narrative.

Meanwhile, under the prevailing conditions in the capital markets, no firm in London sought to entice investors to purchase the debt obligations of the colonial legislatures, for a very sensible reason: almost none existed.[3] Parliament had severely restricted the ability of the thirteen colonies to issue public debt instruments.[4]

In the second phase of the evolution of the Anglo-American market, institutional specialization emerged, and the focus was primarily on the overseas trade sector. Two of the best-known merchant-banking houses – the Barings and the Browns – made commitments to participate fully in the Anglo-American market. These firms not only bought and sold goods on their own account for transatlantic shipment, but in addition offered a range of financial services to other mercantile firms that were likewise engaged in similar trading patterns. The performance of specialized financial services was what differentiated this small group of houses from other less ambitious firms. The leading houses made advances to American shippers against consignments of goods, mainly cotton and tobacco, to British ports; they created active sterling markets in US ports to serve the needs of local and regional importers and exporters; and, for a modest fee, they began the issuance of letters of credit to American importers who were thereby able to purchase goods in foreign markets around the globe on more favourable terms than previously.

This last function, the issuance of letters of credit, was the one financial service in the first half of the nineteenth century that qualified an enterprise as a full-fledged merchant-banking house. Only the elite houses with impeccable international

---

[3]   After 1750 the New England colonial legislatures created a small floating debt of three-year treasury bills. It is possible that a few British nationals acquired a fraction of this debt on the recommendation of an American agent, but there was no attempt to place any portion of the colonial government debt overseas.

[4]   The issue of colonial public debt is closely linked to contentious debates with Parliamentary committees over the issuance of paper money by the thirteen legislatures. See E.J. Perkins, 'Conflicting Views on Fiat Currency: Britain and Its North American Colonies in the Eighteenth Century', in *Business History*, vol. 33, 1991, pp. 8–30.

reputations for financial strength had sufficient prestige to attract customers for their letter-of-credit operations. An enhanced reputation in international financial circles often took years, if not decades, to develop. As a consequence, the leading merchant-banking houses typically had very few serious competitors as issuers of letters of credit. This specialized market had oligopolistic characteristics from the outset, and it remained a highly concentrated field throughout the nineteenth century.[5]

In the period from 1790 to 1820, the Anglo-American merchant banking houses were only sporadically involved in promoting British portfolio investments in American securities. The opportunities to do so were few and far between. In the 1790s the new US federal government funded its outstanding non-performing debt, plus the debts of the several States, without the aid of private bankers. Once President Thomas Jefferson took office in 1801, the federal debt was steadily retired. American banks and insurance companies, which in some cases were capitalized at several million dollars, drew largely on the savings of local investors. A number of American securities subsequently traded on secondary markets in London, but the original placements were overwhelmingly transactions negotiated in the US market.

The third phase in the evolution of the Anglo-American financial market was characterized by a mixture of the existing trade-related services and the emergence of new underwriting services linked to the expanding capital markets. The instantaneous success of the Erie Canal, an ambitious venture launched in 1817, triggered a host of expensive transportation projects. The funds to finance the construction came from diverse sources, some governmental and some private. Anglo-American merchant banking became involved in these transactions in varying degrees. In many instances, the promoters of American canal and railroad projects engaged private bankers with overseas connections to solicit investors in London and other parts of Europe. But the participation of the private bankers was erratic and irregular. Many firms that had agreed to help promoters raise funds in London for American projects on an ad hoc basis later withdrew their services in the aftermath of the economic dislocations associated with the Panic of 1837. In the light of the vicissitudes of the US economy in this period, none of the leading Anglo-American merchant banking houses made the strategic decision to provide investment services on anything approaching a permanent basis during the first half of the nineteenth century. These merchant bankers were already engaged in handling thousands of transactions of all varieties linked to the trade sector, and they considered securities transactions a sideline business rather than a mainstream activity. Nonetheless, given the wide scope of their business activities, which included a mixture of trade financing and occasional investment banking ventures, this era represented the height of the power and influence of those Anglo-American houses engaged in multi-functional merchant banking.

The fourth and final stage in the evolution of the Anglo-American financial markets coincided with the outbreak of the American Civil War. Suddenly, the

---

[5]   Some issuers later added travellers' letters of credit and travellers' cheques to their range of services.

size of the US federal debt grew enormously, and new opportunities for private bankers immediately arose. Almost simultaneously American railroads sought to raise millions of dollars to finance the expansion of track into the far western States plus improvements in existing lines, mainly the purchase of steel rails. The tremendous volume of American securities generated in the second half of the nineteenth century produced favourable conditions for additional specialization by the Anglo-American houses. Some banking partnerships which had previously provided a mix of routine trading and capital-market services decided to forego the trade sector and to concentrate their energies on investment-banking functions. The Peabody/Morgan organization was the most prominent private banking firm to readjust its strategies in response to these changing conditions. Originally a merchant-banking house that offered a full range of diverse financial services in the Anglo-American market, the Peabody firm was carried forward by the father/son team of Junius and John Pierpont Morgan, and under their leadership it had evolved into primarily an investment-banking firm by the 1870s.

The second section of this chapter addresses, in sequence, the activities of the leading Anglo-American banking houses in the nineteenth century. Chronology orders this discussion. I start with the earliest entries into the market and then move forward to the late arrivals. The six firms discussed are the Barings, Browns, Rothschilds, Peabody/Morgan, Seligmans, and Kuhn Loeb.

The Barings

The Barings were the first important Anglo-American merchant banking house, and based on their overall performance, the Barings were the most accomplished within this class of nineteenth-century business enterprises. The partners were involved in more diverse commodity and financial markets over a longer period of time than any of their competitors. The Barings were also more geographically diversified than any of their Anglo-American competitors, since the partners also conducted an extensive business in Canada, Latin America and the Far East. The partners were different from other Anglo-American houses too because of their involvement in loan contracting in the London market for European clients, which included the massive bond issues of several governments, including England and France. In these activities, the Barings competed directly with the Rothschilds.

The firm was established by three Baring brothers in 1763 with offices in both Exeter and London. The partners began as merchants and only later diversified into the provision of supplementary financial services. This same pattern of internal development prevailed in all six of the firms discussed in this chapter. Clear evidence of the Barings' early successes in diversifying the scope of their operations was their inclusion on the list of contractors authorized to market the British government's £20.5 million loan of 1800.

By the end of the eighteenth century, the partners had also turned their attention to the international trade sector in North America.[6] Alexander Baring visited the United States in late 1795. He established agency agreements with independent merchants in Boston, Philadelphia, Baltimore, and New York. More importantly, he signed an agreement with the First Bank of the United States, the federally chartered institution with a huge capital of $10 million, to cooperate on the transfer of various funds between the two countries. On the basis of that mutually advantageous association, the Barings became involved in helping to facilitate the transfer of monies linked to the American purchase of the Louisiana Territory from the French government for $15 million in 1803. In cooperation with Hope & Co. in Amsterdam, the Barings helped in placing $15 million in new US bonds with European investors; these investors proved to be eager buyers given the outstanding credit reputation of the United States after the implementation of the federal debt refunding programme in the early 1790s. Indeed, this transaction in 1803 was one of the few instances before the American Civil War in which the Anglo-American houses had the opportunity to aid the US government in the sale of bonds to prospective investors at home or abroad.

Following the War of 1812, which ended in a stalemate, the Barings were consistently active in the American foreign trade sector. The partners were frequently outright purchasers of cotton in the United States for shipment to Britain, based on the usually reliable advice of their American agents and correspondents. In addition, they periodically made advances to American exporters to attract consignments on which they earned commissions for arranging sales in London or Liverpool. During the 1820s and early 1830s, the Barings operated a lucrative foreign-exchange business in cooperation with the Second Bank of the United States. The Barings' sterling bills always passed at premium prices because the risk of non-payment was judged to be exceedingly low. The partners also authorized their agents in the major US ports to issue letters of credit to American importers with adequate capital resources and reliable reputations. In the capital markets, the partners became loan contractors for several of the new canal and railroad projects in the United States. In sum, the Barings acted as all-purpose merchant bankers in the Anglo-American economy, and they were widely recognized as the unchallenged leaders in this broad field through the 1830s.

Sensing possible danger ahead, the Baring partners were well-prepared for the Panic of 1837, having curtailed their commitments in the American market during the previous year. Most of their main competitors were severely damaged by the panic and the subsequent economic downturn. Immediately after the panic, the Barings reached what was probably their zenith of power and influence in the US market. Rather than taking full advantage of the temporary weaknesses of their competitors, however, the Barings became exceedingly cautious with regard to the entire US market. Interestingly, an American, Joshua Bates, became the de facto

---

[6]   The definitive book on the Barings is R. Hidy, *The House of Baring in American Trade and Finance: English Merchant Bankers at Work, 1763–1861* (Cambridge Mass., 1949).

head of the partnership at about this time. Bates, who was born in Massachusetts in 1788, had emigrated to London in 1816 or 1817, and had steadily progressed in his business career. But Bates showed little partiality to his native land.

Under the leadership of Bates, the partnership exhibited a vacillating attitude toward the American economy in the 1840s and 1850s. Bates recruited Thomas Wren Ward, a Boston merchant, to serve as a general supervisor for all the Barings' operations in the United States, and Ward was even made a junior partner in the firm.[7] But Ward had only limited influence over the independent houses that acted as Baring agents in other US port cities. Always fearful of a repeat of the 1837 disaster, the Baring partners could never bring themselves to make an unshakeable commitment to either the US trade market or the nation's rapidly developing capital market. Periodically optimistic and aggressive in their involvement in the American economy during this period, the partners invariably pulled in their horns at the first sign of potential disturbances.

Rather than taking the initiative and establishing a network of branch offices in the main US ports, the Barings continued to work through a chain of independent American agents. In several instances the partners had working arrangements with two or three agents in the same port city, who competed with one another for new business. In other words, to interject modern Chandlerian terminology into this discussion, the Barings failed to take the steps necessary to build an organizational structure with the potential to take optimum advantage of their enviable competitive position at the end of the 1830s. The appointment of Ward as their primary American agent was only a half-measure. As a consequence of their failure to build a strong organizational network, other firms began to carve out larger market shares in various sectors, leaving the Barings in their wake.

Perhaps one of the main stumbling-blocks to any greater expansion in the US market was the fact that the Barings were simultaneously deeply involved in business affairs in other regions of the world, including continental Europe. The partners were unable to perceive at mid-century that one of their best opportunities for maximizing future profits was in the US market. Other regions seemed equally appealing. In trying to become and remain a global enterprise long before that modern-day terminology had entered our vocabulary, the Barings spread themselves too thin. To compound the problem, the partners regularly withdrew a large proportion of their yearly profits, which kept the capital base stagnant. The maintenance of a luxurious standard of living was more important to many partners than the growth of the enterprise. Several members of the Baring family also served in Parliament and thus became distracted by politics. Reservations about adding new partners, especially permanent non-British residents, may also have inhibited the Baring partners from pursuing expansion plans abroad.

Given all these factors, the Barings' failure to commit greater resources, both capital and personnel, to the United States gave other firms the opportunity to make inroads. By the 1850s the Browns had inherited the leadership position in

---

[7]   Chapman, *Rise of Merchant Banking*, p. 27.

the foreign-exchange and letter-of-credit markets.[8] Meanwhile, upstart firms like Winslow & Lanier that focused narrowly on investment banking had seized the initiative in the rapidly emerging New York capital market. Once the acknowledged leaders within the Anglo-American merchant banking community, the Barings steadily lost market share in the last half of the nineteenth century. The partners' multi-functional strategy and their broad global involvement became, in time, a liability rather than an asset. By the 1870s, they were no longer capable of seizing business from other houses based in New York that had become more functionally specialized and were more strongly committed to serving the American market.

The Browns

The Brown firm was established in 1800 by Alexander Brown, a modestly successful linen merchant who emigrated from Northern Ireland to Baltimore, a port where close relatives had only recently preceded him. Ten years after his arrival in Baltimore, Alexander sent his eldest son William to Liverpool to open what eventually became a branch office of the parent firm. Later, two younger sons opened two additional wholly-owned branch offices in Philadelphia and New York. Like the Rothschilds, the Browns had a unified ownership that functioned smoothly over long geographical distances for many decades. By the 1820s the Browns were involved in a wide range of trade-related financial markets – including the purchase and sale of sterling bills, the making of advances to attract cotton consignments to the Liverpool branch, and the issuance of letters of credit to American importers. In this period the Browns stood just behind the Barings with respect to their overall involvement in the foreign-trade sector of the American economy.

The Browns differed from the Barings and most contemporary merchant bankers primarily because of their reluctance to participate extensively in complementary investment banking activities. The location of their overseas branch office in Liverpool, rather than in London, precluded their involvement in all but a few isolated securities transactions. The absence of a presence in what was then the world's key money centre did not hurt the partnership's profits, however. From 1816 to 1836, the Browns' capital rose from £150,000 to £1.3 million, increasing at an annual rate of 11.5 per cent.

The Browns were hit hard by the Panic of 1837, and only loans from the Bank of England saved them from the embarrassment of repudiating, at least temporarily, their maturing debt obligations. As a result of this crisis, the partners decided to pursue a policy of greater specialization. They entirely gave up trading in merchandise on their own account, which means, strictly speaking, they were no longer acting as merchants – only as bankers. Henceforth, the firm concentrated

---

[8]   Baron Alphonse Rothschild acknowledged the Browns' status in a letter from New York in 1849: 'There is only one banking house here, and that sole concern is that of the Browns'. Quoted in Chapman, *Rise of Merchant Banking*, p. 42.

exclusively on providing financial services for the American foreign-trade market. By the mid-1840s the Browns had supplanted the Barings as the leading Anglo-American house providing services to American importers and exporters, a leadership position that the partners never surrendered throughout the remainder of the nineteenth century.

The Browns were enormously successful in serving the US foreign-trade market because of their truly unique organizational structure. The firm had critically important branch offices, manned by partners or salaried employees, on both sides of the Atlantic Ocean. The offices in New York and Liverpool, with the latter superseded by London in 1863, served as dual headquarters. The entire operations of the firm were carefully coordinated and closely monitored. The Browns adopted uniform policies and procedures at all their offices, which included – in addition to New York, Liverpool, and London – branches in Boston, Baltimore, Philadelphia, New Orleans, and Mobile, Alabama. Many non-family members joined the house as lowly clerks and advanced through the ranks. Except for William Brown, all the directing partners in the British branches were British nationals, among them Joseph Shipley – thus the famous branch office title of Brown, Shipley & Co. At a later date, Mark Collet and Francis Hamilton shared the managerial duties. Collet, incidentally, became governor of the Bank of England in 1887.

Unlike the hesitant Barings, the Browns proved willing to make a strong commitment to the US trade sector. For more than half a century, they assiduously built the organizational capacities to succeed over the long run, and their carefully laid plans eventually translated into a profitable reality. The partners focused on the activity that they knew best, which was serving the requirements of the American foreign-trade sector. From 1840 to 1857 the firm's capital account grew at a rate of 5.5 per cent annually – not as fast in the previous twenty years but still a respectable performance. The Browns constantly reinvested a high proportion of their earnings in their thriving enterprise. In only one exceptionally bad year during this period, 1842, did the partners' withdrawals exceed profits.

Unlike most of their competitors, including George Peabody, the Browns breezed though the worst moments of the Panic of 1857 without seeking aid from the Bank of England and without suffering any serious losses. On the eve of the American Civil War, the partnership was flying high. Reminiscent of the status of the Barings at the end of the 1830s, the Browns were thoroughly ensconced as the undisputed leaders of the Anglo-American merchant-banking community at the end of the 1850s, and the partners were exceedingly proud of their achievements.

But developments subsequently turned sour for the Browns as well, and they eventually fell off the Anglo-American pedestal. Million-dollar underwriting of government bonds and railroad securities became routine in the US capital markets, and portfolio transactions soon overshadowed the volume of activity in the more mundane foreign-trade sector. While the Browns ranked among the leaders in financing the trade sector through the 1890s, that sector's relative importance within the Anglo-American economy continued to fade. In the first decade of the twentieth century, a number of American commercial banks with huge financial resources became competitors in the foreign-trade sector, and the Browns' position correspondingly fell. In time the firm merged with the Harriman family enterprise to create Brown Brothers Harriman, a small private bank with an elite clientele.

The Rothschilds

The partners' involvement began sometime in the 1820s, or possibly in the early 1830s. The firm invested in transportation projects, either for the partners' own joint account or for the portfolios of valued clients. The partners may have also served as loan contracts for certain canal and railroad companies, plus a few state governments, but the exact details are unknown. The Rothschilds worked through independent American agents, although the names and locations of their representatives are incomplete before 1840. Presumably one or more agents were located in Boston, New York, and Philadelphia – the main US money centres.

Our key source of information about the Rothschilds' Anglo-American activities is linked to the career of their long-term US agent, August Belmont, who served the firm in various capacities for over six decades. Born in Alzey, Germany, in 1813, Belmont joined the Frankfurt office as a clerk at age 15. In the early months of 1837 the firm sent him on a mission to Havana, Cuba, via the United States. When he arrived in New York City in March of that year, Belmont found the city in turmoil because of the raging financial panic. The Rothschilds' local agent, the firm of J.L. and S.I. Joseph & Co., had recently suspended payment, with outstanding liabilities of reportedly $7 million. Rather than continuing to Havana, Belmont stayed in New York to protect his employer's financial interests as much as possible. He created an independent firm, titled August Belmont & Co., and became, in turn, the Rothschilds' sole American representative. For the next several years, he tried to reduce as much as possible the Rothschilds' exposure to losses on their American securities and to recover what could be salvaged. The partners were extremely satisfied with his performance, and rewarded him liberally for his efforts.

But that one disastrous experience was apparently enough to stifle the Rothschilds' interest in the American capital market. Although Belmont frequently tried to induce the firm to participate in a series of promising underwriting deals, the partners remained cool to most of his proposals.[9] They joined some syndicates but headed very few. The Rothschilds certainly had the financial resources to dominate the US market had the partners chosen to exert their influence after the investment climate improved in the early 1840s. In 1844 the Rothschilds' capital stood at £7,800,000 versus just £750,000 for the Browns and a mere £500,000

---

[9]   Chapman, *Rise of Merchant Banking*, p. 21.

for the Barings.[10] Frustrated by the Rothschilds' persistent disinterest, Belmont turned to politics, later serving for several years as the organizational leader of the Democratic National Party.[11]

Why the Rothschilds failed to respond to the dramatic changes in the federal government's accelerating debt requirements during and after the American Civil War deserves consideration. Sponsoring very large governmental debt issues had long been the firm's specialty in Europe, and many inviting opportunities in the Anglo-American market arose after 1865. But the Rothschilds held back. To conduct business properly on a grand scale, the partners would have needed to create a genuine branch office in New York City under the direction of a family member. No Rothschilds stepped forward to volunteer for that assignment. Perhaps the family was so closely associated with the monarchical tradition in Europe that none of its senior members ever gave serious consideration to the prospect of dealing regularly with American presidents and cabinet officials who had, in most cases, risen to power from humble and non-aristocratic backgrounds. I am just guessing here, of course, about the snobbery factor; I will leave it to my European colleagues to enlighten me on this issue. Nonetheless, for whatever the reason, the Rothschilds were not major players in what was rapidly becoming one of the most active markets for securities in the entire world.

Peabody/Morgan

Today, the name of J.P. Morgan is universally recognized in financial circles around the globe, but the original enterprise -- the firm that made the Morgan family both rich and famous – was actually founded by George Peabody. A native New Englander, Peabody became a successful Baltimore merchant in the 1820s before migrating to London in the mid-1830s.[12] He rose rapidly in the Anglo-American merchant-banking community. Like the Barings, Peabody adroitly performed several functions simultaneously: trading in commodities on his own account; offering trade-related financial services to American importers and exporters, and acting as a securities promoter and contractor. He differed though, because his geographical focus was narrowly on the US market. Persistently optimistic about the future prospects of the American economy and the fundamental soundness,

[10]   The data on the Rothschilds and Barings is found in N. Ferguson, 'The Rothschilds: Finance, Society and Politics in the Nineteenth Century', paper delivered at the conference *Finance and the Making of Modern Capitalism*, Berkeley, University of California, Center for German and European Studies, 1997. The data on the Browns is from Perkins, *Financing Anglo-American Trade*, Appendix A.

[11]   The one major biography focuses on Belmont's political career; see I. Katz, *August Belmont: a Political Biography* (New York, 1968).

[12]   The definitive biography is M.E. Hidy, *George Peabody: Merchant and Financier* (New York, 1978).

in terms of the risks and associated rewards, of investments in the securities of American railroads, he was the most consistent advocate of capital transfers from England to the United States in the 1840s and 1850s.

But Peabody's run of good fortune ran out in the late 1850s. He was caught short in the Panic of 1857, and his firm had to appeal to the Bank of England for a timely rescue package. That crisis dampened his enthusiasm and led to his withdrawal from the partnership in the mid 1860s. Although outside the scope of our primary interests at this conference, it should, nonetheless, be noted in passing that, during his lifetime, Peabody was renowned in both England and the United States as an extremely generous philanthropist. He established a standard for charitable giving that other wealthy Americans like Andrew Carnegie and William Rockefeller emulated half a century later.

In 1854, Junius Morgan, another native of Massachusetts who had prospered as a merchant in New York City and Hartford, Connecticut, moved to London and joined Peabody as a junior partner. Morgan soon assumed responsibility for the day-to-day management of the busy office. When Peabody retired in 1864, Morgan became the principal owner. Meanwhile, in 1857, the elder Morgan had sent his son John Pierpont, then aged 20, back to the United States to serve as a clerk in Duncan, Sherman & Co., a firm located in New York City that had a longstanding agency agreement with Peabody.[13] A few years later, the younger Morgan started his own firm. Father and son were not, as it happens, members of a jointly-owned enterprise, but they continued to cooperate on a long series of business transactions over many years. In 1871, J.P. Morgan joined forces with the Drexel family of Philadelphia to create Drexel, Morgan & Co. The Drexels had surplus capital; Morgan provided the managerial skills and the vital link to foreign investors through his father and other cooperative European agents.

The Morgans were well positioned to take advantage of the enormous expansion in the US securities market in the post-Civil War era. They helped raise millions for the federal government and the booming railroads. Their deep involvement in this second market – the private corporate market – is one characteristic that distinguishes the Morgans from the Rothschilds. The American railroads and eventually many industrial enterprises grew to become extremely big businesses, and their capital requirements were nearly insatiable. The Morgans had the transatlantic ties to seek out European investors eager to supplement the limited financial resources of American savers.

Within the borders of the United States alone, the Morgans probably exercised more raw financial power than the Rothschilds ever exercised in any single nation state in Europe. Because of the peculiarities of American political and financial history in the first half of the nineteenth century, the United States was left with no

---

[13]   The literature on John Pierpont Morgan is vast. The best sources are V. Carosso, *The Morgans: Private International Bankers, 1854–1913* (Cambridge, Mass., 1987) and R. Chernow, *The House of Morgan: an American Banking Dynasty and the Rise of Modern Finance* (New York, 1990).

functioning central bank. When major financial breakdowns occurred, J.P. Morgan was essentially drafted by his peers in the private sector, with the acquiescence of government officials, to take the unpopular steps necessary to restore equilibrium. Finally, after years of acrimonious debate, Congress created the Federal Reserve System to deal with these recurring problems in 1913. But from 1890 to 1910 or thereabouts, J.P. Morgan reluctantly played the pivotal role of the nation's de facto central banker, since the federal government had long ago abrogated its responsibilities. His decisive role in the Panic of 1907 was especially notable. In sum, Morgan performed both private and public functions, and amassed a fortune in the process. He left an estate of $68 million plus artwork valued at $50 million in 1913. Whether Morgan's wealth exceeded that of the Rothschilds in the early twentieth century is unknown to me.

The Seligmans

Within the Anglo-American merchant banking community, the Seligman family enterprise came the closest in most respects to emulating the Rothschilds' organizational strategies.[14] At the height of its power and influence, the Seligman firm had partners managing key branch offices in New York, London, Paris, and Frankfurt. The Seligman family's success in the United States is a classic 'rags-to-riches' story. Joseph Seligman emigrated from Germany to the United States in 1837. From a base camp in eastern Pennsylvania, he became a country peddler; he used his modest savings to help bring three brothers across the ocean. By the early 1840s the Seligmans had broadened their lucrative peddling routes to include the southern slave States.

In the early 1850s two Seligman brothers, Jesse and Henry, made the acquaintance of a young military officer who would later become one of the firm's important benefactors. This friend was Lieutenant Ulysses S. Grant, a future US president. Even before Grant's war-ending victories on the battlefield in 1865, the Seligmans had expanded their business from merchandizing to include complementary financial services. They were loan contractors for the early war bond issues of the federal government. In 1864, the brothers opened branch offices in London and Frankfurt. They explicitly used the Rothschilds' organizational strategies as an instructive model.

In the late 1860s and 1870s, the Seligmans emerged as major competitors in a wide range of typical merchant-banking fields. They contested the Browns in the foreign exchange markets. Like the Rothschilds, the Seligmans also had influential friends in high places. After his election in 1868, President Grant offered Joseph Seligman, the family patriarch, the cabinet position of Secretary of the Treasury.

---

[14]   R. Muir and C. White, *Over the Long Haul: the Story of J. & W. Seligman & Company* (New York: privately printed, 1964). The firm's surviving nineteenth-century records are located in a special collection at the main library of the University of Oklahoma.

Joseph declined, and his Jewish heritage and formerly immigrant status were allegedly crucial factors in reaching that decision. The Seligmans became the financial agents of the US government for the transmission of funds overseas. Where the Seligmans differed markedly from the Rothschilds was in their involvement in sponsoring securities issues of many of the largest American railroads. With branch offices throughout Western Europe, they were in a favourable position to identify potential investors for millions of dollars' worth of new securities. Like the Morgans, the Seligmans were active participants in underwriting public debt issues and a wide range of corporate securities.

Kuhn, Loeb & Co.

The origins of Kuhn, Loeb & Co. echo the backgrounds of the Rothschilds and Seligmans. Abraham Kuhn and Solomon Loeb were born to German-Jewish parents. They began their business careers as small-town merchants in rural Indiana, then moved to Cincinnati, and finally settled in New York City in 1867.[15] Their firm remained a minor player in the US investment banking field until Jacob Schiff, who married Loeb's daughter Theresa, became directing partner in the 1880s. In time, Schiff rose to become widely recognized as the nation's second leading investment banker, ranking behind only the influential J.P. Morgan.[16]

Schiff was born in Frankfurt in 1847 into a fairly prosperous German-Jewish household. Well-educated in European schools, he migrated to New York City in 1865 and subsequently joined Kuhn Loeb in 1873. Under Schiff's management, the partnership relied on its close connections with a network of correspondents in London and on the continent to identify investors for American railroads searching for new capital. Kuhn Loeb's outstanding performance demonstrates that a transatlantic ownership pattern was not essential for long-term profitability; but its success does suggest quite strongly that at least one important office supervised by a partner with tremendous authority had to be located in the financial centre of the nation from which the demand for investment capital arose – in this case New York City. The Barings and Rothschilds failed to take heed of this organizational imperative; they concentrated on the supply side of the capital equation, not the demand side, and lost their position of leadership in the Anglo-American market.

Kuhn Loeb differed from its competitors in other ways as well. Unlike the Barings, Rothschilds, Morgans, and Seligmans, this firm never depended in its formative years on business originating in the public sector. Instead, Kuhn Loeb tied its fate to the private market – the booming US railroads. Again, an expanding financial market had encouraged further specialization. Kuhn Loeb is the only

---

[15]   Carosso, *Investment Banking in America*, pp. 19–20.

[16]   C. Adler, *Jacob Schiff: His Life and Letters* (Garden City, NY, 1928); and F. Redlich, *The Molding of American Banking: Men and Ideas* (New York, 1968).

investment house in this survey that rose to prominence almost exclusively by serving the financial requirements of corporate enterprises.

Schiff also disagreed with Morgan about the importance of placing representatives of the major investment banking houses on the boards of directors of the railroads that the bankers routinely financed. Morgan thought the presence of his partners on boards of directors was prudent and necessary since they served as watchdogs for investors in cases of gross railroad mismanagement. Schiff believed that regular monitoring was unnecessarily time-consuming – except, of course, in dire circumstances. The exceptions to his general rule applied after a thorough reorganization of a given railroad's capital structure by court-appointed trustees, persons who were frequently none other than the investment bankers themselves. Schiff's reluctance to become closely associated with the management of the railroads that Kuhn Loeb had financed prevented him from becoming a lighting-rod for public criticism to the same extent as J.P. Morgan.

This is an instance where anti-Semitism may have rebounded in Kuhn Loeb's favour. Many American railroad leaders were unwilling, except during a crisis, to add anyone with a Jewish background to their corporate board of directors. That prejudicial attitude helped keep Kuhn Loeb out of the glaring gaze of the public spotlight. In contrast to J.P. Morgan, Schiff was never subpoenaed to appear before a congressional committee investigating the so-called 'money trust'. Under the circumstances prevailing in the early twentieth century, Schiff and his partners were quite happy to play second fiddle to the House of Morgan.

Conclusion

Over the three centuries spanning the period from 1600 to 1900, the Anglo-American financial-services sector became increasingly large and more sophisticated. The general trend was away from an early emphasis on the foreign-trade sector and more toward the burgeoning US capital market, which literally exploded in the second half of the nineteenth century. The flow of money was always westward; Europeans with surplus capital aided US economic development in almost every imaginable way. As the financial markets ripened, greater specialization emerged. The multi-functional merchant-banking houses lost market share as the nineteenth century progressed, and they were superseded by banking enterprises that had a narrower scope.

Initially, the Anglo-American market was institutionally fragmented, but the maturation process advanced steadily after 1750. The leading firms created transatlantic networks of agents or branch offices to expedite transactions of all varieties involving both merchandise and financial services. Trade-related activities predominated through the War of 1812. In the 1820s Anglo-American merchant bankers became simultaneously involved in the US capital markets, helping to locate European investors for a series of capital-intensive transportation projects. These portfolio investments stalled momentarily after the Panic of 1837, but resumed in the 1840s and 1850s. After 1860, the cost of fighting the American Civil War created a huge federal government debt, and soon thereafter the US railroads embarked on a massive expansion programme in the far western States. By the end of the century, the most prestigious and powerful firms in the Anglo-American financial community had largely abandoned their trade orientation to concentrate on investment banking.

The second half of the nineteenth century also witnessed the rise of New York City as the main US money centre. Before the Civil War, Boston had a securities market that rivalled Wall Street. New York investment-banking firms eased ahead of their rivals in the 1850s, when railroad lines were extended into the Midwestern States. In the 1860s New York bankers became the dominant force in the investment market, with Boston houses like Kidder Peabody & Co. and Lee Higginson & Co. falling into the second tier. By the turn of the century, New York was challenging London on the world stage. London was still far ahead in terms of the number of listed bond issues, but the New York securities market had a growing number of choice equity issues.[17]

Investigating the similarities and contrasts among the six leading firms provides enlightenment on several fronts. Two partnerships were essentially family firms – Rothschilds and Seligmans. The Barings had admitted non-family members by the 1820s, and an American actually headed the London office after 1837. The Browns began as a transatlantic family enterprise, but within a quarter century the English branch office was being managed by non-family partners. The Morgans had a close father-son connection in the second half of the nineteenth century, but the mutual-ownership pattern was notably absent. Kuhn Loeb, the last major US entrant into this oligopolistic market, never relied on family connections in Europe for its success. On the other hand, it can be stated that Kuhn Loeb, like Rothschilds and Seligmans, had close ties to the larger community of European Jews. Indeed the principals in all three of the Jewish firms could trace their roots to a single German locale, the city of Frankfurt and its hinterlands. Three houses placed a great deal of emphasis on creating strong transnational organizations with branch offices in key cities managed by partners or salaried employees. The Browns, Rothschilds, and Seligmans were atypical of contemporary firms because of their close internal coordination of operations, and they took advantage of their administrative structure to provide customers with superior services. The directing partners in all three firms insisted on the adoption of uniform policies and procedures throughout the organization. The Browns and Seligmans had branches in the United States, but not the Rothschilds. On the other hand, Barings, Morgan, and Kuhn Loeb demonstrated that it was possible to function as a successful enterprise by relying on a network of agents and correspondents.

When financial services were primarily linked to the trade sector, the location of a branch office in the country where the demand for services arose was not

17   R.C. Michie, *The London and New York Stock Exchanges, 1850–1914* (London, 1987).

critical for success. The Barings were fully capable of serving their American trade customers through a chain of independent merchants in US ports before the middle of the nineteenth century. When the emphasis shifted to the provision of investment banking services for the federal government and the American railroads, then the maintenance of an influential branch office in New York City was a necessity if a house hoped to play a lead role in the transatlantic capital market. Morgan and Kuhn Loeb had singular offices on Wall Street, while the Seligmans made their New York branch their headquarters. The Browns had a New York office but preferred to restrict their business to the trade sector. Without branch offices in New York, the partners of Barings and Rothschilds could not regularly meet with the executives of American railroads to arrange lucrative underwriting transactions. The Browns, Barings, and Rothschilds remained participants in the US capital markets, but they acted primarily as distributors of securities rather than as syndicate organizers.

Over the course of the nineteenth century, the great Anglo-American merchant banking houses underwent a major transformation. The strategy of mixing international trading on their own account with complementary financial services to third parties – foreign exchange transactions, advances against consignments, letters of credit – gave way to greater financial specialization. The Rothschilds abandoned their mercantile activities in the first quarter of the century and immediately stressed investment banking. The Browns ceased merchandising in the late 1830s and concentrated thereafter primarily on the provision of financial services. The Barings, Peabody/Morgan, Seligmans, and Kuhn Loeb shed their mercantile functions at a subsequent date. Except for the Browns, the leading houses in the Anglo-American financial markets at the end of the nineteenth century concentrated on providing investment banking services for governments and large corporate accounts.

CHAPTER 7

The Parisian 'Haute Banque' and the International Economy in the Nineteenth and Early Twentieth Centuries

Alain Plessis

The world of private banking, which was more prevalent than is generally thought in France during the last century, can be separated into essentially two very different groups. On the one hand, the countryside abounded with small local bankers (to which some regional banks can be added), scattered throughout a large number of French towns (a number close to three thousand can be counted), which supplied the whole of the national territory with loans. On the other side was the very small group of powerful houses which formed what is referred to as the 'Haute Banque'.

This expression first appeared during the Restoration in the world of the finance professionals before being widely used by the supporters of the July Monarchy and so entering into current usage. It referred to a small number of 'private' houses established in Paris: these were sometimes individual businesses, but more often a partnership, usually organized as a general partnership. Even if the heads of these businesses were amongst the first to become interested in the new limited companies, none of them were ever tempted to transform their own bank into a joint-stock company.

The term 'Haute Banque', which recalls an eccentric world and implies a considerable, sometimes quasi-magic, power, remains difficult to define. The lists of members of this financial elite, the 'crème des crèmes' according to R. Cameron,[1] were never official, because they did not subscribe to any statutory admission requirements, which explains why their composition may vary a little at any point in time. The membership of the Haute Banque depended on the image made by such and such a house, its reputation, its respectability, a valuation placed on a certain number of factors making up an honourable reputation. The ability to carry out credit activities beyond France certainly featured amongst these factors. The international breadth of the operations of the houses of the Haute Banque seems to fundamentally distinguish them from those bankers who mainly operated in the local, regional or even national markets.

If it is undeniable that the international dimension is one of the specific criteria for the Haute Banque, it is difficult to define what it consisted of, and how it

---

[1] R. Cameron, *La France et le développement économique de l'Europe, 1800–1914* (Paris, 1971), p. 116.

evolved over the course of time. As long as these banks remained private they were not obliged to publish a balance sheet and for a long time remained preoccupied with keeping their business secret. They have therefore left very few archives. Only four or five have apparently preserved any papers, which are moreover very incomplete, and when they were entrusted to the National Archives were quickly transferred into storage at Roubaix. This has rendered it difficult for most French and foreign researchers to consult them. As for historical works based on the consultation of archives, these are very few in number. The main works are those, already rather dated, by Bertrand Gille on the house of Rothschild; but this house held an exceptional place in the world of the Haute Banque, and is therefore not truly representative of the whole of the group. Unfortunately, Gille's study also finishes in 1870.[2]

In this chapter, which aims above all else to incite a revival in research into an historic subject which is too little studied, we wish first to recall how, as soon as they were formed at the end of the eighteenth century and the start of the nineteenth, the majority of the houses were businesses with international interests. We will then attempt to analyse the period during which they reached their peak (1840–60) and understand the importance of their foreign activities in the very complex totality of their operations. Finally, we shall question the alleged decline of the Haute Banque at the end of the nineteenth century and start of the twentieth, and its real position, at least in the international field.

The Men: a World Open to Foreigners

According to the lists established in the middle of the nineteenth century, the banking families which made up the Haute Banque could overall be taken to be of foreign origin. It is certainly true that those which were of the Protestant or Jewish religions were often from foreign countries.

The Protestant families, who were the most numerous, were often descended from French Huguenots who had been refugees in the Swiss cantons, or especially Geneva, not a canton till 1814, before establishing themselves in Paris, often only after some time: from 1723 in the case of the Mallets, at the end of the century

[2]   B. Gille, *Histoire de la Maison Rothschild*, vol.I, Des origines à 1848, and vol. II (1848–1870) (Geneva, 1965 and 1967). On the Haute Banque also refer to H. Bonin, 'The Case of the French Banks', in R. Cameron and V.I. Bovykin (eds), *International Banking, 1870–1914* (Oxford, 1991).

The Rothschild archives have been deposited in the National Archives, where they are classified under series AQ as are the Mallet papers (which we have consulted). The Mirabaud papers, which we have also consulted, have recently been deposited in the National Archives, where they are currently being classified, and in their turn transferred to Roubaix. The archives of the house of Seillière, subsequently Demachy et Seillière, are preserved in Paris by the recently formed Foundation for the History of the Haute Banque.

for the Delesserts, an ancient Waldensian family, and the Odiers. The Hottinguers, originating from Zurich, were also to be found practising as bankers in Paris from 1786, or, arriving at the start of the next century, the Hentsch family from Geneva, as well as the Vernes, who were also Huguenot descendants. The last to arrive were the Mirabauds, also with Huguenot ancestry, who really installed themselves in Paris in 1846 when they became associates of the Paccard-Dufours, who were originally from Geneva.

Among the Jewish families in the Haute Banque one finds the Foulds, who were from Lorraine with distant Germanic ancestry, and, of course, the Rothschilds: it is known that James de Rothschild, the founder of the French branch of the family, arrived in Paris from Frankfurt in March 1811, where he was registered as a banker with the Tribunal de Commerce (Commercial Tribunal) from 1814, but that he remained of foreign nationality up until the end of his life (1868), even though his son, Alphonse, became French naturalized at the start of 1848. Other major Parisian bankers came from various German States, such as the Heines from Lower Saxony (who became allied with the Foulds), and especially the Rhine regions, such as the Cahens from Antwerp.

Among the Catholic families, not an insignificant number, one finds the Pillet-Wills, who may also be considered to be of foreign origin, the founder of this Parisian bank, Frederic Pillet-Will, being born in Savoy in 1781, well before its annexation by France, and having served his commercial and banking apprenticeship at Lausanne. But the other Catholic bankers were of French stock, such as the Périers from the Dauphiné, the Seillières originating from Lorraine, or the Durands, descended from an ancient commercial dynasty based in Roussillon and Montpellier.

If the Parisian Haute Banque remains thought of as a cosmopolitan world incompletely assimilated into the French elite, this is due to the continued links that these great banking families maintained with their parents and friends who remained in the foreign countries. It is also necessary to establish a distinction between the Catholic Haute Banque and the Jewish and Protestant Haute Banque. The major Jewish and Protestant bankers were married, and very often married their children, to foreign wives and husbands, or with people established in France but also with foreign origins, often of the same religion as themselves. These unions sometimes took place within the confines of the same family, as with the Rothschilds. The heads of the French branch were systematically married to other branches of the family: James married the daughter of his brother Salomon, who was located in Vienna, and his son Alphonse was married, in 1857, to his cousin Léonore, the daughter of Lionel de Rothschild the head of the English branch, whilst his sister Charlotte married Nathaniel de Rothschild. Often these marriages united the bankers more closely with foreign, or foreign-origin, families, with which they already had an affinity, or more or less close relationships. Thus, in 1813 and then 1818 two brothers, Louis-Jules Mallet and Adolphe-Jacques Mallet, successively married the two daughters of Oberkampf, a Protestant of Bavarian origin who was a client of their bank, with a factory for painted canvases at Jouy-en-Josas.

Antoine Odier married the daughter of a businessman from Hamburg descended from French reformed ancestors, then married his son, James, to the daughter of an Amsterdam banker. The Hottinguers were allied to Farquhar Jameson, a British associate of the house, with the Delesserts, whose bank they acquired, and with the de Bethmanns, who also belonged to the world of international finance.

These foreign connections were reinforced further by travelling, which allowed the same bankers to receive their parents and 'friends' from various countries and in turn visit them. The members of these families moved around considerably, at least as long as their age allowed them to. Generally, they sent their sons on numerous foreign journeys which were really training to allow them to understand major international business. Naturally, they often started in England, close geographically and ahead in the development of credit. The majority visited this destination, but there were also those who made multiple tours abroad, such as Rodolphe Hottinguer, who left for England at the age of 18. After returning for a year in Paris he then spent some time in St Petersburg, then left for the United States, this already being a well-established tradition in the family: some years later he left for a tour of the Ottoman Empire. Alphonse de Rothschild went to London at a very early age and made frequent and prolonged stays, notably from the age of 19, for experience of the railroad business. In 1848, at the age of 21, he was ready to leave for the United States, exploring the business worlds of New York, New Orleans, and, more briefly, Havana. In 1856, he visited the Ottoman Empire, where his father had already travelled prior to 1848; he also went as far as Alexandria in Egypt.

These journeys had the further objective of prospecting for new markets and, above all, forming a good network of agents in order to develop these markets. The power and prosperity of each house of the Haute Banque in effect depended for its importance and effectiveness on its appointed (and often part-time) agents, especially in foreign countries. Bertrand Gille has shown how the house of Rothschild formed a particularly close network of agents, who could be private bankers also working on their own account, in a large number of financial markets. In the countries where Rothschild's interests were particularly important, they set up their own local agents, paid by the house, 'who acted only on orders, or who generally only acted in very restricted fields'.

In so building up their network, the Rothschilds were not really innovating, but following a path forged by the Protestant bankers in the eighteenth century. The inventories of Mallet Brothers and Co., which was not the most powerful of the houses but held the honour of being the oldest, give a sufficiently precise idea of the geographic distribution of its agents at the end of 1860. At that date the bank listed 1035 holders of current accounts, as many debtors as creditors, and close to 500 of these were for agents domiciled outside France: seventy-five set up in England, as many again in the Scandinavian countries, about fifty in the German States, about forty in Switzerland; about thirty of the accounts came from Belgium and about twenty from Holland. The house had 35 regular clients in Spain, similarly in Italy, around ten in Portugal and around another ten in Austro-Hungary. Russia, including the Grand-Duchy of Warsaw, held around twenty accounts, and such countries as Greece or Romania also supplied a small group of agents. If the European countries, and above all the countries close to France, are the most represented in this inventory, one also finds some agents in the Middle East, the United States, in Bahia and Rio-de-Janeiro, Havana, Bogotá or Calcutta.

We know very little of the foreign distribution for the networks of the majority of the other major Parisian private banks, though one may suppose that the Catholic banks would not have benefited from such a diversified international base. It is always the case that the international spread of all these firms was largely a function of the existence of such networks of agents. The agents constantly reported to the Parisian establishments important information on exchange conditions, the position of the different financial markets and the opportunities to be exploited, and were also able to place considerable capital at their disposal should the need arise.

The Place of International Operations in the Activities of the Houses of the Haute Banque (1840–70)

The available sources do not allow a precise estimate of the volume of business carried out in foreign countries by the major banks based in Paris. Nevertheless, we may shed some light on the subject by analysing the annual inventories available for the house of Mallet for the period around 1860, even if in these inventories the presentation of the different entries for the assets refers to the type of operation (advances on current account, acquisition of drafts and other bills of exchange, and other transferable securities) without establishing any distinction between the parts relating to France and to foreign countries.

Mallet Frères and Co. was of average size in the world of the Haute Banque judged by the size of their capital, which was 3.6 million francs in this period before rising to 4.5 million by 1865. Under the July monarchy, the houses of the Haute Banque for which we have information were founded on share capital of between 1.5 and 5 or 6 million. Périer's was 1.4 million in 1853, increasing to 4 million in 1857 and 5 million in 1865, Davillier's was 2.6 million from 1844, Paccard, Dufour and Co.'s was 3.7 million in 1854, and fell to 2.8 million at the start of 1861 (by which time it was called Mirabaud, Paccard and Co.). The capital of the Paris branch of Rothschild reached far higher figures – 8.4 million from 1818, then 37 million in 1825, and finally, according to our calculations,[3] around 50 million francs under the Second Empire. It therefore had exceptional power at its disposal.

Mallet, like the other houses of the Haute Banque, was a bank that operated in all fields, provided a complex group of services, such as commercial traffic, exchange

---

[3] A. Plessis, *Régents et gouverneurs de la Banque de France sous le Second Empire* (Geneva, 1985), pp. 110ff.

operations, bank and credit business and sale of public and private securities, and, very rarely, engaged in industrial business. This collection of diverse operations still mainly concerned the French economic and financial markets. The majority of the bank's resources came from the investments of its associates, the sums that they left in their current accounts, the current accounts of their relatives and those of the independently wealthy[4] French clients whose fortunes they managed.

Their relations with foreigners can be seen through some entries in each inventory, which allow a little insight into their relative importance. This is how one of them is presented.

Table 7.1   Inventory of Mallet and Co. on 31.12.1860 (in millions of francs)

– Balance Sheet total: 17

Liabilities,   Share capital: 3.6 + deposits from associates: 1.372
                      – Net profit: 0.291

          – Creditors' accounts: 9.9 for 775 named current accounts; 0.514 for 480
               named stockholders (see comment, fn. 4).
          – Acceptances (Notes payable): 1.503

Assets;   – Debtors' current accounts: 5.467
               of which foreign accounts: 2
          – Commercial portfolio: 6.718
               of which 647 bills of exchange on Paris:
               849 bills of exchange on "the provinces and abroad": 3.783
          – Public funds and industrial securities: 4
               of which foreign securities: 0.6

We will attempt to isolate the entries which are able to explain the foreign operations, and to measure their relative importance. First of all, *liabilities*, under the heading acceptances in circulation ('*acceptances and dispositions on ourselves*'), an entry which represents approximately 9 per cent of the total balance sheet at this point in time. An acceptance is a form of credit allowing the transfer of a simple commercial document, a bill of exchange, as a method of payment. These are drafts that the bank is committed to pay on their client's account, therefore giving the drawer the certainty that they will be settled on their expiry; although favoured in the settlement of commercial and financial deals between France and foreign countries, part of these acceptances would still be to finance commercial settlements within France.

---

[4]   Translator's Note: the French word 'rentier' translates either as someone who is of independent means, or as stockholder. In this period the first translation is usually more appropriate, but its appearance on the inventory suggests that there stockholder is the right translation.

Furthermore, under *assets*, three entries include foreign holdings. First, *the current accounts of debtor clients* (who represent a quarter of the total), among which we often find some large foreign accounts mentioned (for example for the Bank of Mauritius) which make up almost half of this entry.

Next *the portfolio of bills of exchange* (some 40 per cent of the assets): here the foreign bills are still mixed with provincial bills, and in this case they together represent a value greater than the amount of bills of exchange on Paris; however, this is often the reverse in the inventories of neighbouring years. A good proportion of the banking business of the house of Mallet therefore concerned internal trade.

The asset heading *'public funds and industrial securities'* includes the securities held voluntarily by the house and the remainder of those that the bank has been charged to issue but has not yet had the time or possibility to place with its clientele or sell on the Stock Exchange. The entry, which represents in this case between 20 and 37 per cent of the jobs for the years considered, is in numbers of securities, four times higher for French securities than for foreign securities. Even if there are sizeable packets among these foreign securities (143,000F of stock in the State of Pennsylvania, 95,000F of securities in Russian railways, 108,000F of shares in Austrian railways, 107,000F of shares in gas in Mechlin, etc.), foreign securities only represent a small part of this portfolio of securities (15 per cent in 1860, and at most 30 per cent in adjacent years).

A quick analysis of the Mallet balance sheets around 1860 therefore leads us to conclude that for this house of the Haute Banque the main portion of its credit openings and transferable securities were still within France. Certainly, these balance sheets do not allow us to measure the considerable volume of operations relating to exchanges, particularly the negotiation of bills of exchange, which was from the start the speciality of these houses. As stated by H. Lefevre, who presented himself in his work of 1880 on *The Exchange and the Bank* as 'the former personal secretary of the late M. le Baron James de Rothschild', the bulk of exchange trading was due to the volume of trade France had with foreign countries. At that time he estimated it to be 8 thousand million francs towards France, made 'through a small number of banking houses of the first order'. in other words through the services of the houses of the Haute Banque: they handled complex operations well, 'in the way in which they carry out the liquidation of reciprocal agreements between the different markets'.[5] Their role was therefore considerable, and they made large profits because the 'small commissions' that they charged for these exchange operations mounted to enormous sums. These exchange operations, which leave little trace in the balance sheets, are also missing from the other sources available to us. These relate more to the subject of extraordinary operations (large credits, large issues of securities) than to daily business, which was boringly routine. We must add that there was a trade surplus between France and Britain up until around 1860, whereas in the same period trade between the rest of continental Europe

---

5   H. Lefevre, *Le Change et la Banque* (Paris, 1880).

and Britain was in deficit. This allowed the Paris market and banks which were established there to play a privileged role in the negotiation of bills of exchange.

There remains little more to say. In credit deals and financial operations the Mallets were at least as much, and undoubtedly more, involved with French than with foreign business during this period. At this time the monetary requirements of the French State were high, and those of some large French businesses (notably the major railway companies) remained considerable. This relative preference for French business by Mallet appears, in so far as it is possible to generalize, to have typified all of the houses of the Haute Banque during this period. There were without doubt houses which devoted themselves more to international trade, such as de Neuflize (with acceptances representing 45 per cent of liabilities around 1860-5),[6] or Hottinguer, who became involved under the Second Empire with Crédit Foncier d'Autriche, with various metallurgical and mining businesses in Spain, with Russian railways and a number of miscellaneous securities in North America. Rothschild de Paris did better as always; having an unequalled network of agents, it was deeply integrated into the international economy. They were also to be found in all the major financial deals of the period concerning the loans of numerous States, the launch of new railway companies, and in international trade in tobacco, cotton, gold and already petroleum. They also had a very strong position in the exchange market, and in their portfolio of bills of exchange, which was worth a very considerable amount, foreign paper must have largely predominated.

At the opposite extreme, many houses of the Haute Banque found themselves less involved with the international economy, particularly among those which belonged to Catholic families, generally of French origin. Even if their various activities are badly understood, it seems correct to say that all were engaged in the negotiation of bills of exchange and involved in major deals, in particular on the Havre market. Firms such as Pillet-Will or Périer had less numerous and more dispersed foreign agents, and they apparently only selectively participated in large foreign deals. For example Périer was very involved with the sugar-refining industry and coal extraction in France (they maintained close links with the coalmining company at Anzin), having hardly any major liabilities beyond the national border except with the Belgian company, de la Vieille Montagne. The case of Seillière is not very different: certainly, following in the steps of Crédit Mobilier, it was involved a little in the Imperial Ottoman Bank and in Crédit Mobilier Spain. They also opened on their own account a Californian branch, entrusted to a certain Abel Guy up until 1870, and in this they regularly invested between 2 and 4 million francs. The rest of their balance sheet, which rose to around 32 million from 1858, consisted mainly of the supply of wood and clothing to the French army and major participation in French businesses (in Etablissements Schneider at Le Creusot, wool mills) and in French railway companies: even if they 'did not limit their

---

6   M. Lévy-Leboyer, 'Le crédit et la monnaie', in *Histoire économique et sociale de la France*, vol. 3, 1789–années 1880 (Paris, 1976), pp. 347ff.

view to the French horizon'.[7] their foreign operations hardly represented a tenth of their work.

Taking everything into account, the international involvement of the Mallets appears to correctly reflect the average behaviour of the Haute Banque, if, that is, it is correct to talk of an average for a group of establishments with such very varied behaviour. On the whole, towards 1860 large French businesses still remained essential to the majority of the houses of the Haute Banque, even if they had long been habitual participants in international financial operations.

The Decline of the Haute Banque or the Strengthening of the International Role of the Haute Banque?

At the end of the 1860s, the Old Bank triumphed over the New Bank, in other words Crédit Mobilier, formed in 1852 by the Pereire brothers, who, it is true to say, profited from the support of many families in the Haute Banque (notably the Foulds and the Mallets).[8] A decline had however already started for the Haute Banque. This can readily be described as relatively rapid and apparently inexorable, so much so that studies of banking history hardly mention the Haute Banque after this time.

It is true that it had to contend with an entire economic and financial environment little in favour of maintaining its traditional activities. As the trade from France to England no longer gave regular trade surpluses, the Paris market lost one of its advantages. It also suffered for too long from forced prices on notes from the Bank of France which isolated it from international monetary agreements from 1870 to 1890. After this, the international supremacy of the London market was indisputable. At the same time, the new credit establishments which were set up as limited companies (Crédit Lyonnais in 1863, Société Générale the following year, etc.) started to organize the systematic draining of savings in the form of deposits: because of the formidable extent of their resources and the multiplication of their agencies over all the national territory, they became very strong competitors for the old houses.

It is nevertheless necessary to understand the reality of this decline in the Haute Banque. Indisputably the number of houses making it up dwindled. It no longer enriched itself with new members, because the few private banks, most often still of foreign origin, that had been able to apply and be accepted were affected by the severe financial crises which exploded in the decade of the 1880s, and then by the Panama scandal, which resulted in their disappearance. At the opposite end, some well-known members of the Haute Banque ceased their operations.

---

[7]   J.-F. Belhoste and H. Rouquette, *La Maison Seillière et Demachy, banque de l'industrie et du commerce depuis le XVIIIe siècle* (Paris, 1977).

[8]   D. Landes, 'Vieille Banque et Banque Nouvelle: la révolution bancaire du XIXe siècle', in *Revue d'Histoire moderne et contemporaine*, vol. 1956, pp. 204ff.

Sometimes it happened to families with no descendants, but these disappearances mainly affected the Catholic Haute Banque and the firms least involved in the international scene, such as the Pillet-Wills, or, at the start of the twentieth century, the Périers.

At this time the Haute Banque therefore consisted of no more than twelve to fifteen banks belonging essentially to Jewish or Protestant families. These were very prudent and wealthy, with directors who had acquired a remarkable ability in the field of exchanges, had a diversified international base endowed with foreign networks which they had built up over a long period, and had solid assets with which to resist the offensive from the new banks. They were also capable of adapting to the new competition and of reacting with dynamism.

It appears to be true that these banks maintained a predominant place in the negotiation of bills of exchange and in all the exchange operations with foreign countries, this incontestably remaining one of their specialities. The everyday operations in this field rarely leave much trace in the archives, but each time an exceptionally large foreign transfer of funds had to be carried out, it appears that it was necessary to call on the Haute Banque. Thus, in July 1872, when it was necessary to settle the indemnity that Germany had demanded from France after the war of 1870–71, the treasury had to reach agreement with a syndicate made up of the banks, just as the major European banking houses did, to guarantee them the supply of 700 million francs of foreign exchange. Similarly in 1890, it was one of the 'traditional' bankers, Jean de Neuflize, who was delegated by a syndicate of French bankers to negotiate, at the request of the Bank of England, an advance of 75 million francs to be made to them with the agreement of the Bank of France. This was at a time when the lowering of Argentinian credit threatened a number of loans issued by Argentina in England.[9]

These banks succeeded to a certain extent in retaining a presence in the major financial deals of the time (launch of State loans, financing large railway companies, etc.). Without a doubt they did not have the necessary resources to guarantee the subscriptions to the largest loans, and they could not from this point of view compete with the new 'public' establishments (in other words those formed by share issues) which could mobilize their multiple branches for such operations. Nevertheless, they continued to place with their small but very rich investment clientele significant packets of new securities, therefore guaranteeing the closing of an issue, and this is one of the methods by which they guaranteed their personal fortune. They also knew how to unite in syndicates which allowed them to carry more weight, and were able to gain support from the new commercial banks that they had largely contributed to the creation of. Thus, with the Imperial Ottoman Bank (1863), one finds represented on the Committee of Paris, at the side of the English bankers of the Committee of London, the Mallets, Hottinguers, Foulds, Pillet-Wills, and André (from the house of Neuflize). The same position was shown when the Banque de Paris et des Pays-Bas was born in 1872, from an

---

[9]   *De Neuflize, Schlumberger et Cie, 1800–1950* (Paris, 1950).

alliance among a number of major private banks. As for the Banque de l'Union Parisienne, this was created at the start of 1904 by five houses of the Haute Banque (Heine & Co., Mallet Frères & Co., Mirabaud & Co., de Neuflize & Co., Vernes & Co.), in association with the Société Générale de Belgique. Due to these links, the Haute Banque continued to retain a not insignificant share in the placing of securities issued by foreign governments and companies.

We would add that these houses still played an often dominant role in the delicate negotiation of the agreements which made the preparation of this type of issue necessary, then in the introduction of these securities to the Paris Bourse, and afterwards they often guaranteed the ensuing regular payment of the coupons. And one again finds the names of some of the major banking families when studying the financial relations between France and distant countries which had attracted French capital, for example Mallet and Mirabaud in the Balkan States or Mirabaud again in Argentina.[10] Even the presence in these regions of the Imperial Ottoman Bank or the BUP had not resulted in the disappearance from these deals of the names of the old banks; in fact quite the contrary, as they were part of the team at the head of these new commercial banks.

A quick examination of the inventories of Mallet Frères & Co. around 1910–13 confirms the fact that this Protestant bank was not content with participating in the BUP, showing an astonishing dynamism on the part of an old firm.

Table 7.2   Inventory of Mallet and Co. on 31.12.1913 (in millions of francs)

– Balance Sheet total: 45

Liabilities;   – Share capital: 5 + reserve: 1.4
+ deposits from associates: 0.722

– Creditors' accounts: 19.887 (in 1,280 named current accounts
and the names of stockholders)
–Acceptances (331 Notes payable in circulation): 18

Assets;   – Debtors' current accounts
(350 names): 22.54
of which foreign accounts: 15.6
– Commercial portfolio: 9.78
of which 279 bills of exchange on Paris: 6
70 on the provinces: 1.95
10 on London: 0.318
57 foreign: 1.474
– Public funds and industrial securities: 12.36
of which foreign securities:
around 10.

10   Cf., e.g., A.M. Regalsky, *Marchés financiers, groupes d'investissement et élites locales. Les investissements français en Argentine, 1880–1914* (thesis, University de Paris I, 1997).

In comparison with the early 1860s, the balance sheet total rose from 19 to 45 million francs (and even 47 million in 1912) and the profits, although very irregular, translate into a strong upwards trend; considering that they were zero in 1913, over 900,000F in 1910 and 1911, and 742,000F in 1912, this gives an average over the four years of more than 600,000F compared to 150,000F in 1860. This progress was achieved with a capital of 5 million francs, which had changed little (it was 4.5 million in 1865).

In France the house no longer resembled its original form: with a certain amount held in the new businesses, overall it satisfied itself by maintaining its position in the sectors where it had operated for a long time, such as insurance.

It was the development of its international operations which undoubtedly allowed this house, which had been involved with the exchange markets since its origin, to find a new dynamism. The number of its foreign agents increased by more than 50 per cent. The acceptances, which from now on served almost exclusively to finance the international trade, had a value ten times higher than in the 1860s, by themselves representing 33 to 40 per cent of the assets instead of 9 per cent.

The three *liability* entries which we have already analysed also point towards a strong move to foreign business. Amongst the *debtors' accounts*, which rose from 5 to 22 million francs, foreign accounts represented 2/3 of the total instead of a third. Amongst these one can pick out Goldman Sachs and Co. of New York, with 900,000F, Portalis & Co., of Buenos Aires, with 700,000F, Pouliloff with 400,000F, Coutts & Co., with 195,000F, Union de Banques Suisses, with 110,000F, etc. In the *portfolio of bills of exchange*, it is difficult to make a comparison, since up until around 1880 the foreign bills were mixed in with the provincial bills, but the fact that from this point they are differentiated (and represent 20 per cent of the total and often close to a third) is a sign of their new importance. Finally, under the heading '*public funds and industrial securities*', the foreign securities are not far off the majority, and they represent 80 per cent of this heading, instead of a third. All these signs point in the same direction: the Mallet bank worked more and more with foreigners, and its position in the international market was considerably stronger. In some regards, one could therefore compare this private bank in Paris to certain merchant banks or accepting houses in the City during the Edwardian era.[11]

One may assume that it was the same for the other houses of the Haute Banque, and in particular, but at a completely different level, for the Parisian branch of Rothschild. One again finds the names of these houses of the Haute Banque on the majority of security issues at this time, which shows that they were successful in maintaining their activity in this type of operation in spite of the competition from the major credit establishments. Thus, when in 1901 the Russian government intended to place a 4 per cent loan of 424 million francs on the Paris market, it was Rothschild which became the 'the director of the syndicate' for the guarantee, and

---

[11]   Cf. Y. Cassis, *Les banquiers de la City à l'époque Edouardienne* (Geneva, 1984); and Y. Cassis, *La City de Londres, 1870–1914* (Paris, 1987).

in the 'participation in the contract', 50.47 per cent fell to the house of Rothschild, followed by Hottinguer which acquired 9.43 per cent, just as much as Crédit Lyonnais, the other major banks only acquiring percentages of 4.72 or 2.36.[12]

Two years later, for an issue of 4 per cent Russian railway bonds for an amount of 173 million francs, fixed value, the direction of the syndicate fell to the Banque de Paris et des Pays-Bas,[13] a new bank, set up as a limited company, but with the support of a certain number of old banking families. The 'participation' of the Haute Banque appeared to be a minority share, since only Hottinguer acquired 25 per cent, the same as the Banque de Paris et des Pays Bas and Crédit Lyonnais. But the 'retrocessions' of securities to be placed show that the majority of the houses of the Haute Banque remained present, due to their remarkable ability to 'close' the new securities within their own clientele, who were rich and trusted them: the 'participants' thus retroceded a million securities to Heine (the successor to Fould), to Vernes, to de Neuflize, and to Mallet, and 500,000F to Mirabaud, Lazard, Cahen d'Anvers etc.

As for Rothschild de Paris, if from this time they kept their distance from the 'Russian loans,' they were converted to other operations, amongst these the placing of Japanese loans (in co-operation with Rothschild of London), issued in three phases, in 1905 (625 million at 4 per cent), in 1907 (290 million at 5 per cent) and in 1913 (200 million at 5 per cent). Each time, the house of Rothschild alone signed the contract and was director of the syndicate, but it retroceded part of the issue to other houses of the Haute Banque, notably to Hottinguer. It made Crédit Lyonnais the beneficiary of a 'retrocession,' again very significant, which shows that the success of these issues of foreign securities drove the houses of the Haute Banque to collaborate closely with the major credit establishments, showing that they did not think of them only as implacable competitors.

But the movement toward internationalization of the financial business of the Haute Banque did not only come about by the development of exchange transactions, by the increased use of finance by acceptances, or by their participation in issues of foreign securities on the Paris market. Many of these houses, with greater or lesser success, launched themselves into grand international speculations involving raw materials and, in particular, non-ferrous metals. Thus, after having taken part in the speculation on copper at the end of the 1880s, the house of Demachy and Seillière participated, at the end of the nineteenth century and start of the twentieth, in another operation regarding tin, in association with Kleinwort & Co. of London, and tied up many millions in this business over a long period of time.

Certain of these houses also made direct investments in various foreign businesses, among others mining businesses. The Parisian branch of Rothschild

---

[12]   The shares of different banks in this security issue and in those which are mentioned afterwards are held in the Crédit Lyonnais historical archives (folders 158 AH 1 et seq.).

[13]   J.P. McKay, 'The House of Rothschild (Paris) as a Multinational Industrial Enterprise, 1875–1914', Conference on *Multinational Enterprise in Historical Perspective* (University of East Anglia, 1985).

thus formed a multinational group for mining extraction and refining of precious metals, including notably the Société minière et métallurgique de Penarroya (created in 1881), the Société Le Nickel and the Compagnie du Boléo (1885), and at a very early date it started to prospect for petroleum in Spain and Russia.

The Mirabauds, who were head of a lesser bank (their capital was 6 million francs from 1897), had closely collaborated with them in many of these industrial companies (in particular in Penarroya and the Compagnie du Boléo). They then created a company specifically for prospecting new mining business, the Société Française d'Etudes et d'Entreprises. It was this that allowed them to start to independently exploit a Serbian copper mine by forming the Compagnie Française des Mines de Bor with a startup capital of 5.5 million in 1904. Meanwhile, keeping sufficient shares to guarantee their control of this business (it was sufficient for them to retain 6.8 per cent), and to retain a commission of 1 per cent on the value of copper sold, they succeeded in placing the rest of the securities with friends and clients whose fortunes they managed (they had close to 3,000, forming what they called their *gens*[14] in the Latin sense of the term). In the same way, in 1908 they were able to achieve an increase in capital of 1.5 million, then through other large deals between the two wars they arrived at a nominal capital of 60 million. They therefore found themselves at the head of a business which had proved exceptionally profitable from before the Great War and throughout the 1920s. These very profitable investments created a goldmine for the Mirabauds, allowing them to take part in numerous other industrial businesses, as much in France as in foreign countries, up until the eve of the Second World War.

The Haute Banque is a group of houses which is more diverse than is often thought. The factor which unifies them is their relationship with foreign countries and their participation from the start in all forms of international operations. They therefore precociously acquired an international culture which they used to acquire a remarkable ability in this field.

This international base, the network of relationships extending to numerous countries, helped them to adapt themselves to developments in international monetary and financial relations, and to profit from them. It is this that, for a long time, allowed them to successfully resist the rising power of the new credit establishments, which for a long time did not have the same resources available. While in the national market the old banks were unable to preserve their market-share when faced with the new competitors, on the international market they succeeded in maintaining themselves and appeared to be indispensable, forcing even the directors of the new banks to use their services.

This continued over a long period: at least up until the Great War, which changed forever the operation of the money markets, and marked the end of a golden age for these houses, during which they succeeded in preserving the essence of their positions in the world scene.

---

[14]   Servants.

CHAPTER 8

Private Banks and International Finance in the Light of the Archives of Baring Brothers

John Orbell

Introduction

The last significant bastion of private banking in Britain was merchant banking, which today, in its modern form, is generally labelled investment banking. Most London merchant banks traced their origins to merchant houses formed by migrants to London from mainland Europe in the late eighteenth or early nineteenth century. As such, they traded internationally in commodities and provided agency services to other merchants in commercial centres around the world. They moved on from this to play a vital role in the provision of short-term finance for international trade and long-term finance for, inter alia, infrastructure development around the world. Their role in mobilizing capital in London's emerging international capital market for use by overseas borrowers was hugely important in the development of the nineteenth-century economy. It won them great prestige and extraordinary influence; they punched well above their weight and in some areas worked as equals alongside giants such as Deutsche Bank and Crédit Lyonnais.

Their names are well known, although in the last 20 years most have disappeared as a result of acquisition by larger banking businesses anxious to establish a presence in the international securities markets and in wholesale banking. Survivors are N.M. Rothschild and Lazard Brothers, while recent departures include Baring Brothers, Brown Shipley, Robert Fleming, Hambros, Morgan Grenfell, Kleinwort Benson and Samuel Montagu. Earlier withdrawals include Brandts, Erlangers, Gibbs, Higginsons, Huths, Japhets, Samuels, Seligmans and Sterns.

Internationally focused private banks existed in other European financial centres. In the eighteenth and nineteenth centuries many prospered, especially in Amsterdam, Frankfurt and Paris, and many London merchant banks did business with them, maintaining an intimate correspondence, forming syndicates and acting on joint account. But none developed the range of activities or the influence of London's privately owned merchant banks, which held their own against the competition – whether real or potential – of Britain's publicly owned joint-stock banks. Although the latter, with their huge balance sheets and customer bases, began to encroach upon the traditional territory of merchant banks before 1914, significant inroads were not made until well after 1945. This was despite the modest resources of merchant banks, which lacked significant customer deposits and, as private banks, were restricted to the personal capital of their partners and to their accumulated reserves. Although it is true that their capital was relatively large in their early days, it shrank massively relative to that of publicly owned, deposit-taking joint-stock banks as the nineteenth century progressed.

What private merchant banks lacked in balance-sheet size they made up for in terms of reputation based on experience, expertise and standing; their 'name' was their greatest asset. For much of their history it underpinned their financing of international trade via the provision of guarantees [i.e. acceptances]. Reputation was equally vital in their securities business, where a respected name behind a bond issue for a remote and unknown borrower sent a signal to investors that the bonds were sound and investment in them would be safe. And smallness had other advantages. It facilitated close contact with customers and markets and quick decision making. New opportunities could be identified and seized far more quickly than at large commercial banks. Ideas, innovation and delivery as well as reputation compensated for smallness of balance sheet.

Another characteristic of merchant banks was their internationalism. They sought their business outside Britain, especially in the eighteenth and nineteenth centuries; only between the two world wars and in the three decades after 1945 did they focus on British-based customers, the result largely of regulations introduced to protect sterling. International business ran in their blood. Their origins had been in Europe, their first work was as international merchants and their correspondent networks always stretched around the globe. They financed international trade and in the nineteenth century were the principal means by which sovereign states, municipalities and large corporations from around the world gained access to the London capital market.

The purpose of this chapter is to explain the international activities of London's merchant banks, to describe the archives these activities generated and to indicate the use of these archives in historical research. It is based on the historical experience and archives of Baring Brothers, for 250 years a leading London merchant bank, acquired in 1995 by ING, the Amsterdam-based and internationally spread financial-services group. Although Barings was established several decades before its rivals and won particularly high prestige through the quality of its business, it is typical of its kind. London's merchant banks possessed remarkable homogeneity in terms of ownership, outlook, management style and activity; such characteristics enabled them for most of the twentieth century to meet quite comfortably in the Accepting Houses Committee, from which platform they promoted their joint interests and excluded unsuitable newcomers. They differed mostly in the balance or focus of their activities.

It follows that Barings' archives are broadly similar in their nature to those of other merchant banks. Where there is difference, it is in the propensity of archives to survive. Without doubt the largest, most comprehensive and most valuable merchant-bank archives are those of Barings and Rothschilds. For various reasons they have survived largely intact, and because of their size and importance are administered by teams of professional archivists within ING and Rothschilds respectively. The surviving archives of other houses – for example Morgan Grenfell,

Kleinwort Benson, Brown Shipley, Hambros and Antony Gibbs – are much more piecemeal, although still of great value. Most are deposited in the Manuscripts Department of Guildhall Library in the City of London, but a few collections are elsewhere – most notably those of Huths at University College London and Brandts at the London School of Economics and Nottingham University.[1]

Baring Brothers

Barings traces its origins to a German family of merchants who established a textile merchanting and manufacturing business at Exeter in 1717. In 1762 a London branch was formed and quickly emerged as the merchant bank of Baring Brothers, a partnership of Baring family members to which outsiders were from time to time admitted when new leadership was needed. In 1890, following a liquidity crisis, the business was reconstructed as a limited-liability company, Baring Brothers & Co. Ltd, but in essence it remained a private bank in Baring family ownership until the end of the twentieth century, when its equity was transferred to a charitable trust.

From the outset the firm acted as international merchants, but soon also provided agency services for other merchants trading internationally. From this base the firm branched into merchant banking through the finance of international trade, mostly through the provision of acceptance credits but sometimes through advances. During the War of American Independence, Barings began to market British government securities, a function which grew in importance during the European Wars, 1793–1815, when the securities of other governments were also issued. By now the firm was reckoned to be the leading merchant bank in London; its influence in the markets was such that in 1818 it was likened to the sixth Great Power in Europe. This position was consolidated in the nineteenth century; its issuing and trade finance activities prospered, although merchanting was in steep decline by mid-century. In the twentieth century issuing and trade finance continued and activities such as corporate finance advice and asset management were added.[2]

The eighteenth- and nineteenth-century archives of Barings fall into two very broad groups; general and customer ledgers and supporting accounts on the one hand and correspondence with customers, agents and correspondent banks on the other. The ledgers are virtually complete from the 1760s; a record exists of almost every transaction for customer or house account through to the 1990s. The correspondence archive is also remarkably complete, but has two significant gaps. Much is missing from the 1760s to the 1820s, while most papers relating to

---

[1]   Series-level descriptions of merchant bank archives are available in J. Orbell and A. Turton, *British Banking: a Guide to Historical Records* (Aldershot, 2001).

[2]   For detailed accounts of Barings' history, see P. Ziegler, *The Sixth Great Power: Barings, 1762–1929* (London, 1988); R. Hidy, *The House of Baring in American Trade and Finance, 1763–1861* (Cambridge, Mass., 1949); and J. Orbell, *Baring Brothers & Co. Limited: a History to 1939* (London, 1985).

United States and Canadian business from the 1820s to 1870 were removed to the National Archives of Canada in the 1920s, although microfilm copies are available in London.

Much of the correspondence archive falls into two broad if somewhat intermingled groups and serves two functions. Most obviously, one records relationships, projects and services provided, is customer- and transaction-specific and deals with security issues, acceptance credits, merchanting transactions, advisory mandates and the like. The second is less obvious but hugely important and comprises intelligence collected in a number of formats about businesses, individuals, markets, commodities, political issues, economic conditions, business confidence and the like. Seen from this perspective, the Baring archive constitutes a vast information bank dealing with a wide range of subjects in many countries and reflects the fact that the systematic collection and careful analysis of information was at the heart of successful merchant banking.

These formats include character reports on businesses, and published materials such as merchant circulars, newspaper reports, prospectuses and the like. But of much greater importance is the extensive correspondence regularly received from correspondents and agents around the world and in particular from Amsterdam, Boston, Buenos Aires, Calcutta, Canton, Madrid, New Orleans, New York, Paris and St Petersburg. This provided information and opinions about a huge range of subjects, especially economic and political factors affecting the markets. An example is the Ward family's correspondence from New York. In 1882 – a year taken entirely at random – several hundred letters to Barings cover, inter alia, the Ohio & Baltimore Railroad; the West Shore & Buffalo Railroad; finance of cotton at New Orleans; Massachusetts state finance; trade in nitrate and guano; failure of merchants at Hong Kong; reports on American iron companies; war risk insurance; and the political and mercantile situation in Chile and Peru. In 1852, another year taken at random, the Paris merchant bank of Hottinguers corresponded about the politics and trade of France; the French Northern Railway; the City of Paris loan; the Paris-Lyon Railway; Austrian credit; the Ottoman Bank; Swiss and Russian railways; and Marshal Soult's picture collection.

By 1900 the organization of Barings' archives was being transformed as the firm assumed a well-defined department structure. Twentieth-century archives are therefore arranged in distinct sections reflecting functions such as security issuance, credit management, securities management, investment management, bookkeeping and administration, although cutting across them are the papers of the partners – known as Partners' Filing – which deal with strategic issues, negotiation of major transactions, and relationships with the most important customers and correspondents.[3]

---

[3]   For more details about the Baring archive, see *Guide to The Baring Archive from the Eighteenth to the Early Twentieth Century*, 3rd edn (London, ING Bank, 2006).

Merchanting and Agency Work

The oldest-established merchant banks were rooted in international trade where, as merchants, they purchased commodities in one international market and sold them in another, and in the process made a speculative profit (or loss). In theory, merchants could deal in a vast range of goods in many different markets but, in order to reduce risk, they specialized in particular markets and commodities and undertook transactions on joint account with other merchants. Most transactions were small but not always. A few were hugely ambitious and envisaged control of entire markets, as in 1787 when Barings, with Hopes of Amsterdam and Ryans of Cadiz, attempted to corner the European market in cochineal, and in 1830–31 when Barings, with the St Petersburg banker Baron Steglitz, sought control of the international tallow market then largely supplied through Russian ports.

Familiarity with commodities, markets and market intermediaries inevitably led merchants to become expert in related areas. As a merchant's reputation grew and as his network of contacts – especially merchants with whom he speculated on joint account – expanded, so it was a small step for him to act as agent for merchants located in other trading centres. The agency services he provided included the purchase and sale of commodities, the organization of warehousing, insurance and shipping, and the arrangement of payments and collections. These services generated a commission income to underpin the speculative profit or loss derived from merchanting; such low-risk business provided much-needed stability. For merchant banks, merchanting and associate agency work remained a significant activity in the early decades of the nineteenth century but fell away rapidly thereafter, although at Barings its remnants were still visible in the Produce Department as late as the 1920s.

Merchanting did not give rise to records of any great note, as the underlying transactions were both repetitive and short-term. Thus, the related correspondence and contractual papers were routine and were not retained long-term; relatively few survive in the Baring archives. Significant exceptions arose in the event of a legal dispute, when financial problems were encountered or when a transaction was particularly large. There are, for example, many papers relating to the 1787 cochineal market ramp while other papers cover disputes involving confiscation of cargo, condition of cargo, debt recovery and disputed insurance claims. Many disputes arose during the period of the European Wars, 1793–1815, the result of the practical and legal difficulties of trading internationally at that time.

Of greater potential interest but difficult to interpret are general and customer ledgers, and supporting accounts such as journals, which detail Barings' own speculations as well as those of its merchant customers. This accounting archive is complete and vast; it has seldom been used, so here there is virgin territory for the persevering historian. Seemingly it touches every part of the world, although the identification of a distinct geographical pattern is not easy. Early on, however, many merchants were located in England, especially the West Country and Yorkshire, and in Europe, especially Spain, Portugal and the Mediterranean. After the War of American Independence, American merchants appear in large numbers, in part because of the burgeoning North Atlantic cotton trade in which Barings was a major participant. From the 1830s and following the final demise of the East India Company's monopoly, accounts of merchants in the Far East, especially on the China coast, become more numerous.

These accounts are, of course, useful in locating details of particular merchants and learning more about particular trading centres, but more generally, their analysis can be expected to yield much about the nature of eighteenth and nineteenth century international trade – underlying commodities, profitability, geographical extent, other parties involved, risk limitation, costs of associated services – and about how this changed over time. Wider issues include trade procedures and variation in them both over time and between commodities; the precise nature of the relationship between the London merchant and the merchants for whom he acted as agent; the nature of the powerful trading alliances existing between groups of merchants in different international markets; marine insurance; shipping; and so on.

The potential of the ledgers is somewhat countered by difficulties in interpretation. The account of a merchant tends to include all work undertaken for him; separate accounts do not seem to exist for different categories of work or different transactions. Moreover, the narrative against each account entry lacks a standard terminology and is sometimes difficult to interpret. Also, to be fully understood, each entry needs to be cross-referenced to journal entries and this, on a large scale, is immensely time-consuming and requires considerable stamina. That said, some pieces of information are very easily extracted for analysis, such as the name and location of a merchant customer, which appear at the head of each account, and the annual turnover of the account. Analysis of Barings' own trading speculations is, however, relatively straightforward as separate accounts appear to exist for separate 'adventures'.

Other groups of papers also shed light on international trade. Amongst them is a small group of memorandum or commonplace books, probably kept by partners as an aide-mémoire, which gives useful details about market procedures and commodities. Character books provide information about the standing and reputation of early and mid-nineteenth-century customers. Much more important are the sets of letters exchanged with overseas agents or correspondents based in places like Amsterdam, Boston, Buenos Aires, Canton, Calcutta, New Orleans, New York, Paris and St Petersburg. These cover a vast range of subjects, but much is about trade and merchants, Notable groups of surviving letters are those with E.J. Forstall & Sons of New Orleans, 1830–90; Gisbourne & Co. of Calcutta, 1830–88; and Russell & Co. of Canton, 1830–83.

In the early nineteenth century, as with other London houses, Barings established a branch in Liverpool to participate in trans-Atlantic trade. The archives of Barings' Liverpool house, especially its correspondence with Barings in London, are a major source for the study of the cotton and wheat trades. Papers within the Statistics of Trade series include merchant circulars for the 1820s to the

1860s; these give details of commodity prices, shipping movements, taxes and regulations, market conditions, etc., for markets around the world.

Other archives worth noting are the private papers of Sir Francis Baring (1740–1810), the founder of Barings. As one of England's leading merchants, he acted as an adviser to British government ministers and others on matters relating to trade and finance and was influential in East India Company affairs as a director and chairman. Through these appointments he accumulated many papers of relevance to international trade.

Finance of International Trade

Agency services provided by merchants came to include the vital work of collecting and making payments for merchant customers. It was a small but seemingly inevitable step from this for the merchant, on the one hand, to advance funds to enable payments to be made and, on the other, to hold deposits as a result of making collections. The merchant was transformed into a merchant banker.

Thus the merchant banker became a financier of international trade, a core activity which in Barings' case endured to the 1920s, after which banking facilities were increasingly restricted to British-based customers, albeit often to finance their international sales and purchases. But as the merchant banker was not a significant deposit taker until well after 1945 so, generally speaking, the advances he made were limited. Far more important was his provision of credits represented by bills of exchange; the so called 'bill on London', accepted by and payable at London's merchant banks, was of vital importance in international trade finance before 1914.

Bills of exchange were guaranteed – more commonly referred to as accepted – by merchant banks in return for a commission. In other words, by guaranteeing bills, merchant banks lent their good name – the product of a widespread acknowledgement of their reputation based on expertise and integrity – rather than their money. In its simplest form, bill finance ran something like this. A merchant customer of Barings located, say, in Shanghai, paid for commodities with a bill of exchange drawn on Barings and payable at Barings in London at a future date, say three or perhaps even six months ahead. If the holder of the bill required funds immediately he could sell the bill to a third party – perhaps another merchant needing to remit funds to London – for slightly less than its face value. In due course the holder of the bill would present it to Barings for payment and payment would be made from funds in the merchant's account. By now, of course, the merchant would have had time to sell the commodities and to forward the proceeds to his Barings' account so that sufficient funds were available for payment of the bill. In the event of the merchant encountering difficulties and not having funds, Barings would nevertheless stand by its guarantee and honour the bill.

This simple and effective mechanism had other uses. It was, for example, a vital means of making international payments. Also, it financed more than international trade. While 'commercial credits' were granted to merchants, 'financial credits' were made available to other categories of business, especially financial institutions. Most notably these included State banks, in order to assist them in making international payments and operating in the foreign exchange markets. In the early nineteenth century, for example, the Bank of the United States figured as one of Barings' most important customers, as did the Banco do Brasil and the Banco de la Nación Argentina at the end of the century. A development of this business during the First World War was the 'rehabilitation' of the sterling-guilder and sterling-rouble exchanges, both of which had collapsed under pressure of wartime conditions. Financial credits, in a somewhat unlikely adaptation, were also used to finance ship construction; at Barings, for example, financial credits were provided to Cunard Steam Ship Co. to fund the construction of early twentieth-century passenger liners.

Until 1900 there is a curious absence of archives relating to trade finance in Barings' archives; the same appears to be so at other merchant banks. While accounts exist in both customer and general ledgers for merchants and institutions in receipt of commercial and financial credits and while the operation of these credits is often referred to in correspondence with customers, no dedicated series of archives exist for the terms and conditions of credits detailing such matters as value, commission or interest, term, security, purpose and other parties involved. Even schedules of credits do not exist. It is hard to think that such archives were not once kept; their loss much reduces our understanding of the merchant banks' role in trade finance.

Nevertheless – as with merchanting – analysis of ledgers and their supporting journals would reveal much about finance of international trade. These ledgers contain a mass of data which – time and stamina permitting – is capable of a degree of scientific analysis to supplement present knowledge, which – as with merchanting – is based largely on case studies. Research would shed light on, inter alia, the obviously close relationship between the provision of agency services and trade finance, the extent to which advances were provided relative to acceptance credits, the credit mechanism, the underlying security, the spread of risk, the nature of financial credits, commissions, defaults and so on.

Barings' archives are vastly more informative about trade finance for the years after 1900 when the business was handled by a dedicated Credit Department. Now memorandum books detail the terms upon which individual credits were granted, while other books provide precise information about their administration. These archives are supplemented by detailed annual reports on the work of the Credit Department dealing with, for example, new accounts, accounts in difficulty, the extent to which credits were drawn upon, the extent to which they were provided on joint account with other banks, their geographical spread, the general environment in which the business operated, the spread of risk and so on. Another supporting series from the 1920s is the Department's 'diary.' These are, in fact, detailed journals summarizing meetings, correspondence and other events on a daily basis. Together these form a rich source for studying the trade-finance activities of a merchant bank in the first half of the twentieth century.

When customers encountered difficulties Barings foreclosed, took possession of assets and administered them until their disposal. When these assets included real estate, disposal could take years, thereby drawing Barings into their management as going concerns. Examples well documented in the firm's archives are the administration of sugar and coffee estates in Ceylon between 1847 and 1896 and of sugar plantations on the West Indian island of St Croix between 1825 and 1876.

Other series touching on trade finance have already been mentioned on account of their relevance also to merchanting. These include reports entered into character books on the standing and resources of customers. They cover details such as capital resources, background, nature of business and standing, and therefore give useful insight into an individual business or group of businesses at a particular location. Examples at Barings include reports on houses at Rio de Janeiro in 1838, Madrid in 1848 and Moscow in 1867. A particularly good set for the late nineteenth and early twentieth centuries, relating especially to North America, survives amongst the archives of Barings' Liverpool house. Other papers, already discussed in connection with merchanting, are correspondence with overseas agents. These also deal with trade-finance issues; the correspondence exchanged with the Ward family and, later, Kidder Peabody of Boston and New York is particularly important.

Security Issuance

Bill finance was essentially short-term, but from the late-eighteenth century demand for long-term funds increased substantially, especially from governments. These funds were raised through the sale to investors of securities, mostly bearer bonds, repayable in, say, 20, 50 or even 100 years. Merchant banks were quick to add this to their portfolio of activities. While bill finance provided a steady income stream, revenue generated from issuance, while less regular, generated far greater profits.

Few Western European countries in the nineteenth century had no internal capital market; most governments, for example, devised means of selling their securities to local investors even if markets were imperfect and ad hoc. That said, there were very few international capital markets in which borrowers from countries experiencing local capital shortage could raise long-term capital. In the eighteenth century Amsterdam was the leading international market, and several European governments issued their bonds there. London overhauled Amsterdam at the turn of the century and dominated the international markets until 1914, being joined in late century by Paris and Berlin and, after 1900, by New York. After 1918, London faded, having been weakened by war and restricted by regulations imposed to protect sterling, while New York was in the ascendancy and unchallenged.

As the nineteenth century progressed so the range of borrowers in the international markets increased. Initially access was limited to governments, a class of borrower that enjoyed the highest standing in the eyes of investors; by 1900 few governments had not issued bonds in London. They did so in order to finance general expenditure, stabilize their currency, construct infrastructure and wage war. By mid-century they were joined by corporate borrowers, mostly formed to build railways – the cornerstone of the modern industrial State,with an unprecedented need for capital – and infrastructure such as water supply, drainage, roads, tramways and municipal buildings to facilitate urban development, another key feature of modernization.

Merchant banks provided these borrowers with access to the London market in order to issue their securities; in capturing such business the banks had many advantages. As international merchants and financiers of international trade their knowledge of countries and governments far exceeded that of other groups of British-based financial intermediaries. Moreover, their standing was as well known to potential foreign borrowers as it was to potential domestic investors, meaning that they were uniquely suited to bringing the two together. As important was their web of international connections – merchants, bankers and other intermediaries – which facilitated their formation of syndicates to underwrite and distribute the securities they issued.

Barings' securities business developed in the 1780s, when British government securities were purchased and marketed to investors in order to fund military and naval expenditure during the War of American Independence. During the European Wars, 1793 to 1815, Barings emerged as a leading marketer of these securities, once again issued to fund war expenditure. This, in turn, led to similar business for other governments; it began in 1801 when Barings and Hope & Co. of Amsterdam marketed Portuguese government bonds to enable the government to fund subsidies payable to France. Far more important was the 1803–4 issue, again with Hopes, of US$11.25 million United States government bonds to fund the purchase of the Territory of Louisiana from France, a transaction which doubled the size of the country through the addition of one million square miles. Few transactions carried out by London merchant banks had greater historical significance.

As the nineteenth century progressed the securities business grew in importance. Between 1816 and 1818 the firm led a massive and politically important, yet unresearched, transaction to fund indemnities payable by France after its defeat in 1815. In the following decades private placements for US State governments and businesses predominated, many of the proceeds being ploughed into railway development and public works but also into banks in order to improve the mobility of local capital needed by the emergent cotton industry.

From mid-century, public issues via the circulation of prospectuses rather than via private placements predominated. Now Barings' geographical specialization in issuing securities for national and provincial governments, municipalities and businesses in the United States, Canada, Russia and Argentina was pronounced. But issues were made for many other governments, including those of France, Belgium, Italy, China, Chile, Japan, Uruguay, Venezuela, Mexico, Austria, Portugal, the Cape of Good Hope and Spain. Many of the proceeds balanced annual budgets but a huge amount was ploughed into railway construction in countries as diverse as India and Italy, China and Chile. These projects sometimes included construction of the first significant railway infrastructure, such as the Grande Société des Chemins de Fer Russes and the Canadian Grand Trunk Railway. Stabilization of the Italian lira was facilitated by two especially large issues in 1881–2 for the Italian government, while the proceeds of an 1850 Russian government issue, ostensibly made to fund the Moscow to St Petersburg Railway, went instead to finance a military expedition against Hungary. In the two decades before the First World War another specialization was issues for North American transcontinental railroads, including the Great Northern, the Union Pacific and the Canadian Pacific.

By the end of the century, the development of competitor markets to London coupled with improved telegraphic communications was undermining the established practice of sole management of an issue in a single market. More and more, syndicates of European and, later, New York banks were formed to handle large issues simultaneously in the different markets. Thus Barings acted as a syndicate member, often as its leader, alongside the likes of J.P. Morgan, Kuhn Loeb and Kidder Peabody in New York, Deutsche Bank and Disconto-Gesellschaft in Berlin and the Crédit Lyonnais and Banque de Paris & des Pays Bas in Paris. That London's private merchant banks could hold their own in such company highlights the influence they exerted.

In the 1920s, bond issuing for the firm's traditional customers in the United States, Canada and Russia dwindled to nothing, although some business was done for customers in Brazil, Argentina, Japan and elsewhere. Often in collaboration with Rothschilds and Schroders, many issues were arranged for European customers – the governments of Czechoslovakia, Hungary, Austria and Belgium and the cities of Hamburg and Berlin – to fund monetary and infrastructure reconstruction required as a result of First World War disruption. Very often this was done with encouragement, sometimes co-operation, from the Bank of England, which sought to promote economic stability in Europe. By the 1930s, access to the London capital market for foreign borrowers was virtually at an end, on account of embargoes introduced to protect sterling. London's merchant bankers turned away from international finance to focus on work for British industry; a generation was to pass before the emergence of a new international role made possible by the Eurodollar and the Eurobond market.

The Baring archives cover in considerable detail all the above transactions and capital-market developments. In particular, they include correspondence with customers and with other participating banks, contracts, prospectuses, certificates and papers relating to the customer. The latter often deal with the underlying project, an excellent example being The Canadian Grand Trunk Railway, for which there are annual reports, statements of account, maps and plans and so on. Others papers touch on the assets or revenue streams on which bonds were secured, such as detailed reports on Japanese railways, for which issues were contemplated in the early twentieth century, and papers referring to Portugal's tobacco industry and monopoly, the tax revenue from which was allocated for interest payments in what amounted to an early form of securitization. Other papers relate to the construction of the Buenos Aires Waterworks, the finance of which was to bring Barings to its knees in a liquidity crisis in 1890.

Of slightly less importance are the very many 'proposals for business' that were turned down as unattractive. Many were for conventional bond issues for governments and businesses, but the range is much wider and includes funding for the construction of the Schleswig-Holstein Canal in 1880 and exotics such as the purchase of the Château Margaux vineyards in 1835.

A highly important group is the correspondence exchanged with agents acting as local negotiators or correspondents of Barings; these firms and individuals have already been encountered in the sections on merchanting and trade finance. When it came to the securities business they were the firm's eyes and ears, maintaining contact with customers, reporting on economic and political events, sending market intelligence, giving opinions on investor sentiment and individuals, referring on proposals, and so on; their correspondence is of interest to political as well as economic historians. When a bond issue was contemplated they played a vital negotiating role. Many long runs of correspondence exist, but of particular value is that with Alexander Baring in the United States (1796–1803); Thomas Ward at Boston (1828–50); SG and GC Ward at New York (1872–85); Kidder Peabody at Boston and New York (1878–1920s); Hope & Co. at Amsterdam (1822–1900s); Hottinguer & Cie at Paris (1820–1900s); Stieglitz & Co. at St Petersburg (1825–84); Charles Jutting also at St Petersburg (1863–79); Ericksens at Vienna (1848–61); Nicholas Bouwer at Buenos Aires (1876–90); and Essex Reade also at Buenos Aires (1891–1900).

As the international capital markets grew larger and more sophisticated, better organized and more extensive records were needed in place of the somewhat ad hoc procedures of the early century when issues were smaller. At Barings this is reflected in the creation of new archive series to record the underlying underwriting and issuing process. Of greatest significance here are the new issue registers running from 1876, which identify syndicate banks behind the issue, sub-underwriters and subscribers, and record the extent of their participation. They allow analysis of investors and an understanding of market mechanisms such as the evolution of risk distribution.

While the above archives shed light on particular transactions, customers and processes, they also have much to offer in understanding the changing nature of the international capital markets. Most obviously, they trace the emergence of new markets such as Berlin and New York and the ways in which they were co-ordinated in syndicates. A particular feature highlighted is the extraordinary competition for business that arose between syndicates and markets.

Another area covers the relationship between customer and bank and the means by which they worked together to build and maintain a market in the customer's securities. This took the form of careful control of issuing in order to foster the market; it might require the bank to advance funds as a stopgap measure, especially to fund interest payments, when market conditions for further issues were unfavourable. Such reputation-building was at the heart of, for example, Barings' relationship with the government of the Province of Upper Canada. A hundred years later it was present in Barings' connection with the government of the newly formed State of Czechoslovakia. This also touches on the resolution of differences between customer and bank and the fiscal and economic policies required of the sovereign customer in order to maintain its standing in the markets.

There is also much in Barings' archives about default and debt reconstruction. While a merchant bank sought to protect its reputation by issuing securities that would maintain their market value, misjudgements occurred and losses were sustained by investors through default soon after issue. Barings was certainly no exception, and several groups of papers deal with debt reconstruction. The earliest cover the 1824 Government of Buenos Aires loan, its default in the late 1820s and its conversion in the 1850s. Here Barings' archives cover Argentine government finance generally, negotiations with bondholders and negotiations undertaken by a succession of emissaries dispatched to Buenos Aires to treat with the government. Other early papers were accumulated by, for example, George White, a Barings' clerk and trouble-shooter sent to Mexico on behalf of the Mexican bondholders for two years in the 1860s to deal with the Mexican government. Although he was unsuccessful in his negotiations to reschedule the government's debt, his extensive papers provide extraordinary insight into Mexican economy and politics at that time. Later examples, in the late 1920s and 1930s, are extensive files covering debt rescheduling by Argentina, Brazil and Germany.

The role of the merchant bank as a formal and informal agent of government is another area of interest. Co-operation and competition between merchant banks, supported by their national governments, for control over bond issues for the Chinese government is well known, but Barings' archives also shed light on similar developments elsewhere, not least the extension of British economic power in the eastern Mediterranean before 1914. For this there are papers touching on Turkey and Egypt, and especially on the proposed Baghdad Railway promoted to link the railway networks of Asia and Europe. Other areas where strong political undertones are present include the Russo-Japanese War, in which Barings managed to assist both sides, finance of the Imperial Russian government between 1914 and 1917, and issues for European governments, especially Czechoslovakia, between the wars.

Corporate Finance Advice

In the twentieth century, especially after 1945, corporate-finance advisory services for British and overseas businesses became a mainstay of London's merchant banks, its origins being in mid nineteenth-century bond issues for railway companies outside Britain. It was a short step from this to issuing equity and debt for British-based businesses, but this work soon became more complex and wide ranging. Early on, in the 1880s, for example, it included the conversion of old-established but very large private partnerships, such as Guinness and Whitbread, into publicly owned limited companies through flotation on the London Stock Exchange. Such transactions came to involve more broadly based advisory work, dealing with such matters as shareholder rights, valuation and stock-exchange regulations, in addition to relatively straightforward issuing work. This activity came gradually to be labelled corporate finance advice.

Although largely Britain-focused until the first wave of cross-border transactions in the 1980s, there were important exceptions. When the Atchison, Topeka & Santa Fe Railroad of the USA, a business for which Barings had already made debt issues, encountered difficulties in the 1880s, the firm worked closely with Kidder Peabody of New York in its reconstruction. Similarly the firm, via its New York house, was active in financing the wave of mergers which swept across United States industry in the decade or so before 1914. In the same period, Barings was drawn into other corporate and anti-trust issues thrown up by issuing work for the aggressively competitive North American transcontinental railways. Later on, in the 1920s and 30s, links existed with United States businesses such as Goodyear Tire & Rubber and Pressed Steel in their establishment of British-based operations for the first time. Also notable is the firm's work in injecting North American management practice into moribund British manufacturing businesses such as Armstrong Whitworth and the Lancashire cotton textile industry in the 1920s through the work of Barings' Canadian-born senior partner, Sir Edward Peacock, and the company doctor, James Frater Taylor.

Paying Agencies

Other functions grew out of the issuance of securities for sovereign and occasionally business customers. One was paying-agency work whereby the merchant bank made interest payments to holders of a government's (or business's) securities and operated sinking funds for their gradual redemption. This generated a commission income, a lucrative spin-off from issuing. Sinking-fund registers survive, giving details of bonds redeemed, but this function was essentially routine and only of note when the customer experienced difficulty in funding interest and redemption payments. In such cases, Barings was likely to advance funds to enable payments to be made.

Financial Agencies

An especially sensitive role of London's merchant banks was that of general financial agent; for much of the nineteenth century Barings acted as London agents for the governments of the United States, Russia and Canada, plus others from time to time. At its most routine, this involved managing the government's bank accounts in London, making payments and collections for the government's account, not just in Britain but in countries where Barings had correspondent banks. As an extension to this, the accounts of the government's officials and agents might also be kept. By the end of the nineteenth century, this role had all but disappeared, passing to the government's home bankers which had, by then, established reliable international connections.

From time to time, the role embraced particular commissions such as the purchase or sale of commodities or equipment. During the American Civil War, for example, Barings was charged by the United States government with purchasing for its account munitions in Europe. More regular work involved the provision of credits to captains of United States warships for use in purchasing supplies when absent from home ports. Similar functions were undertaken for the Imperial Russian Government, especially during the First World War when Barings assisted the government in its fund-raising negotiations with the British government and subsequently made payments for the purchase of war supplies. The volume of this business was enormous, and a particularly large archive of correspondence, telegrams and contracts accumulated. Throughout its history Barings received numerous commissions from the British government despite no formal agency existing. Most notably, these commissions included the remittance of funds to Britain's allies during the European Wars, 1793–1815, and the supply of grain to Ireland during the Irish Famine in the late 1840s.

The management of financial agencies was discreet work which seldom came to general notice, but it nevertheless created real conflicts of interest. On the eve of the Crimean War, for example, when Britain and France confronted Russia, the head of Barings was accused in the House of Commons of being a private agent of the government of Russia on account of the government's bullion supposedly being removed from Barings' vaults prior to the declaration of war. Of greater historical note was the 1803–4 transaction whereby Barings, with Amsterdam merchant bankers, marketed United States government bonds to finance that government's purchase of the Territory of Louisiana from France at a time of war between France and Britain. In effect it amounted to financing an enemy of the British Crown, and Barings was in due course obliged to curtail its role.

Comparatively little financial-agency correspondence survives in Barings' archives, as presumably most of it was routine. By far the most important source, however, is the ledgers and their supporting journals, which survive in their entirety and quite clearly show the nature of the business undertaken. This aspect of Barings' work has scarcely been researched.

Private Banking Services

The provision of financial services to merchants, governments and big businesses inevitably drew merchant banks into providing banking services to individuals associated with them. These included current accounts, advances, safe custody, security dealing, travel facilities and trustee services, but in terms of revenue generated this was never of great significance at Barings, unlike at other merchant banks where it was developed more purposefully. It did, however, notably add to the firm's prestige, as customers included statesmen such as Napoleon III, the King of the Belgians, many US Presidents including James Monroe, and the Prince de Talleyrand, as well as numerous ambassadors, other diplomats and leading businessmen.

Another group comprises the private customers of Barings' agents and correspondent banks in Europe and in North America who wished to have banking facilities in London, and in particular to hold part of their capital assets there in the form of securities. Others, travelling or living temporarily in Europe, required travel facilities which their home banks were unable to provide as they lacked the well-developed correspondent network already established by Barings. This applied especially to American travellers in the early and mid-nineteenth century and accounts for the existence in Barings' ledgers of unexpected names ranging from the writer Nathaniel Hawthorne to the sculptor John Gibson. Accounts of the Count of Monte Cristo and Phileas Fogg, who went around the world in eighty days, are also supposedly included.

Security Management

An overlooked aspect of merchant banking is security management, whereby portfolios were administered for customers, especially those in mainland Europe. Securities were purchased and sold and held in safe custody, while dividends and interest were collected, credited to current accounts or paid away. At Barings this activity resulted in the creation of security registers arranged both by name of customer and name of security; they date back to the 1830s, although early volumes, of which there are only a few, appear to have been somewhat haphazardly kept and are difficult to interpret. From 1891, however, they provide a clear statement of sales and purchases per customer and per security and provide an excellent resource for the study of investor behaviour.

Investment of Resources

The focus of published work on merchant-banking history has been on activities most in the public eye, such as trade finance and security issuance. An altogether more discreet side existed, reflecting the deeply etched sense of entrepreneurship at the heart of merchant banking; it was the partners' management of the bank's private treasury and of their personal capital kept outside the bank's balance sheet. Allocation was across a wide range of instruments and other assets including bills, short-term loans made via the money market and in particular to brokers, equities, gilts, corporate and government debt, medium-term customer loans, property and so on. Such balance-sheet analysis is well possible for Barings, given its detailed and comprehensive accounting archives.

Much of this was routine work, but sometimes it involved major investment with a strong international dimension. An example close to home was speculative investment in the 1850s in the important Weardale Coal & Iron Co., a potential supplier of iron rails to the United States and Russian railway companies for which Barings marketed securities. Another example is the 1796 investment, with Hopes of Amsterdam, in one million acres of land in Maine, USA; it not only represented a safe haven for surplus funds outside an unstable Europe, but underlined the firm's credibility in the USA, where it was building a major presence. While relatively few papers touching on the Weardale Company survive, a large number do for the Maine Lands transaction giving, inter alia, fascinating insight into United States trade and government finance and, not least, eighteenth-century life in New England. Other wide-ranging investments include the National Bank of Turkey, Caucasus Copper Co. Ltd and the British-based Pressed Steel Co. in the 1930s.

Summary

The above account deals with the main functions of London's merchant banks and the archives that these functions gave rise to. It is a generalized account, short on detail and with much omitted. It nevertheless serves to show the vital function of merchant banks in international finance from the late eighteenth to the early twentieth century, especially through their short-term finance of international trade via the accepting of bills of exchange and their long-term finance of governments and businesses via the issue of securities. These were the principal means by which overseas borrowers accessed the London capital market at a time when London was far and away the most important source of international capital. Given the importance of this role, it is extraordinary that it should have been carried out by privately owned banks employing family capital and family management. It highlights the vital importance in private banking of elements such as reputation and goodwill, contacts and networks, market intelligence and quick decision-making.

CHAPTER 9

German Private Banks and German Industry, 1830–1938

Dieter Ziegler

If the old Gerschenkronian hypothesis that the German banks were of indispensable importance for mobilizing the capital needed for an industrialization process that was based on a much more capital-intensive leading-sector complex than that of the industrial pioneers is right,[1] then it is not the universal bank that deserves the praise but the private banker.

This fact was overlooked by Gerschenkron and others for two main reasons. First, by the 1850s the demand for capital and credit from the railway companies and emerging heavy industry was already outrunning the private bankers' resources, and initiatives for joint-stock credit banks were emerging, while only a quarter of a century later these joint-stock banks began to dwarf even the largest private banks in the credit market. Second, the famous cosmopolitan banking dynasties of German origin, such as the Rothschilds, the Bethmanns, the Mendelssohns and the Erlangers, were not among the banking pioneers of German industrialization.

In addition, until recently historical research unanimously agreed that after the turn of the century German private banks underwent a period of steady decline, interrupted only by an illusory flowering during the inflation. In the logic of this interpretation the de facto disappearance of private banks in Germany after 1945 is seen as a 'natural' result of market forces. This article attempts to get both the role and importance of private bankers during industrialization and the reasons for their disappearance as a major component of the German financial markets into perspective.

Private Bankers and German Industrialization

In the early nineteenth century the role and function of the private banking houses depended on the peculiarities of the place where they operated. Despite Germany's economic backwardness, banking in Germany was not underdeveloped as such, but as yet not geared towards the financing of industry and trade. The only exception was Hamburg, the outstanding North Sea port for Central Europe. Hamburg's intermediate position between the Atlantic and its vast economic

---

[1]   A. Gerschenkron, *Economic Backwardness in Historical Perspective* (Cambridge, Mass., 1962), pp. 5–30; see also R. Sylla, 'The Role of Banks', in R. Sylla and G. Toniolo (eds), *Patterns of European Industrialization: the Nineteenth Century* (London, 1991), pp. 45–63.

hinterland demanded an efficient financial backing. Thus, the Hamburg bankers, such as Berenberg, Gossler & Co., Salomon Heine, L. Behrens & Söhne, C.H. Donner and M.M. Warburg & Co., specialized in a particular service, the financing of overseas trade – merchant banking.[2]

While the economic fragmentation of the German territory before 1834, when the Zollverein was founded, had been one of the reasons for the poor state of internal trade and thus for the country's economic decline relative to its western neighbours, the political fragmentation was one of the reasons for Frankfurt's position as a first-rank European financial centre. After the German map had been reshaped at the Congress of Vienna, the new German States were near to declaring themselves bankrupt. In addition to their mainly unfunded war debt, these States developed an enormous additional credit demand in order to build up a State bureaucracy and to integrate their newly acquired, often politically, economically and mentally incoherent parts. In economic terms political fragmentation also meant coinage chaos. Hundreds of different types of coins circulated in Germany, and in many cases the manipulation of the coins' specie content had been a means of the smaller territories' fiscal policy. Long-distance trade, therefore, suffered from exchange risks despite seemingly stable specie standards, and payment settlements often required professional assistance. Exchange dealings thus formed a large market for Frankfurt banking houses.[3]

Both markets – merchant banking (in Hamburg) and State financing and exchange dealings (in Frankfurt) – were not at all declining when a new demand for capital and credit appeared. By the mid-1830s the first German railway companies had proved that the building of railways could become a profitable business, not only for the prospective customers (by speeding up the transport of goods and passengers and by reducing transport costs), but also for prospective investors. Capital was not scarce in Germany during the 1830s and early 1840s, but the wealthy public was not yet used to investing in shares of joint-stock companies.[4] In addition, during the early period of railway development the German States did not support private railway initiatives, while the States themselves were not inclined to take control of railway development by building the tracks on their own account. The reasons were different – the Postmaster General feared railway competition with the State-owned Prussian post services, the finance minister feared the railways' competition with the newly erected State-owned

---

[2]   M. Pohl, *Hamburger Bankengeschichte* (Mainz, 1986), pp. 55–71.

[3]   U. Heyn, *Private Banking and Industrialization: The Case of Frankfurt am Main 1825–1875* (New York, 1981), pp. 206–61; H.P. Ullmann, 'Der Frankfurter Kapitalmarkt um 1800: Entstehung, Struktur und Wirkung einer modernen Finanzinstitution', in *Vierteljahrschrift für Wirtschafts- und Sozialgeschichte*, vol. 77, 1990, pp. 75–92; C.-L. Holtfrerich, *Finanzplatz Frankfurt* (Munich, 1999), p. 155.

[4]   K. Borchardt, 'Zur Frage des Kapitalmangels in der ersten Hälfte des 19. Jahrhunderts in Deutschland', *Jahrbücher für Nationalökonomie und Statistik*, vol. 173, 1961, pp. 401–21, here p. 414.

Prussian turnpikes, the smaller States' finance ministers shied away from the then necessary and unprecedented addition to the State debt, the landed interest feared that additional credit demand by the States would result in a 'crowding out' of mortgages in the capital market – but the result in almost all German States was that the railway promoters were left alone.[5]

The leading Frankfurt bankers quickly realized the potential of the railway business, and in 1836 a committee of bankers, lead by Gebr. Bethmann, M.A. Rothschild & Söhne and Grunelius & Co., was set up to plan the underwriting and building of the first railways around Frankfurt. But by contrast with the Paris and Vienna Rothschilds, the Frankfurt branch soon retreated from this risky adventure and returned to its traditional business.[6] With the exception of Gebr. Bethmann – the leading Frankfurt bank of the eighteenth century, which was dwarfed by the Rothschilds in the government loan market after 1815 – during the early years of railway development only a handful of newcomers among the Frankfurt banks sustained their interest in this new mode of transportation.[7]

At the same time, commodity merchants in several commercial centres other than Frankfurt and Hamburg had begun to finance trade transactions and at times even specialized in banking. In Cologne, for example, during the 1830s several 'bankers' abandoned commodity trade and became proper bankers: Abraham Schaaffhausen, Sal. Oppenheim jr. & Cie., I.H. Stein, I.D. Herstatt and others. Schaaffhausen and Oppenheim had been the most dynamic, and both engaged in local railway committees, such as the Rhenish Railway (Cologne-Aachen) and the Rhine-Weser Railway (Cologne-Minden, as a component of a trunk line between Berlin and the Rhineland).[8]

Although Cologne was one of the outstanding centres of early railway development, its situation was not unique. However, railway committees attracted bankers first and foremost in those places where government financing was of no importance, but railway promoters were particularly active: besides Cologne also in Elberfeld, Leipzig, Breslau and later Berlin. Bankers of these cities did not simply finance railway companies, but were themselves always among the most active railway promoters.[9]

---

[5] D. Ziegler, *Eisenbahnen und Staat im Zeitalter der Industrialisierung* (Stuttgart, 1996), pp. 37f.

[6] N. Ferguson, *Die Geschichte der Rothschilds. Propheten des Geldes*, 2 vols (Stuttgart, 2002), vol. 1, pp. 497–9.

[7] Heyn, *Private Banking*, p. 291.

[8] R. Tilly, *Financial Institutions and Industrialization in the Rhineland 1815–1870* (Madison, 1966), p. 92, 97.

[9] W. Hoth, 'Zur Finanzierung des Eisenbahnstreckenbaus im 19. Jahrhundert', in *Scripta Mercaturae*, vol. 12, 1978, pp. 1–19; D. Ziegler, 'Banking and the Rise and Expansion of Industrial Capitalism in Germany', in A. Teichova et al. (eds), *Banking Trade and Industry: Europe, America and Asia from the Thirteenth to the Twentieth Century* (Cambridge, 1997), pp. 136f.

Personal links between the bankers and wealthy (and influential) landowners were crucial in this respect. Since the agrarian reforms had produced substantial surplus funds in the hands of the big landowners, the latter relied on the bankers' advice on how to invest their personal property. The available investment opportunities such as government loans and mortgage bonds, however, either produced a low (and declining) return or involved high risks. It was in their common interest, therefore, that the influential Westphalian nobility pressed for State guarantees in Berlin in order to minimize the risks involved in subscribing railway shares. This, in turn, induced other, more reluctant wealth-holders to invest in railway shares of guaranteed companies such as the Cologne-Minden or Berg-Mark railway companies via the Rhenish private bankers.[10]

Outside Prussia, particularly in Southern Germany, the situation was somewhat different. Wealth-holders shied away from investing even in guaranteed shares, and the States were thus forced to build State railways.[11] In order to fund their investment projects governments had to go to the Frankfurt capital market, so that in this indirect way even the most risk-adverse Frankfurt bankers became involved in the financing of railways. Despite the close connection between the leading Frankfurt banks and railway building States, hardly any banker became directly engaged in domestic railways. M.A. Rothschild & Söhne and the other leading Frankfurt bankers became content with the introduction of foreign railway issues in the Frankfurt market. Apart from that, railways became important only as part of governmental transactions.[12]

The activities of Erlanger & Söhne, after the mid-century the outstanding Frankfurt competitor to the Rothschilds, are a telling example in this respect. Erlanger's engagement began in 1865, when for political reasons Bismarck tried to buy up the formerly Danish Southern Schleswig Railway Company, which was built and largely owned by the English railway contractor Morten Peto. From then on, Erlanger became the leading Frankfurt 'railway bank', but it hardly invested in German railway companies, instead specializing, like the Frankfurt market as a whole, in foreign railways, Russian and US railway bonds in particular.[13] The market in domestic railway shares and bonds was left to Berlin, since the leading Berlin banks had taken on the challenge. Already in 1848 Gebr. Schickler held a strong minority interest in nine railway companies. Schickler was thus the leading

---

[10]   W. Treue, 'Das Privatbankwesen im 19. Jahrhundert', in H. Coing (ed.), *Wissenschaft und Kodifikation des Privatrechts im 19. Jahrhundert*, vol. 5 (Frankfurt/Main, 1980), p. 103.

[11]   H. Winkel, 'Kapitalquellen und Kapitalverwendung am Vorabend des industriellen Aufschwungs in Deutschland', in *Schmollers Jahrbuch*, vol. 90, 1970, pp. 275–301, here pp. 288–9; Ferguson, *Geschichte*, vol. 1, p. 497.

[12]   Heyn, *Private Banking*, pp. 264–71.

[13]   N. Klarmann, 'Unternehmerische Gestaltungsmöglichkeiten des Privatbankiers im 19. Jahrhundert - dargestellt am Beispiel des Hauses Erlanger & Söhne', in H.H. Hofmann (ed.), *Bankherren und Bankiers* (Limburg, 1978), pp. 27–43.

Prussian 'railway bank' – besides Sal. Oppenheim jr. & Cie. (Cologne) and von der Heydt-Kersten & Söhne (Elberfeld).[14]

The financing of railway companies induced several private bankers to develop a primitive mixed banking by diversifying their activities into both large and risky transactions and the carrying out of payment transactions (including trade credit and current account transactions). This metamorphosis is well documented in the case of Sal. Oppenheim jr. & Cie. This bank was not only heavily engaged in the management and financing of the first West German railway, the Rhenish Railway Company Cologne-Aachen (-Antwerp), but also realized that the introduction of railways was linked to an as yet unknown demand for coal, while at the same time the future prospects of goods produced near the track would become more than promising. Already by 1832 Oppenheim had granted a mortgage loan to a coalmine near Aachen. Although it cannot be proved positively, it is very likely that Oppenheim's 1836 initiative to concentrate coalmining in the region by the creation of a joint-stock company combining almost all the mines was strongly influenced by its parallel activities in the Rhenish Railway Company.[15]

The Frankfurt bankers, lacking the experience of financing railway companies, did not engage in funding industrial undertakings. In general, they favoured cutting their risks and preserving and administering their assets rather than exposing them to the vicissitudes of the industrial age. In 1838, Moritz von Bethmann, who had every reason to look for new business opportunities if he wanted to withstand the Rothschild competition, declined the application for an involvement in a lignite mine near Frankfurt by pointing out that 'a project of this nature lies entirely outside the sphere of activities of my firm'.[16]

Historical research is unanimous that this attitude became one major reason for Frankfurt's decline as the leading German financial centre, while from the same (viz. ex post) point of view the enterprising business strategy of the Cologne and Berlin bankers finally proved to be more farsighted. In the short run, however, the risks involved in the financing of industrial undertakings were substantial and at times even threatened the existence of the bank itself. Almost all 'banking heroes' of German industrialization experienced the situation of near bankruptcy when major industrial clients came into difficulties. In the case of the already mentioned Oppenheim-bound mining company, short-term profits turned out to be much smaller than the expected margin, while at the same time additional capital was needed to become a profitable business in the long run. When by the late

[14] Treue, 'Privatbankwesen', p. 110; M. Stürmer et al., *Wägen und Wagen: Sal. Oppenheim jr. & Cie.: Geschichte einer Bank und einer Familie* (München, 1989), pp. 84–92; D. Krause, *Garn, Geld und Wechsel. 250 Jahre von der Heydt-Kersten & Söhne* (Wuppertal, 2004), pp. 31–4.

[15] G. Teichmann, 'Das Bankhaus Oppenheim und die industrielle Entwicklung im Aachener Revier von 1836–1855', in M. Köhler und K. Ulrich (eds), *Banken, Konjunktur und Politik* (Essen, 1995), pp. 10f.

[16] Heyn, *Private Banking*, p. 306.

1830s business in general slackened, local investors were no longer prepared to fund such a risky venture. In 1839, Oppenheim held about three quarters of the company's stock. The bulk of this was funded by the bank's own resources, while only a small portion was deposited on behalf of the bank's customers.[17]

Although the bank's resources consisted largely of the proprietors' personal capital, the liquidity position of the bank became dangerously strained, since at the same time the not-yet-opened railway was facing the same difficulties. When the cost estimate proved to be insufficient, the depression of the late 1830s (plus seemingly hostile Prussian railway legislation) from the outset made every effort to raise additional finance through the market a lost cause. Since the Prussian State was also very reluctant to support the company, it relied heavily on its bankers. In 1838 a consortium consisting of Oppenheim, Stein and Herstatt agreed to pay for the total of a new stock issue of 1.5 million thalers. Yet downward price movements of stock soon rendered the shares held by the banks unsaleable, and the 'lock-up' of the bankers' resources posed a serious threat to the latters' solvency. By the end of 1838 the bankers urged the board of directors to repurchase a substantial part of the company's stock in order to stabilize the price. At first the directors were very restrained, hiding themselves behind the argument that the company statutes did not allow such manipulation. Finally, however, when the bankers threatened to unload their holdings of stock completely and without regard to the losses involved, the directors agreed to take back the whole issue of 1.5 million thalers. The price which the bankers had to pay for this concession was the stipulation that they lost the whole amount of calls already paid (20 per cent) if the shares were kept in the hands of the company until mid-1839. Later, the period was prolonged until the end of that year, but the situation did not ease. In order to make sure that the Rhenish Railway was connected to the Belgian State Railway, the Belgian government finally agreed to pay for the stock before the bankers had to write off their calls.[18]

It is pointless to speculate about the outcome of the crisis if the negotiation with the Belgian government had failed, but it is quite clear from this case that a banker having realized the potential of this new venture had to invest an extremely high portion of his own resources. He could not rely on an anonymous capital market, but had to resort to private contact with the limited circle of his wealthy clients. As a consequence, the fate of the banker was intertwined with that of his industrial customers. Some banks, particularly those which had options other than industrial credits, decided to avoid such risk and to retreat from this business. An outstanding example is the Berlin bank Mendelssohn & Co. This bank, which had been both a first-rank State financier and an active 'railway bank', got into trouble from its involvement in the Cuxhafen-Stade Railway Company in 1875. As an emergency measure the Mendelssohns sold their entire interest in industrial and

---

[17]   Teichmann, 'Bankhaus', p. 13.
[18]   Stürmer et al., *Wägen*, p. 88.

railway companies and even decided to decline any invitation to join a joint-stock company's supervisory board in the future.[19]

An alternative for those who decided to stick to their interest in industry and transport was involvement in the client company's management. In the case of the Oppenheim interest in the Rhenish Railway Company, the senior partner Abraham Oppenheim had become executive director and thus combined the position of a director of the company and its banker. Conflicts of interest were unavoidable, and both sides, the shareholders and the bankers, were keen to get rid of this interlocking position. The non-bank enterprises (shareholders other than the banking interest and the non-bank bound management) supported an independent executive board, since a banker-director was much too powerful simply by the combination of these two functions. As competition among banks increased, non-bank general meetings rarely fell into such straits as to elect a banker onto the executive board. On the other hand, when the bankers came into the position of diversifying risks because investment opportunities became more widespread, they were no longer in a position to spend as much time as demanded by an executive directorship. Instead, they restricted their activities to a supervisory role.[20]

After having diversified their business activities, many bankers also 'diversified' board representation, i.e. some of them 'collected' supervisory-board seats and created a network of personal linkages between banks and up to twenty (and at times even more) industrial enterprises. The management regarded the bankers on the board not only as a necessity for ensuring injections of capital and credit in case of need, but also as most valuable advisers in business and financial matters and as sources of information on business, economics and politics.[21]

From the mid-nineteenth century on, railway companies and heavy industrial concerns grew very quickly, and the bankers' resources, which were only reluctantly replenished by customers' deposits, became insufficient in relation to the needs of big industry. This problem was realized by many bankers who then started initiatives for getting governmental concessions for joint-stock credit banks. The German States, however, Prussia in particular, were not at all willing to liberalize joint-stock legislation, and, as concessions for industrial joint-stock

---

[19] W. Treue, 'Das Bankhaus Mendelssohn als Beispiel einer Privatbank im 19. und 20. Jahrhundert', in *Mendelssohn Studien*, vol. 1, 1972, pp. 29–80, here p. 54.

[20] H. Wixforth and D. Ziegler, '"Bankenmacht": Universal Banking and German Industry in Historical Perspective', in Y. Cassis et al. (eds), *The Evolution of Financial Institutions and Markets in Twentieth-Century Europe* (Aldershot, 1995), pp. 256ff.

[21] H. Wixforth and D. Ziegler, 'The Niche in the Universal Banking System: the Role and Significance of Private Bankers within German Industry', in *Financial History Review*, vol. 1, 1994, pp. 99–119, here p. 104; M. Reitmayer, 'Der Strukturwandel im Bankwesen und seine Folgen für die Geschäftstätigkeit der Privatbankiers im Deutschen Reich bis 1914', in idem, *Der Privatbankier: Nischenstrategien in Geschichte und Gegenwart* (Stuttgart, 2003), p. 14.

companies were only very reluctantly granted, banking concessions were almost always rejected until the 1860s.[22]

A major exception was the Bayerische Hypotheken- und Wechselbank, founded in 1835. This bank, a combination of mortgage bank, discount house and bank of issue was founded on the initiative of the Bavarian King. At first, the Munich and Augsburg bankers, including the court banker Simon von Eichthal, were not prepared to subscribe the bank's capital, but the King succeeded in interesting the Frankfurt banker Carl von Rothschild and thus forced all major Bavarian bankers to join the initiative. Eichthal even became one of the bank's two honorary directors.[23]

Occasionally, joint-stock banks were founded by the conversion of existing private banking houses – in some cases because the family business with its limited resources could no longer withstand their customers' demand for capital and credit and in some cases because the family was no longer in a position to supply able successors when senior partners retired. Two examples are outstanding. The Bayerische Vereinsbank was founded by taking over the business of the leading Munich bank, Robert von Froelich & Co. (formerly known as A.E. von Eichthal),[24] and the Dresdner Bank was established by the conversion of the Dresden private bank Michael Kaskel. Kaskel was one of the very few successors of former court Jews who successfully transformed their business not only into State financing, but also towards granting credits to modern industry and transport. Carl Kaskel, a brother-in-law of Simon Oppenheim, had also been a railway promoter and became the supervisory-board chairman of the Austrian Aussig-Teplitzer Railway Company. As in many other cases, the successor problem determined the fate of this bank too. The family decided to join the Dresden banking house Gutmann and to convert the business into a joint-stock bank. Although Gutmann had been a much smaller bank, it had recently overcome the generation break thanks to an able and enterprising young family member, Eugen Gutmann. While the senior member of the Kaskel family, Felix Kaskel, was elected supervisory-board chairman, Gutmann became a member of the Dresdner Bank executive board;[25] he kept the position as head of the bank for more than forty years.

---

[22]   J.M. Brophy, *Capitalism, Politics, and Railroads in Prussia 1830–1970* (Columbus, 1998), pp. 87–106.

[23]   F. Jungmann-Stadler, 'Die Gründung der Bayerischen Hypotheken- und Wechselbank 1834/35', in *Zeitschrift für Bayerische Landesgeschichte*, vol. 60, 1997, pp. 889–924, here p. 920.

[24]   M. Pohl, *Konzentration im deutschen Bankwesen (1848–1980)* (Frankfurt/Main, 1982), p. 39.

[25]   J. Kaskel, 'Vom Hoffaktor zur Dresdner Bank: Die Unternehmerfamilie Kaskel im 18. und 19. Jahrhundert', in *Zeitschrift für Unternehmensgeschichte*, vol. 28, 1983, pp. 159–87, here p. 162; D. Ziegler, 'Eugen Gutmann – Unternehmer und Großbürger', in *Eugen-Gutmann-Gesellschaft – Gründungsversammlung* (Frankfurt/Main, 2003, unpublished), p. 23.

Schaaffhausenscher Bankverein, the first Prussian joint-stock credit bank, was founded in 1848 on the wrecked private bank Abraham Schaaffhausen, formerly the leading bank in Cologne. Like the Oppenheims, Schaaffhausen had begun to finance Rhenish industry during the 1830s, at first by short-term loans to textile firms, but later also by long-term loans to shipping and railway companies, insurances and coalmines. As outlined above, these activities involved substantial risks, but Schaaffhausen was not as fortunate as Oppenheim ten years earlier and had to suspend payments during the revolutionary weeks in March 1848. Luckily, the revolution had brought liberal Rhenish railway entrepreneurs to power in Berlin, who temporarily lifted the ban on joint-stock credit bank concessions and approved the establishment of Schaaffhausenscher Bankverein by converting the bank's debts into stock. The continuity between the former private bank and the new joint-stock bank was striking. Despite the bank's failure the former partners, Victor Wendelstadt and Wilhelm Deichmann, kept their positions and were elected members of the executive board of the bank.[26]

By this time a joint-stock bank was no 'managerial enterprise' in a modern sense, but rather an enlarged private bank. The head of the bank as a particular person was at least as important for the bank's success as the enlarged resources. Not surprisingly therefore, other joint-stock banks that were erected upon failed private banks also resorted to former partners, as in the case of Gustav Adolf Fischer, partner in the failed Barmen private bank Gebr. Fischer. He became a member of the executive board when the Barmer Bankverein Hinsberg, Fischer & Co. was founded on the remnants of the liquidated private bank in 1867.[27]

It cannot be denied that the French Crédit Mobilier was seen as a model for the German credit banks founded in succession to the Schaaffhausenscher Bankverein, but it is also true that the mixed-banking experience gained by several private bankers proved to be the decisive factor for the nascent universal banks' success.[28] Thus, almost all successful joint-stock banks were founded by experienced private bankers:

> – Darmstädter Bank (by the Cologne banker Sal. Oppenheim jr. & Cie. and by the Frankfurt bankers Gebr. Bethmann and Goll & Söhne),
> – Berliner Handelsgesellschaft (by the most important Berlin bankers including S. Bleichröder, Mendelssohn & Co., Breest & Gelpcke and Robert Warschauer, but also by Oppenheim again),
> – Mitteldeutsche Kreditbank (by a group of less important Frankfurt bankers consisting of R. Sulzbach, J.J. Weiller Söhne, S.M. Schwarzschild and the Leipzig banker Becker & Co.),

---

[26]   Tilly, *Financial Institutions*, p. 112; Brophy, *Capitalism*, p. 91.

[27]   *Hundert Jahre Commerzbank*, 1870–1970 (Frankfurt/Main, 1970), pp. 109ff.

[28]   R. Tilly, 'German Banking, 1850–1914: Development Assistance for the Strong', in *Journal of European Economic History*, vol. 15, 1986, pp. 113–52, here p. 118.

– Deutsche Bank (by almost all important Berlin bankers led by Delbrück, Leo & Co. and many other bankers from Bremen, Cologne, Frankfurt and other places),
– Commerz- und Discontobank (by several Hamburg bankers including Hesse, Newman & Co. and C.H. Donner, but also by the Berlin banker Mendelssohns & Co.).[29]

In contrast to Schaaffhausenscher Bankverein and Barmer Bankverein, these founding activities can be interpreted as an attempt to institutionalize some form of cartel for those transactions which had become too large for a single private banking house. Consequently, the relationship between the bankers and 'their' joint-stock banks was more or less cordial and the bankers still kept both an influential position and adequate quotas in all syndicate agreements.[30] In international syndicates their foreign partners at times even refused the participation of the novel joint-stock banks and cooperated only with the established private bankers. In all, the 1830s to 1880s can be seen as the 'heyday' of private banking in Germany.

Private Banking in Decline?

Until recently, the substantial decline in the number of private banks after the turn of the century has led to an unwarranted overestimation of their relative decline in importance for the functioning of the universal banking system. A glance into the statistics which reflect the quantitative development of private banking during the first half of the twentieth century suggests that the significance of this type of bank has declined considerably. Such quantitative data can be interpreted to the effect that while many private bankers had played an important role in the early phase of German industrialization, in the process of maturing economic development their significance and influence in industry and commerce constantly declined. The weakening of the formerly dominant position of the private bankers in the banking system cannot and will not be denied on principle, but the simple fact has to be qualified.

Despite some notorious cases of formerly first-rate private banks – M.A. Rothschild & Söhne was sold to the Discontogesellschaft in 1901 and Robert

[29]   M. Pohl et al., *Deutsche Bankengeschichte*, 3 vols (Frankfurt/Main, 1982), vol. 2, pp. 182–6, 264–8; Pohl, *Konzentration*, pp. 67–74, 107–16; C. Burhop, *Die Kreditbanken in der Gründerzeit* (Stuttgart, 2004), pp. 90–106.

[30]   P. Hertner, 'German Banks Abroad Before 1914', in G. Jones (ed.), *Banks as Multinationals* (London, 1990), pp. 99–119; R. Tilly, 'International Aspects of the Development of German Banking', in R. Cameron and V. Bovykin (eds), *International Banking 1870–1914* (Oxford, 1991), pp. 90–112; B. Barth, 'Deutsch-jüdisch-europäische Privatbankengruppen vor und nach dem Ersten Weltkrieg', Arbeitskreis für Bankgeschichte der GUG, Arbeitspapier no. 5 (1997, unpublished).

Warschauer & Co. to the Darmstädter Bank in 1904[31] – until the banking crisis of 1931 it was rather the provincial and smaller metropolitan bankers who fell victim to the concentration process. By the turn of the century the local joint-stock banks had begun to tap local middle-class savings by opening branches and using the backing of these resources to compete for the financing of the 'Mittelstand,' which had been the domain of local private bankers. In addition to their larger means, the provincial joint-stock banks began to supersede current-account credit by the cheaper acceptance credit, in which the local private banker with his limited credit standing was also unable to compete. This 'evolutionary' displacement of the provincial banker was reinforced by stock-exchange legislation reforms during the 1880s and 1890s, which privileged Berlin and Frankfurt bankers, particularly the Berlin great banks, in the stockbroking business.[32] These most unfavourable circumstances forced many private bankers to sell their businesses to a provincial joint-stock bank, to convert the bank into a branch, and to become a director of the bank (in the case of larger private banks) or at least to become the manager of the branch (in the case of smaller houses).[33]

In order to keep up with the growth potential of the competing provincial joint-stock companies, some of the larger provincial private banks reacted by adopting limited liability and becoming provincial joint-stock banks themselves. The Meiningen private bank B.M Strupp was converted into Bank für Thüringen vorm. B.M. Strupp AG in 1905. In the same year, the Stuttgart private bank Stahl & Federer was converted into Stahl & Federer AG. Until 1919 this bank adopted an aggressive amalgamation policy by taking over thirteen provincial private banking houses and thus building up a dense network of branches in Württemberg.[34] Also in 1905 the Mannheim private banking house W.H. Ladenburg & Söhne, which was for decades closely connected with one of the largest German chemical firms, the Badische Anilin und Soda Fabrik (BASF), was converted into Süddeutsche Discontogesellschaft, in order to keep up with the fast-growing demand from the Mannheim and Ludwigshafen industry. Thanks to the participation of the (Berlin) Discontogesellschaft, the Ladenburg bank became one of the largest South German credit banks. However, despite the great bank's interest the Ladenburg family kept control of 'its' bank. The Discontogesellschaft was only allowed to hold stock worth 8m. Marks, while the family kept the rest, 12m. Marks.[35]

---

[31]   Pohl, *Konzentration*, p. 237; Ferguson, *Geschichte*, vol. 2, p. 294.

[32]   C. Meier, *Die Entstehung des Börsengesetzes vom 22. Juni 1896* (St Katharinen, 1993); C. Wetzel, *Die Auswirkungen des Reichsbörsengesetzes von 1896 auf die Effektenbörsen im Deutschen Reich* (Münster, 1996).

[33]   K. Donaubauer, *Privatbankiers und Bankenkonzentration in Deutschland von der Mitte des 19. Jahrhunderts bis 1932* (Frankfurt/Main, 1988), p. 99.

[34]   M. Bergner, *Das württembergische Bankwesen: Entstehung, Ausbau und struktureller Wandel des regionalen Bankwesens bis 1923* (St Katharinen, 1993), p. 333ff.

[35]   B. Kirchgässner, 'Zur Geschichte der Deutschen Bank Mannheim und ihrer Vorgänger (1785–1929)', in *Beiträge zu Wirtschafts- und Währungsfragen und zur*

These examples clearly indicate that by the turn of the century at the latest even the largest private banks were facing the problem of limited resources. Those banks which were not prepared either to follow the Ladenburg example of cooperating with a great bank in order to enlarge the capital base or to follow the Stahl & Federer example by building up a branch network in order to develop the deposit business had to give away some of their formerly most important business activities. Even outstanding private banking houses like Sal. Oppenheim jr. & Cie. had lost major industrial customers to the great banks,[36] as their means became insufficient to supply the growing demand for capital and credit by big industry.

Issuing foreign loans and financing international trade constituted a second field of competition between the great banks and the leading private bankers. The great banks' (and their overseas subsidiaries') attempts to gain a foothold in overseas finance was limited. Many private bankers kept their position, partly because of their expertise, partly because the international syndicates were still led by Paris and London private (and merchant) bankers, and, later, New York investment bankers, all of whom had not only been in close contact with their German counterparts for decades, but were often even related by kinship. For these reasons, the most internationally orientated of the great banks, Deutsche Bank, failed to supersede the Mendelssohns as the leader of the Russian State loan syndicate; and similarly, the Deutsche Bank's attempts to attack the leading position of the Rothschild and Baring syndicates in the Latin American State loan market were equally unsuccessful.[37]

Although the private bankers' continuing success in international finance is seemingly of no importance for the purpose of this chapter, during the interwar period, and particularly during the 1920s, their former international orientation became a major factor for survival, because it turned out to be a competitive advantage in the provision of funds for big industry. Before 1914, Germany had been a net exporter of capital, and access to foreign capital markets had been of little importance for German industry. After the War, however, and particularly following the inflation, due to dramatically diminished working capital, almost all industrial companies were forced to fund necessary rationalization and reorganization schemes by credit. Since German capital markets were unable to meet this demand, big industry turned overseas. In this situation some old-established private banks scented their chance quickly and revived their old contacts overseas in order to facilitate the capital flows – but now in the opposite direction as compared with the Kaiserreich.[38]

The Essen banking house Simon Hirschland was particularly successful. Already in early 1924 it managed to secure for the big steel concern Gutehoffnungshütte

---

Bankgeschichte, vol. 23, 1988, pp. 59–92, here p. 81.

[36]   W. Feldenkirchen, 'Kölner Banken und die Entwicklung des Ruhrgebietes', in *Zeitschrift für Unternehmensgeschichte*, vol. 27, 1982, pp. 81–106, here p. 102.

[37]   Barth, 'Privatbankengruppen'.

[38]   Wixforth et al., 'Niche', pp. 113–16.

AV a £100,000 sterling credit, granted by a group of London bankers. Not only was this credit renewed several times during 1924/25, but Hirschland also acted as an intermediary for further credits, variously denominated in either Sterling or Dollars, supplied internationally to Gutehoffnungshütte. The Essen bank obtained comparable facilities for Mannesmann Röhrenwerke, August Thyssen-Hütte, Gelsenkirchener Bergwerks AG, Rheinisch-Westfälische Elektrizitätswerke, Klöckner, Phoenix, Krupp and Vereinigte Stahlwerke.[39]

No less important than Hirschland in the intermediation of foreign capital – in this case particularly US capital – were Warburg, the Hamburg bankers. Paul Warburg, a brother of the Hamburg banker Max, was a founder of the International Acceptance Bank, established in New York in 1921, which specialized in granting dollar-denominated credits to foreign industrial concerns. The International Acceptance Bank not only collaborated with the Equitable Trust Company, one of the largest New York banks, but also had an interest in the banking house Dillon, Read & Co., one of the most important New York issuing houses. Several German industrial companies (Thyssen, Rheinelbe-Union and Vereinigte Stahlwerke) utilized the connection between M.M. Warburg & Co., the International Acceptance Bank and Dillon Read to issue stock in New York on substantially better terms than those then obtainable in Germany.[40]

There are other examples of private banking houses putting their international contacts at the disposal of their industrial customers. Sal. Oppenheim jr. & Cie., which had traditional close ties with French banks, negotiated franc-denominated credits for German customers during inflation and stabilization. Even Mendelssohn & Co., which had terminated its contact with industrial customers in the 1870s, obtained foreign credits for some large industrial customers (Phoenix and Vereinigte Stahlwerke) between 1924 and 1932 through its Amsterdam[41] and New York branches.[42]

---

[39]   H. Wixforth, *Banken und Schwerindustrie in der Weimarer Republik* (Cologne, 1995), pp. 118, 138; K. Ulrich, 'Von Simon Hirschland zu Burkhardt & Co.: Die Geschichte des traditionsreichsten Bankhauses des Ruhrgebietes', in J.-P. Barbian and L. Heid (eds), *Die Entstehung des Ruhrgebietes* (Düsseldorf, 1996), pp. 430–33; K. Ulrich, *Aufstieg und Fall der Privatbankiers: Die wirtschaftliche Entwicklung von 1918 bis 1938* (Frankfurt/Main, 1998), pp. 115–18.

[40]   R. Chernow, *Die Warburgs: Odyssee einer Familie* (Berlin, 1994), p. 285; Ulrich, *Aufstieg*, pp. 106–8; E. Kleßmann, *M.M. Warburg & Co.: Die Geschichte eines Bankhauses* (Hamburg, 1999), p. 77.

[41]   The Amsterdam new-issue market was dominated by two syndicates. The most important syndicate, responsible for a market share of about 40 per cent during the second half of the 1920s, consisted of the Nederlandsche Handel Maatschappij, Pierson & Co., Mees & Zoonen and Mendelssohn & Co. See C. Kreutzmüller, *Händler und Handlungsgehilfen: Der Finanzplatz Amsterdam und die deutschen Großbanken (1918–1945)* (Stuttgart, 2005), p. 42.

[42]   Wixforth et al., 'Niche', p. 115.

The outstanding importance of several private banks for the mobilization of foreign capital during the 1920s and particularly after the inflation contrasts significantly with their generally declining involvement in industrial finance before the First World War. One reason for their ability to raise foreign finance more easily, more rapidly and on more favourable terms than the great banks arose from their overseas connections. These stemmed from their tradition of conducting mutual business across international centres, long-established kinship linkages between the various cosmopolitan banking dynasties, and common behaviour patterns resulting from the particular social pre-eminence of the international banking elite. Second, the financing of international trade remained a domain of the largest international private bankers. After the war, and particularly after the inflation, the German great banks faced substantial internal problems. Their managerial capacities were absorbed in handling these problems to a much greater extent than the smaller and more flexible private banks. In addition, the restrictive policy pursued by the Reichsbank after the hyperinflation forced the great banks to shy away from risky ventures. Many private bankers – even those who, like Hirschland, were not among the most important houses before 1914 – perceived the unique opportunity for diversifying their business of financing international trade through additionally negotiating international loans. During the stabilization period of the mid-1920s private bankers predominated in this segment of the finance markets. The great banks began to compete once more in international finance only from 1926 or 1927.[43]

The flowering of private banking during the inflation was thus not simply illusory – this was true only for small local bankers, which had been large in numbers, but had not even then been an important component of the financial markets. Instead, the pre-1931 second flowering of the leading German private banks was well founded, and there was no sign of a sudden fading. They were able to utilize the niches of the universal banking system, that is, they provided those services which neither the great banks nor the savings banks were able to supply: besides their international contacts the private bankers' inside knowledge derived from their intimate contact with other bankers, diplomats, politicians and industrialists as well as their fairly independent position as neither major shareholders nor big creditors, while both qualified them for advisory services in all financial and business matters.

The network of personal linkages among various big industrial concerns, and between banks and industrial undertakings, which arose from the accumulation of board seats in these companies, is more than simply a proxy of the private bankers' importance in the financial markets. In 1906, leading bankers Louis Hagen (A. Levy, Cologne), Ludwig Delbrück (Delbrück, Leo & Co., Berlin) and Eduard v. Oppenheim (Sal. Oppenheim jr. & Cie., Cologne) held up to about forty joint-stock company supervisory-board seats each. Hardly any great bank director held more. Until the late 1920s private bankers continued to occupy a central position in the

---

43   Wixforth et al., 'Niche', p. 116.

bank-industry network constituted by interlocking directorships. In 1927 their pre-eminence had even increased, since Louis Hagen, Simon Alfred v. Oppenheim, Heinrich v. Stein (I.H. Stein, Cologne) and Johann Friedrich Schröder (Schröder Bank KGaA, Bremen) held between 41 and 58 supervisory-board seats each. Only the former private banker Jacob Goldschmidt (Darmstädter und Nationalbank) and Curt Sobernheim (Commerz- und Privatbank), descendant of a former Breslau private-banking dynasty, had accumulated more seats.[44]

It is a significant contrast to their relatively small capital resources that about one third of all bank representatives among those persons with more than 15 supervisory-board seats were private bankers. While the presence of great bank directors and 'big' industrialists can be explained by the importance of the financial resources they commanded, the private bankers were 'outsiders' having few financial resources, but were qualified by their capability to coordinate business policies beyond the scope of an individual company.

In addition to the number of supervisory-board seats occupied by private bankers, a second indicator, being named as dividend payment office for joint-stock companies, also proves the bankers' growing involvement in the financing of industry and commerce during the 1910s and 1920s. Between 1906 and 1927 the average number of namings of the leading houses had increased by about 20 per cent. This held for the leading private bankers of the Kaiserreich such as Delbrück, Schickler & Co., which increased its number of namings from 76 (combined Delbrück, Leo & Co. and Gebr. Schickler) in 1906 to 98 in 1927, and Gebr. Arnhold (from 78 to 96 namings), but in particular for the 'newcomers' in industrial finance such as M.M. Warburg & Co. (from 7 to 61 namings) and S. Hirschland (no namings in 1906, but 36 in 1927).[45]

The number of namings as dividend payment office is not only instructive as regards the importance of private bankers as a component of the financial market as such, but also proves the continuing success of the leading houses during the first three decades of the twentieth century. None of the twenty most important banking houses of 1906 (defined by this indicator) had failed by 1927, and only two of these banks had been taken over by a great bank. Those which disappeared between 1906 and 1927 had merged with another private bank and reappeared as a 'new' bank. Mergers between private banks were no common feature of the amalgamation movement of German banking in this period, but at times important provincial private bankers attempted to merge with a Berlin bank in order to get their foot in the door of the Reich's most important financial market. The two outstanding cases are the mergers of the leading Frankfurt private banks of Dreyfus & Co. and Lazard, Speyer-Ellissen with the Berlin banks of S.L. Landsberger

---

[44]   D. Ziegler, 'Geschäftliche Spezialisierungen deutscher Privatbankiers in der Zwischenkriegszeit: Ein vergeblicher Überlebenskampf?', in idem, *Der Privatbankier: Nischenstrategien in Geschichte und Gegenwart* (Stuttgart, 2003a), table 5, p. 221.

[45]   H. Wixforth and D. Ziegler, 'Deutsche Privatbanken und Privatbankiers im 20. Jahrhundert', in *Geschichte und Gesellschaft*, vol. 23, 1997, pp. 205–35, here table 4, p. 220.

(1919) and C. Schlesinger-Trier & Co. (1929) respectively. By the early 1930s these amalgamated banks had become the two leading Frankfurt private banking houses (as defined by this indicator) and had reached the 'Top Ten' of German private banks.[46]

The crisis of 1931 had changed the situation completely. No doubt the fact that many private bankers had speculated in foreign exchange and in stocks backed mainly by interbank loans was a major reason for the breakdown of several of the leading private banks after 1931. But this is not the whole truth. The reluctance on the part of the Reichsbank to refinance private banks during the banking crisis and the one-sided Government aid for the great banks between 1931 and 1933 were at least as important. The de facto State guarantee for great-bank deposits induced many customers to turn their backs on their former house bank and reduced the bankers' liquidity even further.[47]

While the banking crisis ended a period of remarkable stability for the leading private banks, the crisis is not sufficient to explain the termination of the private banks' importance as a relevant component of the finance market as such. In addition to the non-economic factor of one-sided State aid in favour of the great banks, the final reason was purely political: anti-Semitism as an accepted factor in business after the seizure of power by the National Socialists in January 1933.

From the early stages of industrialization, a majority of private bankers – not to speak of the court bankers – was Jewish or at least of Jewish origins. Of the leading twenty-five German private banks of 1933 (as defined by dividend payment office namings) twenty-one were described as 'Jewish'. As the period between the outbreak of the crisis (July 1931) and the National Socialist seizure of power was very short, it is not always possible to clearly identify the final reason for the breakdown of a given bank. In some cases, such as A. Levy (Cologne), Hagen & Co. (Berlin), Ephr. Meyer (Hanover) and Lazard, Speyer-Ellissen (Frankfurt), it is quite probable that these banks would have had to be liquidated even without the political changes.[48] But these cases are exceptions. The rest survived the repercussions of the crisis, but were either liquidated (4) or 'Aryanized' (12) between 1936 and 1938. The only exception was Sal. Oppenheim jr. & Cie., which was labelled 'Christian' and survived until the final stage of the War on condition that the Jewish partners (as defined by the Nuremberg Laws) left the bank and that the bank was renamed Pferdmenges & Co.

When the forced 'aryanization' set in, the 'Jewish' banks had already lost their former importance in many respects. First, the bankers' international connections

[46]   Wixforth et al., 'Privatbanken', table 4, p. 220. See also R. Heilbrunn, *Das Bankhaus J. Dreyfus & Co. 1868–1939* (Frankfurt/Main,1962, Unpublished).

[47]   W. Winterstein, 'Privatbanken', in H. Pohl (ed.), *Das Bankwesen in Deutschland und Spanien 1860–1960* (Frankfurt, 1997), p. 98.

[48]   Ziegler, 'Spezialisierungen', p. 35; I. Köhler, *Die 'Arisierung' der Privatbanken im Dritten Reich: Verdrängung, Ausschaltung und die Frage der Wiedergutmachung* (Munich, 2005), pp. 53ff.

saved many of the banks from violent action by the radical mob, but they became less important as a comparative business advantage, because from about 1937 the autarkic economic policy of the Third Reich made access to foreign capital markets obsolete. Second, the 'outside' bankers' consultative services were equally no longer required. The Jewish private bankers lost many important supervisory-board seats, which seriously impaired their consultative capacity. More generally, self-financing predominated and the capital and credit markets were highly regulated, so that industrial companies only rarely had to decide between alternatives in financial matters for which an independent adviser was needed. Third, many customers had terminated their business relations with 'Jewish banks' as they feared negative effects, especially if they were dependent on State orders.

By late 1938, when the 'Aryanization' of the German private banks was completed, the result was that those private banks which were 'Aryanized' but remained independent, such as M.M. Warburg & Co. (from 1941 Brinckmann, Wirtz & Co.) and S. Hirschland (from 1938 Burkhardt & Co.), had already become too weak to recover their former importance. None of the new proprietors entered the top ranks in the bank-industry network of interlocking directorships. Only those 'gentile' private banks which had 'Aryanized' a 'Jewish' bank by merger, such as Hardy & Co. (itself purged of its Jewish managing directors) and Merck, Finck & Co. kept their position. But with the exception of the leading Nazi banker Kurt von Schröder (I.H. Stein, Cologne), hardly any private banker was playing a leading role in the German economy when the war began.[49]

Conclusion

This chapter has attempted to show that private banking played an important role for the mobilization of funds during the crucial period of early industrialization in Germany. Several private bankers, particularly those from larger provincial towns such as Cologne and Elberfeld, did not simply introduce the Crédit Mobilier style of banks (and banking) into the 'German' economy, but played a decisive role in the intermediation of funds, and at times even provided funds for industry and transport from their own limited resources. By the mid-1850s, when the first joint-stock credit banks were founded, the basic railway network connecting almost all important German Zollverein States was already built. By that time its aggregate length (5,850 km by 1850) was second only to the British network.

---

[49]   A. Fischer, 'Jüdische Privatbanken im "Dritten Reich" ', in *Scripta Mercaturae*, vol. 28, 1994, pp. 1–53, p. 38; C. Kopper, *Zwischen Marktwirtschaft und Dirigismus: Bankenpolitik im 'Dritten Reich' 1933–1939* (Bonn, 1995), pp. 254–91; H. James, *Verbandspolitik im Nationalsozialismus. Von der Interessenvertretung zur Wirtschaftsgruppe: Der Centralverband des deutschen Bank- und Bankiergewerbes 1932–1945* (Munich, 2001), pp. 263–8; Ziegler, 'Spezialisierungen' pp. 36–45; Köhler, *'Arisierung'*, pp. 173–91.

When the big heavy industrial concerns appeared, the establishment of joint-stock credit banks became inevitable, since the resources of individual private bankers soon became insufficient compared with the credit demand of big industry. This did not mean, however, that private bankers became superfluous, whether in the short or the long term. Industry and commerce were not confined to big concerns and, in particular, medium-sized industry in the provinces relied on local private bankers well into the twentieth century. Only by the turn of the century did the larger provincial joint-stock banks begin to build up their regional branch networks. For the local private banks the situation became additionally strained by the First World War, when the savings banks developed as local universal banks too. Thus, even before the banking crisis of 1931 this segment of private banking had fallen victim to the concentration process in banking; but the leading private bankers were hardly touched by this development.

The substantial decline in the number of private banks has led to an unwarranted general overestimation of their relative decline in importance for the functioning of the universal banking system. Until the end of the Weimar Republic, a significant number of private banks was able to withstand the competition of the great banks by supplying services which the latter were unwilling on principle (because of the administrative centralization and the necessary bureaucratization and hierarchicalization of management decisions), and at least at times (obtaining foreign credits during the stabilization crisis) unable to provide.

This means that, first, we have to postpone the decisive weakening of the German private banks to the 1930s, and second, that we have to provide an alternative to the contemporary explanation that stresses the declining competitiveness of the private banks in the long run. The evolution of the German universal banking system did not render private banks generally superfluous. On the contrary, the evolutionary development had created a division of labour in which a limited number of private banks had gained an important position. Consequently, we need additional non-economic, exogenous factors in order to explain the interruption of this evolutionary process. In addition to the destruction of many niches, the most important of these factors was the racist policy of the Third Reich.

CHAPTER 10

Private Bankers and Italian Industrialisation

Luciano Segreto

Introduction

The role of private bankers in the process of Italian industrial development has never been studied in depth and detail. On the other hand, studies on the relations between banks and industry have, in general, focused on the changes wrought in the Italian financial system by the process of reorganisation of the entire Italian banking system that began in the mid-1990s. The emergence of the Banca d'Italia generated the initial reorganisation of the issuing banks, and the consolidation of the mixed bank brought the Italian banking world significantly closer to the European standards. Effectively, since according to many economic historians this process was functional to if not actually decisive for Italian industrialisation, over the last thirty years studies on banking in Italy have concentrated specifically on the development of the relations between the mixed banks and the sphere of industrial enterprise, through an attentive examination of Gerschenkron's model for Italy. An initial phase, marked by a substantial confirmation of the validity of this explicative model, was followed by a partial decline (and the consequent strengthening of revisionist positions), which nevertheless opened the path to a clearer understanding of the role played by the Bank d'Italia and the State, not only in the modernisation of the financial system, but above all in the definition of a stable framework within which mechanisms of accumulation were guaranteed in a country on the road to industrialisation.[1] This evolution of the debate paved

[1]   A. Gerschenkron, *Il problema storico dell'arretratezza economica* (Turin, 1965); S. Fenoaltea, 'Decollo, ciclo e intervento dello stato', in A. Caracciolo (ed.), *La formazione dell'Italia industriale* (Bari, 1969); S. Fenoaltea, 'Riflessioni sull'esperienza italiana dal Risorgimento alla prima guerra mondiale', in G. Toniolo (ed.), *Lo sviluppo economico italiano 1861–1940* (Bari, 1973); A. Confalonieri, *Banca e industria in Italia* (Milan, 1975, 3 vols); F. Bonelli, 'Il capitalismo italiano. Linee generali di interpretazione', in *Storia d'Italia, Annali 1* (Turin, 1978), pp. 1193–255; P. Hertner, *Il capitale tedesco in Italia dall'Unità alla prima guerra mondiale: Banche miste e sviluppo economico italiano* (Bologna, 1984); G. Toniolo, *Storia economica dell'Italia liberale 1850–1918* (Bologna, 1988); more recent S. Battilossi, 'The History of Banking in Italy: the Debate from the Gerschenkronian Mixed Banks to the Financial Road to Development', in G.D. Feldman et al. (eds), *The Evolution of Modern Financial Institutions in Twentieth Century*, B 12, Proceedings, Eleventh International Economic History Congress (Milan, 1994), pp. 117–39; A. Polsi, *Stato e banca centrale in Italia. Il governo della moneta e del sistema bancario dall'Ottocento a oggi* (Rome Bari, 2001).

the way for the application to the Italian case also of Goldsmith's conceptual instruments of a statistical-accounting nature.[2] This made it possible, in the first place, to show how in Italy, in the period following the emergence of the mixed banks, the financiatial intermediation ratio indicator (FIN) was higher than that of other industrialised countries and that there was an elevated and precocious institutionalisation of the credit system, and that consequently the Italian case came within the financing schema. In the second place, it showed that the increase in the financial inter-relation ratio (FIR) was very high in the interwar period (1914–1938), but very low in the period of industrialisation (1881–1914). Thus, at a merely quantitative level, exploding 'the theory that in the initial launch of Italian industry, given the "forced" nature of the process, the overall role of finance [...] was more important than in other periods'. Such considerations, nevertheless, ended up by strengthening rather than undermining Gerschenkron's theory, confirming that the credits of the financial intermediaries, and in particular those of the mixed banks 'replaced others rather than augmenting them' and that, in view of the considerable contribution made by such credit institutes to the increase of the FIN they must have had 'a specific 'qualitative' tendency [...] to foster the industrial and economic development of the country' between 1895 and 1913.[3]

Nonetheless, all these studies very carefully avoided considering the role played by private bankers both before the reorganisation of the credit system and after the birth and consolidation of the mixed bank. References to the importance of these economic entities had not been lacking in the past. As observed by Franco Bonelli,[4] in the 1920s Luigi Einaudi had already drawn attention to the role played by the minor banks and by private bankers in enabling the major credit institutions that emerged at the end of the last century (Banca Commerciale Italiana, Credito Italiano) to expand their sphere of action to a clientele traditionally bound to the private banks by relations of trust, and at times even family connections.[5] About thirty years ago, the same concept was confirmed by the then governor of the Banca d'Italia, Guido Carli.[6] The difficulty – up until very recently – of accessing direct archive sources was for a long time a serious impediment to the progress of such studies. Recently, however, several important steps forward have been made, primarily thanks to a younger generation of scholars who have adopted an

---

[2]   R.W. Goldsmith, *Financial Structure and Development* (New Haven, 1969).

[3]   A.M. Biscaini Cotula and P.L. Ciocca, 'Le struttura finanziarie: aspetti quantitativi di lungo periodo (1870–1979)', in F. Vicarelli (ed.), *Capitale industriale e capitale finanziario: il caso italiano* (Bologna, 1979), pp. 65–75 (quotations are on pp. 67, 70 and 75).

[4]   F. Bonelli, *La crisi del 1907: Una tappa dello sviluppo industriale in Italia* (Turin, 1971), p. 14.

[5]   L. Einaudi, 'Prefazione' to M. Segre, *Le banche nell'ultimo decennio con particolare riguardo al loro sviluppo patologico nel dopoguerra* (Milan, 1926), p. III.

[6]   See his preface to R. De Mattia (ed.), *Banca d'Italia, I bilanci degli Istituti di emissione italiana dal 1883 al 1936, altre serie storiche di interesse monetario e fonti* (Rome, 1967), vol. I, p. XVI.

original approach to the study of private bankers. The two most significant cases are those of the Milanese and the Florentine bankers in the pre-unitary period. In the first case, the activity of the private bankers is considered as functional not only to the provision of resources for productive investments, but also to fostering dynamic processes for the creation and management of means of payment, fruitfully exploiting the vast body of theoretical literature on the subject.[7] In the second case, they swiftly rule out the idea that there was no financial market in Tuscany in the first half of the nineteenth century.[8] This idea was derived from the general conviction that, for the entire nineteenth century and a good part of the twentieth, any real financial market in Italy was insubstantial or even non-existent. This concept was in its turn linked to the view – for long prevalent in Italian historiography – that the financial system of the new unified State, and even more so in the pre-unitary States was underdeveloped, governed within the territory by regional traditions that exacerbated its backwardness and was in a subordinate relation to the international finance of England and France.[9] This vision began to be partially called into question by global studies of the national banking system, which among other things also began to focus the research on the private bankers.[10]

The specific objective of this chapter is to offer an initial, albeit summary, overall reconstruction of the role played by the Italian private bankers in the period from the mid-nineteenth century up to the First World War, although the emphasis will be placed above all on the decades following national unification.

The Private Banker in Pre-Unitary Italy

The very definition of the entity is somewhat complex. Effectively, the term 'private banker' has an ambiguous connotation that goes beyond the Italian

---

[7]   G. Piluso, *Dalla seta alla banca: Moneta e credito a Milano nell'Ottocento (1802–1860)*, Università Bocconi, dottorato di ricerca in Storia economica e sociale, VIII ciclo, anni accademici 1994–96, p. 11; G. Piluso, *L'arte dei banchieri: Moneta e credito a Milano da Napoleone all'Unità* (Milan, 1999) and G. Piluso, *Il mercato del credito a Milano dopo l'Unità: strutture e dinamiche evolutive*, in *Banche e reti di banche nell'Italia postunitaria*, ed. by G. Conti and S. La Francesca, vol. II, *Formazione e sviluppo di mercati locali del credito* (Bologna, 2000), pp. 503–56.

[8]   A. Volpi, *Banchieri e mercato finanziario in Toscana (1801–1860)* (Firenze, 1997).

[9]   L. De Rosa, 'La formazione del sistema bancario italiano', in *Società Italiana degli Storici dell'Economia, Credito e sviluppo economico in Italia dal Medio Evo all'Età contemporanea*, Atti del primo convegno nazionale, 4–6 June 1987 (Verona, 1988), pp. 543–61; V. Zamagni, *Dalla periferia al centro: La seconda rinascita economica dell'Italia 1861–1981* (Bologna, 1990), pp. 173–86.

[10]   A. Polsi, *Alle origini del capitalismo italiano: Stato, banche e banchieri dopo l'Unità* (Turin, 1993); the most recent results of this new research line are in the two volumes *Banche e reti di banche nell'Italia postunitaria*, cit.

national context. While in Great Britain the so-called 'private bank' is a private deposit bank, on the continent the term is frequently confused with the French 'haute banque', even though the activities performed by the representatives of the latter are closer to those of the English merchant banks.[11] In Italy, the pre-unitary fragmentation of the State undoubtedly contributed to the emergence of types of banking institution which were extremely differentiated, but nor can it be said that the process of national unification after 1861 led to a rapid standardisation of the numerous different figures that were comprised within the definition of private banker. A slim volume on Italian private bankers, published in 1921, listed the numerous activities which such 'capitalists', conveniently defined as private bankers, were in a position to perform: loan operations backed by bills of exchange (then rediscounted at ordinary commercial banks), long-term loans, mortgages, advances on the salaries of public sector workers, loans against pledge, sale-purchase of real estate, purchase and sale of currency and securities on the exchange, ending up with what the author himself defined as 'elegant usury'.[12] In some ways, this book, which was not written by a historian, appeared too late, so that a further, vast range of activities escaped the author. In the first half of the nineteenth century, and in the northern regions (in Piedmont and Lombardy) even later, the work of the private bankers or the so-called *negozianti banchieri* (which is semantically even closer to the English term 'merchant banker') comprised commercial mediation of various kinds, flourishing and structured in a sometimes quite complex manner, especially in the silk trade (in particular in the reeling) which was one of the most important and internationalised industries, even from the early nineteenth century. [13]

Thus, while at a functional level the evolution of banking activities over the course of the centuries went through a progressive de-specialisation in comparison to the functions performed by the first bankers of the mediaeval and modern period, in terms of corporate structure the nineteenth-century private banks did not differ substantially from the older banking institutions. They were in fact prevalently individual enterprises, often involving sons and/or brothers, and with room for a few partners at the most, whose names did not always appear in that of the firm. The first limited partnerships did not emerge until the early twentieth century,

---

[11]   Y. Cassis, *Les Banquiers de la City à l'époque Edouardienne* (Geneva, 1984) and S. Chapman, *The Rise of Merchant Banking* (London, 1984).

[12]   P. Palumbo, *Banchieri privati* (Turin, 1921), p. 14.

[13]   S. Angeli, *Proprietari, commercianti e filandieri a Milano nel primo Ottocento: Il mercato delle sete* (Milan, 1982); A. Moioli, *Il commercio serico lombardo*, in *La seta in Europa (secc. XIII–XX)*, Atti della XXIV Settimana di studio dell'Istituto internazionale di storia economica 'F. Datini' (Florence, 1993); G. Federico, *Il filo d'oro: L'industria mondiale della seta dalla restaurazione alla grande crisi* (Venice, 1994); S. Levati, *La nobiltà del lavoro: Negozianti e banchieri a Milano tra Ancien Régime e restaurazione* (Milan, 1997); G. Piluso, *L'arte dei banchieri*.

and the first public limited companies not until the end of the First World War, although even then such types of companies continued to be the minority.[14]

However different the economic and financial systems that evolved in the various States of the peninsula may have been, the divergences in the social-professional figures that we have defined as private bankers resided more in the specific content of the activities they performed than in the restraints placed on them by the variations of the institutional fabric. Nevertheless, it is clear that the fact that Lombardy was embroiled in the economic-financial system of the Austro-Hungarian Empire imposed upon the Milanese bankers 'the need for a sectorial diversification of the assets, [a choice] imposed by the absence of a creditor of last resort to which they could apply at times of cash crisis in a system devoid of its own mechanism of discount.'[15] This was a problem, for example, which was less marked for the bankers of the Kingdom of Sardinia (who had the Banca Nazionale at their disposal since 1848) or of the Kingdom of the two Siciles (which already had a central bank from 1816, the Banco delle Due Sicilie, renamed Banco di Napoli in 1860, and from 1850 actually boasted two, when the Banco Regio dei Reali Dominii was set up beyond the lighthouse, later named the Banco di Sicilia in 1860) and which the Tuscan bankers did not resolve until 1857, when the Banca Nazionale Toscana was created.[16] If anything, the low rate of circulation of paper money in pre-unitary Italy (restricted to the most important operations and circumscribed at geographical level to the commercial centres of Liguria, Tuscany and Piedmont) ended up by representing a further element of distinction between the banking dealers themselves.[17]

In this highly segmented framework, in the middle of the nineteenth century the shared features of the sphere of private Italian banking lay in the close enmeshment with the political institutions and the links with the foreign *haute banque*, as well as

---

[14]   *Storia di Milano*, vol. 15, *Nell'Unità italiana 1859–1900*, Fondazione Treccani degli Alfieri per la storia di Milano (Milan, 1962), pp. 1022–23; Associazione Bancaria Italiana, *Annuario delle aziende di credito e finanziarie 1941–49* (Rome, 1949), pp. 155 and 165; *Uomini e denaro: Banche e banchieri italiani dal 1222 ad oggi* (Rome, 1952), pp. 363–4; E.D. Becattini, *Firenze bancaria* (Florence, 1913), p. 80.

[15]   Piluso, *L'arte dei banchieri*, pp. 11f.

[16]   R. De Mattia (ed.), *Gli istituti di emissione in Italia: I tentativi di unificazione (1843–1892)* (Rome Bari, 1990); V. Sannucci, 'Molteplicità delle banche di emissione: ragioni economiche ed effetti sull'efficacia del controllo monetario (1860–1890)', in *Ricerche per la storia della Banca d'Italia*, vol. I (Rome Bari, 1990).

[17]   G. Piluso, 'Sulla struttura dell'offerta di credito in Italia: mercati e squilibri regionali (1860–1936)', in *Storia e problemi contemporanei*, vol. VIII (Rome, 1995), pp. 13f; G.B. Pittaluga, *La monetizzazione del Regno d'Italia*, in *Il progresso economico dell'Italia: Permanenze, discontinuità, limiti*, ed. by P.L. Ciocca (Bologna, 1994).

in an economic culture that revealed a predisposition, and above all a preference, for business capable of generating high profits in the short term.[18]

In fact, the financing of the public debt represented one of the most significant and profitable aspects of the business of the private bankers, even if they had to share – frequently from minority positions – a relation with the governments that effectively hinged on the English and French *hautes banques*. The Rothschilds were particularly adroit in insinuating themselves into a dominant position in many of such operations in the pre-unitary decades in Piedmont (which a French historian rechristened 'le règne des Rothschild'), in the Papal State and in the Kingdom of the Two Sicilies. The Hambros too – especially in the Kingdom of Sardinia – and various Parisian houses, both there and in other States of the peninsula, managed to carve out a niche for themselves in the issuing of government securities, and above all in the major loans contracted by several of the pre-unitary States. However, the private bankers' subordination to competitors (and more frequently, in fact, to business partners) should not be conceived as a one-way affair. These connections with international finance also served to cream off the world of Italian private banking, allowing several of the entities that were more dynamic and better prepared in technical and professional terms to come to the fore. Moreover, these contacts were also functional to the opening up of the financial market of the peninsula – undoubtedly small-scale, but not provincial – if it is true that (for example in Tuscany) not only public debt securities but also a varied range of European securities were to be found.[19] Hence, along with a not insignificant fertilisation of the Italian banking environment, these international relations also brought to light another aspect that helps to cast further light on the type of private banker operating in nineteenth-century Italy. In effect, we should not overlook the fact that a small number of the Italian private bankers, often those with the strongest foothold in international relations, were foreign or of foreign origins (French, Swiss, English and German) and that the category also comprised a significant minority of Jewish or Protestant religion, very frequently transplanted to Italy between the end of the seventeenth and the beginning of the nineteenth century.[20]

---

[18]   L. Conte, *La Banca nazionale: Formazione e attività di una banca di emissione (1843–1861)* (Naples, 1990), p. 25. This evaluation, that the author offers for the Turin and Genoa private bankers, can be enlarged also to those operating in the other Peninsula states before national unification.

[19]   B. Gille, *Les investissements français en Italie (1815–1914)* (Turin, 1968), pp. 75–174; V. Castronovo, *Economia e società in Piemonte dall'Unità al 1914* (Milan, 1969), pp. 43–59; J.A. Davis, *Società e imprenditori nel Regno borbonico, 1815–1860* (Bari, 1979); D. Felisini, *Le finanze pontificie e i Rothschild* (Naples, 1990); Volpi, *Banchieri e mercato*, pp. 121–99.

[20]   B. Gille, *Les investissements français en* Italie, pp. 43–55; V. Castronovo, *Economia e società in Piemonte*, pp. 43–6; Volpi, *Banchieri e mercato*, pp. 121–99; Piluso, *L'arte dei banchieri*, pp. 71–115; G. Maifreda, 'Banchieri e patrimoni ebraici nella Milano

Apparently, only in the case of the construction of the railways (which in Italy as in the rest of Europe was launched primarily in the 1840s and 50s) was short-term profitability a secondary factor, precisely because it was taken over by a form of state guarantee of the return on investment. This was probably the real reason that drove many private bankers to support the financing of railway construction projects in Naples, and in Turin and Florence. Despite this, the investment in infrastructures was also the first occasion on which the Italian private banking world demonstrated that it at least shared the expectations of medium-long term economic development that other sectors of the society of the pre-unitary States revealed in a more open and marked manner.

Other basic elements, already mentioned above, also contributed to the interest in the investment in the railways; in particular the frequently subordinate relationship with the big foreign banks, within a context which both before and after unification featured a highly significant presence of foreign capital and know-how in the railway construction sector.[21]

Then, in the 1850s, the opportunities for investment beyond the two sectors (public debt and railways) on which many private bankers had hinged their business began to be intensified, thus attracting even the banking houses, which had previously restricted their activity almost exclusively to advances to merchants or, as in Genoa, to shipbuilders. Nevertheless, although the signals were more than sporadic, it is still difficult, and essentially also mistaken, to generalise this trend to the entire country.

In Milan, certain banking houses traditionally linked to the silk trade also began to examine other openings for financial investment. Generally, however, such intervention was focused on very specific cases, where there were property guarantees and certified market openings for the products involved. Some of the most famous Milanese merchant banks (Mylius, Esengrini, Decio, Kevenhüller) in 1846 financed the setting up of the Elvetica company, which produced rolling stock for the Milano-Monza railway company and for the Lombardo-Veneta railroad company. Another banking house, that of Felice Noseda, offered financial backing to a company engaged in supplying railway carriages to the Lombardo-Veneta, the Grandona & C., but in this case, as well as the guarantee offered by the contract with the railway company, there were also family ties (Grandona had married Noseda's sister) which in a certain sense underpinned the entire operation. Another and different case is that of Giulio Richard, who moved to Milan from

ottocentesca', in D. Bigazzi (ed.), *Storie di imprenditori* (Bologna, 1996), pp. 97–157; D.L. Cagliotti, 'Imprenditori evangelici nel Mezzogiorno dell'Ottocento', in *Archivi e imprese*, vol. 8, 16, 1997, pp. 245–81; B. Armani, 'Banchieri e imprenditori ebrei nella Firenze dell'Ottocento: due storie di famiglia tra identità a integrazione', in *Archivi e Imprese*, vol. 16, 1997, pp. 333–64.

[21]   G. Guderzo, *Vie e mezzi di comunicazione in Piemonte dal 1831 al 1861* (Turin, 1961); Davis, *Società e imprenditori*, pp. 143–8; A. Giuntini, *Leopoldo e il treno: Le ferrovie nel Granducato di Toscana 1824–1861* (Naples, 1991).

Turin in 1840 to exploit his experience in the sector of porcelain manufacture, and in 1847 became the owner of the firm that he had been managing for the previous seven years. In the corporate title, alongside his own name was that of Vittorio De Fernex, a famous Turin banker, thanks to whom Richard had managed to establish valid contacts with the economic and banking milieu of Milan.[22]

In the Kingdom of Sardinia, the two main economic and financial centres featured a somewhat different approach. While in Turin the banking houses did not modify their traditional strategies (backing of the silk trade, small loans backed by collateral, operations on public debt securities etc.), in Genoa the private bankers were much more active in the incorporation of companies operating in the sector of public services (maritime transport, aqueducts, local railways), and even engaged in dealings with industrial enterprises (in the footwear sector).[23]

In Tuscany the free trade policy of the ruling classes had left little room for new initiatives in the industrial sphere. Nevertheless, the very decision to introduce the Grand Duchy into the international labour division as a supplier of raw materials opened up interesting opportunities for investment for the private bankers in the mining sector, which was particularly florid and evolved within the regional panorama. The Livorno banker Pietro Bastogi, friend of Mazzini and financial backer of Giovane Italia (the political organisation founded by Giuseppe Mazzini to fight for national unification), was at the head of a group of capitalists which, in the middle of the century, rented the State-owned mines of Maremma and the Pistoia Apennines, and above all the iron mines of Elba; the mineral was extracted, after which half of it was exported abroad, and the other half transformed into cast-iron in the furnaces of Follonica and Piombino.[24] Another banker, Emanuele Rosselli, a member of the Jewish community of Leghorn, in 1860 took over from another Jewish family, the Modigliani, in exploiting the mercury mines of Monte Amiata. In this case, too, the mineral was largely exported. Its launching on the international markets was taken care of by the Rothschilds, who were able to fix the price, since they had obtained from the Spanish crown exclusive rights for the marketing of the production of the largest and richest mines in the world, situated in Almaden (in the centre of the Kingdom, close to Ciudad Real).[25] Nevertheless, such cases still appear to be exceptions, since – and this observation also embraces the first three decades following unification – the local bank capital was responsible

---

[22]   G. Fiocca, 'Credito e conoscenze: le condizioni dell'ascesa imprenditoriale', in G. Fiocca (ed.), *Borghesi e imprenditori a Milano dall'Unità alla prima guerra mondiale* (Rome Bari, 1984), pp. 28f and 34f.

[23]   Castronovo, *Economia e società in Piemonte*, pp. 43–7; G. Doria, *Investimenti e sviluppo economico a Genova alla vigilia della prima guerra mondiale*, vol. I, *Le premesse* (Milan, 1969), p. 163.

[24]   G. Mori, *L'industria del ferro in Toscana dalla Restaurazione alla fine del Granducato (1815–1859)* (Turin, 1966).

[25]   L. Segreto, *Monte Amiata. Il mercurio italiano: Strategie internazionali e vincoli extraeconomici* (Milan, 1991), pp. 30f.

only for a 'casual and fairly unconvinced' contribution to the development of the Tuscan industrial heritage.[26]

In any case, it was precisely some such new commitments that underscored the need for financial organs of greater dimensions, a trend which was considerably reinforced after the emergence of the Kingdom of Italy. For example, the Cassa del Commercio and the Cassa di Sconto both emerged in Turin between 1852 and 1853, supported by two different groups of private bankers. Just a few years later, in 1856, two banks were set up in Genoa: the Cassa Generale (which numbered among its shareholders the Piaggio, later one of the most relevant industrial family of that area) and the Cassa di Sconto, the latter founded by some of the most important local banking houses (Bartolomeo Parodi, the Cataldi brothers, Leonardo Gastaldi and Francesco Oneto), with the added support of a Turin banker, originally from Geneva, Emile De la Rue, a personal friend of Cavour. The connections between Turin and Genoa were further strengthened when the Casse di Sconto of the two cities merged to form the Banco di Sconto e Sete di Torino, which was set up in 1856 with a capital of 4 million lire, through the initiative of the leading Turin bankers (De Fernex, Ogliani, Soldati, Dupré and Ceriana). This initiative, designed to meet the requirements of the silk manufacturers of Piedmont and Liguria and the Genoese merchants and shipbuilders, almost immediately expanded its objectives to other banking operations (discount, rediscount, trade bills, current account holdings, issuing of bonds).[27]

The example and the success attained by the Crédit Mobilier in France induced above all the Piedmont bankers to prepare projects for the creation of similar credit institutions in the Kingdom of Sardinia too, but the opposition of the government blocked these plans for almost a decade. Despite this, the difficulties in which the railway companies became embroiled in the 1850s forced the political powers to slacken the restrictions on the operations the banks were allowed to perform. In fact, in 1856 the Cassa del Commercio began to operate on the model of the Crédit Mobilier, underwriting railway bonds, while the Cassa di Sconto was allowed to purchase the shares left by delinquent debtors.[28]

In Tuscany, a different approach was adopted, modelled not so much on the French model of the Crédit Mobilier as on the Belgian example of the Société Générale. In 1846, the Società Generale delle Imprese Industriali was set up through a highly diversified combination of financial contributions, ranging from the high finance of the leading aristocratic landowners to agrarian capital and mercantile capital of medium dimensions. Its purported objective was the promotion of industrial initiatives of all kinds, but in practical terms the favoured sector was

---

[26]   Mori, *L'industria del ferro in Toscana*, p. 235.

[27]   Doria, *Investimenti e sviluppo economico a Genova*, vol. I, pp. 163–5; Castronovo, *Economia e società in Piemonte*, p. 53; Polsi, *Alle origini del capitalismo italiano*, pp. 6–13; G. Berta, *Capitali in gioco: Cultura economica e vita finanziaria nella City di fine Ottocento* (Venice, 1990), p. 108 .

[28]   Polsi, *Alle origini del capitalismo italiano*, pp. 13–15.

that of the railways, both in Tuscany and in the other States of the peninsula. A few years later, in 1855, the Società Generale was transformed into an authentic industrial credit institute (changing its corporate title for the occasion into Istituto Toscano di Credito Mobiliare, which was later changed again into its definitive form as Società Industriale Italiana), adopting the model of the Credit Anstalt of Vienna, considered at the time the most updated evolution in temporal terms of the bank of the Péreire brothers. Nevertheless, despite a consistent increase in capital, in which English and French investors also participated, the enterprise did not succeed in fulfilling its designated role, which was possibly too advanced for the times and above all for the socio-economic context in which it operated, still loath to make a coherent commitment to industrial development.[29]

New Investment Opportunities in the First Thirty Years after Unification: Old Fears and Novel Leadership

In a certain sense, the birth of the Kingdom of Italy represented an extraordinary opportunity for the private bankers to augment their business, even if, in effect, those who actually exploited the new situation – and above all the emergence of a State which rapidly became the prime economic agent in the peninsula – were only the few, trusted and rigorously selected bankers who had for some time entertained close-knit relations with the political sphere. The catalyst of many processes was the new transport policy of the early governments of liberal Italy, the objective of which was an effective rail coverage of the entire country. The emergence in 1862 of the Società per le Strade Ferrate Meridionali, the first president of which was Pietro Bastogi, symbolically represented the unification of the finances and interests of the private bankers who, up to that time, had operated more at regional, or possibly international, level than with other states within the country.[30] Effectively, among the major underwriters of the capital of the company, along with the Cassa del Commercio (which actually underwrote securities for a value greater than its own capital) and the Cassa Generale di Genova and the bankers of Florence and Livorno, there were also bankers from Genoa, Turin, Milan and other smaller centres.[31]

The size of the enterprise, which Bastogi managed to wrest from the Rothschilds, demanded the creation of a 'safety net', which essentially concealed the need to find similarly powerful allies after the estrangement of the eminent banking house.

---

[29]   Volpi, *Banchieri e mercato finanziario in Toscana*, pp. 217–63.

[30]   From this point of view the banking sector was not at all different from the merchants community in the Peninsula, which had very similar relations and habits (M. Romani, *Storia economica d'Italia nel secolo XIX* (Bologna, 1982).

[31]   G. Capodaglio, *Fondazione e rendimento della Società Italiana per le Strade Ferrate Meridionali* (Bologna, 1962), pp. 5–7, but also Polsi, *Alle origini del capitalismo italiano*, p. 29.

In fact, in 1863, through the transformation of the Cassa del Commercio di Torino, the Società Generale di Credito Mobiliare was set up, with a capital of 50 million lire, which not only referred explicitly in its name to the model of institute set up by the Péreire brothers, but was also the Trojan Horse which could engineer the retrieval of the French interests, in competition with the Rothschilds, which had like them been excluded from the major business of the railways by Bastogi's adroit manoeuvres.[32] Thus, thanks to the good offices of Balduino, the Péreire got back into the big business of the railways just in time to share out equally – between themselves and the English group headed by Brassey Parent & Buddicon and that of the Italian entrepreneurs Vanotti and Finardi – the works for the construction of the rail network, amounting to an overall value of 250 million lire.[33] In the same year the Banca di Credito Italiano was founded in Turin on the initiative of the Paris group of the Societé de Crédit Industriel et Commercial in collaboration with several local bankers (Vincenzo Bolmida, Barbaroux, Levio and Minoli). Again in the same year, and again in Turin, the merger between the Cassa di Sconto and the Banco Sete took place, generating the Banco Sconto e Sete, which also included a major shareholding on the part of the Rothschilds.[34]

The weakness of the new emergent state and its enormous financial requirements offered a leading role to several major bankers who were particularly adroit in negotiating between the government, Parliament, the central banks and the international financial centres. In particular, Bastogi, Domenico Balduino, Director of the Credito Mobiliare, and Carlo Bombrini, Director of the Banca Nazionale (the most important of the six central banks that existed in the country in the first post-unitary decades) managed, despite their official or semi-official appointments (or precisely by virtue of them) to obtain the contract for the sale of the public property in 1862 and for the monopoly of tobacco in 1868, while they did not flinch from the most fraudulent manoeuvres for the sake of saving the Credito Mobiliare from difficulties in 1866.[35]

Beyond certain pathological aspects, the affair clearly indicated the importance wielded by the banking sphere in the new State. Moreover, the government warmly welcomed the initiatives of many bankers aimed at strengthening the Italian credit

---

[32]   E. Piscitelli, 'Figure di grandi banchieri italiani: Domenico Balduino', in *Bancaria*, vol. 41, 1958, p. 1292; M. Da Pozzo and G. Felloni, *La borsa valori di Genova nel XIX secolo* (Turin, 1964), pp. 303–5.

[33]   Balduino Archives (Genova), Crédit Mobilier a Domenico Balduino, no date (but of the second semester of 1862); this letter is reproduced in the appendix of B. Balduino, *Un banchiere privato al lavoro: Ritratto di Domenico Balduino*, Tesi di laurea, Università degli Studi di Firenze, Facoltà di Scienze Politiche, anno accademico 1998–99, pp. 240 and 264–65.

[34]   Castronovo, *Economia e società in Piemonte*, p. 53; Polsi, *Alle origini del capitalismo italiano*, pp. 29–37, but see also G. Luzzatto, *L'economia italiana dal 1861 al 1894* (Turin, 1968), p. 50.

[35]   Ibid., pp. 28 and 37.

system, which effectively in the twenty years following unification experienced a major growth in both quantitative terms and territorial expansion (which nevertheless continued to favour the northern regions) and in relation to the types of bank. Between 1861 and 1870 86 banks were set up, and between 1871 and 1878 no less than 242, an explosion comparable in numerical terms to that which took place in the United States in the first three decades of the nineteenth century or in Japan in the first years following the Meiji Restoration.[36]

In the general process of growth and strengthening of the national banking system, Milan was probably the economic centre that revealed the greatest dynamism from the 1870s on, albeit mostly due to the fact that the pre-1860 policy of the Austro-Hungarian administration, hostile to the emergence of banks of any importance, had left it lagging seriously behind. The Milanese bankers were particularly active in setting up commercial banks, which they needed not only to strengthen the local banking structure, but also to expand the connections with the bankers of other centres. In fact, in 1871 the principal Milanese banking houses joined up (from positions of strength) with those of Turin and Genoa to create the Banca Industriale e Commerciale (with a capital of 8 million lire, 3.2 paid up), an initiative in which the major exponents of the industrial sphere also took part on a joint basis; in 1872 the Banco Sete Lombardo (capital 12 million, half of it paid up) and, in the same year, the Banca di Costruzioni, which was to finance railway building in Poland and Hungary.[37] Of no lesser significance was the decision, again taken in 1871, to set up the Banca Lombarda di Depositi e Conti Correnti, an institute that managed to combine various operational functions, since it was a deposit and investment bank, while also being able to operate abroad. Its foundation was the result of a sort of general understanding between all the major bankers of Milan and the upper echelons of the Lombard aristocracy, Pisa, Weill-Schott, Vonwiller, Duke Visconti di Modrone, Duke Melzi d'Eril and others, who divided the 9600 shares representing the initial capital of the bank into 25 exactly identical packages.[38]

---

[36]   The complete list of the banks set up in Italy between 1858 and 1878 is in the appendix of Polsi, *Alle origini del capitalismo italiano*, pp. 334–55; for the USA and Japan see A.D. Chandler jr, *Stati Uniti: L'evoluzione dell'impresa*, in *Storia economica Cambridge*, vol. 7, *L'età del capitale*, II, *Stati Uniti. Giappone: Russia*, ed. by M.M. Postan and P. Mathias (Turin, 1980), p. 98 and K. Yamamura, 'L'industrializzazione del Giappone. Impresa, proprietà e gestione', in A. Chandler et al., *Evoluzone della Grande Impresa e Management* (Turin, 1986), p. 271.

[37]   *Storia di Milano*, vol. XV, pp. 984–7; P. Cafaro, 'Finanziamento e ruolo della banca', in S. Zaninelli (ed.), *Storia dell'industria lombarda*, vol. II.1, *Dall'Unità politica alla Grande Guerra* (Milan, 1990), pp. 176, 189 and 198.

[38]   E.D. Becattini, *Milano bancaria* (Milan, 1907), p. 53; S. Licini, 'Banca e credito a Milano nella prima fase dell'industrializzazione (1840–1880)', in E. Decleva (ed.), *Antonio Allievi: dalle 'scienze civili' alla pratica del credito* (Milan Rome Bari, 1997), pp. 556–9; Cafaro, 'Alle origini del sistema bancario lombardo', pp. 487–8.

Nevertheless, more generally, the world of the private bank in the main centres of the country was quicker and nimbler in concretely implementing a process of unification between the financial circuits, as demonstrated by the participation of the most famous bankers of the various national financial centres in the setting up of banks of both large and medium dimensions, operating both on a prevalently local basis and on a national basis in cities other than that in which their own business had its premises.[39] The best example is provided by the birth of the Banca Generale in 1871, the initial 30 million lire capital of which was put up, in addition to the Austrian Union Bank (the leading underwriter), by the banking houses of Morpurgo e Parente, Weill-Schott, Giulio Belinzaghi, Zaccaria Pisa, Ulrich e C. and Vonwiller of Milan, Geisser e C. and Ceriana of Turin, Weill Weiss, Spada Flamini e C. of Rome, Jacob Levi of Venice, Emanuele Fenzi e C. of Florence, and Maurogordato e Bondi of Livorno, among others.[40]

An initial attempt to expand the sphere of influence of the private bankers from the centres of northern Italy towards the south of the country took place in 1871. In that year a consortium of Milanese bankers, associated in their turn with Austrian, English and Swiss banks and with influential Neapolitan banking houses (including Felix Herman & Figli, Meuricroffe & Co., Minasi & Allotta and the Cilento firm) founded the Banca Napoletana with an initial capital of 11 million lire. This initiative enjoyed a certain success in the following years, representing a benchmark for many economic enterprises undertaken in the area, especially in the construction and real estate sector, but without neglecting contributions to the formation of industrial capital too. In 1885 then, under the aegis of the Banca Nazionale nel Regno d'Italia, the bank was transformed into the Società di Credito Meridionale, increasingly taking on the connotations of an industrial credit institute. Provided with a capital of 12 million lire and dominated at the level of shares by the Turin banking groups (Ulrico Geisser & Co., Banca di Torino, Banca Subalpina), it nevertheless also boasted a significant presence on the Board of Directors of local private bankers such as Mario Arlotta (Chairman), Giovanni Auverny (Vice-Chairman) and Antonio Cilento (Secretary).[41]

---

[39] A detailed picture can be found in the appendix to the volume by Polsi, *Alle origini del capitalismo italiano*, pp. 358–70.

[40] Confalonieri, *Banca e industria in Italia*, vol. I, p. 277; G. Mori, 'Dall'unità alla guerra: aggregazione e disgregazione di un'area regionale', in G. Mori (ed.), *Storia d'Italia. Le regioni dall'Unità a oggi, La Toscana* (Turin, 1986), p. 113.

[41] M. Marmo, 'Speculazione e credito mobiliare a Napoli nella congiuntura degli anni '80', in *Quaderni storici*, vol. 2, 1976, pp. 647–50 and 672; A. De Benedetti, 'Il sistema industriale (1880–1940)', in P. Macry and P. Villani (eds), *Storia d'Italia. Le regioni dall'Unità a oggi, La Campania* (Turin, 1990), pp. 44f: V. Fagiuolo, *I banchieri privati napoletani dall'Unità nazionale alla Prima Guerra Mondiale*, Tesi di laurea, Università degli Studi di Firenze, Facoltà di Scienze Politiche, anno accademico 1999–2000, p. 119.

On the other hand, the Neapolitan banking houses figured as shareholders of a certain importance in the constitution of commercial banks, operating principally in other centres. The banker Onofrio Fanelli was a shareholder in the Banco di Torino (set up in Turin in 1872) the Credito Siciliano (Rome, 1873), and the Banco di Ferrara (Ferrara, 1873). Feraud & Figli were part of the Società Generale di Credito Provinciale Comunale (founded in Florence in 1860) and in the Banca Italo Germanica (Rome, 1871). Meuricroffe & Co., the most renowned of the Neapolitan banking houses, was among the shareholders of the Banca Nazionale, the Società Generale di Credito Mobiliare and the Cassa Marittima (set up in Milan in 1872).[42] Some of these same bankers, then, had an even more pre-eminent position when it was a question of taking part in the foundation of local banks: this is the case of the Banca Popolare di Piano di Sorrento, set up in 1891, with an important shareholding underwritten by Meuricroffe & Co., by the Banca Holme & Co. and by the Aselmeyer, Pfister & Co.; an analogous case is that of the Banca di Facilitazioni, Depositi e Conti Correnti, set up in 1907 by the banker Giovanni Pasquazza and other partners.[43]

Moreover, we cannot overlook the fact that certain private bankers already managed to play their part as shareholders in important financial operations at international level. This is the case, for example, of the banker Giulio Belinzaghi (who was also mayor of Milan from 1868 to 1884 and from 1889 to 1892, before becoming a Member of Parliament and later Senator) whom we find among the founders of the Crédit Lyonnais in 1863 and, the following year, of the Anglo-Italian Bank (set up by Italian and English capitalists to strengthen the economic links between the two countries). Rare as they were at the time, such events indicate that the opening up of the Italian private banking sphere to the major international circuits, and its integration within the same, had made very significant forward progress.[44]

In the absence of specific studies we can only make conjectures, but it is probable that the private banks succeeded in exploiting the new opportunities offered by this situation, above all in terms of offering them to their clients, considering that at the time and in the following decades banks that had branches in other cities were fairly rare, and that they normally operated in the latter through correspondents and commission agents.[45]

---

[42] Polsi, *Alle origini del capitalismo italiano*, Appendix II.

[43] Fagiuolo, *I banchieri privati napoletani*, p. 121.

[44] F. Bouvier, *Le Crédit Lyonnais de 1863 à 1882: Les années de formation d'une banque de dépôt* (Paris, 1961), p. 128; N. Foà, 'Giulio Belinzaghi', in *Dizionario biografico degli italiani*, vol. V (Rome, 1965), pp. 583–4; Cafaro, *Finanziamento e ruolo della banca*, p. 176.

[45] Palumbo, *Banchieri privati*, p. 17. According to the *Annuario generale d'Italia*, before 1913 the only private banks with more than a branch were the M. Bondi and Sons of Leghorn, which between 1886 and 1896 had branches also in Florence and Rome, while in 1913 they had one in Florence and another one in Genoa; the Wagnière & Co. of Florence,

These financial initiatives had few repercussions in the industrial sphere, at least in the first twenty years following unification. The sole exceptions are to be found in the textiles sector where, starting from the 1870s and above all in the 1880s, in Lombardy the private banks began to emerge from the circuit (and from the protective shell) of the silk industry and showed signs of willingness to offer finance also to the cotton industry, probably the fastest-growing industrial sector and hence also that which offered extensive guarantees of liquid assets and return on investments. However, such signals were accompanied by others of an opposite bent; while in the same years the cotton industrialists of Busto Arsizio were obliged to set up their own bank, the Banca di Busto Arsizio, to guarantee industrial financing, several major textile enterprises – the Rossi woollen mill of Schio and the Società per la Filatura dei Cascami di Seta (dealing in the spinning of silk waste), with plants in Vienza and Novara – moved their administrative headquarters to Milan, which was evidently considered a rich market for capital.[46]

Several events, different from each other but all dense with significance, demonstrate that even by the 1880s not all the reservations of the banking world in terms of its attitude to industrial development had been dissipated, even though the number and qualitative importance of these mean that they cannot be defined as more than simple exceptions. The first brings us to the enterprise that can possibly be considered symbolic of the industrialist shift of the Italian ruling classes. In 1884 the Terni was founded, the first major Italian steel company, the purpose of which was first and foremost to supply to the Ministry of the Navy the steel necessary to build the armour-plating for the warships. The operation was conducted by a Venetian entrepreneur who had done important business in the sector of public works and building, Vincenzo Stefano Breda, who boasted close links of friendship with the Minister of the Navy, Benedetto Brin. The success of the initiative was guaranteed by the government, which offered a large sum as advance on contracts, and three years later, in 1887, strengthened the strategy of trade protectionism as an industrial policy for the younger and weaker sectors of the Italian industrial panorama. The foundation of the company was sustained by Breda himself, by the Società Veneta per Imprese e Costruzioni Pubbliche and by a group of Venetian bankers and capitalists led by Baron Alberto Treves de'

---

which in 1886 had a branch also in Rome; the Mylius of Milan, which in 1886 had a branch also in Turin. In 1896 the Kuster of Turini opened a branch in Florence which was operating until 1911, when it was acquired by the bank Conti & Co. (Becattini, *Firenze bancaria*, p. 83).

[46]   A.M. Galli, 'Credito e finanza. La Cassa di Risparmio e la crescita economica e sociale', in G. Rumi et al. (eds), *Milano nell'Unità nazionale 1860–1898* (Milan, 1991), p. 441; Cafaro, *Finanziamento e ruolo della banca*, pp. 254–5; R. Romano, *L'industria cotoniera lombarda dall'Unità al 1914* (Milan, 1992), p. 181; Cafaro, *Alle origini del sistema bancario lombardo*, pp. 500–502.

Bonfili, head of the Venice banking house of the same name and Vice-President of the Banca Veneta di Depositi e Conti Correnti.[47]

If at first sight this presence can, and in a certain sense must, be read as a confirmation of behaviour that was nothing new (the guarantee of the outcome of the production, combined with tariffs protection, offered extensive guarantees even to the most cautious and conservative of financiers), it is also true that the complexity of the operation implied, we might say, the overreaching of the 'point of no return'. In fact Treves sustained Terni at length, offering it constant financial support and actually opening up the circle of backers to other private bankers (Lenci of Genova and Ambron of Florence) and various German banks: the Berlin banking house Warschauer & Co. and the Nationalbank für Deutschland, also in Berlin, the same banks that, along with several Italian shareholders, in 1895 had given birth to the Credito Italiano. Terni entrusted its cash services to the Credito Mobiliare, but during the most acute phase in the crisis of the bank, in 1893, it was only the presence of Treves and the other private bankers that saved the company from bankruptcy in 1893. From that time on, and up to 1904 (when the steel enterprise came under the sphere of influence of the Banca Commerciale), it was the bank of Baron Treves that took care of all the Terni banking operations.[48]

Alongside such demanding operations there were also many other initiatives which, despite globally requiring fewer resources, were nevertheless symptomatic of a growing diversification of the activities of the private bankers in the industrial sphere. Two recent studies, one dealing with the private bankers of Turin and the other with those of Naples, underline converging innovations in this direction from the 1890s on. As regards the former case, among the many examples we might mention those relating to the presence of the Turin bankers in the foodstuffs sphere, where Kuster was among the shareholders of the Società Anonima di Esportazione Agricola Cirio and of the Boringhieri e C., a company dealing in the production and marketing of beer and ice; the Marsaglia brothers were part of the Molini (mills) of Collegno and Fellizzano Brothers Tavolaj & Co. In the mining sphere, the Ulrico Geisser and De Fernex banking houses offered their support in the guise of shareholders to the Monteponi company; in the services sector, Kuster was among the shareholders of the Società Italiana Elettricità Sistema Cruto (together with the private bank Sacerdote Ezechia & Co. and the bank Fratelli Nigra). Geisser appears in the list of shareholders of the Società Metallurgica Italiana and, through the house of Molvano, Olivetti e C., the banker Alessandro Molvano is in 1885 among the co-founders of the Tardy e Benech of Savona. Antonio Kuster is again to be found among the founders of the Società Elettrometallurgica Italiana. The same banker also took part – along with Schläpfer and Wenner, two important

---

[47] F. Bonelli, *Lo sviluppo di una grande impresa in Italia: La Terni dal 1884 al 1962* (Turin, 1965), pp. 3–16; S. Lanaro, 'Genealogia di un modello', in S. Lanaro (ed.), *Storia d'Italia: Le regioni dall'Unità a oggi, Il Veneto* (Turin, 1984), p. 86.

[48] Bonelli, *Lo sviluppo*, pp. 42–4.

families of Swiss origin (as was Kuster himself) active in the cotton sector in the Salerno district (South of Naples) since the 1820s – in the incorporation of the company Schlaepfer e C. in 1885, set up to work in the same area in the mechanical and metallurgical sector. This is at once a sign of dynamism and of new interests in the industrial sector on the part of the Turin banking community, and also proof of the 'negligible interest of the Turin banking system in the Turin mechanical industry.'[49]

As regards the second line of investigation, from the Neapolitan case it clearly transpires that, even in areas traditionally less equipped, even in cultural terms, to tackle the many unknowns linked to an initiative in the industrial sphere, new phenomena were emerging, especially in the 90s and in the course of the first decade of the new century, to which the local private bankers were anything but extraneous. The main difference to the Turin case related to time – 'the darkest years of the economy of the new Kingdom'[50] were now in the past – and precisely this fact indicates that the general new economic climate was generating novel opportunities even in areas that had long been excluded from all new ferment. Thus it is in no way incidental that, in the early years of the century, Naples was the testing ground for the first law designed to favour industrial settlements in depressed areas.[51] The initiatives in which the private Neapolitan bankers took part were fairly numerous, and some of a certain significance. For example, the bankers Anselmi and Meuricroffe were the major shareholders of the SA Petrolio of Naples, a company set up in 1894, closed down and reincorporated in 1869, and strengthened by the entry of new shareholders in 1898, when the company name was changed to Società Meridionale per il Commercio del Petrolio – Napoli, a firm to trade oil. Then, in 1899, the firm Pavoncelli F. e G. was among the founders of the Società Napoletana per Imprese Elettriche, set up through the initiative of big electrofinance groups of Geneva. While the sector of the remittances of the emigrants was, in a certain sense the bread and butter business of the Neapolitan private bankers,[52] especially from the early twentieth century on we find the most famous names of the financial sphere in other sectors too: the banker Achille Minozzi took part in the incorporation of the Società Meridionale per Industrie Metallurgiche, and Tommaso Astarita in that of the Metallurgica Napoletana, set up in 1905; the firm Aselmeyer, Pfister & C. was the owner of the Officine di Sarno, while the bankers Meuricroffe, Cilenti, Labona and De Angeli were

[49]   I. Balbo, *Banche e banchieri a Torino: identità e strategie (1883–1896)*, in *Archivi e imprese*, vol. 21, 1, 2000, pp. 79–85 (quotation is at p. 85).

[50]   Luzzatto, *L'economia italiana dal 1861 al 1894*, p. 177.

[51]   R. Petri, *La frontiera industriale: Territorio, grande industria e leggi speciali prima della Cassa per il Mezzogiorno* (Milan, 1990), pp. 20–23.

[52]   L. De Rosa, *Emigranti, capitali e banche (1896–1906)* (Naples, 1980), pp. 109–12 and 445.

among the most committed underwriters when the Società Nazionale d'Industrie Meccaniche was set up.[53]

More widely known, instead, is the engagement of several families of entrepreneurs of Swiss origin (like Aselmeyer, Schläpfer, Wenner) in the cotton industry in the Salerno district. In a couple of cases, the Aselmeyer and the Schläpfer, they not only greatlyexpanded this activity but transformed themselves from industrialists into bankers. In the same sector, we should also mention the two Neapolitan bankers, who were at the same time Members of Parliament, the Pavoncelli and Arlotta (the latter, among other things, General Director of the Banco di Napoli from 1895 to 1897, when he was elected to the Chamber from the third constituency of Naples) who were the local leaders of the initiative which in 1905 led to the construction of the plants of the SA Ligure-Napoletana di Filatura e Tessitura in the duty-free area of the city. In 1906 instead, it was the Amedeo Berner firm (the owner of which was, inter alia, discount manager at the Neapolitan branch of the Banca d'Italia) and the Meuricroffe house that took part in the setting up of the Canapificio Napoletano, while just a few months later we find the Holmes and Alsemeyer firms among the shareholders of the newly set up Iutificio Napoletano.[54]

Instead, events of a completely different kind reveal how a large part of the banking world was still in thrall to a short-term speculative logic, to which the private bankers were not immune. In the 1880s, in fact, the urban development and the building speculation that had been launched practically in the wake of national unification reached giddy heights. In the first two post-unitary decades, activity in the building sphere represented the ideal terrain for the conjunction of interests and capital of different provenance (from banking, commerce, real estate, the land and agriculture) and the opportunity for financial combinations between private and public interests. The crisis came in 1887, in coincidence with the highest ever marked value of the 5 per cent Treasury Bonds issued to pay the debt of the pre-unfication States,[55] when it appeared clear that the growth potential of a market that aimed predominantly at the middle-upper brackets was not infinite, and expanded rapidly in the following years until it swept away precisely those who had been the prime movers in the construction boom, the property companies and the major banks in the country, the Credito Mobiliare and the Banca Generale.

Most of the private bankers escaped the most dire consequences of this development, even though many of them were involved in property business at both local and non-regional level. The most important property company operating on the Roman market was from Genoa, the Impresa dell'Esquilino, in the foundation

[53] L. De Rosa, *L'industria metalmeccanica nel Mezzogiorno, 1840–1904* (Naples, 1968), pp. 73–4 and 260; Fagiuolo, *Il banchieri privati napoletani*, p. 148.

[54] Ibid., pp. 154–5.

[55] Bianchi, *Appendice statistica*, p. 152.

of which the entire banking world of Genoa had taken part.[56] Moreover we also find the Milan house of Zaccaria Pisa, the Leghorn bank of the Bondi family, the Turin banking houses of Levi and Ceriana all engaged in the most important business connected with the urban redevelopment of Naples.[57] And this is not all. Once the storm had blown over, a number of new banking houses very adroitly insinuated themselves into the spaces left open by those who had succumbed to the property crisis of the late 80s, a clear sign that the sector offered interesting new opportunities. Thus, for example, the Banca Feltrinelli, which emerged after the most acute phase of the crisis, was able to exploit the chance of an important investment in Rome when it entered the liquidation of the Banca Tiberina, and in 1899 purchased a hefty slice of the properties of the Esedra; in 1903, through one of its affiliates, the Società Italiana per il Commercio degli Immobili, the same bank secured for itself a significant block of land parcels and real estate in Naples, Milan and Rome originating from two important liquidations administered by the Banca d'Italia.[58]

Effectively, that of the bank of the Feltrinelli family was not an isolated case. Having overcome the major slump of the late 1880s and early 90s, property fever began to rage again, even though this time it concerned the industrial areas and those destined to housing projects, while the Italian economy, by now much stronger, had developed potent antibodies that defended it against further crises originating from the property sector. The role of the private banks was not, on the whole, diminished, even if they were now flanked by the large commercial banks. As we can see in Table 10.1, between 1883 and 1894 only 5 new property companies were set up and of the 93 founder-shareholders, only 11 were bankers, while in the period 1895–1907 the new companies numbered 57 and among the 223 shareholders the bankers recorded were 12, and in the period 1907–1913 81 new property companies were set up with 318 shareholders of whom, again, 12 were bankers. The proportionately greatest involvement of private bankers took place in the second period, when we more frequently find the names of various private banking houses: Del Vecchio of Florence, Belloni e Friedschien, Feltrinelli and Zaccaria Pisa of Milan, and Ceriana of Turin.

---

[56]   Doria, *Investimenti e sviluppo economico a Genova*, vol. II, pp. 349–67.

[57]   Marmo, *Speculazione edilizia e credito mobiliare a Napoli nella congiuntura degli anni '80*, p. 668.

[58]   L. Segreto, 'La formazione del patrimonio dei Feltrinelli', in Società Italiana degli Storici dell'economia, *Tra rendita e investimenti: Formazione e gestione dei grandi patrimoni in Italia in età moderna e contemporanea*, atti del Terzo Convegno nazionale, Torino, 22–23 novembre 1996 (Bari, 1998), p. 438. Banca Feltrinelli was set up in 1889 with the name of Banca Feltrinelli, Colombo & Co. and was renamed in 1896, when Colombo and other shareholders who were not members of the family sold their parts (ibid., pp. 436–8).

Table 10.1   Property companies set up in Italy and professions declared by the founders (1883–1913)

	1883–1894	1895–1907	1908–1913
companies	5	57	81
landowners	24	57	81
aristocrats	3	11	19
engineers	11	19	20
lawyers	8	14	21
industrialists	3	24	28
bankers	11	12	12
merchants	10	6	25
MPs	1	7	3
officials	–	–	2
accountants	1	7	16
retail traders	1	8	7
clerks	1	–	10
architects	–	5	4
master builders	–	1	3
surveyors	–	1	1
freelance professionals	–	–	3
clergy	1	8	21
women	–	12	13
not indicated	18	32	50
Total	93	223	318

Source: Ministero dell'Agricoltura, Industria e Commercio, Direzione generale del credito e della cooperazione, *Bollettino Ufficiale delle società per azioni*, parte I, *Atti costitutivi*, Roma, 1883–1913.

The Private Bankers and the Birth of the Mixed Banks

The period that opened with the setting up of the Banca Commerciale e del Credito Italiano did not, in general, lead to attenuation in the business of the private banks or to their being overshadowed. Undoubtedly, however, it induced a process of selection among the merchant banks which, nevertheless, in quantitative terms was revealed only by a reduction of their number in the major centres of the country, while in qualitative terms it materialised in the presence of the directors of some of the most prestigious – though not necessarily the oldest – of the banking houses in the management bodies of the mixed banks, in the syndicates set up to found or finance some of the most important industrial undertakings or in considerable operations of trading.[59] The quantitative data recorded in Table 10.2, moreover, underscore an undeniable fact: the birth of the mixed bank and its increasingly capillary presence within the national territory did not cause any significant reduction in the number of banking houses in the major financial centres of the country up until the First World War. The demographic trends prove very irregular, and call for specific studies and analyses of the various local situations. What is certain is that the financial capital of the country, Milan, despite being home to the headquarters of three mixed banks, did not penalise the private bankers, since their number actually increased from 18 to 26 between 1896 and 1913. This was not the case in Rome, on the other hand, where the fourth mixed bank, the Banco di Roma, had its headquarters, and where the reduction was quite marked, with a drop in the number of banking firms from 23 to 16. The overall reduction in the number of private banks is a process that the sources can illustrate only for a limited period, but which had probably been under way for some time, and in any case illustrated the progressive reduction of the economic and financial importance of certain areas of the country,[60] as well as indirectly confirming the increased impact of the other credit institutes. If anything, what emerges is the fact that it was the years of the crisis in the building-property sector and the ensuing difficulties that also contaminated other industrial sectors, with very few exceptions, which generated an initial and much harsher process of selection among the private banking houses operating in the most important financial centres of the country, the number of which fell sharply by about 25 per cent over a period of ten years, dropping from 197 to 157.

Table 10.2   Private banking houses in the major Italian financial centres (1886–1913)

	1886	1896	1913
Milan	24	18	27
Turin	36	35	25
Genoa	32	34	35
Venice	17	5	7
Florence	22	15	12
Rome	35	13	16
Naples	31	37	19
Total	197	157	141

Source: *Annuario generale d'Italia*, various years

---

[59]   The bank Manzi of Rome was used by the Banca Nazionale to trade the Italian bonds in Paris in 1890, M. De Cecco (ed.), *L'Italia e il sistema finanziario internazionale 1861–1914* (Rome Bari, 1990), p. 717.

[60]   In Florence, for exemple the private banks were 27 in 1860, i.e. more than the double of their number in 1913 (Volpi, *Alle origini del capitalismo italiano*, pp. 289–90).

The growth of Milan, even for the private bankers, demonstrates the absolutely pre-eminent role of the city in the new industrial and financial equilibrium of the country, determined in a decisive manner by the mixed banks. As we know, these were set up principally by the German, Swiss and Austrian banks. Nevertheless, certain private bankers also played a far from secondary role in the affair. In fact, the founder members of the Banca Commerciale also included Giovanni Marsaglia, a member of the Turin banking house of the same name, who was later also a Director from 1894 to 1897, while another member of the same family, Luigi Marsaglia, became a Director in 1907 and remained on the Board up to 1919, and in the last four years even rose to the rank of Vice-President. Another private bank, the Raggio of Genoa, put forward two Directors, Edilio, Director from 1895 to 1906, and Carlo, in office from 1906 to 1926.[61] The Banca Marsaglia rapidly assumed a decisive role in the equilibrium of the Banca Commerciale. Effectively, starting from the increase of capital of 1907, the Turin house became the Italian representative in the syndicate for placing the shares of the bank, with a holding of 42.5 per cent alongside the Austrian-Swiss-German group led by the Bleichröder bank (42.5 per cent) and the Banque de Paris et des Pays Bas (15 per cent).[62] This was a clear sign that the Directors of the Banca Commerciale considered this private bank and its interlocutors in the private banking sphere the best instrument for penetrating the medium-high and high brackets of the Italian savers.

In the case of the Credito Italiano the bonds were even tighter. The German banks that had taken part in the founding of the bank had for some time been in business with the Treves house of Venice, which was not among the founders, but became a shareholder in 1903 when there was an increase of capital. The following year, the Venetian banker Alberto Treves became no less than Vice-President of the bank, coinciding with the passage of the Terni company into the orbit of the Commerciale – a sort of backdated recognition for the series of activities performed by Treves in favour of the steel company over the previous twenty years. Moreover, among the founder members were three important banking houses from three different centres: the Kuster of Turin, the Vonwiller of Milan (which simultaneously ceased activity, transferring its entire personnel to the Credito Italiano) and the Manzi house of Rome (it too in business relations with one of the German banks that founded the Credito Italiano, the Warschauer), which put at the disposal of the new bank one of its best men, Giacomo Castelbolognesi, who became first Director, and then later, from 1903, Vice-President.[63]

The third of the mixed banks, the Società Bancaria Milanese (renamed Società Bancaria Italiana from 1904 on), was also the smallest: it was in fact set up in 1898 with an initial capital of just 8 million lire, following the transformation of

[61]   Banca Commerciale Italiana, Archivio storico, collana inventari, Serie I, vol. I, *Presidenza e consiglio d'amministrazione (1894–1934)* (Milan, 1990), pp. 28–9.

[62]   A. Confalonieri, *Banca e industria in Italia. Dalla crisi del 1907 all'agosto 1914* (Milan, 1982), vol. I, pp. 383–4.

[63]   Hertner, *Il capitale tedesco in Italia*, p. 175; *Storia di Milano*, vol. XV, pp. 1011–12.

the private Weill-Schott bank, founded in Milan shortly after the mid-century by a Jewish family that had emigrated to Milan from the Austrian Baden, and which was one of the most active and important of the city in the following decades.[64]

The constant presence of the principal private banks of the major financial centres of the country in the incorporation and/or the expansion of the capital of the mixed banks possibly represents the most telling clue on the path of research first proposed by Luigi Einaudi after the First World War. This impression is corroborated by other clues relating to the new clientele of the private banks from the 1890s on, even before the setting up of the mixed banks. The most crucial example is possibly the presence, alongside the Banca Generale, of the Banca Zaccaria Pisa and the Banca Feltrinelli among the financiers and shareholders of the Edison, the leading Italian electricity company, from 1894 on and – in an even more significant position – from 1896, when the intervention of the Banca Feltrinelli (and very probably of its friends and clients) was decisive in maintaining the majority of the capital of the company in Italian hands in the face of the offensive of the AEG and of the swiss electroholding Bank für Elektrische Unternehmungen.[65] From that time on, the two private banks continued to figure among the components of the banking pool that the Edison could count on, both after the replacement of the Banca Generale with the Banca Commerciale (in 1894), and when, in 1918, the Banca Italiana di Sconto took over from the Commerciale.

Another highly relevant factor consists of the project, conserved in the Feltrinelli archive and most probably dating to 1895–96, illustrating the guidelines for a prospective merger between the Società Metallurgica Italiana and the Società delle Miniere di Montecatini. The project was drafted in French, a circumstance that can be explained by the interests in the Montecatini company of the French groups led by the Parisian banker Jules Rostand, Vice-President of the company up to 1893, and by Maurice Piaton, Director from 1894 to 1899 and Managing Director in 1895. The text effectively shows how this private bank was acting like a modern merchant bank, knitting up relations with international finance that were no longer aimed simply at operations of a strictly banking kind, but rather of financial engineering in the industrial sphere.[66]

From the 1890s on, therefore, the private banks not only accompanied, but at times even anticipated or paved the way for the mixed banks in the relations that the latter were beginning to knit up with frequently pre-existent industrial enterprises. There is no business deal of a certain importance that does not feature one or more private

[64]   V. Poggiali, *Storia della Banca Morgan Vonwiller* (Milan, 1969); Bonelli, *La crisi del 1907*, pp. 29–30; Hertner, *Il capitale tedesco in Italia*, p. 191; G. Maifreda, 'La costruzione di un rapporto fiduciario: Francesco Crispi e la banca Weill-Schott', in *Archivi e imprese*, vol. 16, 1997, pp. 285–6.

[65]   C. Pavese, 'Le origini della Società Edison e il suo sviluppo fino alla costituzione del "gruppo" (1881–1919)', in B. Bezza (ed.), *Energia e sviluppo: L'industria elettrica italiana e la Società Edison* (Turin, 1986), pp. 72–8.

[66]   Segreto, *La formazione del patrimonio dei Feltrinelli*, p. 436.

banks in a decisive position. The works of Antonio Confalonieri are packed with references to financial operations – the setting up of joint stock companies, frequently following the transformation of pre-existing private firms or limited partnerships, the formation of syndicates for shares placement on the occasion of capital increases, credit facilities – implicating the private bankers, frequently alongside the mixed banks. For ease of reading, we reproduce below a table that has been constructed utilising simply this source, which, as illustrated by the cases cited above from Turin to Naples, by now appears as solely indicative and in no way exhaustive.

Table 10.3   Private bankers involved in financial operations in favour of industrial enterprises (1884–1913)

Sector	Enterprise	Private banker
cement	Industrie calce e cementi	Prandoni
chemical	Unione Concimi Carburo Fabbriche riunite fiammiferi	Jarach, Pisa Nast Kolb Prandoni
cotton	De Angeli Cotonificio Veneziano other non-specified companies	Pisa De Fernex, Marsaglia, Sella, Prandoni Pisa, Vonwiller, Prandoni Belinzaghi, Weiss, Ceriana
electricity	Edison Forze Idrauliche della Maira Idroelettrica Ligure Illuminazione di Venezia Cellina Sviluppo Imprese elettriche Trazione elettrica su ferrovia Unione Esercizi Elettrici Negri Illuminazione di Firenze	Treves, Feltrinelli, Pisa Pisa Manzi Treves Papadopoli Manzi Manzi Bellon Belloni Bondi, Wagnière
foodstuffs	Ligure Lombarda Semoleria Italiana	Raggio Bozano, Borgnini
mechanical	Officine Ansaldi Fiat Carminati e Toselli	Pisa Ceriana, De Fernex Marsaglia
mining	Montecatini Fernex Ligure Ramifera	Grasso, Vonwiller, Kuster, De Ferrari
oil	Società Oli Minerali Reinach	Kuster Prandoni
steel	Piombino Falck Metallurgica Tempini Terni	Bondi, Raggio Feltrinelli Feltrinelli Treves, Lenci, Ambron

To mention only the most outstanding cases, we go from the setting up of Fiat in 1899 (which featured the Ceriana house among the founder members), to the financial intervention in Montecatini on the part of Vonwiller and the Turin bankers Kuster, Grasso and De Fernex in the early years of the twentieth century, to the participation of the Manzi house in the foundation of the financing company for the electrical sector of Siemens, the Società Nazionale per Industrie e Imprese Elettriche in 1898, to the growing involvement of the Bondi bank in the Società degli Alti Forni of Piombino, which progressively became the principal investment of the family starting from 1905–06, to the financial connections between Feltrinelli and Metallurgica Tempini and the Falck, to the financing of the Unione Concimi by Jarach and Zaccaria Pisa. The presence in the cited cases of almost all the sectors of the second industrial revolution confirms that certain ancient bonds (with the silk sector and the textile sector in general) were by now only one of the aspects – and certainly not the most important – of the new relations between private banks and industry.

The insistent recurrence of certain names probably indicates that, towards the end of the nineteenth century, a new process of functional 're-specialisation' was taking place among certain major private bankers after a very lengthy phase of de-specialisation that had led all the operators in the sector to deal with a huge variety of activities (from banking in the strict sense to commercial activities and stock trading). The term 'private banker' continued to comprise a vast variety of figures, but the professional profile of certain of these began to be more in line with the economic climate of the time.

This new functional specialisation does not appear to have been at the expense of other factors and characteristics that had up to then distinguished the world of the private bank: a relationship of personal trust, and the most absolute discretion and confidentiality. Practices and relations of trust that had gradually developed from the end of the 1880s, networks of friendship and personal connections, explain the reasons at the basis of many of the relations which the private bankers managed to set up with the industrial entrepreneurs. We can moreover plausibly argue that, when the prime mover in a financial transaction was a mixed bank (as was increasingly more the case from the mid 1890s on) it was in the interests of the latter to aggregate the private bankers in certain operations, not so much or not only to alleviate its own position, as much as to guarantee the complete success of certain operations, such as the placement of a security, with the various urban élites (*rentiers*, aristocrats, freelance professionals, etc.). Effectively, on account of their status and habits, the latter groups had a greater ease and frequency of relation with the private banker who, in a certain sense, was part of the same system of social and cultural values professed by such milieux, and unquestionably more so at the time than a high-ranking bank official.[67]

---

[67] A.M. Banti, *Storia della borghesia italiana: L'età liberale* (Rome, 1996); M. Meriggi, *Milano borghese: Circoli ed élites nell'Ottocento* (Venice, 1992); P. Macry, *Ottocento: Famiglia, élites e patrimoni a Napoli* (Turin, 1988).

Writing in 1921, Pietro Palumbo confirmed that the banker was 'in a fairly favourable position in relation to competition with the banks. Many operations could be performed by him alone, and once he had managed to set up around himself an environment of trust and esteem, the capitalists, merchants and industrialists found it easier to apply to him than to a banking institute'.[68] This statement may appear paradoxical, but it highlights a certain truth which the financial historian has taken little account of. Only in much more recent times have a handful of studies begun to consider as essential to the training of a banker that set of personal and professional values that are functional to the consolidation of his business,[69] encouraging a different way of observing the world of the private bankers. Then there is another element that provides indirect confirmation of the pregnancy of such observations. The opening of a branch of a mixed bank in a city, which on more than one occasion took place through the acquisition of the control and then the takeover of a leading local banking house, should be interpreted not so much and not only as the inevitable victory of the giant over the financial pygmy, but rather as a tangible recognition – which was frequently also formalised through the assignment of management positions – of the role of the private banker in paving the way for the new, powerful bank entity. We can consider the case of Credito Italiano (certainly not an isolated case, a more profound study would be certain to bring out a string of other viable examples) which opened its Naples branch in 1905 after having taken over the Meuricroffe house, entrusting the management to John Meuricroffe, the last descendant of the family of Swiss origins that had founded the banking company towards the end of the eighteenth century.[70]

On the other hand, if we take even a swift glimpse beyond the outbreak of the First World War that marks the implicit temporal horizon of this contribution, we can note elements that confirm the notion of the private banker's enhanced capacity to 'intercept' – or at least to be the first to do so – a certain type of demand, such as that emerging from the more complex articulation of Italian society that was partly coincidental and partly a direct consequence of the conflict and of the phenomena of enrichment permitted by the particular conditions in which business was performed. This possibly explains the substantial stability in the number of private bankers in the decade 1913–24, but also the growth of the war years which brought the figures for the seven major financial centres of the country back to the levels of 1896. As against this, precisely the greater complexity of the requirements of this new clientele, and above all the combination of these with the greater restraints and controls introduced by the political and monetary authorities in the 1920s and 1930s, help to explain the literally vertical plunge that the private bankers experienced in the years leading up to the new banking law, issued in 1936.

---

[68]   Palumbo, *Banchieri privati*, p. 14.

[69]   Maifreda, *La costruzione di un rapporto fiduciario*; Maifreda, *Banchieri ebrei*; Garruccio, *Otto Joel alla Banca Generale*, pp. 159–99.

[70]   B. Gruber-Meuricroffe, *Die Familie Meuricroffe in Neapel*, s. l., 1970, pp. 29–32.

Table 10.4   Private banking houses in the major Italian financial centres (1913–1936)

	1913	1917	1924	1936
Milan	27	26	35	6
Turin	25	32	22	7
Genoa	35	39	29	8
Venice	7	7	5	0
Florence	12	12	9	6
Rome	16	17	30	4
Naples	19	18	11	11
Total	141	153	141	42

Sources: *Annuario generale d'Italia* (Rome, 1913); *Annuario delle banche italiane – Guida statistico-monografico della Industria bancaria* (Naples, 1917); U. Gozzini, *Dizionario delle banche, banchieri e casse di risparmio* (Ancona, 1924); Banca d'Italia, *Struttura funzionale e territoriale del sistema bancario italiano 1936–1974* (Rome, 1977).

Obviously, the comparison between private bankers and the mixed banks cannot be posed in merely quantitative terms (and this is moreover prevented by the sources at least up to the mid-1920s, and even after they render it of little interest).[71] Nevertheless, it appears clear that, at least in the period between the mid-nineteenth century and the First World War, the role of the private bank in the process of Italian industrial development cannot be ignored, and on the contrary needs to be attentively appraised. In this way, very plausibly, not only will the private banker be given the attention he deserves, highlighting all the transformations which one of the most ancient economic and social figures went through in this period, but it will also be possible to better appreciate the modes and paths through which entities extraneous to the Italian banking culture, that is the mixed banks, managed to consolidate their position in the country.

---

[71]   R. De Mattia (ed.), Banca d'Italia, *I bilanci degli istituti di emissione italiani 1845–1936* (Rome, 1967), vol. II, p. 913.

CHAPTER 11

Private Banks and Industry in the Light of the Archives of Bank Sal. Oppenheim jr. & Cie., Cologne

Gabriele Teichmann

The Oppenheim Bank and its Role in the History of Industrialization

In 1789, the 17-year-old youngster Salomon Oppenheim jr. from Bonn founded a commission agency and bill-trading business on his own account. He came from a family belonging to the group of so-called court Jews who provided the splendid court of the Prince Elector in that city with luxury goods and money. In 1794, however, the Rhineland was conquered by French revolutionary troops and the Prince Elector left, never to return. Salomon Oppenheim realized that Bonn held no future for him, and therefore moved to the ancient trading city of Cologne, where the bank has retained its principal seat ever since.[1]

The time and place of the bank's establishment are important in order to assess its role in the industrialization process. After the French conquest and the formal integration into the French Republic in 1797, the Rhineland suddenly shared the most advanced and dynamic political, social and economic system of the day. The *Ancien Régime* was abolished, while the introduction of the *Code civil* and the *Code de commerce* offered a degree of freedom for the individual never experienced before. The Rhenish Jews benefited to an even greater extent from the new order because they were granted full emancipation for the first time in history, at least until Napoleon's *Décret Infâme* of 1808 again cut back on their civil rights. Thus, the modern age began earlier in the Rhineland than anywhere else in Germany, and French rule paved the way for modern industrial Cologne.[2]

Around 1800, banking in Germany was dominated by the private bankers of Frankfurt – among them most prominently Meyer Amschel Rothschild – who siphoned off almost the whole public loan business. Accordingly, bankers elsewhere found themselves forced to open up new business fields. Those of Cologne turned

---

[1] For overall information about the history of the Oppenheim Bank, see M. Stürmer, G. Teichmann and W. Treue, *Wägen und Wagen: Sal. Oppenheim jr. & Cie.: Geschichte einer Bank und einer Familie* (Munich, 3rd edn, 1994); English edition: *Striking the Balance: Sal. Oppenheim jr. & Cie. A Family and a Bank* (London, 1994).

[2] R. Tilly, *Financial Institutions and Industrialization in the Rhineland 1815–1870*, (Madison, 1966), p. 12–13.

to the financing of industry as early as the first decade of the nineteenth century and for many years had this field almost exclusively to themselves. It was a high-risk business which other banks for a number of reasons felt reluctant to embark on.[3] Among the handful of Cologne bankers active in venture-capital lending, the Oppenheim Bank was by far the most active and creative, and thus helped to shape emerging capitalism and industry in Germany.

For the scholar of banking history this means that the Oppenheim Archive is a must if doing research on the industrialization process in Germany between 1825 and 1870. The archive, formally established in 1939 as one of the first banking archives in Germany, was not initially supposed to be used by outsiders, but to serve as a quick-and-easy means of information for members of the Oppenheim family. The establishment of the archive came at a time when the family was under high pressure from the Nazi regime because of its Jewish ancestry. The archive therefore became a symbol of the family's unbroken sense of tradition and its will to persevere. As the main structuring element, the easily accessible principle of pertinence was chosen while priority in contents was laid on the great achievements of the bank in the nineteenth century, which is why these records still form the bulk and core of the accessible material.[4]

The Specific Commitments of Sal. Oppenheim jr. & Cie. during the Process of Industrialization

By and large, the bank showed commercial interest in all branches of industrialization. The archival records pertaining to these activities are arranged in files devoted to the different companies. In addition, there is the business and private correspondence of the two Oppenheim brothers who ran the bank at that time.

There are four main headings under which commitments can be grouped:

1. shipping and railways
2. mining and heavy industry
3. the insurance business
4. banking.

[3] H. Pohl, 'Das deutsche Bankwesen (1806–1848)', *Deutsche Bankengeschichte*, ed. im Auftrag des Instituts für bankhistorische Forschung, vol. 2 (Frankfurt am Main, 1982), pp. 18–33.

[4] For further information about the Oppenheim archive, see G. Teichmann, 'Archive Survey: Sal. Oppenheim jr. & Cie., Cologne', in *Financial History Review*, vol. 1, 1994, pp. 69–78.

Shipping and railways

Considering Cologne's long tradition as a trading city, it seems a matter of course that the transport industry became one of the first fields of investment for the Oppenheim Bank. In 1825, it belonged to the founders of the *Preußisch-Rheinische Dampfschiffahrtsgesellschaft* (Prussian-Rhenish Steamship Company), specializing in goods trade on the Rhine. About a decade later, Sal. Oppenheim took part in establishing and financing some of the first major railway lines in Germany, the first of which was the *Rheinische Eisenbahn* (Rhenish Railway Company) established in 1837, linking Cologne with Aachen; on the Belgian side, the railway ended in Antwerp. Only two years later, the company went through a severe crisis triggered by speculation in railway shares, and it was only through close cooperation between the Oppenheim Bank and the Belgian government that the company could be saved. Geographically, the bank's activities first of all focused on the Rhineland, but soon broadened out to other parts of Germany, notably the North and East, e.g. the *Köln-Mindener Eisenbahn* (Cologne-Minden Railway Company) as part of the highly important line to Berlin. After the major railway lines in Germany had been established, the bank turned in the 1880s to the funding of local lines, showing that investment in railways continued to be a profitable business.

From the 1850s onwards, the Oppenheim Bank also engaged in financing foreign railway lines, e.g. in Italy, in the Austro-Hungarian Empire, in Romania and in Russia. Its most important foreign commitment was its participation in the international *Gotthardbahn* (Gotthard Railway) project linking central Europe and Italy.

Mining and heavy industry

This leading sector of industry became a major focus of interest for the Oppenheim Bank as early as the 1830s. Its first commitments were centred in the region around Aachen, which had a long-standing tradition of coal mining. There the bank merged the numerous small coalmines operating on a local level into the *Vereinigungsgesellschaft für Steinkohlenbau im Wurmrevier*, a company which was one of the first to operate on a rational, profit-orientated capitalist philosophy and gives an early example of horizontal concentration. A few years later, the bank became active in zinc mining in the same area as co-founder and major shareholder of the *Stolberger Zink AG*. It is important to note this company's close connection with French business partners: the top management was French, most of the capital was raised on the French market and the company was quoted on the Paris Stock Exchange.[5]

---

[5]   G. Teichmann, 'Das Bankhaus Oppenheim und die industrielle Entwicklung im Aachener Revier (1836–1855)', in M. Köhler and K. Ulrich (eds), *Banken, Konjunktur und Politik. Beiträge zur Geschichte deutscher Banken im 19. und 20. Jahrhundert* (Essen, 1995), pp. 16–17.

When the Ruhr area developed into the industrial heart of Germany, from the 1850s onwards, the Oppenheim Bank was also present, taking part in the establishment of several coalmining and heavy industry companies like the *Bochumer Verein*, the *Gelsenkirchener Bergwerksverein* or the *Dortmunder Union*. In the immediate vicinity of Cologne, the Oppenheims became owners of major lignite mining concessions in 1870 and introduced opencast mining in this area.

It seems, however, that the bank's commitments in mining and heavy industry soon overstretched its financial resources and did not meet with its expectations of profit; nor did the bankers feel they could sufficiently control risks. This is why Simon Oppenheim beseeched his sons in his testament of 1863 '*never* after my death [to] participate in any industrial enterprise, whatever its name, and especially avoid like the plague any dealings in mining'. Even if the sons did not completely follow their father's advice, it is clearly noticeable that activities in mining and heavy industry played a less important role thereafter in the bank's investment policy than those in other branches of industry.

The insurance business

This line of commitment was opened up in 1818 when the Prussian customs tariff made the monarchy a large economic area without internal frontiers. Salomon Oppenheim participated significantly in the establishment of the *Rheinschiffahrt-Assekuranz-Gesellschaft* (Rhine Shipping Insurance Company), a Rhine navigation insurance company which, in fact, marked the beginning of the investment business for the bank.

In 1839, Salomon Oppenheim's sons Simon and Abraham founded *Colonia*, the first private fire insurance in Prussia, cooperating closely with other Cologne private bankers as well as Rothschild from Frankfurt and the Paris firm of Fould, owned by their sister and brother-in-law. A few years later, the Oppenheim Bank initiated the *Kölnische Rückversicherung*, the world's first reinsurer, set up with the backing of the Frankfurt, Paris and London Rothschilds. Other companies insuring special risks followed, until the 1880s. The establishment of insurance companies was a logical answer to the expansion of industrial credit, insofar as they could serve as a means of security against the risks of investment credit.

Banking

This also holds true for the Oppenheim Bank's commitments in the banking business. The necessity to look for further means of controlling risks became ultimately clear to the Oppenheims during the 1848 revolution, when A. Schaaffhausen, another powerful Cologne private banker, had to suspend payments. In order to avoid a complete crash, Schaaffhausen was restructured as the first joint-stock bank in Prussia, with the active participation of the Oppenheim Bank.

Four years later, in 1852, the Oppenheim Bank was one of three foreign institutions to take part in founding the *Crédit Mobilier* in Paris, the first joint-stock investment bank in Europe. A year later, Oppenheim was the leading founder of the first bank of this type in Germany, the *Darmstädter Bank für Handel und Industrie*, aimed at challenging the power of the Frankfurt Rothschilds, who in vain tried to prevent the establishment of this bank.[6]

The Oppenheims as well as some Cologne and Frankfurt business partners used these two banks as a model for the *Banque Internationale à Luxembourg*, founded in 1856. With a share capital of 40 million francs – the whole budget of Luxembourg came to 3.1 million francs – it was designed right from the start as an international investment bank.[7] The last in the series of banks founded on the initiative of Oppenheim was the *Preußische Central-Boden-Credit AG* of 1870, the first mortgage bank on a joint-stock basis in Prussia.

A Discussion of Possible Fields of Research

While it can be in no way exhaustive, this approach is designed to point out some topics of research connected with the history of industrialization for which the Oppenheim Archive holds valuable records.

Issues of economic history

The first batch of topics is obviously connected with issues of economic history. The Oppenheim Archive holds interesting records for scholars of the actual founding process of joint-stock companies in the early days of industrialization and the problems the founders were faced with. One of these was capital raising. As mentioned before, the Oppenheim Bank often used foreign, especially French, capital, thus assuming a turn-table role for the capital market of western Germany until the 1850s. This was necessary because German capital owners continued to show little inclination for high-risk industrial investment, while preferring public loans and property.

Another problem was risk management. The Oppenheim history provides numerous examples of how newly founded companies soon ran into trouble. For the Oppenheims, the risks were especially high because the bank often played a double role of financial intermediary between capital supply and demand on the one hand, and of major shareholder on the other. The latter role may have developed because of the scarcity of venture capital in Germany just mentioned,

---

[6] For further information on the role of Oppenheim and other private banks in the foundation process of joint-stock banks, see M. Pohl, 'Die Entwicklung des deutschen Bankwesens zwischen 1848 und 1870', Institut für Bankhistorische Forschung (ed.), *Deutsche Bankengeschichte* (Frankfurt am Main, 1982–1983), pp. 159–60, 166–86.

[7] W. Treue, 'Die Gründung der Internationalen Bank von Luxemburg vor 125 Jahren', in *Bankhistorisches Archiv*, vol. 7, 1981, pp. 3–15.

and at the same time the bank's will to exert as much control on its corporate clients as possible.

The activities of the Oppenheim Bank also give an example for the development of 'mixed banking' in Germany with its typical combination of corporate finance and investment banking, a banking culture quite different from the Anglo-Saxon world. Another German peculiarity is that of the wide representation of bankers on supervisory boards. The Oppenheims, for example, held seats on almost all supervisory boards of companies they had helped to establish and used their position to control and influence these companies' policies.

My last suggestion for further research is the question of synergies. Through its wide commitments in so many branches of industry and the intensity of involvement in the individual companies, the Oppenheim Bank was bound to gain a survey of the economic situation unparalleled by any other institution – state or private – at least in the Rhineland. It seems logical that the Oppenheims used this key position to make one project benefit from another for maximum profit. This is suggested by, for example, the fact that when the Oppenheim Bank established the Rhineland railway it advocated a more costly routeing – the only one among the Cologne founders to do so. The reason was that the coalmines around Aachen they were investing in at the same time would thereby secure a railway link, opening up a much greater market for these mines.[8]

Banking and the state

There was a considerable clash of cultures and mentalities between the old Prussia east of the river Elbe, dominated by the agrarian interests of an ultra-conservative aristocracy, and Prussia's western territories acquired after 1815, governed by liberal political, social and economic ideas. Until at least the 1840s, the Prussian administration showed little understanding of the problems and needs of banking and industries developing in the Rhineland. Specifically, this meant that the Oppenheims could, for some time, neither expect financial support even for projects of public benefit like railways, nor meet with administrative support when trying to get concessions for new companies. Quite the contrary, the administration often used arguments like the fear of developing monopolies to delay such concessions. Interestingly, the administrative bodies in the Prussian Rhineland usually supported the bank's interests. The retarding attitude of the Prussian State was a motive behind the foundation of the *Banque Internationale à Luxembourg* as well as the *Darmstädter Bank für Handel und Industrie*. As they were situated on foreign soil, they could bypass Prussian legislation and restrictive fiscal policies.[9]

---

[8]   Teichmann, 'Das Bankhaus Oppenheim', p. 21.
[9]   Tilly, *Financial Institutions*, pp. 13–15.

Social studies

Finally, research may benefit from the Oppenheim records concerning the wide field of social studies. One important topic is certainly that of social rise and social mobility: the founder of the bank grew up in the Jewish ghetto of Bonn while his heirs rose to the ranks of nobility in the 1860s. Another subject comprises the history of Jewish emancipation and assimilation in the nineteenth century. The archive also provides us with records that may help to assess the mentality and lifestyle of the bourgeois class, its charitable commitments and its political attitudes.

For a business in family ownership like the Oppenheim Bank, the whole sphere of family relations is an important topic. Did the Oppenheims pursue any marriage strategies? To what extent were family ties inside and outside Cologne used for business purposes? This leads on to the subject of personal networks in general. Who were the persons the Oppenheims cooperated with regularly, and on which projects? It is known, for instance, that they used their influence to have business friends voted into the management of industrial companies which would give them access to insider information.[10]

Personal networks also played a decisive role in risk management, as a forthcoming dissertation based to some extent on the records of the Oppenheim Archive will show.[11] Hence the assessment of risks did not, in the end, rest on rational analysis of the market, of technologies etc., but on a common code of bourgeois values shared by the decision-makers in banking and industry. The trustworthiness of potential partners did not necessarily depend on their wealth but on their connection with or recommendation by the right kind of people.[12] Thus, the assessment of character plays an ever-recurring role in the correspondence of the Oppenheim bankers. Crucial business situations were also often assessed from a psychological point of view. For example, just after the establishment of a new company the Oppenheim bankers wrote to other shareholders that it should be their first and foremost aim to create public trust in the new firm and therefore cut down on their expectations of quick profits for a while.[13]

We have attempted to show that the Oppenheim Archive is a valuable source of information on the industrialization of western Germany, on the interplay between the emergence of industries and the development of financing tools and strategies and on the history of the upper bourgeois class in the nineteenth century. Access policy is handled liberally.

---

[10]   Tilly, *Financial Institutions*, p. 107.

[11]   Monika Pohle, author of the dissertation, has already dealt with this problem in her article 'Risk, Onformation and Noise: Risk Perception and Risk Management of French and German Banks during the Nineteenth Century', in *Financial History Review*, vol. 2, 1, 1995, pp. 25–39.

[12]   Tilly, *Financial Institutions*, p. 85.

[13]   Oppenheim Archives, Nr 194, letter by Abraham Oppenheim to Regierungsrat Ritz, 15 October 1839.

CHAPTER 12

Jewish Private Banks

Ginette Kurgan-van Hentenryk

Trade lies at the core of the history of Jewish private banks. From the *Hofjude* in eighteenth-century German States or the pedlar immigrant in nineteenth-century America to Lazard Brothers today, Jewish private banks have built their fortune on trade, be it trade in commodities, trade in capital during their golden age before World War I, or trade in ideas and services during the late twentieth century. Those who survived the golden age kept the basic methods of their ancestors, while adapting themselves to the economic environment and anticipating new activities and financial products.

This chapter focuses on the evolution of Jewish private banks in Europe during the nineteenth and twentieth centuries, from three angles. First, it discusses their economic role and the factors of their success and decline. Second, it analyses the social position of the Jewish banker in different countries. Third, it considers its political influence, often overestimated by anti-Semitic campaigners.

Economic Role of Jewish Private Banks

During the first half of the nineteenth century the banking structure of European countries was dominated by private banks. In these family businesses, personal wealth intermingled with capital invested in business. Deeply rooted in the local milieu, their financial development rested on the experience accumulated by their owner and the network of family and personal business connections he built throughout the country and abroad. Two elements played a significant part in networking: wedlock alliances and the apprenticeship of the heirs in family businesses or allied banks in the country and abroad. Thus the personal factor played an essential part in dealings with partners and customers.

In England, private banks were founded by merchant bankers who had developed banking activities accessory to their business in international trade during the eighteenth century. Progressively, discount activities and the development of the endorsement and acceptance of bills of exchange tended to replace speculation in commodities. Since the mid-eighteenth century, the City banks, i.e. the London private bankers, were considered members of a specialized club in the market for short-term commercial credit. A few Jewish merchant bankers appeared during or after the Napoleonic wars. The most prominent of them was Nathan Rothschild.

In the Netherlands, private banks originated from the securities business of the eighteenth century. Traders in securities were merchants, usually Sephardic Jews of Spanish or Portuguese origin, who came to specialize in this field.

During the wars of the French Revolution and Empire eighteenth-century merchant bankers had to refine their techniques in financing trade. Paris then emerged as a national and international payments centre. Indeed, as the only country undertaking reciprocal exchange with Latin America and also having a positive balance of payments with the Anglo-Saxon world, France played a significant role in the international payments system. Whilst the English and Americans sought to procure bills on Paris to pay their imports of French goods, continental merchants turned to Parisian banks to manage their debts to Anglo-Saxon countries. Foreign banks had also set up offices in Paris, chiefly Swiss Protestants and German Jews. While keeping busy in international trade, they placed government loans for the restored monarchies. As a result the *haute banque* came into being in Paris during the Bourbon Restoration. It was an informal but closed circle of twenty private banks, some of them established well before the Revolution. Among them were German Jews such as Louis d'Eichtal, James Rothschild, Salomon Oppenheim. Other Jewish bankers joined later: Fould, Cahen d'Anvers, Stern, Bischoffsheim.

Until 1870, private banks enjoyed a privileged position in Germany. Most of them originated in trade and business of the *Hofjuden* of the numerous eighteenth-century German States. By the turn of the century, one hundred and fifty court Jews' families had been raised to the nobility, mainly in south Germany and Austria. Thus, Aron Elias Seligman of Mannheim, who did the king of Bavaria services during the Napoleonic wars, was ennobled in 1814 as Leonard, Freiherr von Eichtal; then he converted to Roman Catholicism. Similarly, the Kaulla family founded a bank with Duke Frederick of Württemberg in 1802; it became the bank to the Kingdom of Württemberg's court after the Napoleonic wars.

Frankfurt-am-Main was especially favoured as a financial centre because of its status as a free city, as well as because of its geographic position at the crossroads of major European commercial and water routes. The early nineteenth century confirmed its rise as the pre-eminent commercial and banking centre of Germany, a rise which had begun in the previous century. Private bankers made it their preferred market for broking international government loans – especially the Bethmann firm, whose activities in this market were eventually to be overtaken by the Rothschilds. Cologne also figured among the important financial centres from which the Oppenheims built their international network. At that time the Berlin banking houses could not compete with Frankfurt in the Prussian government loan market. At Hamburg, the Warburgs, whose first known ancestor worked as a money changer and pawnbroker during the sixteenth century, established a banking house in 1798.

The rise of the house of Rothschild fascinated contemporaries because of the size of its operations throughout Europe. The dynasty's founder, Meyer Amschel Rothschild, was trained by the Oppenheims at Hanover. He was one of the many businessmen who made a fortune in military procurement during the wars with

France. The father of five sons, he went into partnership with the two eldest, Amschel and Salomon, and in 1798 he sent his third and most gifted son, Nathan, to England. Starting in Manchester, Nathan accumulated a fortune as a textile merchant before settling in London by 1804. He managed to make his way into the circle of merchant bankers who were issuing British government loans, and created a network of agents covering the whole of Europe. Nathan's youngest brother Jacob, better known as James, arrived in Paris in 1811 and founded his bank there in 1814.

Having become the bankers of Europe's conservative monarchies, the Rothschilds settled in Vienna, where Salomon founded a bank, and in Naples, where the fourth brother, Charles, established himself. Links with other centres developed, with privileged correspondents like Samuel Bleichröder and his son Gerson in Berlin, or August Belmont in New York. In other places the Rothschilds had direct representatives like Louis Richtenberger, who looked after the Parisian branch's interests in Brussels, and his stepson Samuel Lambert in Antwerp. Through their extended network of financial relations, the Rothschilds played a prominent role in international gold and silver flows. They achieved a very efficient system of couriers which offered a level of security and rapidity in business communications never surpassed until the appearance of the telegraph. For years, the Rothschilds were better informed about international events than governments were. Ministers and diplomats often relied on their information.

The case of the Rothschilds is far from being a unique example of the scattering of German private bankers throughout Europe. The Oppenheims, linked with the house of Fould in Paris, were present in Brussels during the Napoleonic era, and Adolphe Oppenheim became the first treasurer of the Banque de Belgique. They patronized two prominent bankers at Brussels, Jacques Errera, the son of a Venetian Jewish banker who married Oppenheim's daughter, and Franz Philippson, who became the wonderboy of the Brussels market. Likewise, the Bischoffsheim brothers, from Mainz, set up banks in Amsterdam, Antwerp and Brussels.

Contrary to the Rothschilds, who had their representative in Belgium until the end of the century, Jonathan Bischoffsheim set up his business in Brussels and developed his network throughout Europe with numerous German Jewish bankers' families, among them Goldschmidt, Bamberger, Cassel and Stern, whose youngsters were trained in his bank and settled in Belgium. Similarly, one of their relatives, Germain Cassel, founded a bank in Brussels in 1839 and allied through marriage with the Frankfurt bankers Stern, who also expanded their operations to London and Paris. In the same way Bischoffsheim's son-in-law, the famous baron Maurice de Hirsch, founded his own bank in Brussels in 1862 as a partnership with his brother-in-law Fernand Bischoffsheim.

The development of the German Jewish private bankers' New York community followed in a way the pattern observed in Europe, although it occurred later in the century. Having emigrated to the United States between the late 1830s and the 1850s, they started business trading in commodities, whether retail, wholesale or international trade. Like the Revolution and Napoleonic Wars in Europe, the

Civil War created opportunities for developing banking activities, and the postwar decade was decisive for the rise of German Jewish private banks in New York. Among them, following the example of Rothschild, the numerous Seligman brothers established houses in London, Paris and Frankfurt, thereby building the strongest network of all.

Government loans made up an essential part of private banking operations for the first two-thirds of the nineteenth century. After the Aix-la-Chapelle Congress of 1818, thanks also to their privileged connection with Metternich, the Rothschilds dominated the continental market. National debts then consisted partly of long-term amortizable loans and perpetual stock, and partly of short-term, floating debt made up of Treasury bills. The amortizable loan gave rise to repayment of the capital in annual instalments, for a fixed term of several decades. In the case of perpetual loans, however, the State contracted to pay out annual interest in perpetuity, known on the Continent as a *rente*, on the capital advanced by the lender, without ever redeeming the principal. On occasions the government could retire part of the funded debt by buying out the *rentier*. Whenever possible, a government which enjoyed a good credit rating would offer its loans by public subscription, the normal practice being to farm the loans out to a banker or a financial syndicate. These would undertake to contract for a given price or guarantee a minimum part of the issue. They might either retrocede part of the loan to other bankers, or organize a public issue, or sell the bonds on the stock exchange. The banker's reward consisted of the commission received from the government for placing the loan and the underwriting margin. While long-term securities and amortizable loans easily found investors amongst a public increasingly familiar with stock exchange and speculation, only banks could respond to the needs of State treasuries as far as the issue of short-term government stock was concerned.

At the start of the nineteenth century, a factor impeding the placement of government loans in foreign capital markets was uncertainty about the terms of interest payment. These were due in the country of origin at undefined dates and liable to exchange fluctuations. A major innovation in this respect was introduced by the Rothschilds, who issued loans contracted with the regimes of the Holy Alliance. Their interest was paid in London on fixed dates with a fixed rate in relation to sterling. All public credit operations undertaken on the continent were subject to preliminary discussion with the London branch, which played a key role in the flotation of continental loans during the 1820s. As a result, the greater security of new loans granted in Prussia, Austria, Naples, France, Spain and Russia attracted a larger clientele. Between 1813 and 1830, the Rothschilds were able to float four billion francs in loans at London and Paris.

When Belgium achieved independence in 1830, the assistance of the Rothschilds enabled the young State to obtain its first loans on the capital market, and to maintain a credit rating then threatened by the contemporary scepticism about the country's viability. At the same time, Jonathan-Raphaël Bischoffsheim founded the Administration Générale des Rentes Nationales et Etrangères with Cahen d'Anvers in 1834. It issued securities in Belgian currency with a fixed interest rate, guaranteed by foreign obligations. The influence which Bischoffsheim acquired in the Belgian financial market led him to play a key role in setting up national capital. In 1835, he was one of the founders with James Rothschild and Adolphe Oppenheim of the Banque de Belgique whose objective was to counterbalance the power of the Société Générale, supposedly linked to the King of the Netherlands. He decisively assisted the liberal governments in reforming the credit system by creating a central bank, the Banque Nationale de Belgique, in 1850, and other public credit institutions several years later.

Negotiations for government loans gave bankers excellent opportunities to develop close relationships with politicians and royalty. Private bankers were not necessarily associated with a particular political faction and their main desire was to preserve their financial interests. However, with the growing internationalization of their operations they naturally came to favour the balance of power in European politics.

Meanwhile, wars still gave exceptional opportunities to private Jewish bankers to rise to the top of the financial markets, thereby following a pattern very close to that of their ancestors, the *Hofjuden*. This process lasted certainly until the 1870s. Let us recall the case of Abraham Camondo, 'the Rothschild of the Orient'. Heir of a Sephardic family of bankers originating from Spain, who moved to Venice then to Istanbul, he lived among the *sarraf*, the bankers settled in the Galata quarter. He succeeded in becoming the banker of the Ottoman government and made his fortune by financing the Crimean war and supporting the Sardinian monarchy during the wars for Italian unification. Similarly, the rise of banker Gerson Bleichröder, later nicknamed the Rothschild of Berlin, began with providing Bismarck with the funds to finance the war with Austria, after the Prussian parliament had refused to oblige. In 1867 Bismarck switched from the Frankfurt Rothschilds to Bleichröder for the management of his personal finances. At the same time, the Berlin banker became his close associate for the building of the German empire. Thanks to his close relationship with the Rothschilds of Paris and Vienna, Bleichröder capitalized on his position as one of the best-informed persons in Berlin.

With the early specialization of the British banking system, the main task of the London Jewish merchant bankers was financing international trade through acceptance and floating foreign loans. As a consequence, the prominent position of private bankers in the City lasted longer than on the continent, and they maintained their influence by sitting on the boards of the big joint-stock banks which developed at the end of the century. Yet Alfred de Rothschild was the only Jewish private banker who was admitted to sit on the board of the Bank of England before World War I.

On the continent, where bankers were involved early in financing railway building and industrialization, Jewish private bankers were very active. Although they belonged to a religious and more or less discriminated minority, they did not escape harsh rivalries with each other. At the core of that competition was the wish of some bankers to free themselves from the leadership of the Rothschilds. Nonetheless, it was not until the 1870s that they really succeeded.

In France and Germany Jewish bankers played a significant role in promoting railway companies in the 1830s. When Emile Pereire, his former employee, launched the Paris-Saint Germain line, James Rothschild was one of the main shareholders in the company, with Louis d'Eichtal. Its success focused attention on the market for railway stock. In 1837 the launching of the Paris-Versailles route by the Rothschilds gave rise to numerous stock-exchange transactions, stimulated by a press campaign announcing the creation of a number of projected lines throughout Europe. The financial crises of 1838 brutally suspended railway building. And in spite of the 1842 law which laid down the basic principles of French railway construction, many years passed before the bankers became decisively involved in railway business. While the Rothschilds got the concession for the Paris-Belgian frontier line, which was the starting point for the expanding network of the Compagnie des Chemins de Fer du Nord in the North of France and South-Western Belgium, the great Parisian bankers speculated on rail mainly by investing heavily in stocks of various important railway companies. Thus, the Pereire brothers were promoting the PLM (Paris-Lyon-Méditerranée).

In Germany, Jewish private banks invested early in railway construction. The initiative there was taken by four private bankers of Cologne – J.H. Stein, A. Schaaffhausen, J.D. Herstatt and Salomon Oppenheim Jr – with the foundation in 1837 of the Rheinische Eisenbahngesellschaft with a capital of 325,000 thalers, of which the Rothschilds of Paris contributed 50,000 and the Oppenheims 35,000. Originally mandated to build a line from Antwerp to Cologne, the company managed to construct a network of railroads between the western frontier of Prussia, the Rhine and the Saar. The banks supported the railway company through its difficult early years by overdrafts and brokerage services. Their reward lay in share issue and speculation in railway stocks. Their policy of holding stocks assured them of voting rights and influential positions on the board of the railway company. Among other similar enterprises, let us recall the alliance of the Rothschilds and the Bethmanns for developing Frankfurt as a railway centre for the whole of Germany.

While financing railway construction, bankers also took an interest in the industrialization of the regions served by the companies they supported. Thus, the Rothschilds of Paris acquired important interests in coalmining in Belgium and extended their railway network in such a manner that they controlled Belgian coal imports to France. The Pereire were long-standing shareholders in the Compagnie d'Anzin. The Oppenheims were tied to the iron industry in the Rhineland.

Jewish private bankers became aware that the demands of railway and industrialization finance could no longer be satisfied by their limited resources. It was necessary to mobilize public savings by creating joint-stock banks. In Belgium, the model of the universal bank had been adopted early with the founding of the Société Générale in 1822. In 1835 James Rothschild, Jonathan-Raphaël Bischoffsheim and Adolphe Oppenheim had helped King Leopold I in founding the Banque de Belgique which invested in coalmining and ironworks to supply the construction of the railway network by the State. Conversely, governments in France and in the German States deeply mistrusted joint-stock banks, and it took the crisis of 1848 to change their minds. A second motive also inspired the bankers: creating a counterweight to the financial might of the Rothschilds.

In France, the Pereire brothers promoted the mixed banking model, which prevailed from the foundation of the Crédit Mobilier until the collapse of the Union Générale in 1882. Influenced, like Louis-Napoléon Bonaparte, by Saint-Simonian ideals, the Pereires took advantage of his rise to power. With the founding in 1852 of the Crédit Mobilier they stamped their own imprint on the revolution in the banking system, both by the broadness of their vision and by the energy with which they defended and promoted their ideas.

The Crédit Mobilier's vocation lay in financing the development of railways and heavy industry, carrying out all operations with the public authorities, and sustaining the companies' share values on the stock market. The bank's originality was in its proposed method of collecting savings by issuing short- and long-term redeemable bonds to mobilize all available funds. In this way, the Pereires aimed to centralize the financial operations of the great railway and metallurgical companies in order to merge all the firms from a given industrial sector into a single company. The Crédit Mobilier, following one of the most fruitful ideas of the Pereires, would eventually substitute its own shares and debentures, in a so-called omnium equity share, for all the securities currently in circulation, in such a way as to establish a joint and several obligation and thus gain the public's confidence.

These schemes, with their monopolistic vision of the future great industrial firms, extended far beyond France; they had particular appeal for continental countries yet to engage fully in industrialization, like Austria, Switzerland, Italy, Spain and the Russian Empire. After a promising start, favoured by political and economic conditions, the Crédit Mobilier's plans united the Rothschilds, the regents of the Banque de France (many of whom belonged to the *haute banque)* and the great railway barons against it. James de Rothschild was undoubtedly the greatest opponent of the Crédit Mobilier. Not only did he attempt – unsuccessfully – to dissuade Louis-Napoléon Bonaparte from supporting the Crédit Mobilier, but he also struggled continuously against the Pereires on the stock market as well as in all the sectors where they were involved in France and abroad. Thus, the Rothschilds participated in all the railway and banking coalitions which opposed the Pereire enterprises. Their opposition went as far as creating a Crédit Mobilier-type institution in Austria, the well-known Credit-Anstalt, and in Italy where they participated in founding the Caisse de Turin.

The Pereires collapsed. But it is worth noting that the Rothschilds were unable to convince governments of the dangers of the type of credit institution they had created. As a consequence, they chose to adapt to that type to preserve their own position in European finance. But that choice was dictated by necessity.

In the German States, the promoters of mixed banking were frustrated during the 1850s and 1860s by strong resistance from the Prussian government to the creation of joint-stock banks. The circumstances of the foundation of the first D-

Banks, the Darmstädter (1853) and the Disconto-Gesllschaft (1851–6), on the initiative of several Jewish private bankers are revealing in this respect.

The first of these houses was established on the initiative of a group of Cologne private bankers who had participated in the rescue and conversion to a joint-stock bank of the Schaaffhauser Bank during the crisis of 1848. At the outset, Abraham Oppenheim, Gustav Mevissen and their partners encountered a double obstacle, the Prussian government's opposition and the Rothschilds' hostility, which ruled out any possibility of setting up the new bank in Frankfurt. However, thanks to Oppenheim and Mevissen's family connections, they were supported by the grand-duke of Hesse, and on 13 April 1853 the Bank für Handel und Industrie opened in Darmstadt. More than half of the initial capital of 10 millions florins was subscribed by the Crédit Mobilier. The new bank wasted no time in increasing its capital to 25 million florins by 1856 in order to reduce the influence of the Pereire brothers. Since setting up branches or subsidiaries in Prussia or accessing the Frankfurt money market was impossible, its expansion was focused on the rest of Germany and abroad through partnerships with existing banking firms.

Despite his significant role in the management of the Bank of Prussia, David Hansemann failed to convince the Prussian rulers that joint-stock banking offered advantages. Indeed, after his own efforts to create such an establishment in Berlin lost him his post, he chose to develop a different type of banking institution by creating a discount house, the Direction der Disconto-Gesellschaft, under a cooperative structure. Thanks to rapid growth in membership and in the volume of its operations, Hansemann was soon able to convert the cooperative into a limited partnership, the Disconto-Gesellschaft, with a capital of ten million thalers, thereby raising it to the first rank of Prussian banks and second place in the whole Zollverein behind the Darmstädter Bank für Handel und Industrie.

Meanwhile, a group of leading Jewish private bankers including Bleichröder and Mendelssohn, with the help of Oppenheim and Mevissen, founded a rival establishment, the Berliner Handelsgesellschaft. Its pattern was inspired by those of the Crédit Mobilier and Darmstädter Bank.

In Germany, France and other countries of the continent, the Franco-Prussian war decisively accelerated competition between private banks and joint-stock banks. At the time, liberalization of legislation on joint-stock companies in both countries as well as the huge business generated by financing the five billion francs indemnity imposed upon France by the new German Empire promoted the birth of new joint-stock banks. In January 1870, several Jewish bankers and politicians, among them Ludwig Bamberger, the builder of the future Reichsbank, and Herman Wallich, had participated in founding the Deutsche Bank with the aim of financing international trade; the bank soon entered the same field as the other D-banks and the Berliner Handelsgesellschaft. On the other hand, the indemnity loans raised in 1871 and 1872 by France, whose financial success stunned Europe, had multiple benefits for the banking system. The *haute banque* and the new banks competed to take up loans, thereby collecting guarantee commissions, underwriting fees and profits from arbitrage dealings and bills. While the Rothschilds put together an international syndicate of the *haute banque*, deposit and investment banks set up their own syndicate in August 1871 on the initiative of the Banque de Paris to benefit from operations undertaken by the French government. Providing the government with foreign currency and bills led the syndicate to promote underwriting abroad through a wide network of correspondents. The Bischoffsheims federated these partners in 1872 by constituting the Banque de Paris et des Pays-Bas with numerous members of the European *haute banque* as well as German, French, Belgian, Dutch, Swiss, Austrian and Danish bankers. Jewish bankers like Henri Bamberger, Maurice de Hirsch, Goldschmidt of London, Edouard Fould and Antoine Stern sat alongside Protestant and Catholic ones.

The most striking feature of the competition between private banks and joint-stock banks was the ability of the latter to collect growing external resources. However, until World War I, Jewish private bankers preserved their influence on the financial markets. During the last quarter of the nineteenth century, newcomers settled on the main European markets while the New York German Jewish bankers' community prospered. The former founded investment banks like Lazard Brothers in London and Paris, the Camondos moved from Istanbul to Paris, the Seligman Brothers were established in most of the European places, and the young Franz Philippson founded his bank in Brussels in 1876 and won a high reputation negotiating lottery loans with Belgian municipalities. Above all, Ernest Cassel, the son of a Cologne banker who arrived in London in 1870 at the age of 18, became the most famous financier of that generation. On the eve of World War I, Simon Lazard's wealth amounted to but a tenth of the French Rothschilds'. Indeed, when he died Gustave de Rothschild's fortune was evaluated at £10 million, while Sir Ernest Cassel at the time reached £7.5 million.

On the other hand, many private bankers kept influence by participating in the foundation of the new joint-stock banks and sitting on their boards in England and on the continent. In Belgium, Jewish private bankers were deeply involved in the foundation of the Banque Bruxelles by Jacques Errera and several German Jewish bankers in 1871, and of the Brussels branch of the Banque de Paris et des Pays-Bas. The latter evicted the Rothschilds from the top of the Belgian financial market which it, with the Société Générale, went on to dominate by the end of the century. In some joint-stock banks, the first general managers belonged to the milieu of Jewish private bankers. Let us recall the case of Herman Wallich at the Deutsche Bank. As for Raphaël de Bauer, head of the Banque de Paris et des Pays-Bas in Brussels from 1872 to 1916, he began his career as an employee of the Banque Bischoffsheim-de Hirsch, married the daughter of Samuel Lambert, the Rothschilds' representative in Brussels, and was linked by matrimonial alliances with the Rothschilds, Oppenheim, May, Goldschmidt and the Russian Jewish family Gunzburg. One generation later, Horace Finaly, the influential manager of the Banque de Paris et des Pays-Bas, also belonged to a family of private bankers. Nevertheless, when analysing the leadership of the joint-stock banks in several European countries, one cannot but observe that Jewish membership faded away more or less rapidly after their foundation. In Germany, the private bankers very quickly lost control of the joint-stock banks, especially in the D-banks. One may consider the case of Horace Finaly as an exceptional one after World War I; however, anti-Semitism was a not insignificant factor in his fall in 1937.

At this stage one may wonder why the rise of joint-stock banks with a huge capacity to collect funds failed to affect the world of private banks much. While the joint-stock banks attained a dominating position in the national markets of the industrialized countries of the continent, private bankers kept a privileged position in penetrating the markets of less-developed countries. They were also ideal channels for covert action in colonial activities. To open new markets, they took advantage of their widespread international family and business links, their discreet way of operating, and their numerous contacts with political and diplomatic circles. In light of the specialization of the British banking system, the question does not concern the merchant banks until World War I.

Mendelssohn, Bleichröder and Hansemann had become the main bankers to Russia in the 1880s. They issued Russian public loans in the West European markets until the *Lombardverbot* of 1887, which had the consequence of transferring no less than 60 per cent of the Imperial Russian foreign debt to the French market. Thus, Paris overtook Berlin as the main market for Russian securities; the Rothschilds and the Banque de Paris et des Pays-Bas took over the leadership of the syndicates for negotiating with the Russian government.

Colonial expansion also gave Jewish private bankers new opportunities. Ernest Cassel, who was close to Maurice de Hirsch, built his fortune partly through his large operations in Egypt under the British protectorate. Several Jewish bankers helped King Leopold II to achieve his scheme of founding a colony in Africa at a time when Belgian opinion and the business community were anticolonialist. Thus, Bleichröder played an important part on behalf of the king at the Berlin conference of 1885 which was decisive for his acquisition of the Congo. In Belgium, private bankers like Franz Philippson and Léon Lambert collaborated closely to build the Etat Indépendant du Congo, while the Société Générale and the Rothschilds were hesitant about the king's colonial enterprise. Thanks to its colonial involvement initiated by his links with Albert Ballin, one of the few Jews in the upper echelons of German shipping, the bank MM.Warburg of Hamburg leapt into the first rank of world banking. Whereas Bleichröder was regarded during the 1890s as the richest banker in Berlin, with assets of about 36 to 40 million marks, the Warburgs' assets expanded from 46 million marks in 1900 to 127 million in 1914. Allied by marriage with Jacob Schiff of Kuhn, Loeb and Cy, the main competitor of the Morgan bank in New York, Max Warburg, together with his brothers, introduced American securities to the German market. At the beginning of the twentieth century they led German banks in securities underwriting with the Deutsche Bank, and sat on about twenty corporate boards. As a significant feature of the evolution of the banking system, we may observe that at the time this prominent private bank employed 111 employees, whereas the Deutsche Bank's staff numbered about 6,600.

After World War I, most of the private bankers were unable to compete successfully with the large joint-stock banks, be it in long-term investments or financial services to industry. On the continent, postwar inflation eroded their resources while large banks were able to rebuild deposits. This was the beginning of a new process in the economic role of Jewish private bankers, which was accelerated by the rise of Nazism in Germany and World War II. To diversify their income, those who survived developed a fee-based business in providing advisory services and arranging credits instead of making loans and taking positions. In Germany, Max Warburg and Carl Melchior were from the start the most important figures on the reparations question. This was not only because they enjoyed a broad international experience, but also because they had excellent connections in Great Britain and the United States. Two of Max Warburg's brothers were American bankers through their partnership in Kuhn, Loeb & Co. One of them, Paul Warburg, was a founder of the Federal Reserve System. With Franz von Mendelssohn, who operated in Amsterdam, the European centre for German currency and trade operations during the inflation period, the Warburgs contributed to facilitating capital flows to Germany after the war.

When Hitler came to power, Schacht failed to protect the Jewish bankers on whom he depended as a source of foreign exchange to finance rearmament. In 1938, the Jewish banks had to choose between liquidation, selling out to an Aryan bank, or being Aryanized. Aryanization meant that the Jewish partners could sell their stakes to non-Jews and preserve the firm. As a consequence, almost two hundred private banks disappeared and most of the Jewish families fled abroad. The same process occurred in the countries occupied by the Nazis during World War II. Many of those who survived did not return to the home country and settled in Great Britain or in the United States. Some very old families came back after the war to Germany, like the Oppenheims who controlled Colonia, the second insurance group in Western Germany, which they sold in 1989 with the aim of centring their business on banking. In Belgium, the Lambert and Philippson families came back. Léon Lambert rebuilt his bank and developed investment banking. After merging his group with the Banque de Bruxelles, he progressively lost influence and was supplanted by financier Albert Frère. To-day only the Philippson family is still present in private banking, through Banque Degroof, which adopted the name of their wartime Aryan partner.

In both the United States and Europe, Jewish private bankers developed innovation in finance by leveraging their experience and dense network of international business and political connections to advise governments and big business. Creativity had become the key to their fortune. Lazard Brothers is the paradigm of this new type of bank. They are still today at the top of merger and acquisition business, through keeping the tradition of the *haute banque* of privileging quality of services over capital investment. Similarly, the rise of Siegmund Warburg, who emigrated from Germany to London in 1934, deserves a mention. Besides traditional activities like issuing the first long-term postwar dollar bond for a European institution, the European Coal and Steel Community, he became famous by creating the Euromarkets. He gained worldwide fame by conducting successfully for Reynolds Cy the hostile takeover of British Aluminium.

During the 1960s he became known as the master in the art of takeovers whether he belonged to the attacking or defending camp. In reaction, merchant banks, and later large banks, set up corporate finance teams before the latter actively pursued mergers with the former in the last decade. By buying out Seligman Brothers in 1957, Simon Warburg became one of the seventeen member firms of the select Accepting Houses Committee, thus acceding to the top of the *haute banque* in London. At the time his firm, which had been founded with a group of first-rate Austrian and German Jewish refugees, numbered eighty employees. In 1995 the Swiss Bank Corporation bought out S.G. Warburg, while other famous London merchant banks fell under the control of foreign banks.

By developing investment trusts beside their traditional activities, private bankers like Schröders have adapted themselves to the accelerating concentration in banking. This process does not hinder the rise of individual talented financiers. The case of the Hungarian Jew George Soros is striking in this respect; his influence on world money markets today may be compared to the power attributed to the Rothschilds during the last century.

Social Position of the Jewish Banker

The social position of Jewish private bankers raises two main questions. The first one concerns the nature of their networks, which proved to be a major factor in their success. Second, the problem of integration needs to be analysed in relation to the conditions prevailing in the various countries where they settled.

Whereas banking history of the nineteenth century early pointed out the importance of kinship relations, this basic factor has to be combined with two others, religion and geographic origin, as far as Jewish private bankers are concerned.

The importance of kinship in network building has been explained by several factors: capital accumulation ability, low transaction costs, confidentiality and trust, supposedly best attained through working with close relatives, and informal business connections useful for information and credit. These factors are widely described in the literature on merchant banking. At this point, kinship has been generally considered from the perspective of the continuity based on family ownership. However, two conceptions of kinship emerge from the case studies of private banks. The first one relies on a strict selection of male heirs for acceding to top management of the family bank or banking group. The Rothschilds' and Lazards' cases are well known. The history of the Warburg family reveals how talented sons were subject to strong pressure to enter the banking business. Contrary to that strict conception of kinship, some banks built broad networks including numerous wedlock alliances, and recruited in-laws. The Bischoffsheims' case is a typical one. Similarly, two prominent leaders of Kuhn, Loeb & Cy in New York were in-laws, viz. railroad financier Jacob Schiff, Salomon Loeb's son in-law, and Paul Warburg who married Schiff's daughter.

At this stage, intermarriage and the role of women in networking need to be considered. In the merchant banking world, strict endogamy aimed at consolidating the family's wealth by preventing inheritance partition. The Rothschilds attained an extreme degree of intermarriage in this respect, with fourteen marriages between members of the family among eighteen marriages celebrated from 1824 to 1870. However, intermarriage was not specific to the Jewish bankers' community. In the City of London, the old banking aristocracy and the Quaker families who founded Barclays were also used to it. In France, the Protestant families of the *haute banque* adopted the same behaviour. What was specific to wealthy Jewish bankers was having numerous relatives abroad and building wide international networks through their social and business connections. Most of them followed the Rothschilds' model, some of them being settled both in Europe and North America, like the Seligmans and the Warburgs. By marrying Eva Philippson, whose Jewish father managed Svenska Handelsbank, Siegmund Warburg became allied to the main rival bank of the Wallenbergs in Sweden. That specific feature undoubtedly inspired the image and the myth of the powerful Jewish cosmopolitan banker which became so popular during the nineteenth century.

There is perhaps another feature specific to the Jewish bankers' community. For most bankers, marriage was less a means of upward mobility than a means of conserving or increasing their wealth. Thus, contrary to other bankers, who were anxious to contract alliances with aristocracy by marrying their children, business connections and money prevailed over social relations. One may object that a long past of discrimination and struggle for survival influenced their behaviour. Perhaps the woman's role in the Jewish family should also be kept in mind. Despite the lack of systematic studies, existing monographs about bankers' dynasties reveal the authority of Jewish women inside the family and their major role in the banker's social life. From the second or third generation, education and culture became essential for women who had charge of the organizational work of networking and cultivating useful contacts. Thus they complemented their husband's economic position by cultural habits and an aristocratic way of life.

The longevity of private bankers' dynasties has been related to their membership of a religious minority. During the early nineteenth century emancipation and social mobility meant for many bankers in Central Europe the necessity to convert. But many others followed Jewish custom strictly during several generations. In Britain and France they adhered earlier to Reform, which introduced a more secular Judaism. As in the Rothschilds' case, loyalty to Judaism was less a question of religiosity than a clannish attitude, the family considering that religion was part of the cement which held it together and that remaining Jewish was an integral part of their good fortune. Men belonging to the financial elite like Gerson Bleichröder and his friend Moritz von Goldschmidt, the Rothschilds' main partner in Vienna, were both faithful Jews who considered their Jewishness as a special bond between them. In consequence, most of the wealthy Jewish bankers participated fully in communal and philanthropic activities and felt it was their duty to help their poor co-religionists.

Beyond religion, geographic origin was of primary importance for intermarriage and networking. This was typical among the bankers of German background. Thus, the German-Jewish banking community in New York cultivated its national characteristics, with the consequence that through their linguistic, social and cultural affinities, they promoted investment banking between America and Germany, whereas the New Englanders drew on the capital resources of Britain. Jacob Schiff wrote in German to Sir Ernest Cassel and so did many other international bankers at the time. Similarly, the discriminating behaviour of the German-Jewish New York bankers versus Jews originating from other countries, especially Sephardic Jews, played a significant part in the Lazards' decision on settling in Paris and London in the last quarter of the nineteenth century.

Paradoxically in Germany, where Jewish bankers felt the strongest sense of national identity and acceded to the upper echelons of society before World War I, they were never entirely accepted, and were condemned to disappear when the Nazis came to power. Gerson Bleichröder's story is the paradigm of the problem of integration in Germany and Stern's book is a brilliant demonstration of the ambiguity of Jewish success. The fact that, despite their close collaboration during thirty years, Bismarck did not even mention him in his memoirs, is perhaps one of the most revealing feature of that precarious condition.

When comparing integration of Jewish private bankers in different European countries, their position in the banking community and the social structure of the country where they lived influenced their integration. The case of Germany undoubtedly contrasts deeply with that of other West European societies. First, contrary to other countries, the German private bankers, especially in Berlin, were almost all Jews or of Jewish origin. Second, Germany's economic growth at the end of the nineteenth century was not immediately followed by modernization of society and full integration of businessmen into the dominating elite. Until World War I, although numerous *Junker* were in relationship with the private bankers, money was still a taboo in the Ancien Régime aristocracy of the German Empire and as such constituted an insurmountable barrier to integration. Thus, contrary to other Western countries, wealth was far from being a condition of acceptability into the higher circles. Bleichröder's life is revelatory of the Jewish parvenu's hunger for respectability. Despite his ennoblement for having undertaken to salvage the fortunes of Prussian junkers who had been caught in the collapse of Strousberg's railway projects in Romania, his growing visibility and luxurious way of life made him a target for those who despised the rise of Jewish plutocrats. With him as a symbol, the conjunction of anti-Judaism and anticapitalism stimulated the rise of German anti-Semitism during the 1870s. Higher education in select schools and universities was not a channel of social integration into the upper classes either; this may perhaps explain why the German bankers had a lower level of education than their colleagues in Britain or in France before 1914.

In England, successful bankers were generally integrated by the second generation. While they adopted an aristocratic way of life, their attitude to landownership, work and leisure was different from that of aristocrats. Thus, buying an estate was less a source of status or revenue than a source of leisure used as an instrument of business and social networking. The banking community being heterogeneous in matters of religion since the eighteenth century, this factor did not hinder Jewish bankers' ascension. Even though anti-Semitism was less virulent than elsewhere and many Jewish financiers were close to King Edward VII, before World War I only Lord Alfred Rothschild had been admitted to sit on the board of the Bank of England.

In France, most of the members of the *haute banque* belonged to the Protestant and Jewish minorities. In the second generation, the Jewish bankers assimilated without leaving their religion, by adopting the upper classes' education and way of life and obtaining French nationality. However, Jewish bankers suffered anti-Semitic prejudices, which worsened during the Dreyfus affair. The birth of the Banque de l'Union Parisienne, founded in 1904 by six houses of the Protestant *haute banque* and the Société Générale de Belgique, gives proof of the persistence of religious solidarities and rivalries in the banking world.

Moreover, even in such a liberal country as Belgium, the Société Générale had never had a Jew on its board. While the bank had for a long time to share the Belgian market with the Rothschilds and was in relationship with Mendelssohn since the 1870s for the Russian loans issues, it declined offers to do business from both the Warburg and Bleichröder banks. After the mid-1850s, when the growth of the Rothschilds' industrial interests in Belgium and the project for a Crédit Mobilier promoted by a group of the international *haute banque* brought strong opposition in Parliament and public opinion, the Jewish private bankers or at least their sons got used to asking for naturalization once they were well established in Belgium. In this way, they increased their integration in the national capitalism while at the same time stimulating the internationalization of the Brussels financial market. Although a few of them were able to become members of Parliament or were ennobled, the Jewish *haute banque* did not reach such a high degree of integration as in Britain. As intermarriage inside the Jewish international community suffered few exceptions, as religious practice and philanthropy towards the growing waves of poor Jews migrating from Eastern Europe prevailed, assimilation was rather difficult in high society before World War I, where Catholicism prevailed.

Jewish Private Bankers and Politics

The rise of Jewish bankers gave birth to new stereotypes in anti-Semitic propaganda after the late nineteenth century. One of those was their supposed omnipotence in world affairs. Without going into debate, we may point out some aspects of their relationship to politics. In calling Siegmund Warburg 'un homme d'influence', Jacques Attali stresses a significant feature of the role some prominent Jewish private bankers have played in politics, be it at national or international level. Few of them were directly active in politics in Parliament or government.

In Britain, Cassis has listed forty-six active bankers belonging to thirteen prominent banking families of the City who sat in Parliament between 1832 and 1918. Among them there were four members of the Rothschild family and two of the Samuels, not to mention the three Hambros whose family had been converted since the eighteenth century and belonged to the old banking aristocracy. In government, they were still less represented, the most-known figure being the liberal minister Sir Herbert Samuel. This weak political representation was not specific to Jewish bankers but a common feature of the banking community of the City. However, members of the bankers' families who were not in business might still go into politics, thus forming a link between the banking world and political circles.

In France, few members of the Jewish *haute banque* were openly in politics. The case of Achille Fould was rather exceptional. He began his political career during the July Monarchy, and became Minister of Finance during the Second Republic. He was called back to the Ministry of Finance by Emperor Napoleon III in 1860 to remedy the budget deficit. With the support of major interest groups, particularly the Rothschilds, Fould acted more as a representative of high finance than as a docile servant of the Emperor. However, some gentile politicians were close to the Jewish *haute banque* and defended their interests. The case of Léon Say, one of the Rothschild's Compagnie du Nord managers who was several times Minister of Finance during the Third Republic, is well known. Say's refusal to join the Gambetta cabinet in 1881 wrecked the republican left's project to nationalize railway companies.

Direct involvement in politics was also unusual among private Jewish bankers in other countries. However, some of them played a prominent role in politics concerning the monetary and credit system of their country. In Belgium, indeed, Jonathan Bischoffsheim was a member of the Liberal party, holding a seat on Brussels municipal council and on the Senate for twenty years. He was an influential counsellor of Minister Frère-Orban, who thoroughly reformed the Belgian monetary system by creating a central bank and developed municipal credit and saving by the lower classes by establishing public specialized institutions. In Germany, the famous banker and National Liberal politician Ludwig Bamberger, whose mother was Jonathan Bischoffsheim's sister, started his career in his uncle's bank at Amsterdam. During the foundation of the Empire, despite his political opinions, he played a major role as a close adviser of Bismarck in unifying German currency and setting up the German central bank, the Reichsbank. Although during the Empire Jewish bankers had some involvement in politics at a local or national level, the rise of anti-Semitism after World War I turned them away from the political scene. Significantly, Max Warburg refused to enter the Cabinet in 1921. He also refused to be German ambassador to the United States, in a desire to reduce his political visibility.

Though open political activity was uncommon among the Jewish private bankers, it did not mean that they were not interested in politics at all. Indeed, bankers' concern for politics was generally linked to their business interests. Despite their strong support for the restoration and stability of the conservative monarchies in continental Europe, the Rothschilds appear to have adapted themselves to the successive regimes in France after the fall of the monarchy. Similarly, through its broad international interests the family might be involved with both sides in conflicts between a conservative regime and its opponents. Thus, during the wars for Italian unification, the London house underwrote an Austrian loan while at the same time the Rothschilds of Paris were negotiating with the Piedmontese government.

As information obtained through personal contacts with business, political and diplomatic circles lay at the core of the private bankers' business, it is not surprising that government tried to use them as intermediaries and entrusted them with discreet missions. Thus, on several occasions Bleichröder was an intermediary between Bismarck and the liberal opposition in Prussia. We cannot tell his numerous diplomatic missions, but it is worth stressing that after the 1870s his position in Berlin so impressed the Russian Ministers of Finance that they corresponded secretly with him about not only financial but also political matters.

Despite appearances, the political influence of Jewish private bankers should not be overestimated. Its efficiency was correlative with the convergence of their interests and the aims of the government they served. Bleichröder's decline after the fall of Bismarck is a revealing case. The Romanian question is a yet more revealing one. During the 1870s Western Jews decided to use their power and influence in order to organize collective European pressure on East European governments to improve the lot of Jewish minorities. Bleichröder devoted himself to the case of the Romanian Jews. So long as German railway interests in Romania were threatened, Bismarck supported the campaign for emancipating the Romanian Jews. When in 1878 the Powers imposed their liberal principles on Romania at the Berlin Congress, Bleichröder celebrated his triumph sumptuously. It did not last very long. Once the railway question was solved with the Romanian government two years later, Bismarck cynically gave up his support to the Romanian Jews and their emancipation was forgotten.

Without debating the financing of the Zionist movement by certain prominent Jewish financiers, let us recall that the deteriorating situation of Russian Jewry also influenced their international business. Indeed, outraged by the pogroms against Russian Jews, Jacob Schiff decided to finance and support Japan during the war of 1904–5, and Japanese bonds were sold on the German market by the Warburg bank with the agreement of the Wilhelmstrasse.

On the whole, peace seems to have been the main concern of the international Jewish *haute banque*. The dread of war inspired Sir Ernest Cassel's and Max Warburg's efforts to unite Britain and Germany on the eve of World War I. Siegmund Warburg's action in favour of European Union after World War II was also motivated by his conviction that prosperity and close Western ties were the best way to prevent Nazi revival. Anyhow, the private bankers' political influence remains largely an unknown. By the end of the twentieth century, the private Jewish bank had lost its specific place in the banking system. A few houses have survived thanks to their strength and their ability to keep family control and adapt to banking evolution. The banking revolution of the last decade raises the question whether they will integrate the growing international groups or like their ancestors use their traditions to open up new pathways in the banking industry.

CHAPTER 13

Protestant Banking

Martin Körner †

The previous chapter has addressed Jewish private banks. This chapter will address Protestant banks. The explicit choice of the two groups mentioned implies a special sense given here to the term 'minority.' It is the affiliation to a distinct religious or confessional minority that makes their exploration attractive and interesting. But regarding these two particular minority groups, I would say that the second cannot easily be compared with the first.

It seems undisputed that Jews were a minority in all the countries where they lived during the medieval age and all over early modern and modern Europe. The case of the Protestants is not so clear. In Lutheran and Calvinist countries, Protestants undoubtedly became the majority during the sixteenth century and even kept the position of an exclusive confessional group until the end of the Ancien Régime. As regards economic activity, we may say that in most Protestant countries there is no knowledge of Roman Catholic private bankers' activities. At least with regard to Switzerland, we do not find any of them in the Protestant towns of Basel, Geneva, Bern or Zurich from the sixteenth to the end of the eighteenth century.[1]

With regard to the definition of private banking I wish in my chapter to discuss the various forms of banking as generally related in the historiography of the subject: merchant bankers, investment bankers, financiers. The important thing is that during the whole early modern period bankers were generally merchants too, and had at their disposal an international network for payment and capital transfer as well as being able to export the sums entrusted to them by their clients and place them at interest in public loans, industrial and colonial investments.[2] In addition to this, we should do well to remember that these special aspects of banking must be seen as an almost exclusively urban phenomenon. First of all, we shall answer

---

[1]   J.-F. Bergier, *Wirtschaftsgeschichte der Schweiz von den Anfängen bis zur Gegenwart* (Zurich, 1983, 1990), pp. 329–33.

[2]   J.-F. Bergier, 'Le dynamisme de la banque privée (VIIe–XIXe siècles)', in A. Vannini Marx (ed.), *Credito, banche e investimenti, secoli XIII–XX* (Florence, 1985). For general and specific information on economic history with regard to this chapter, see also P. Léon (ed.), *Histoire économique et sociale du monde, vols I–IV* (Paris, 1977–8); F. Vittinghoff et al. (eds), *Handbuch der europäischen Wirtschafts- und Sozialgeschichte*, vol. 3–4 (Frankfurt, 1986, 1993); L.H. Mottet, *Geschichte der Schweizer Banken: Bankier-Persönlichkeiten aus fünf Jahrhunderten* (Zurich, 1987); A.-M. Piuz et al. (eds), *L'Economie genevoise de la Réforme à la fin de l'Ancien Régime, XVIe–XVIIIe siècles* (Geneva, 1990).

the question when and how a so-called Protestant private-banking network came
to be set up in Europe.

Towards a Protestant Financial Solidarity and Banking System in the Sixteenth Century

After the Reformation, one observes a political, demographic and financial change
in Europe creating confessional antagonism and separate solidarities. The so called
Religious Wars for territorial or dynastic domination ended in Switzerland in 1531
and in Germany in 1555, but began in France in 1562 and in the Netherlands in
1567. Support for the Protestant party in France became reinforced in Calvinist
Switzerland and Germany through the arrival of French refugees mainly at Geneva
and Frankfurt.

From the reign of Francis I (1515–47), the Kings of France got loans to finance
their wars mainly from their principal financial centre, which until the end of the
Grand Parti was Lyons. But they also used to issue loans at Basel, which was
the main Swiss financial centre in the sixteenth century. From 1553 to 1558, an
important confessionally mixed group of Swiss merchants and mercenary officers
was still committing sizeable amounts to some of the last loans issued by Henry II
(1547–9) at Lyons before the insolvency of the French Kingdom. Like his father
Francis I, King Henry II used these to bring about a kind of backflow of all the
money he regularly paid to Switzerland by way of pensions and subsidies. In
addition, through these loans the Swiss mercenary officers were at least in part
financing the French war against Spain in Picardy and Flanders and hoped in this
way to save the jobs for their military troops.[3]

But from the beginning of the Religious Wars[4] until 1570, the French Kings got
further loans only from the Swiss Roman Catholic Republics, while the Protestant
Republics preferred to financially support first the Republic of Geneva, as they had
done since 1530, and second the Calvinist Bourbon King Henry of Navarre. Minor
loans were given to the Count Palatine for his military interventions, notably in
support of the Protestant party in France. Most of these financial activities were
carried out on the one hand by the Public Bank of Basel through loan issues with
prefabricated individual obligations, and on the other by private bankers or
merchant bankers at Geneva and Basel. And in order to partially pay his debts
toward the Swiss troops after the Peace of St. Germain in 1570, even King Charles
IX (1560–74) was allowed to issue loans among the Protestant Cantons for more

---

[3]   For this paragraph and the following developments concerning the sixteenth and the
beginning of the seventh centuries see M. Körner, *Solidarités financières suisses au XVIe
siècle: Contribution à l'histoire monétaire, bancaire et financière des Cantons suisses et
des Etats voisins* (Lausanne, 1980).

[4]   Concerning the French Religious Wars, see G. Livet, 'Les guerres de réligion', *Que
sais-je?*, 1016 (Paris, 1962).

than 170,000 of a total of 200,000 écus he was able to get from Switzerland through his ambassador.

Just before the outbreak of the eighth religious war in 1586, Antoine of Vienne, Henry of Navarre's main agent in Switzerland, secured a loan of 70,000 écus from the Duke of Württemberg. This affair was arranged at Basel by banker Niklaus Wasserhuhn and notary Peter Rippel. Queen Elizabeth of England (1558–1603) sent 100,000 écus in 1587 to the Count Palatine John Casimir to finance new troops in support of Henry of Navarre. And after the alliance of the two Henrys in France against the Catholic Guise Party in January 1589, Swiss Protestants added a further 250,000 écus. Finally in 1596 King Henry IV (1594–1610), the former King of Navarre, obtained an additional 20,000 écus from England.

After the end of the religious wars in France and the promulgation of the Edict of Nantes in 1598, King Henry IV found himself with the total of all the debts contracted by the French Kings. The total burden of debt against Catholic and Protestant Switzerland amounted to more than 11,000,000 écus or about 36,000,000 livres tournois. When he started to reimburse part of it after 1602, the payments of interests and amortizations passed either through direct money transports to the French Embassy at Solothurn or via the payment network of some Protestant merchant bankers and the Public Bank of Basel.

How do we know about this Protestant network for financial transfers at the end of the sixteenth century? It is known because of the Protestant solidarity with the Republic of Geneva all over Calvinist Europe and Anglican England. The young Republic of Geneva had always been in great difficulties with its public finances since the Reformation and its independence from Savoy and the exile of the former Bishop of Geneva to Annecy in 1535. The accounts ended with a deficit almost every year until the end of the sixteenth century, particularly during the war against Savoy in 1589–93. Geneva got used to receiving large loans – a total of about 211,000 écus – from all the major Swiss Protestant Cantons and from Strasbourg. This money was partially transferred by merchants through letters of change and *cédules obligatoires* from Basel to Geneva during the second half of the sixteenth century. But in 1583–93 Geneva also got some financial help from the French, Dutch, German and Eastern European brethren as well as from the English and Scottish church communities. In these countries an amount of more than 46,000 écus was put together into specially arranged collects for Geneva.[5]

How was this money transferred to Geneva? This question has something to do with the Genevan proto-industrial and commercial activities, especially those of the French and Italian Protestant immigrants after the Reformation. This first immigrant group brought new activities to Geneva, Zurich and Basel and also stimulated traditional branches in these towns. The growth of the production and export of Swiss silk and woollen materials during the sixteenth century was mainly the result of the innovative power of these Italian and French entrepreneurs, who became citizens of Geneva, sometimes also associated with old Swiss entrepreneurs

---

[5]   For more details, see Körner, *Solidarités*, p. 391.

at Basel and Zurich as we know from the publications of Walter Bodmer, Herbert Lüthy, Hans-Conrad Peyer, Jean-François Bergier and Liliane Mottu-Weber.[6]

Now, as regards the international transfers, we do not know if the merchants and bankers who acted as a relay station on the way to Geneva were actually all Protestants. But our research has clarified how the money went through. For instance, in 1582 Jean Mallet of Geneva was able to collect about 5,730 Pounds Sterling in England. Since the exportation of real coins from England to the continent was not allowed, he entrusted the money to a merchant in London, John Bodley, who continued to cash further sums collected after Jean Mallet's departure. Bodley credited the money to the accounts of his clients Guillaume Collabaud and Raymond de Not at Lyons. Then these two merchants credited the money to Horace Micheli, who was a rich Genevan silk manufacturer with excellent connections in Lyons. Finally, a number of other merchants from Lyons, Geneva, Switzerland and Germany helped to transfer the money from Lyons to Geneva. These transfers were brought about in two ways: passing through Geneva, one of these merchants would pay a certain amount of money to the Public Treasurer and get a letter of exchange on Horace Micheli at Lyons, or receive a short-term loan from Horace Micheli at Lyons to pay the merchants at Lyons against *cédules obligatoires* which became payable a few days later at Geneva. In 1583–4, the Republic of Geneva received about 18,000 écus which were transferred in this way from Lyons.

Duke Casimir, the Count Palatine, in 1585 reimbursed a loan of 2,000 écus he had received two years before from the Republic of Geneva. This money was transferred by a letter of exchange sent by Paulus Formberg, Hans Bosch & Co from Nuremberg to Geneva but drawn on the Genevan merchant Gabriel Rinstevand at Frankfurt. A lot of other smaller and larger sums were transferred to Geneva during the following years by letters of exchange or *cédules obligatoires* from Frankfurt, Strasbourg, Basle, St Gallen and Lyons. In 1589–96 about 22,000 écus arrived in this way for the public treasury of the Genevan Republic. During these years we notice the following merchants or merchant-bankers engaged in these transfers: Joseph Fosses, Janneto Motta, Jacob Gradelle, Julien Péaget, Jean Jaillet, Jean Dupré, David Deroche, Mr Calandrin, Jean Combe, Jean and Thibaud Morlot at Geneva, Anton Legalio and Jeromino Mieg at Basel, and Hans Piguel at Strasbourg.

After 1590 Frankfurt became more and more important as a turning point for Genevan capital transfers. When a group of merchants of St. Gallen gave out a

---

    6   W. Bodmer, *Der Einfluss der Refugianteneinwanderung von 1550–1700 auf die schweizerische Wirtschaft: Ein Beitrag zur Geschichte des Frühkapitalismus und der Textilindustrie* (Zurich, 1946); H. Lüthy, *La Banque Protestante en France de la Révocation de l'Édit de Nantes à la Révolution*, 2 vols (Paris, 1959–1961); H.C. Peyer, *Von Handel und Bank im alten Zürich* (Zurich, 1968); Bergier, *Wirtschaftsgeschichte*; L. Mottu-Weber, 'Vie économique et refuge à Genève à la fin du XVIIe siècle', in *Genève au temps de la Révocation de l'édit de Nantes 1680–1705* (Geneva, 1985); L. Mottu-Weber, *Genève au siècle de la Réforme: Economie et refuge* (Geneva Paris, 1987).

loan of 10,000 écus at Lyons to the representatives of King Henry of Navarre, they stipulated Frankfurt as the place for all payments of interest and reimbursement. In 1590–2 the sums of money recently collected in England were transferred by letter of exchange directly or via Hamburg from London to Frankfurt and then mostly by Genevan merchants home to their Republic. Now it was a Mr Castel who arranged this business in London. Then the money was managed at Frankfurt by the Calvinist pastor Canon. Over the year, Genevan merchants and publishers came to all the four fairs at Frankfurt, which were very important international book markets. There we several times meet Louis Maupon, Jean Lepreux, Jean Dupan, Jacques Delacort, Pierre Patru, Jean and Julien Péaget. Finally, the sums collected in the Protestant Low Countries were sent in 1594 by letter of change from Amsterdam to Frankfurt and taken over from there by the above mentioned Genevan trustees.

At the beginning of the seventeenth century King Henry IV transferred from Paris via Lyons the considerable sums he designated as support for the financially weak Republic of Geneva. All this royal money and other sums from private intermediaries came to Geneva mainly via letters of exchange on Lyons. Some of the letters also came directly from Paris. Another sum collected by Jean Anjorrant in England did not travel via Frankfurt to get to Geneva but through Lyons. In 1603–5 about 42,000 écus arrived by letter of exchange in these two ways from London and Paris at Geneva.

All these facts known about Protestant financial activities during the sixteenth century bring us to a first or intermediate conclusion. The foundation of Protestant banking was first the result of ordinary economic activities of merchants and merchant bankers passing from the Catholic to the Protestant confession. Protestant solidarity began in Switzerland among the towns of the Reformation and Calvin's Geneva and continued between European Protestants and the Calvinist party in France, especially with King Henry of Navarre. Protestant banking became internationally visible in history through all kinds of financial and political activities during the French civil and religious wars. It appears that together with England, the Elector Palatine and the Duke of Württemberg, Swiss Protestants became the main foreign financial supporters of the French Protestant party. Capital transfers were brought about in different ways: by real monetary transports, by letters of exchange, by *cédules obligatoires*. It was possible to use the last two techniques mentioned because of the existence of a new international payment network especially among Protestant merchants and merchant bankers existing beside the traditional one concentrated on Antwerp.[7] Of course, the existing traditional network for international payments at 1575–80 had a rather different geographical

---

[7]   According to empirical data found in the accounts of the Republic of Geneva of the sixteenth and seventeenth centuries. See Körner, *Solidarités*, pp. 368–76. This mainly Protestant payment network was also used during the seventeenth century by Swiss Catholic merchants and military entrepreneurs in France. See H. Steffen, *Die Kompanien Kaspar Jodok Stockalpers: Beispiel eines Soldunternehmers im 17. Jahrhundert* (Brig, 1975), pp. 219–21.

appearance.[8] It was obviously that of the then usual payments between the existing dominant economic centres of the Catholic world. About twenty years later, both systems, the Catholic and the Protestant, were on the way to integration.[9]

Consolidation and Domination of Protestant Banking in France in the Seventeenth to Eighteenth Centuries

To repeat: at the beginning of the seventeenth century the French monarchy owed to the Swiss Republics, the private financiers, bankers and mercenary entrepreneurs a sum of around 11 million écus or 36 million livres tournois. This was the result of the growing credit given by the Swiss, rather earlier than generally related in the dominant literature on finance and bank history. In fact, the growth of Swiss financial power in France began in the early sixteenth century and grew from about the late sixties, when one observes the diminishing activities of rivals at Genoa and in Catholic Southern Germany, manifestly turning its capital flow toward the German and Spanish Empire.[10]

Already in the sixteenth century, the French Crown became interested in Protestant Swiss financiers as counsellors. Just after the great loans at the time of the *Grand Parti* of Lyons and the insolvency of the Crown in 1559, the Catholic Caspar Pfyffer from Lucerne and the Protestant Benedikt Stokar from Schaffhausen acted as intermediaries for the representatives of King Charles IX and the Swiss lender consortium.[11] However, in 1562 the French ambassador in Switzerland, Pomponne de Bellièvre, chose two Protestants as his special counsellors for financial affairs between France and Switzerland. Of the two mentioned, he kept Stokar and added the new Hans-Heinrich Lochmann from Zurich.[12] The preference for the Protestant Swiss Republics can also be shown after 1602, when King Henry IV solemnly renewed the military alliance of 1521 with the Swiss Republics and confirmed the old privileges for all Swiss merchants in the Kingdom of France. Henry engaged himself to pay the accumulated interest on capital, part of the principal owed and especially the subsidies

---

[8]   See M.A. Denzel, *'La Practica della Cambiatura': Europäischer Zahlungsverkehr vom 14. bis zum 17. Jahrhundert* (Stuttgart, 1994), p. 529. For the quotations of bills of exchange in 1575–80, see M.A. Denzel (ed.), *Währungen der Welt, vol. IX: Europäische Wechselkurse von 1383 bis 1620* (Stuttgart, 1995), p. 32, map 2. For more examples, see M.A. Denzel, 'Die Integration Deutschlands in das internationale Zahlungsverkehrssystem im 17. und 18. Jahrhundert', in E. Schremmer (ed.), *Wirtschaftliche und soziale Integration in historischer Sicht, Vierteljahrschrift für Sozial- und Wirtschaftsgeschichte*, vol. 128 (Stuttgart, 1996).

[9]   For the quotations of bills of exchange in 1595–1600, see Denzel, *Währungen*, p. 106, map 3.

[10]   Körner, *Solidarités*, pp. 416–30.

[11]   Ibid., p. 421.

[12]   Ibid., p. 422.

from his predecessor, King Henry III, which had not been paid since 1587. While the French treasury transferred exactly the expected sums to the Protestant Republics, the Catholic ones were forced to write off a great part of their assets.[13]

During the reign of Louis XIII (1610–43) the Treasury of the French State was under permanent and growing pressure because of the King's politics of territorial expansion.[14] Swiss and French merchant bankers, mainly Protestants, played an important role in offering the demanded capital to the Treasury. In addition to the traditional Swiss financiers, the descendants of French Protestant refugees in Geneva during the religious wars were now going to act as merchants and bankers in French, Italian and other European economic centres. At the end of the sixteenth and all through the seventeenth centuries they were successful in the production and trade of silk, precious metals and watches as well as in merchant banking. Because of the existence of international family groupings, a result of the refugees dispersing to countries where they were admitted, these former French merchant bankers were present and economically active in London, Amsterdam, Geneva, Genoa and Cadiz, but also as 'new Catholics' in Paris, Lyons and Marseilles. Their common fate created among them a special religious and economic solidarity. Herbert Lüthy spoke of this community force as the 'international Huguenot bank'. They deployed an excellent international information network which allowed them to trade on optimum terms. They offered short-term credits on letters of exchange, principally to merchants but sometimes also to ruling princes. During the reign of Louis XIV (1643–1715), the capital demand of the French monarchy grew even more than before, greatly benefiting the Genevan bankers, who consequently won more and more influence in France in general and at the French court in particular.[15]

After having cherished their traditional connections with Lyons and Paris during the last decades of the sixteenth century, the Genevan merchant-bankers set up in

---

[13]   Ibid., pp. 423–8.

[14]   For more details, see R. Bonney, *The King's Debts: Finance and Politics in France, 1589–1661* (Oxford, 1981). Concerning the general problem of the State's expenditures and indebtedness, see M. Körner, 'Expenditure', in R. Bonney (ed.), *Economic Systems and State Finance* (Oxford, 1995); M. Körner, 'Public Credit', in R. Bonney (ed.), Economic Systems and State Finance (Oxford, 1995).

[15]   Concerning Protestant banking in France during the seventeenth and eighteenth centuries, see Lüthy, *La Banque Protestante*. For the eighteenth century: J. Bouvier, 'Activités bancaires et groupes bancaires', in P. Léon (ed.), *Histoire économique et sociale de la France*, vol. II (Paris, 1978), pp. 310–21; P. Léon, 'Prestige du monde de la finance', in P. Léon (ed.), *Histoire économique et sociale du monde*, vol. II (Paris, 1978), pp. 622–33. Actually, the descendants of the Huguenot refugees in Germany had acted similarly, and some of them created common trading societies with Swiss Protestants in France. See P. Fierz, *Eine Basler Handelsfirma im ausgehenden 18. und zu Beginn des 19. Jahrhunderts: Christoph Burckhardt & Co. und verwandte Firmen* (Zurich, 1994); and M.A. Denzel, *Der Preiskurant des Handelshauses Pelloutier & Cie aus Nantes (1763–1793), Beiträge zur Wirtschafts- und Sozialgeschichte*, vol. 73 (Stuttgart, 1997).

the second half of the seventeenth century in these two centres a number of branch banks which very rapidly became independent Protestant private banking places. Together with Geneva and Lyons, Protestant banking at Paris became at the end of the seventeenth century even more important than all the native French financiers together. The influence and power of the Genevan bankers at Paris upon French State finance became so dominant that they were able to go on operating in France in 1685 when the French Huguenots were officially eliminated from all economic activities by the revocation of the Edict of Nantes.[16] They even reinforced their position by organizing the transfer to foreign countries of the wealth of the exiled French Huguenots. The sums entrusted to them were invested into the French State treasury and paid to the owners in various foreign locations.

Parisian Protestant banking came to a new peak of influence with regard to French State finances particularly during the Nine Years' War (1688–97) and the War of the Spanish Succession (1701–14). The historiography stresses the dominant role played by Samuel Bernard, a Parisian Protestant banker from Sancerre who abjured. Samuel Bernard furnished the Crown with enormous loans for the acquisition of war materiel in France and for the maintenance of the operating armies in Flanders, Bavaria, Alsace and Italy. A group of rich Protestant bankers, among them the Fatios from Geneva and the Hogguers from Lyons, discounted promissory notes of the treasury to the Crown, several financiers and fiscal tenants. They paid the credits in advance, using the money entrusted to them by their clients in France. Outside the country they transferred the money for the account of the Crown by letters of exchange in foreign places. In 1702–5 the royal Almanach also mentions names like Hogguer, Mallet, Tourton and Guiger. These two latter families constituted a Company which was present simultaneously at Geneva, Lyons, Amsterdam and London. Because of their international relationships and the respect the Protestant bankers had won over the decades, they were able to use an important part of the commercial capital flows to finance the French State.

The problem with this kind of public credit funding was that the letters of exchange accepted by the Parisian bankers for the State treasury were not covered by ordinary commercial transactions. They were guaranteed only by the promissory notes of the treasury. But the excessive expenditures caused by the lengthy French wars made the option of reimbursement of the State's debt impossible. The crown tried to save its public credit by reducing the interest rates, promulgating a moratorium on the reimbursement of debts and other urgent appeasements. But all these interventions were without success. In 1709 and subsequent years quite a number of the Parisian Protestant bankers and some others were forced to apply for bankruptcy. One of the consequences was a temporary diminution of the Protestant bankers' influence.

However, some of them survived this payment crisis and even that of the Law System in 1720. Let us give a portrayal of one of these bankers, who was to later

---

[16]   The native Protestants were officially readmitted to French society in 1786 by a new edict of tolerance under King Louis XVI.

lead one of the most powerful banks in Paris. Born in 1690 as a son of a Genevan merchant, Isaac Thellusson, related to Louis Guiguer, arrived in Paris in 1707 after his apprenticeship and further training in Amsterdam and London. A few years later he became the managing director of the 'Jean-Jacques Tourton and Louis Guiguer' firm for 'banking, change and trade'. Herbert Lüthy describes him as the typical representative of the new banker generation in the eighteenth century: overbearing, ruthless, authoritarian and violent, with the terrible good conscience of the just. He was a decided enemy of the Scot John Law and held himself and his affairs back from the System. The Thellusson family continued the profitable management of their own bank. In 1757–68 the firm was called 'Thellusson, Necker & Co' and in 1789 'Greffulhe & Montz'. In 1770 'Thellusson, Necker & Co' was known as one of the three biggest private banks in Paris. The second one, 'Tourton & Bauer', was also a Protestant bank. But the third one, 'Lecouteulx & Co', was Catholic. This shows that not all the important private banks were the property of Protestants.

With the reorganization of the French monetary system and its stabilization after the Law crisis, Protestant banks again became very important in financing French foreign trade and serving the Royal Treasury. A new generation of Genevan bankers – Isaac Mallet and Robert Dufour – introduced themselves in Paris in order to administer the French bonds, mainly shares of the Indian Company, rents on the town-hall and royal lotteries of Genevan and Swiss capitalists. 'Tourton & Bauer' were highly implicated in the affairs of the King of Poland in 1733–8, transferring French subsidies on behalf of the King. During the critical supply situation in 1738–41 Thellusson in his function as minister of Geneva at Versailles played a dominating role in financing the grain provision of Paris. After 1760, the Royal Treasury got more used to accepting the services of the international Protestant bankers at its highest level. One of them, Jacques Necker, citizen of Geneva, merchant and banker, ascended also to the position of resident of the Republic of Geneva at the court and under Louis XVI (1774–93) became the head of the royal finances in 1776, and prime minister of the kingdom until 1788. During these years, officially he was no longer a private banker, but he still continued to be Georges-Thobie Thellusson's partner in the Company.

Since the Swiss economy suffered during the eighteenth century from a great capital overhang, the Genevan bankers present for generations in Paris, and increasingly also those from St. Gallen, Zurich, Basel, Bern, Lausanne and Neuchâtel, were looking for all kinds of investment opportunities.[17] In addition

---

[17]   For more details concerning the capital overhang in eighteenth-century Switzerland, see J. Landmann, *Die auswärtigen Kapitalanlagen aus dem Berner Staatsschatz im XVIII. Jahrhundert: Eine finanzhistorische Studie* (Zurich, 1903); J. Landmann, *Leu & Co. 1755–1905: Ein Beitrag zur Geschichte der öffentlichen und privaten Kreditorganisation* (Zurich, 1905); J. Landmann, 'Der schweizerische Kapitalexport', in *Zeitschrift für schweizerische Statistik und Volkswirtschaft*, vol. 52, 1916, pp. 389–415; H. Büchi, 'Solothurnische Finanzzustände im ausgehenden Ancien Régime (ca. 1750–98)', in *Basler Zeitschrift für Geschichte und Altertumskunde*, vol. 15, 1916, pp. 56–116; B. Wehrli, *Das Finanzsystem*

to the business with the above-mentioned royal bonds, they also bought for their clients shares of semi-public and private firms in industry, trade, navigation and banking. By making good use of their relationships with the world of trade and with old Protestant banking in France these Swiss newcomers did not have any difficulties in introducing themselves into the society of Parisian high finance. Through their offer of foreign capital they appeared as very attractive partners for French merchants and manufacturers. The Genevan Antoine Saladin easily became a shareholder and managing director of the royal mirror manufactory of Saint-Gobain. And we find Jacques-Louis Pourtalès from Neuchâtel at the head of a multinational trading and banking house with bases at Lyons, Paris, Pondicherry, Lorient, Hamburg, London, Philadelphia and Constantinople.

Alongside all the Genevan bankers in Paris such as 'Girardot, Haller & Co' – Necker's old firm – as well as Mallet, Bontemps, Lullin, de Candolle and Calandrini, etc. with all their well-trained business activities, we find in particular five Protestant Swiss bankers among the seven members of the administrative board of the Caisse d'escompte founded in 1776: Isaac Panchaud from Lausanne, the promoter of this new trading bank, Jean Pierre Louis de Montguyon from Geneva, an associate of 'Pache frères & Cie' in Paris, Jean Werner Marck from Basel, founder of 'Marck & Lafabre,' which changed its name in 1775 to 'Banque Lafabre & Doerner' at Paris, Paul Schlumpf from St Gallen, associated with the 'Sellonf & Perregaux' bank at Paris, and Etienne Delessert, the head of the 'Banque Delessert & Fils' at Lyons and of its Paris branch 'Delessert & Cie'. These initiators of the Caisse d'escompte were specialists in maritime trade hoping to be more successful than the French Indian Company which recently had lost its monopoly in the colonial trade. Even the new generation of private bankers that Necker called into this bank in 1778 after the eviction of Panchaud and the 'traders' were representatives of the *haute banque* of Paris, and all Protestants – Girardot, Louis Tourton, Jean-Louis Cottin, Jacques Rilliet, etc. – except Lecouteulx, who was a Catholic. Finally, after 1780 new Swiss Protestant bankers arrived in Paris – Rougemont and Perrégaux from Neuchâtel and Hottinguer from Zurich, who after the French Revolution and the early nineteenth century became some of the big private bankers of the *haute banque*.[18]

Zürichs gegen Ende des 18. Jahrhunderts (Aarau, 1944); H.C. Peyer, *Von Handel und Bank im alten Zürich* (Zurich, 1968); E.W. Monter, 'Swiss Investment in England, 1697–1720', in *International Review of the History of Banking*, vol. 2, 1969, pp. 285–98; B. Veyrassat, *Négociants et fabricants dans l'industrie cotonnière suisse 1760–1840: Aux origines financières de l'industrialisation* (Lausanne, 1982); M. Körner, 'Banques publiques et banquiers privés dans la Suisse préindustrielle: Administration, Fonctionnement et rôle économique', in Banchi pubblici, banchi privati e monti di pietà nell'Europa preindustrale, Atti del Convegno, Genoa, 1–6 October 1990 (Genoa, 1991).

[18] For the period of the French Revolution and the early nineteenth century, see M. Lévy-Leboyer, *Les banques européennes et l'industrialisation internationale dans la première moitié du XIXe siècle* (Paris, 1964). A good summary can be found in M. Lévy-

Protestant Banking During Early Modern Times in Some Other Catholic Countries

In Germany[19] the most important merchant bankers like the Fuggers, Welsers, Höchstetters and Imhoffs remained Catholic after the Reformation. We do not have much information on Protestant firms doing their business in the sixteenth and early seventeenth centuries mainly in Catholic towns or countries, except for the Lutheran Rehlinger merchant bank which acted in and out of Augsburg. The Rehlingers were related to German and Italian firms at Venice and Antwerp in the sixteenth century, and additionally in Piacenza and Lyons in the seventeenth century. They made loans to the courts of Austria, Spain and England. In the early seventeenth century they orientated their investments more to the Protestant low countries with shares in the 'East-India Company' in Amsterdam and the 'West-India Company' in Rotterdam. During the Thirty Years War, Max Conrad Rehlinger (1575–1642) got into difficulties because of his Protestant partisanship. He fled in 1629 to Bern just before being outlawed by the Emperor. With the part of his wealth he had saved from confiscation he continued to advance money to the Protestant faction. He died in 1642 at Geneva, where he had become influential in Protestant international banking. After his death, his son Ferdinand (1619–87) lived and worked in Lyons in 1643–9 and then returned to Germany, but without continuing his career as a merchant banker.

In the later eighteenth century we find more Protestant German merchant bankers doing their business in Catholic countries, e.g. members of the Metzler and Bethmann families from Frankfurt in Bordeaux and Vienna.[20] The banking house of Johann Philipp Bethmann was also an innovator, using the technique of the partial obligation to float more than fifty bond issues in Austria with a total sum of 38 million Austrian florins by the last decades of the eighteenth century. One may now ask the reasons for the offering of these lucrative activities to a Protestant banking firm. One must admit that some tolerance was given to them under the

---

Leboyer, 'Les banques européennes et l'industrialisation internationale dans la première moitié du XIXe siècle', in P. Léon (ed.), *Histoire économique et sociale du monde*, vol. III, *L'avènement de l'ère industrielle (1789-années 1850)*, vol. 1 (Paris, 1976); H. Großkreuz, *Privatkapital und Kanalbau in Frankreich 1814–1848: Eine Fallstudie zur Rolle der Banken in der französischen Industrialisierung, Schriften zur Wirtschafts- und Sozialgeschichte*, vol. 28 (Berlin, 1977); L. Bergeron, *Banquiers, négociants et manufacturiers parisiens du Directoire à l'Empire* (Paris, 1978); M. Körner, 'Banquiers et financiers suisses en France', in *Marchés et Techniques Financières*, vol. 12, 1989, p. 40; F. Baudequin, 'Clavière', in *Marchés et Techniques Financières*, vol. 12, 1989, pp. 42–3.

[19] For more information on banking in Germany, see E. Klein, *Deutsche Bankengeschichte*, vol. 1, *Von den Anfängen bis zum Ende des alten Reiches (1806)* (Frankfurt, 1992).

[20] Klein, *Bankengeschichte*, pp. 246–56.

Emperors Ferdinand III (1637–57) and Leopold I (1658–1705).[21] Dickson thinks that the 'permission given in 1653 and 1664 for Protestant widows to continue the business of their husbands in Vienna implies that toleration was of long standing.'[22] Protestant foreigners are found on the list of retailers all through the eighteenth century and on those of the college of wholesalers in 1774. The edict creating this institution in 1774 explicitly provided for the access of foreigners and Protestants. Among them Steiner from Winterthur, Labhard, Ochs and Rieger from Basel, Fries from Mühlhausen, Paldinger from Ödenburg, Wiesenhütter from Frankfurt am Main and probably Castelmur from Graubünden can be definitely identified as foreign Protestants. Under Joseph II (1765–1790) and later, the Protestants Fries & Co. as well as Ochs & Geymuller were still the leading banking firms in Vienna, together with Arnstein & Eskeles and Brentani Cimaroli.

With regard to the 'Wiesenhütter & Co.' firm, which had been started at Vienna by Franz Wiesenhütter (1720–86), the eldest son of Johann Friedrich, a Protestant banker from Frankfurt am Main, one must underline that its head became a Catholic in 1743 and was made a Bohemian baron after his marriage with Maria Elisabeth, the daughter of Baron Bertenstein. He was prominent as a banker of the court only for a few years. He rapidly got into an impossible financial situation and went bankrupt in 1746.[23]

The Steiners were known as the main merchants in the salt trade from Austria to South Germany and Switzerland in the seventeenth century. They were still known in Vienna throughout the early eighteenth century. One of them entered in 1768 into the group of privileged retailers. In the same year, he created together with Johann Christian Schuster the 'Melchior Steiner & Co.' firm. This firm was not listed among the bankers of Vienna in 1774, but in 1779 actually raised an important war loan for the Austrian crown in Holland. And his nephew Melchior in 1816 became a director of the National Bank.[24]

One of those who assumed a dominant role in government finance after 1750 was Johann Fries (1719–85). This Swiss Protestant banker from Mühlhausen remained pre-eminent from his settlement in Vienna until his death. His strength derived partly from his excellent foreign connections, particularly a close relationship with bank houses in the Austrian Netherlands as well as with Dutch and Italian correspondents. Dickson describes the 'Freiherr von Friess & Co.' as responsible for a range and scale of official finance and contracting unknown since the days of Samuel Oppenheimer in the late seventeenth century. Fries was the eldest son of Philipp Jakob, who was in 1742–6 the town mayor of Mühlhausen. 'In 1744 Johann entered the "English commissariat" charged with supplying the

[21]   For all details on the following developments at Vienna, see P.G.M. Dickson, *Finance and Government under Maria Theresa 1740–1780*, 2 vols (Oxford, 1987), for Toleration Patent, see especially vol. I, pp. 60–65.

[22]   Dickson, *Finance*, vol. I, p. 156.

[23]   Ibid., pp. 171–2.

[24]   Ibid., pp. 170–71.

"pragmatic army" of Austrian, Dutch, English and Hanoverian troops in the Low Countries. He must quickly have made his mark, since he was asked in 1748 to go to London to negotiate for a stipulated £100,000 subsidy the English government was refusing to pay. Fries' mission, which lasted a year, was successful. The English government paid up in March 1749. The empress, impressed, summoned him to Vienna. ... From April 1752 he was responsible for marketing a good portion of the state's silver thalers, and made large profits for the government and for himself. In the Seven Years War he handled receipts of French subsidies, and of Belgian and Italian loans and taxes to a total of nearly 45 million florins.'[25]

Almost every year he was on foreign mission for subsidies, loans and short-term credits, for paying the Austrian army in good coins, and was in charge in 1759–83 of commercializing the production of the state mines. When in Paris in 1764, he married in the Dutch chapel Anne d'Escherny, daughter of a burgess from Neuchâtel, who was also consul at Lyons for the King of Poland. After 1763 most of the government's external loans were emitted under Fries's responsibility. As well as this, there were also a great many other trading affairs we cannot enumerate, e.g. with two Greek partners in 1774 in Constantinople. Changing his business partners in the firm rather often, in 1766 he admitted Johann Jacob Gontard who came from a Frankfurt banking family of French refugee origin. When he died in 1785, he left a very large fortune calculated at more than three and a half million Austrian florins. One thinks that he probably committed suicide because of the public resentment against this foreign Protestant who grew rich at the state's expense. His son Moritz Christian was not at all a successful banker. He systematically dissipated his inherited fortune, so that the firm went bankrupt in 1826.

At this point the question may arise as to why some of the Protestants could rise to the position of dominant financiers and bankers in Catholic Vienna. Dickson thinks that the phenomenon is 'consistent with contemporary statements that Austrian mercantile and banking resources were weak, and bankruptcies frequent, and that domestic entrepreneurs needed to be strengthened from outside'[26]first by Jewish financiers, who were prominent under the empress's father Charles VI (1711–40), and into the 1740s and even later with the Hönigs, Poppers and some others who still had considerable capital. Another move of the government was its willingness to tolerate Protestant finance as an expedient for escaping from Jewish finance. And Dickson concludes: 'The qualified freedom for Protestant Wholesalers conceded in 1774 was an example of this. The career of Johann Fries demonstrates it very vividly. He was a man of immense competence, able to build up a huge fortune partly as a result of monopolies conceded to him by the state.... He thus stands with ... others, whose varied backgrounds and policies gave the Austrian state in this period a more mixed and interesting character...'[27].

---

[25] Dickson, *Finance*, vol. I, p. 173.
[26] Ibid., p. 177.
[27] Dickson, *Finance*, vol. I, p. 178.

We could easily continue the description of the world of Protestant banking in the towns of other non-Protestant countries of Europe: in Italy, in Portugal, in Spain. In lieu of a complete map of all the towns where Protestant commercial and banking activities can be made out, we have been able to address one of the localities where Swiss merchants and bankers were present at the end of the eighteenth century. We find them between Lisbon and Cadiz in the south-west and Moscow and Petersburg in the north-east as well as from Bergen and London in the north-west to Constantinople and Smyrna in the south-east.[28]

Outlook on the Nineteenth Century

Some of the Protestant banking firms we have spoken about went bankrupt during the French Revolution and the Napoleonic Wars. But some of them not only passed through these troubles intact, but were even able by simple opportunity or progressive conviction to adapt themselves to the political and economic change of the period. That is the reason why in 1798 the most important Protestant banks of the vanishing Ancien Régime continued their activities. One of them was Jean Conrad Hottinguer, a banker from Zurich, who after having got his training at the 'Passavent, de Candolle and Bertrand & Co' firm at Geneva, arrived at Paris in 1780. In 1794 he left France for three years for some trade and banking business in the United States of America. When he came back to Paris in 1798, he founded the 'Hottinguer & Co.' bank and immediately opened branches at Le Havre and other French ports. He became a financial counsellor of Talleyrand and is known as one of the first regents of the Banque de France.

Another Swiss Protestant banker in Paris, Jean-Frédéric Perregaux from Neuchâtel, acted during the French Revolution, with his 'Perregaux & Co.' firm founded in 1786, as banker of the Comité de Salut Public. He also brought his financial support to the Directoire until its last days and played a further important role in the early political and financial actions of the Consulate. Having actively participated in the creation of the Banque d'Escompte in Paris in 1776, he also became in 1800 one of the first shareholders of the Banque de France. After his death in 1808, the bank changed to 'Banque Perregaux, Laffite & Cie.' and was to remain on a high rank among the Haute Banque in Paris together with other Protestant banks of mainly Huguenot and Swiss origin, such as 'Mallet Frère & Cie', 'Sartoris & Cie' and also 'Hottinguer & Co.', which after the Bourbon

---

28   L. Bergeron, 'Pourtalès & Cie (1753–1801): apogée et déclin d'un capitalisme', in *Annales. Economies, Sociétés, Civilisations*, vol. 25, 1970, pp. 498–517; Veyrassat, *Négociants*; C. Aubert, *Les De la Rüe marchands, magistrats et banquiers, Genève, Gênes 1556–1905* (Lausanne, 1984); N. Röthlin, 'Ein Blick auf die Bezugs- und Absatzgebiete des schweizerischen Grosshandels anhand einiger Bilanzen aus dem 18. Jahrhundert', in P. Bairoch et al. (eds), *Die Schweiz in der Weltwirtschaft / La Suisse dans l'économie mondiale* (Zurich, 1990).

Restoration became the most important creditor of the French cotton industry. But more and more during the nineteenth century the Protestant bankers in France became a real banker minority, because of the rise of other French private banks on the one hand and of that of Jewish banks, particularly the Rothschilds, on the other[29].

A rather similar evolution can be observed at Vienna, where the Swiss Protestant private bankers, such as 'Melchior Steiner & Neffe', 'Geymuller & Co.' and 'Fries & Co.' together with 'Arnstein & Eskeles' dominated banking life until the 1820s. But as already mentioned, Fries and Geymuller announced their bankruptcy in 1826 and 1841, while 'Arnstein & Eskeles", 'Simon G. Sina' and Rothschild advanced after 1830 to become the most powerful banks of Vienna. In the Italian towns, where Protestant private bankers were active discreetly and as a minority from the late seventeenth and during the eighteenth century, e.g. the De la Rüe at Genoa, they remained on this level during the nineteenth century too.[30]

Main Characteristics of Protestant Banking in Early Modern Times and the Early Nineteenth Century

Upon reflection one may say that Protestant Banking was the business of a social group acting with a complex combination of trading, financial and banking activities in non-Protestant countries. In Protestant countries, they were of course part of the dominant majority. But what exactly differentiated them from their Catholic contemporaries? Their distinguishing feature is that they must be considered as a typical minority phenomenon, of a convinced religious minority in Catholic countries. One also may include among them the former Protestants who became 'new Catholics' by the opportunity of 'conversion', remaining in most cases in the circle of international Protestant trade, finance and banking. It might be that their particular role in history was to have been sometimes the dominant bankers in Catholic countries, inasmuch as historical research does not demonstrate the analogy for Catholic Banking in Protestant countries.

With regard to the *Internationale Huguenote* explored by Herbert Lüthy, one must point out that the international network of Protestant Banking is far older and more widespread than that, because it linked up with that of the traditional Swiss and German Protestant bankers in the sixteenth century. Even in the eighteenth century Austria knew foreign Swiss and German Protestant bankers who did not descend from French Huguenots. That is the reason why we suggest using the term *Internationale Huguenote* only in a restrictive way for the connections

---

[29]   Lévy-Leboyer, *Les banques européennes* (1964), p. 191; Lévy-Leboyer, *Les banques européennes* (1976). *Großkreuz, Privatkapital*, H. Van der Wee (ed.), *La banque en occident* (Gent, 1991), pp. 281–98; H. Pohl (ed.), *Europäische Bankengeschichte* (Frankfurt a.M., 1993), pp. 196–202.

[30]   Aubert, *Les De la Rüe*.

within the Calvinist banking world, which came out of the religious persecutions in sixteenth- and seventeenth- century France. The term 'International Protestant Banking' is perhaps better for the larger network, of course including Huguenot Banking but not only that.

The Protestant bankers in Catholic as well as in Anglican, Protestant and other foreign countries remained in direct and close relationship with their homelands. Generally the banks of the home town – Geneva, Basel, Zurich, Lyons, Amsterdam, London, Strasbourg etc. – were older. The foreign branches at Lyons, Paris, Genoa, Vienna and other towns in Catholic countries arose later. Of course, most of the first French Protestant banks were branches of the merchant-banks opened by Huguenots in the towns of their refuge, e.g. Geneva, Lausanne, Vevey, Neuchâtel, Frankfurt am Main, Amsterdam, London etc. It may be that sometimes, the same thing happened in the opposite way.

In spite of all kinds of persecutions in the Catholic countries against the native Protestants, a select group of mainly foreign Protestants was allowed to do business as merchants or bankers. The basis of these activities was either economic privileges set out in treaties or alliances, e.g. between France and the Swiss Republics since the early sixteenth century, or the liberty afforded to Protestants through special edicts, e.g. in seventeenth- and eighteenth-century Austria. The motivation for all this was the need for all kinds of useful political and financial services the privileged bankers were able to offer to their Catholic host-states: mainly mercenary troops on the one hand and the knowledge essential for concentrating and furnishing all the immense and indispensable sums of money nourishing the dynastic wars.

That is the reason why one finds most of the Protestant bankers rising to socially high positions in foreign Catholic countries. By their theoretical and technical know-how as well as their excellent relationship with other financiers and bankers, some became financial counsellors of the crown, others consuls, ambassadors or ministers of their own State at various courts. Some got into possession of one or several royal monopolies: salt, the mint, copper or other mines. Because of their inestimable services many of these Republican Protestants were ennobled.

Their special behaviour was the maintenance of Protestant faith and culture for generations in the foreign countries of their choice. They always found an opportunity to get married to Protestant brides of their social standing, in this way keeping their families within the elite world of international Protestant banking over generations in Catholic countries. This culture might have been maintained within the majority of Protestant families even in the nineteenth century and later. But the general rise of confessional tolerance in an increasing proportion of the Constitutions of European nations makes it very difficult to continue arguing the problem of a Protestant minority, as was the case during the time of the Ancien Régime.

CHAPTER 14

Private Bankers and Philanthropy:
the City of London, 1880s–1920s

Pat Thane

Philanthropy and the British Elite

The location at which the lives of the very poor and the very rich touched, glancingly, in late Victorian and Edwardian England was that of philanthropy. In recent years historians have become increasingly aware of the importance of philanthropic giving in the culture of the period, thanks, in particular, to the work of Frank Prochaska[1]. Few of the substantially wealthy did not make substantial charitable donations; many also gave considerable amounts of time to charitable administration. How much was given by how many is unknown, and probably unknowable since much of this activity went unrecorded or the records of dead charities have been lost. The commitment to philanthropy among the elite was led by the Royal Family. As Prochaska has shown with fascinating detail,[2] royal patronage of and donations to charities were well established in the eighteenth century. These became a more prominent role of monarchy under the influence of Prince Albert. He needed to find a role, was seriously committed to public service and the improvement of social conditions and was early to appreciate the importance of securing the popularity of the monarchy and of building direct links with the wider population through involvement in the provincial, as well as metropolitan, charities with which professional and business families were closely involved.

After Albert's death, Victoria continued this philanthropic crusade. Though she offended her politicians by withdrawal from political functions, she took care not to offend her people by withdrawal from public displays of philanthropy. For many years she did not open Parliament, but she did open hospitals.[3] She spent about ten per cent of her private income on charitable giving.[4] This can be compared with

---

[1] F. Prochaska *Women and Philanthropy in 19th Century England* (Oxford, 1980); F. Prochaska, 'Philanthropy', in F.M.L. Thompson (ed.), *The Cambridge Social History of Britain, 1750–1950* (Cambridge, 1990), vol. 3, pp. 357–93; F. Prochaska, *The Voluntary Impulse: Philanthropy in Modern Britain* (London, 1988); F. Prochaska, *Philanthropy and the Hospitals of London: the King's Fund 1897–1990* (Oxford, 1992); F. Prochaska, *Royal Bounty: the Making of a Welfare Monarchy* (Yale, 1995).

[2] Prochaska, *Royal Bounty*.

[3] Ibid., pp. 110 ff.

[4] Ibid., p. 78.

between four and seven per cent given by those (few) landed aristocrats whose
charitable expenditure has been studied.[5]

The Role of King Edward VII

Victoria and Albert encouraged their children as well as their subjects to be
actively involved in philanthropy. From the early 1870s, this became an important
preoccupation of the Prince of Wales, the future King Edward VII. Like his father,
this middle-aged man needed a role and preferably one acceptable to his mother
and to the Prime Minister, William Gladstone. He was also aware of the need for
the monarchy to hold its popularity with the people, not only in Britain but in the
Empire. This awareness grew in the later years of his mother's reign and throughout
his own (until his sudden death in 1910), as an emerging labour political and trade-
union movement seemed to some to threaten the social order, and there were signs
of dissidence within the Empire. Edward believed strongly that voluntarism was
one of the bonds which held society together, and he resisted the emergence of
State welfare that was visible in the last years of his reign. He visited charitable
institutions during his visit to India in 1875–6 and became patron of and donor to
a host of imperial charities[6]. In his case as in his mother's the patronage was worth
more to the charities than the donations, since other donors scurried to give where
royalty had bestowed patronage.

Political calculation and self-preservation apart, there is every sign that Edward
became seriously interested in social questions and the promotion of philanthropy.
This was one thing he had in common with his wife, the future Queen Alexandra,
who was also an active patron of charities; though his mistress, Frances, Countess
of Warwick, a future socialist, also encouraged him to join her charitable ventures.[7]
During his reign, despite his debts, Edward VII was patron of about 250 charities
and gave away about £9,000 per year, about ten per cent of his Privy Purse income,
to charities in Britain and the Empire and also in other European countries. Queen
Alexandra also gave lavishly to a variety of charities.

In his turn, Edward drew his associates into his favoured philanthropic
activities. His close contacts with City men of widely varying reputation are well
known. He met them not only at the race-course, the gambling table and the dining
room, but in the committee rooms of hospital and other charities. Their motives for
involvement in philanthropy were, of course, mixed. Association with Edward's
favoured charities helped further to secure his favour and was also a passport to
social respectability for those members of his circles who knew their status to be
insecure among the established elite because they were social *arrivistes*, or Jews,

[5]   F.M.L. Thompson, *English Landed Society in the 19th Century* (London, 1971), p. 210.
[6]   Prochaska, *Royal Bounty*, pp. 119ff.
[7]   Thompson, *English Landed Society*, p. 123.

or both. Edward nurtured their allegiance with reciprocal favours. As Prochaska has put it:

> In an unwritten social contract, Edward VII offered good shooting, respectability and honours to the moneyed elite, but at a price; and the price was, more often than not, support for his favoured charities. In 1899 for example, he had a whip-round of 24 of his friends including [Ernest] Cassel and Henry Bischoffsheim when his bridge-playing friend Agnes Keyser sought to turn her house into a hospital for officers returning from the Boer War (it later took the name King Edward VII's Hospital for Officers).... Edward VII was quick to lavish gifts and honours on his entourage in exchange for voluntary service and contributions.[8]

Medicine was the most favoured object of Edward's charitable interests. In this he was encouraged and guided by Sir Henry Burdett, his unofficial but indefatigable advisor. Burdett, son of a provincial clergyman, worked first in a Birmingham bank, then as administrator of hospital charities. From 1881 to 1898 Burdett was Secretary to the Shares and Loans Department of the Stock Exchange, and networked energetically in the City whilst maintaining his commitment to hospital philanthropy, winning the confidence of Edward, and gambling enthusiastically and successfully.[9] Along with Ernest Cassel, Burdett advised Edward on his personal investments. He drew financiers into royal circles and persuaded both royalty and financiers into support for his favoured charities. In 1889 he greatly enhanced the prospects of the National Pension Fund for Nurses by securing the patronage of the Prince and Princess of Wales and the sponsorship of the bankers Junius Morgan, Lord Rothschild and Everard Hambro[10].

Shortly before his death, Edward persuaded Cassel and Lord Iveagh (Edward Guinness) to make major contributions to the foundation of Britain's first radium institute, modelled on that in Paris, which opened in Portland Place in 1911.[11] However, his major medical endeavour, encouraged and assisted by Burdett, was the foundation in 1897 of the Prince of Wales' Hospital (later, and still, the King's) Fund for London. This was founded to commemorate the Queen's Diamond Jubilee, to raise funds to meet the growing funding crisis in the London voluntary hospitals, the chief providers of medical and nursing training, research and much medical treatment for poorer patients.[12] It was governed by a Council to which large donors were automatically elected, and whose membership was otherwise hand-picked by the Prince. It was a striking example of the manner in which charitable gatherings reinforced influential networks. As Prochaska puts it: 'No other voluntary society of the day brought together the monarchy, the great and the

---

[8]   Ibid., p. 143.
[9]   Ibid., pp. 129–30.
[10]   Ibid., p. 130.
[11]   Ibid., p. 153.
[12]   This account of the King's Fund is derived mainly from Prochaska, *Philanthropy*.

good, and the not so good but rich, in such profusion.'[13] It included Lord (N.M.) Rothschild, the Governor of the Bank of England, Lord Lister and other Presidents of the Royal Colleges of medicine, the Chief Rabbi, the Bishop of London, Ernest Cassel, Julius Wernher, Edward Guinness, Everard Hambro and Lord Revelstoke of Barings. These and other figures from the City and other areas of public life gave time and money to the Fund. Most of the merchant banks, led by J.S. Morgan and Co. and N.M. Rothschild and Sons, and the clearing banks, led by Lloyds, contributed to the initial appeal in 1897. The Bank of England gave the modest annual subscription of £250. Support came also from the Prudential Assurance Co., the City of London Corporation and, more reluctantly, City livery companies. Cassel and Guinness each contributed £60,000, the financier Edgar Speyer gave £25,000. N.M. Rothschild was the Fund's treasurer and his banking house gave £15,000. Revelstoke succeeded him in the role and left the fund £100,000 on his death in 1929. In 1912 Julius Wernher bequeathed an impressive £390,000 to the Fund. Finally, another South African millionaire and associate of Edward, Alfred Beit and his brother Otto, gave £125,000. Henry Bischoffsheim and his wife gave a more modest, but still substantial £14,000 between 1899 and 1906.[14]

By 1910 the Fund had total assets of almost £2 million and was distributing £150,000 per annum to the grateful and, on the whole, deserving, hospitals of London, for which it provided ten per cent of their combined income.[15] The money was not given unconditionally: the fund encouraged efficient administration and high-quality medical treatment. Probably, never had a charity amassed so much income so fast. The Fund was carefully managed by a Finance Committee consisting initially of Lords Rothschild and Revelstoke, Cassel and Robert Fleming.[16]

Whilst it may be true that 'The monarchy and the plutocracy rallied round philanthropy partly to dish socialism and to defend the Empire',[17] neither this nor the desire for social acceptance, status and titles can wholly explain the amount of time and money (especially money donated after death had removed any personal social advantage from giving) donated to charity by some, probably most, City figures. At this time, especially before 1914 when levels of taxation were light, there were no significant taxation advantages to stimulate charitable giving in Britain. Nor could possible fiscal gains explain the personal time given by financiers to philanthropy. An entirely real concern for the sufferings of others was clearly one motive, as was the influence of a variety of forms of religious belief. For Jewish financiers, another motive was the problem posed by the influx of poor Jewish immigrants to Britain from the early 1880s.

---

[13]   Prochaska, *Royal Bounty*, p. 153.
[14]   Prochaska, *Philanthropy and the Hospitals*, pp. 27–30.
[15]   Prochaska, *Royal Bounty*, p. 167.
[16]   Prochaska, *Philanthropy and the Hospitals*, p. 43.
[17]   Prochaska, *Royal Bounty*, p. 147.

Jewish Philanthropy

The great diaspora of Jews fleeing persecution in the Russian Empire occurred just as British Jews were experiencing the formal symbols of social acceptance. Only from 1866 could observant Jews take the oath which would enable them to sit as members of the House of Commons and only from 1871 could they enter Oxford and Cambridge Universities. The wealthy sections of the established Jewish population greatly, and with good reason, feared that their new and fragile social acceptance would be destabilized by the inflow of impoverished immigrants.

Jews who fled to Britain congregated in a small number of urban centres. The largest number settled in East London where the, previously small, Jewish population probably stood at 120–140,000 by 1914.[18] The established Jewish population felt not only fear but compassion for the misery of their co-religionists. In consequence, Jewish financiers and others devoted a great deal of time and effort to philanthropic activities designed to provide for the material needs of poor Jews, and to prevent their becoming a burden on the British taxpayer; also to socialize them into modes of behaviour which would make them acceptable to the British – hard-working, law-abiding and English-speaking – whilst retaining a Jewish identity.[19] They also encouraged and financed the onward movement of the migrants to the United States or to less-crowded countries such as South Africa or Argentina.[20]

Jewish financiers, lawyers and businessmen funded and ran the Jewish Board of Guardians, an alternative for impoverished Jews to the publicly funded Boards of Poor Law Guardians. They financed and administered schools such as the Jews Free School in East London, which provided an English Jewish education and to which N.M. Rothschild, among others, was a generous benefactor. Another major problem was housing. The Jews were accused of causing public health hazards as they crammed into the already miserable housing of East London and Manchester, unable to afford better. Rothschild again took the lead in setting up a semi-philanthropic company to provide tenement housing for the poor. Perhaps in part he was responding to the reported plea of his mother, Charlotte de Rothschild, on her deathbed in 1884, that he should devote his energies to improving the housing of Jewish workers.[21] At a meeting at the Rothschild banking house in 1885 Rothschild planned with Samuel Montagu, F.D. Mocatta and other prominent members of the Jewish community the establishment of the Four Per Cent Industrial Dwellings Company. This was to raise capital for the building of homes for poor Jews.

[18]   D. Feldman, *Englishmen and Jews: Social Relations and Political Culture, 1840–1914* (Yale, 1994), p. 172.

[19]   V.D. Lipman, *A Century of Social Service, 1859–1959: The Jewish Board of Guardians* (London, 1959).

[20]   Feldman, *Englishmen*, pp. 299–306.

[21]   J. White, *Rothschild Buildings: Life in an East End Tenement Block, 1887–1920* (London, 1980), p. 19.

Investors would accept a return fixed at four per cent – a philanthropic gesture, because a higher dividend could be expected from conventional investment. Similar non-Jewish companies already existed, normally offering five per cent. The Four Per Cent Company raised £20,000 within four days. Rothschild was active in bringing about the design and building of the tenement blocks opened in Spitalfields in 1887 as Charlotte de Rothschild Buildings. These eventually accommodated 228 families.[22]

These are just examples from a larger world of Jewish philanthropy that has been described elsewhere[23] and is an important aspect of the philanthropic activity of a prominent group of City men. Since a quantitative assessment of the philanthropic contribution of such men – notably often working closely with their wives – is impossible, the range and importance of their work is perhaps best conveyed through biographical examples.

Baron and Baroness de Hirsch

Moritz von Hirsch (1831–96), later known as Maurice de Hirsch, was not primarily active in the City of London, though he was an associate of Edward VII, but he was an active, influential and immensely rich figure in international finance and his career illustrates especially well how prodigious industry in the financial world could be accompanied by prodigious philanthropic work, and how such activities were not confined to Britain.

He was born in Munich, on 9 December 1831. His grandfather Jacob had established the family as one of the first Jewish families to acquire great wealth and social acceptability in Bavaria, becoming a court banker and substantial landowner. His younger son Joseph (1805–85) carried on his business activities, which became centred in Munich. Moritz was the third of Joseph's ten children. His mother, Karoline Wertheimer, came from an orthodox Frankfurt family and ensured that the children were properly instructed in Jewish matters.

At age 13 Moritz was sent to Brussels for schooling, receiving, according to his obituary in the *Jewish Chronicle*, a 'plain but sound education'. At 17 he joined the banking house of Bischoffsheim and Goldschmidt in Brussels. He was soon regarded as a financial genius, with a special interest in railway promotion. Speculation in sugar and cotton shares also brought him rapidly accumulated wealth and promotion. In 1855 he married Clara Bischoffsheim (1833–99), daughter of the senior partner, Senator Jonathan Bischoffsheim. After his marriage, he moved to Paris to join the board of the Paris branch of Bischoffsheim and Goldschmidt. The heads of the firm followed his speculations with a certain amount of trepidation and refrained from making him a partner, though they allowed him to use the

---

[22]   Ibid., pp. 20–24.
[23]   Feldman, *Englishmen*; Lipman, *A Century*; L.P. Gartner, *The Jewish Immigrant in England, 1870–1914* (London, 1960).

firm's facilities for making transactions. Thereafter, he built his fortunes on the finance of railway construction, including the building of the Orient Express line. He faced accusations of dubious practice but they were never proved. By 1890, besides his huge railway interests, banking houses and a number of industrial firms, Hirsch owned vast estates in Austria-Hungary and France and was one of the wealthiest men of his day, with assets whose worth was estimated at between 16 and 30 million pounds sterling – that estimates were so much at variance indicates the scale and complexity of his operations, which probably no-one but himself could fully comprehend. He worked sometimes in association with other financiers, including, in Britain, Ernest Cassel, whose early career he appears to have nurtured, but the details of such associations remain mysterious. His personal financial activities within Britain appear to have been few and no information is known about them. He attributed his success to mastery of detail, economy in small things and close personal watch over his transactions, which he combined with inexhaustible energy and industry and undeniable financial flair. His working day typically began at 5 a.m. and lasted far into the night.

He was a well-known and ubiquitous member of the 'smart set' in Paris, the South of France and London. He was a lavish host, with homes in London, France and Hungary, though he was personally frugal, as was his wife. Every year he came to London for the Season. He belonged to the circle of the Prince of Wales and shared his interest in horse-racing. His racing stables were famous and his colours were often successful. Like many of Edward's circle, he was more popularly known in Britain for his activities on the turf (and indeed for his philanthropy) than for his business dealings. He was elected as a foreign member of the Turf Club. This followed his rejection by the Jockey Club in Paris, in response to which he purchased the Club's premises and evicted it. Thereafter he lived more in London than in Paris. It was not well known that his winnings on the English turf were always donated to London hospitals, often through the Prince of Wales' Fund. His *Jewish Chronicle* obituary retailed that he liked to tell friends that his horses 'raced for charity'. Substantial sums were involved: £7,000 in 1891, £35,000 in 1892. When in 1893 his horses won only £7,500 he doubled the amount before giving it to the hospitals, saying that they should not suffer for the poor performance of his stable. Over the years he gave some £100,000 in total to the hospitals.

His wife, Clara, took little pleasure in the social scene, though she often travelled with him. She had more interest in philanthropic activity, especially after the death from pneumonia of their only son Lucien (born 1856) in 1887. The parents had previously lost their only other child, a daughter, in infancy and were inconsolable. Shortly thereafter, Hirsch retired from business and both devoted themselves to humanitarian causes. Apparently he wrote in response to a letter of condolence: 'My son I have lost, but not my heir, humanity is my heir'.[24] Retirement or semi-retirement from business to devote time and accumulated

---

[24]   S. Adler-Rudel, 'Moritz Baron Hirsch. Profile of a Great Philanthropist', *Leo Baeck Yearbook*, 1971, p. 39.

wealth to philanthropy was not unusual for nineteenth-century businessmen of all religious persuasions, though few could make donations to match the size and range of those of Hirsch.

He had become active in humane causes before his son's death, probably due to his wife's influence but also to his observing the poverty of the Jews of Turkey and the Balkans as he travelled in connection with his railway transactions. He primarily exerted himself to relieve the poverty and persecution suffered by Jews in Turkey, the Balkans, and later in Russia and Galicia. Clara had been secretary to her father when he was a member of the General Committee of the Alliance Israélite Universelle, which was the major channel for assistance from rich Jews of prosperous parts of the world to the poor and persecuted. Hirsch also became a committee member in 1876. In December 1873 he donated a million francs to the Alliance for the furtherance of education in Turkey. From 1879 he contributed an annual 50,000 francs for the artisans training scheme of the Alliance. From 1882 he underwrote its large annual deficit, keeping it in independent existence. In 1882 he contributed a million francs to an emergency fund for refugees from the Russian pogroms. By the time of his death he had donated at least 12 million francs to the Alliance. An equivalent amount went primarily for the education and training of Jews in Austria, in the face of opposition from the government of Austria. In 1889 he opened welfare agencies in towns in central and eastern Europe, dispensing aid to those in need. These also he supervised closely. His policy was only to give relief in such a way as positively to assist people to become self-supporting, for example through acquiring training or the tools of a trade. He claimed not to give to communities which had substantial other sources of relief, such as the poor of London and Paris, though he evidently made an exception for the hospital charities favoured by the Prince of Wales.

He sought to introduce relief schemes in Russia, but faced with the resolute opposition of the government, sought instead to assist mass emigration of Jews. He gave large sums to poor Jews arriving in America through the Baron de Hirsch Fund, which was established in 1891.

Above all, Hirsch wished to establish and endow a safe Jewish colony. He initially expected this to be located somewhere in the Americas, through the instrument of the Jewish Colonization Society which he established in 1891, with headquarters in London, to raise money for this enterprise and make it a reality. It was floated with a capital of £2 million issued in shares of £100 each. He held 19,993 of these, the others being taken up by prominent London Jews. He distributed his shares around prominent European Jewish organizations. He was to invest at least £38 million in this enterprise before his death. He had high hopes of establishing a colony in Argentina, where a large amount of land was purchased and Jews settled. Smaller colonies were funded elsewhere, including Palestine, after Hirsch's death.

Jewish colonization had become the centre of Hirsch's life and of his incessant work (though his financial dealings never ceased) by the time of his sudden death in Hungary in 1896. He was interred in the family vault at the Montmartre Cemetery, amid, according to the *Jewish Chronicle*, 'demonstrations of sympathy from all classes of society, from the Head of State and the bearers of the proudest names in the old French aristocracy, down to the meanest Christian *ouvrier* and the poorest Polish Jewish immigrant'. He left a million francs for various charities.[25]

His wife, Clara, was his main heir and she carried on the philanthropic and colonizing work on which they had previously worked jointly, until her death in 1899. The importance of her work in the Jewish community is suggested by the fact that her death gave rise to almost as many column inches in the *Jewish Chronicle* as that of her husband. Her obituary credited her with inspiring her husband's devotion to philanthropy and with close involvement in his business affairs: 'For a long time she was also his secretary and to such an extent that she wrote and copied the most important letters he wrote. Often when at home and always when abroad, he had no other assistance'.[26] But for long before his death her main activity had been philanthropy, conducted in meticulous, business-like fashion, expending vast sums from an office in Paris. She read, investigated and filed letters of appeal. The scale and range of her and her husband's philanthropy is suggested by her bequests, which included: 4 million francs to the Teachers' Training School of the Alliance Israélite Universelle, Paris; 3 million for a pension fund for the same school; 3 million for clothing and feeding children in the Alliance Israélite schools; 6 million to the Baron de Hirsh fund, New York; 3 million to the loan fund of the London Board of Guardians; 3 million to the Home for Jewish Working Girls founded by the Baroness; 5 million to the Comité de Bienfaisance Israélite, Paris; 1 million for housing and maternal care in Paris; 200,000 to the City of Vienna for philanthropic purposes; between 100,000 and 300,000 each to the Progressive Jewish Communities of Vienna, Budapest, Paris, Brussels, Frankfurt, Mainz, Munich and to the Jewish Community of Britain; 100,000 francs to the Bischoffsheim Foundation, Paris; 25,000 to each of the 20 Bureaux de Bienfaisance in Paris; 10 million to the Jewish Colonization Society; 3 and a half million to the fund she had founded for the support of Boys and Girls in Austria; 2 million to the Baron Hirsch Foundation for Elementary Education in Galicia. The total in charitable bequests was 46,750,000 francs, equivalent at the time to £1,870,000. Added to the millions she and her husband had donated during their lifetimes, this was a charitable endeavour few in Britain, or anywhere, could match.

---

[25]   Hirsch is elusive to the historian. The main sources on which this account is based are Adler-Rudel, 'Moritz Baron Hirsch'; and obituaries in *Jewish Chronicle*, 24 Apr. 1896 and *The Times*, 22 Apr. 1896.

[26]   Obituary of Baroness Clara de Hirsch, *Jewish Chronicle*, 7 Apr. 1899.

The Bischoffsheims

Baroness de Hirsch's close relatives in Britain, her uncle Henri (Henry) Bischoffsheim, born in Amsterdam, and his wife, the Vienna-born Clarissa, exhibited a similar pattern but with less extraordinary resources. Henri came to London in 1849 to serve in the London branch of his father's business, which had been founded in 1836. It was under the management of his uncle, S.H. Goldschmidt, who subsequently retired to Paris and became (1882) President of the Alliance Israélite. Henri subsequently became an active partner, but in the 1870s, still in his forties, he ceased to take a major part in the affairs of the firm, although still attending his office for a few hours on most days of the week and giving advice, though apparently initiating no transactions. By this time, Ernest Cassel was a successful manager in the firm.

Henri occupied his semi-retirement with a glittering social life and with philanthropy, in both of which his wife was his close partner. The couple were notable donors to charity, especially to Jewish charity. His *Jewish Chronicle* obituary commented: 'That he accumulated a considerable fortune is a fact well-known, and even more notable is the generous use to which he put his wealth, of which he devoted large sums to general and communal purposes.... No movement of importance has gone forward in the community to which Mr Bischoffsheim did not contribute munificently and readily'.[27] As well as giving, he was actively involved in serving on the Committee of the Jews Free School, the Council of the Anglo-Jewish Association and the Roumanian Committee and as a Trustee of the Jewish Convalescent Home. He was one of the founders of the Imperial Cancer Research Fund. He was the founder and sole owner of the Metropolitan Hospital Ambulances which were erected in various parts of London to provide first aid for injured people. He financed the building of the children's wing of the Jewish Convalescent Home, Hampstead, which was established by Baroness de Hirsch. Together with his wife he founded the Daneswood Sanatorium at Woburn Sands, Bedfordshire, for Jewish consumptives. When the Bischoffsheims held their golden wedding anniversary in 1906 they celebrated by giving a total of £100,000 to charity. The largest sum, £40,000, was given to the Imperial Cancer Research Association, £10,000 each to the Daneswood Sanatorium and to King Edward VII's Sanatorium; a further £10,000 went to various Jewish charities. Though the public credit for these philanthropic activities often went to Mr Bischoffsheim alone, the initiative often lay at least equally with his wife. She was independently active as Vice-President of the Union of Jewish Women, a committee member of the Jews Infant Schools and the Ladies West End Charity and of various hospitals, dispensaries and help societies. In none of these activities was she merely an ornamental 'Lady Bountiful', but was an active, serious, professional participant.

When Bishoffsheim died in 1908 he was described by the *Jewish Chronicle*, with perhaps a touch of the exaggeration to be expected at such a moment, but

---

[27]   *Jewish Chronicle*, 13 Mar. 1908.

certainly with some truth, as 'an ideal type of the rich Jew. He gathered his vast wealth by means at which the sternest moralist could set no cavil, he took a pride and a pleasure in distributing huge amounts of it with an unsparing hand, an example to Jews of what a rich Jew should be – an example to the world of what a rich Jew can be'.[28]

Ernest Cassel (1852–1921)

Another 'rich Jew' whose philanthropic activities were more popularly known than his business dealings was Ernest Cassel. Of course, not all City philanthropists were Jewish, but the patterns of philanthropy did not differ substantially between Jews and non-Jews, though the objects might. Cassel, in any case, had converted secretly to Roman Catholicism on the early death of his wife and rarely identified publicly with Jewish causes, though this did not protect him from anti-Semitism.

Cassel came from a modestly successful banking family in the Rhineland. He migrated to Liverpool at the age of seventeen with few resources. He obtained a clerkship with Bischoffsheim and Goldschmidt. This move was probably facilitated by an introduction from de Hirsch. Cassell was closely associated with Hirsch until the latter's death, but as with much in the lives of both men the details of their transactions remain mysterious.

Cassel achieved rapid financial success. When he married, in 1878, aged 26, he was able to put aside capital of £150,000. His wife died of tuberculosis three years later. They had one daughter, Maud. Cassel was a devoted father. He never remarried. His fortune and the scale of his international activities grew. He was an active member of Edward VII's social set, an owner of racehorses with some success, mixed in theatrical and artistic circles and amassed an impressive collection of paintings and other valuable items. He was an active donor to charity, and not only to those patronized by Edward. He made much profit in the 1890s through financing the Aswan dam, also from the development of sugar production, of agriculture and railways in Egypt. In 1903, Cassel also donated £341,000 to equip and operate travelling eye hospitals in Egypt. This may have been motivated at least partly by a desire to mollify opposition to his business ventures. Whatever the motive, the outcome was a major contribution to combating the ravages of such eye diseases as trachoma in poverty-stricken rural Egypt.

In 1910–11 came a turning point in Cassel's life, for a mixture of personal and political reasons. He felt great personal grief at the death of Edward VII. With his friend, he also lost much of his social and political influence, to the undisguised and often openly anti-Semitic glee of certain members of high society. The friendship between Edward and 'Windsor-Cassel' was close and strong. They met at the racecourse around 1896, possibly introduced by Hirsch, and were friends thereafter. Even more tragically, in 1911 his only daughter died after a long battle

---

28   Ibid.

with tuberculosis. Cassel devoted much care to her in her last years. In 1901 she had married a Conservative MP, Lt Col. Wilfred Ashley, grandson of the great Earl of Shaftesbury and great-grandson of Lady Palmerston, through whom he had inherited Broadlands House in Hampshire. After his daughter's death, Cassel's affection centred upon his two grand-daughters, especially the elder, Edwina, later Countess Mountbatten.

In 1910, partly in response to these tragedies, but perhaps also in anticipation of war disrupting international finance, Cassel decided to reduce though not to eliminate the scale of his business activities. Before and after his semi-retirement he gave away at least £2 million in charitable donations, including £200,000 in 1902 for the founding of the King Edward VII Sanatorium for Consumption at Midhurst, with a further £20,000 in 1913; £10,000 in 1907 to the Imperial College of Science and Technology; in 1909 a £46,000 half share with Lord Iveagh for founding the Radium Institute; £210,000 in 1911 for setting up the King Edward VII British-German Foundation for the aid of distressed people in Germany; £30,000 for distressed workmen in Swedish mines (some of his earliest financial gains had been the outcome of investment in the mining, transportation and processing of Swedish iron ore); £50,000 to Hampshire hospitals in memory of his daughter; in 1913 £10,000 to Egyptian hospitals and £50,000 for the sick and needy of Cologne. His main contribution to Jewish charity was to devote a considerable amount of money and effort to Hirsch's favoured cause of acquiring a national home for Jews. During the First World War Cassel gave at least £400,000 for medical services and the relief of servicemen's families. In 1919 he donated £500,000 for an educational trust fund which was used to establish a faculty of commerce at the London School of Economics, to support the Workers' Educational Association, to finance scholarships for the technical and commercial education of working men, to promote the study of foreign languages by the establishment of professorships, lectureships and scholarships and to support the higher education of women. He gave £212,000 for founding a hospital for functional nervous disorders at Penshurst, Kent.

When he died he left £7,551,608 (net personalty £7,329,033) mainly to his family, with very little bequeathed to charity.[29]

Schroders

There is no reason to believe that philanthropy was the preserve of Jewish bankers, though their charitable activities have been more fully documented than those of other groups in the City of London. Richard Roberts's work[30] provides a vivid glimpse into the philanthropic works of one other important group, the Lutheran,

---

[29]   P. Thane, 'Cassel, Sir Ernest Joseph', in D.J. Jeremy (ed.), *Dictionary of Business Biography* (London, 1984), vol. 1, pp. 604–14.

[30]   R. Roberts, *Schroders: Merchants and Bankers* (Basingstoke, 1992).

Anglo-German banking community, which further indicates the extent of banking philanthropy and its transnational scope. Johann Heinrich Schroder (1784–1883) of Hamburg founded banking houses in Hamburg, London and Liverpool, of which the London firm became the most prominent. In 1849, approaching the age of sixty-five, he retired. Much of his time thereafter was absorbed by charitable works in the region of Hamburg, most notably the erection of a home for elderly people, the Schroder Stiftung, which in 1850 he endowed with 1.5 million Bancomarks, £110,000 sterling equivalent at the time, the equivalent of around £4.5 million in the 1990s.[31]

Johann's son, John Henry, inherited control of the London firm. In the mid nineteenth century the partners and clerks of the firm lived in the leafy suburbs of South London, with the exception of John Henry, who preferred fashionable Bayswater. In general, the Anglo-German banking families remained distinct from other groupings in the City. They were neither socially prominent nor politically active. They did not become large landowners or associate closely with the English aristocracy. Rather 'they remained wedded to the values of their continental bourgeois background'.[32] They were devout Lutherans. This helped to inspire their charitable endeavours. A German Evangelical Church was founded in Denmark Hill, South London, in 1854. Prince Albert headed the list of contributors to the building fund, which included the names of partners of the Schroders, Kleinworts and Huths banking houses, many of whom remained active in the affairs of the church.

John Henry Schroder was active in a range of charities. He subscribed in 1843 to the building of a hospital in Hackney, to serve the impoverished German community of London's East End. Partners in Schroders in both London and Hamburg also subscribed, and John Henry served as its treasurer. When it got into financial difficulties in the 1870s he paid off its debts. He left a bequest of £10,000 to the hospital on his death in 1910.[33] He and other family members and partners in the firm were also long-time trustees of the German Lutheran Church in London. John Henry's philanthropic activities continued throughout his life and increased as he went into semi-retirement from the 1880s. He was an active member of the Royal Horticultural Society and an active plant-breeder. He 'contributed handsomely' to the Royal Gardeners' Benevolent Association.[34] He continued to give generously to German philanthropic causes in Britain. In 1908 he endowed a convalescent home for the German Hospital, in 1879 the German Orphanage in Hackney, in 1900 the German Work Colony in Hertfordshire. The German Sailors Home in the London docks was erected at his expense and opened after his death, in 1912. An obituary commented that he 'gave more in charity than all the rest of the Germans in this country put together'.[35] He did not give only to German

[31]   Ibid., p. 41.
[32]   Ibid., p. 113.
[33]   Ibid., p. 112.
[34]   Ibid., p. 111.
[35]   Ibid., p. 112.

charities but also to local charities in the area around Windsor where he lived, notably a gift of five acres of land to Egham District Council for the erection of an isolation hospital. In recognition of his contributions to the welfare of the locality he was presented with an illuminated address by the Corporation of Windsor on the occasion of his Golden Wedding in 1900. John Henry Schroder was on friendly terms with members of the Royal Family, without seeking to merge into the English aristocracy as did members of other banking houses. In 1892 Queen Victoria conferred a baronetcy upon him 'as a mark of personal friendship and esteem, and for the help he had given to the household on matters of finance and accountancy'.[36]

His partner Henry Tiarks was similarly active in his local community in Kent. Though also Anglo-German by origin he became active in his local Anglican church. He was president of the Chislehurst and Cray Valley Medical and Surgical Aid Society, which administered a cottage hospital, the building of which he initiated in the 1880s and generously endowed. He was also active in local government and, like Schroder, in horticultural associations.[37]

John Henry was succeeded by his nephew, Bruno Schroder, who was born in Hamburg. He retained close links with Hamburg and was a generous benefactor to Hamburg charities. His German connections made him one of the victims of virulent anti-German sentiment in Britain during the First World War. This was intensified by the nature of some of his benefactions: the endowment of a professorship of German at Cambridge University in 1910 and his charitable contributions to the relief of German internees and prisoners of war in England, as well as of British prisoners of war in Germany.[38] To escape vituperation he retreated to his home in Surrey for most of the war, resuming work in the City after the Armistice. He remained active until the 1930s both in business and in philanthropy. In 1937, on his 70th birthday, he was presented with an honorary doctorate of the Medical Faculty of Hamburg in acknowledgment of his benefactions to the charities of the city. His son and successor in the firm, Helmut, was the first of the family to marry an Englishwoman, Meg Darell of Gloucestershire, in 1930. The wedding was marked by the presentation of a radio set to every blind person in the county, at a cost of £10,000.[39]

Conclusion

These examples suggest the vast total sums flowing in charity from City businessmen and their colleagues in other countries. Their more general impact upon the recipients or upon social conditions – perhaps even upon politics

---

[36]   Ibid., p. 113.
[37]   Ibid., p. 113.
[38]   Ibid., p. 119.
[39]   Ibid., p. 263.

– cannot be measured, but cannot have been insignificant. Philanthropic activity was an important facet of the impact of financiers upon the world at large. To give some quantitative estimation of the relative importance of the sums transferred: in 1890 the total cost of public expenditure on Poor Law relief in England and Wales (including capital and salary costs) was £8,434,000; in 1900 it was £11,588,000.[40] Equally hard to measure, but perhaps also significant, was the impact upon the business and social opportunities of the donors. If we are fully to understand the role of financiers in the international culture of the later nineteenth and early twentieth centuries, philanthropy is a dimension which cannot be ignored and which deserves more detailed examination.

---

[40]   K. Williams, *From Pauperism to Poverty* (London, 1981), p. 171.

CHAPTER 15

Hereditary Calling, Inherited Refinement: the Private Bankers of the City of London, 1914–86

David Kynaston

'My own feeling is that the private firms are on their trial', Gaspard Farrer of Barings wrote shortly before the end of the First World War to a like-minded Dutch merchant banker. 'If they have not gone back during the war', he added, 'they have at least not made the progress of the Joint Stock Banks.'[1] If the challenge for the City's merchant banks was to return to the pre-1914 glory days – a nostalgic ambition that was the primary motive for their enthusiastic endorsement soon afterwards of Britain's misguided return to the gold standard – a couple of striking quotations, one retrospective and the other contemporary, would suggest that it was a challenge that proved too much for them. In his novel *The Conscience of the Rich*, that perceptive chronicler of the corridors of power, C.P. Snow, gives a portrait of a rich Jewish family which had made its fortune as bankers in the nineteenth century before retiring from the fray as early as 1896. 'Everything's on too big a scale for a private firm', Leonard March laments in the 1920s. 'Look at the Rothschilds. They used to be the most influential family in Europe. And they've kept on going after we finished, they've not done badly, and what are they now? Just merchant bankers in a fairly lucrative way of business.'[2] The other assessment, in a typically memorable passage, was made by Keynes in 1934:

> The capitalist has lost the source of his inner strength – his self-assurance, his self-confidence, his untameable will, his belief in his own beauty and unquestionable value to society. He is a forlorn object, heaven knows.... Lord Revelstoke the First, Lord Rothschild the First, Lord Goschen the First, Sir Lothian Bell, Sir Ernest Cassel, the private bankers, the ship-owning families, the merchant princes.... Where are they now? There are no such objects on the earth. Their office-boys (on salaries) rule in their mausoleums.[3]

---

[1]   P. Ziegler, *The Sixth Great Power: Barings, 1762–1929* (London, 1988), p. 339.

[2]   C.P. Snow, *The Conscience of the Rich* (New York, 1958), p. 90.

[3]   K. Martin, *Editor: a Second Volume of Autobiography, 1931–1945* (London, 1968), p. 98.

Keynes perhaps exaggerated the rise of the office-boy in the merchant banking sector – a species of humanity kept pretty firmly in his place in Rothschilds, Barings and Hambros, to name but three; while Lord Bicester of Morgan Grenfell had sufficient belief in his own beauty to favour wearing a tie knotted through a wedding ring;[4] but Keynes's overall thrust – that the modern world was proving too much for the old-pre-1914 order, an order in many ways epitomized by the private bankers – had considerable force.

This is not the place to give a considered appraisal of the merchant banks' business performance during the City's 40 or so more or less stagnant years after the catastrophe of 1914. There was some recovery in the 1920s, but the German banking crisis of 1931 had the effect of practically writing off the rest of the decade for several of the leading houses. Then, of course, came another war, reducing most of the merchant banks to little more than a care and maintenance basis. In 1942 the Bank of England's George Bolton assessed their postwar prospects:

> The revival of the old conception of the foreign banker appears improbable, although there may be individual examples due entirely to the personal element. The private Houses may also have difficulty in avoiding unfavourable criticism based on comparative credit ranking [i.e. with the joint-stock clearing banks]. But it is possible that the merchant banks may regain their original status of merchants, provided that they leave banking to the deposit bankers and develop their foreign connections with a bias towards merchanting and not banking.[5]

In practice, despite the City's continuing problems after 1945, things did not work out quite so poorly for the merchant banks. In particular, on the back of the 1948 Companies Act, they effectively supplanted the stockbrokers in the potentially lucrative area of domestic new-issue finance; while in the field of investment management, there were one or two, such as Helbert Wagg and later Barings, that skilfully anticipated the rise of the institutions, above all the pension funds.[6] Even so, in what was still for the most part a rather stultifying macro-economic environment, few would have contended in, say, the mid-1950s that the merchant banks represented an especially thriving sector of the financial scene.

Nor, despite the unfortunate absence of systematic empirical research on the subject, is there any reason to doubt that the picture that Cassis has drawn of the pre-1914 City elite still essentially applied in the four decades after the First World War: a largely closed world, in which family, wealth and social connections counted for more than either industry or ability. The utter dominance of the Hambro family at Hambros, the Kleinwort family at Kleinworts, and the Rothschild family

[4]   Interview with Gerald Ashfield, 20 Nov. 1997.
[5]   Bank of England Archives, ADM 14/3, 19 Feb. 1942.
[6]   D. Kynaston, *Cazenove & Co.: a History* (London, 1991), p. 195; R. Roberts, *Schroders: Merchants & Bankers* (Basingstoke, 1992), p. 410; J. Orbell, *Asset Management and Barings: a Note on the Origins* (privately published by ING Barings plc, 1966), pp. 6–8.

at Rothschilds – here were three houses in which the concept of meritocracy could hardly have been less on the agenda, certainly in terms of the very highest positions. Almost as strong as the instinctive attachment to keeping things in the family was the urge to recruit Old Etonians. 'The O.E. tie was worth £200 a year in the City', the Master of Wellington College was informed in 1940, and that was probably an underestimate.[7] The future corporate financier Andrew Carnwath, for example, could not have had a simpler route to 8 Bishopsgate, where he arrived in 1928 at the age of nineteen. 'I had never heard of Barings', he would dryly reminisce about Eton recommending him to that bank, 'but inquiries showed that I would probably be wise to explore the matter further.'[8] Or take a rather more flamboyant merchant banker, Michael Verey, three years younger than Carnwath. Born into a family that invariably sent its sons to Eton, he came down from Cambridge in 1934 and began to consider the City:

> I talked to my father [a solicitor] and he said, 'I will speak to my friend, Alfred Wagg.' He and Alfred [chairman of Helbert Wagg] had been friends since they were little boys at the same private school together and were very close friends at Eton and Cambridge and thereafter. There was a, for me, ghastly, agonizing dinner party which was held in Alfred's very grand flat in Berkeley Square with a butler and footman.... My father and I wore dinner jackets and I said to my father, 'I'll just stay doggo so that he can't take against me. You do the talking.' So my father was frightfully good and swept Alfred along....[9]

The wider point, with no disrespect to the individual ability of either Carnwath or Verey, hardly needs labouring. 'To the Old Etonians', concluded the stockbroker and financial journalist Nicholas Davenport in his memoirs, 'every financial door in the City was open.... It was a sort of Mafia in reverse – a gang based on honest dealing instead of blackmail, on good "hard" money (lots of it) instead of easy loot and on simplicity instead of cunning. The only rules were playing safe, resisting change, opposing new ideas, upholding the Establishment and being willing to dress up and go on the pompous dinner parade in the City halls....'[10]

How easy was it for outsiders up to the 1950s to break into this charmed circle? Probably about the same as during the long nineteenth century: difficult, but not impossible. Three obvious examples, all coming through soon after 1945 as heavyweight merchant bankers, were Siegmund Warburg, Lionel Fraser of Helbert Wagg, and Kenneth Keith of Philip Hill. Verey, in the *City Lives* anthology of oral history, talks revealingly as well as entertainingly about the first two:

---

[7] D. Newsome, *A History of Wellington College, 1859–1959* (London, 1959), p. 361.

[8] *The Times*, 5 Jan. 1996.

[9] C. Courtney and P. Thompson, *City Lives: the Changing Voices of British Finance* (London, 1996), p. 36.

[10] N. Davenport, *Memoirs of a City Radical* (London, 1974), pp. 42–3.

Lionel Fraser was the son of a butler and a housemaid and in the end he became chairman of Helbert Wagg. He had left school at eighteen and had been a clerk in a little merchant bank which Alfred Wagg bought, and just through sheer hard work he became an absolutely leading merchant banker. He was straight as a die. He took night classes to teach himself French. He was driven by ambition to make money, to live in Cadogan Square, to be a member of White's and the St James's Club. Very few people knew that he was a butler's son, most people thought he was an Old Etonian. He was distinguished looking, beautifully dressed – not overdone – and excellent manners. Most people regarded him as the *crème de la crème*....

I wouldn't have worked for Siggy Warburg. At Helbert Wagg we were mixed in our views. We knew he was tenacious and cautious and all the rest of it but I don't think he regarded there being any other life but business and we regarded business as a means to an end. We wanted to have fun and crack some jokes. Jokes were not cracked at Warburgs – not more than once, anyhow. He was frightfully concerned about change and getting things properly organized, and most of us didn't give a damn about that. We took a bit of change in our stride but we certainly didn't want too much. He was an upsetter of the existing Establishment. He wasn't a member of it and he didn't like it and was trying to get rid of it. At the start, the Establishment was dismissive and he was regarded as a squirt, an upstart. Very few people would have regarded him as a personal friend. People took off his foreign accent....[11]

As for Keith, the driving force behind what ultimately became Hill Samuel, he may have been disconcertingly brusque in manner and aggressive in business, but his background was acceptably public school (Rugby), he was a good shot and possessed a tall, military bearing, and above all – like Fraser, like Warburg – he was manifestly top-notch at his job. Back in the 1930s, Montagu Norman had tried to circumscribe the City ambitions of Philip Hill himself, whom Norman regarded as an out-and-out bounder; but a generation later Kim Cobbold, whose approach to the City was quite as papal as Norman's, could do little to stem Keith's ambitions. There was a telling episode early in 1955 when Churchill's private secretary, Jock Colville, used a mutual friend, the politician and press magnate Brendan Bracken, to sound out the governor of the Bank about a possible berth at Philip Hill once Churchill had left office. 'I said that from the City point of view', noted Cobbold after his conversation with Bracken, 'I was in favour of Philip Hill being "respectabilized" and I should be quite glad to see somebody like Colville there. I was bound to say that if I were advising my own brother I would still raise an eyebrow and, as Lord Bracken knows, there are people in Philip Hill who are not generally liked.' Cobbold's warning – quite literally, the raising of the gubernatorial eyebrow – proved futile, for Colville soon afterwards took the shilling.[12]

---

[11] Courtney et al., *City Lives*, pp. 8–9.
[12] Bank of England Archives, G 3/113, 27 Jan. 1955.

Earlier, from the inter-war years, there had been one particularly interesting merchant-banker outsider who had made it to the very top. 'He is absolutely straight, very level headed, not a talker, but goes and does things and does them well', Farrer informed an American banker shortly before Edward Peacock, the son of a Canadian schoolmaster, joined Barings in 1924. 'He has of course had a different upbringing from any of us here', Farrer conceded to another correspondent about the new recruit, 'but the set of his mind and all his ways are on the same lines as ours.'[13] Peacock quickly established himself as the power behind the throne, and after Revelstoke's death in 1929 he was acknowledged as the bank's leader, especially in the areas of international and corporate finance. Cecil Baring may have privately called him 'The Paycock', but neither he nor the other active members of the family imagined that they could do without him.[14]

Peacock was also at the centre of a fascinating moment in merchant banking history – a moment that makes one realize the importance of nuance, prejudice and cultural assumptions, and equally the limitations of a baldly sociological, head-counting, what one might call *Who's Who* approach. It came in the autumn of 1942, some eight months after the death of Lionel de Rothschild left Rothschilds (already badly hit by the Credit Anstalt smash of 1931) in a parlous financial position – almost certainly, from the evidence of Norman's diary, dependent on the Bank of England in order to stay afloat. Schroders was also in a poor state then, and on 8 September that bank's Albert Pam called on Norman in order to float an idea. 'Why shd not Schroders, Rs & Barings amalgamate?' recorded Norman's diary in typically clipped fashion. 'Or why shd not Barings take over the other 2?' Two days later, Norman put the idea to Peacock: '?BB & Co + JHS & Co + NMR & S:; he will consider'. Peacock duly returned three weeks later with Barings' answer: 'BB & Co not willing, after consideration, to join with JHS & Co, whose methods are impossible and unpopularity great – nor with NMR & S who are entirely a Jewish family concern'.[15] Some twenty years after Barings, Rothschilds and Schroders had become the City's so-called 'Trinity', doing a series of important issues together on a consortium basis, this was a strikingly *personal* basis on which to reach a not unmomentous decision. At the very least it serves, to reiterate, as a warning against simplistic readings of the City elite.

The episode in 1942 is one of many not mentioned, let alone illuminated, in *A Gilt-edged Life*, the charming, recently published memoirs of Edmund de Rothschild, a benevolent man with few enemies. His father Lionel liked to call himself 'a banker by hobby, a gardener by profession', and young Edmund after his birth in 1916 was brought up in country-houses in Hampshire. Fishing and

---

[13]   Barings Archives, Dep 33.21, 23 May 1922, Dep.33.22, 9 Nov. 1923.

[14]   J. Orbell, *Baring Brothers & Co., Limited: a History to 1939* (privately published by Baring Brothers, 1985), pp. 82–3; D. Pollen, *I Remember, I Remember* (privately published, 1983), p. 229.

[15]   Bank of England Archives, ADM 20/31, 15 Apr. 1942, 8 Sept. 1942, 10 Sept. 1942, 2 Oct. 1942.

shooting with the gamekeeper, riding, cruises on the family's 800-ton yacht – it was a golden childhood marred only by anti-Semitic abuse when he was sent away to school. A round-the-world tour followed Cambridge, and in Auckland some spontaneous words about Hitler to a local journalist earned a parental rebuke:

> It has always been a tradition of the Rothschild family never to give interviews. I always refuse. I sometimes see the City Editors of *The Times* and *Daily Telegraph* and I talk to them quite freely because they know that if they ever once quoted me, they would never see me again...

Soon after the war, just as he became a partner, Edmund was sent to New York for a period of training at the investment bank Kuhn Loeb. There the 'drudgery' in the book-keeping, stock transfer and credit departments was bad enough, but the statistical department proved 'even worse', and 'it soon dawned on me that the nuts and bolts of banking were never going to be my greatest strength'. Nor they were, though over the years Edmund provided valuable continuity at Rothschilds, especially after his uncle Anthony's stroke in 1955, and he was good at ensuring a happy ship. Through the memoirs as a whole, there is a sense of the author moving comfortably enough through the upper reaches of British society – though relatively seldom perhaps the stratospheric heights, and with little sense of being near the political action of the day. Domestic life in his Hampshire country-home during the 1950s and 1960s seems to have been resolutely middle-brow (tennis, croquet, Mickey Mouse film shows, mah-jongg, card games), consistent with the almost entire absence in his book of either the world of art, literature and ideas, or any sense of changes in British life and society, or indeed almost any reflection on even the City itself. A book for which the adjective 'amiable' might have been invented, and the only autobiography we have of a twentieth-century merchant banker born into the purple, it will be mined almost as much for what it does *not* say as for what it does.[16]

It was mid-way through Edmund de Rothschild's career, in 1957, that there occurred the celebrated Bank Rate 'leak' and ensuing tribunal. Powerful City figures like William Keswick of Mathesons and Lord Kindersley and Oliver Poole of Lazards were acquitted of wrong-doing, but for the first time the City's inner circle found itself subjected to public gaze and even mockery. Much was made of intimate links with Tory ministers and of decisions taken to sell gilts while grouse-shooting on the Scottish moors.[17] 'We cannot defend a system', declared the shadow Chancellor, Harold Wilson, in the Commons debate on the Tribunal, 'where merchant bankers are treated as the gentlemen and the clearing bankers as the players using the professionals' gate out of the pavilion.'[18] A year later,

---

[16] Edmund de Rothschild, *A Gilt-Edged Life* (London, 1998), including pp. 66, 133–4, 220–1.

[17] P. Ferris, *The City* (London, 1960), pp. 129–57.

[18] *Hansard*, 3 Feb. 1958, col. 859.

with heavy use made of the Tribunal's proceedings, there appeared in the journal *Manchester School* the pioneering analysis by Lupton and Wilson of 'The Social Background and Connections of "Top Decision Makers"', arguably the academic dry-run for Anthony Sampson's massively influential *Anatomy of Britain* that would be published in 1962. One of their categories comprised the directors and partners of fourteen merchant banks or discount houses. For them, Eton easily outnumbered all the other schools put together; White's and Brooks's were the most favoured clubs, with the more intellectual Reform scoring a duck; and a series of intricate diagrams demonstrated the interplay of kinship connections in this privileged sector and at the top of the City generally.[19] Overall, on the eve of the 1960s, the more perceptive of the merchant bankers surely felt that their image did not chime well with the desire for a professional meritocracy that was palpably starting to become the national mood, a mood that at a political level would culminate with Wilson coming to power in 1964 and Heath becoming Tory leader the following year. Could the merchant banks, seldom reticent about boasting of how they lived on their wits, re-invent themselves?

Inevitably, taking the 1960s, 1970s and first half of the 1980s as a whole, the answer is mixed – not least in strictly business terms, where a particularly authoritative assessment is to be found in the 1984 edition of the so-called 'Annual Report' on the City's accepting houses issued by the leading stockbrokers Laing & Cruickshank. They identify a particular cycle, repeated several times in this period, comprising three distinct phases: first, innovation, reflecting the generally small and flexible scale of operation; second, profits, reflecting the way in which (in the report's words) 'as inflation in the 1960s and 1970s swelled corporate banking requirements', so 'lending became a lever into fee-earning services provided in conjunction with more complex transactions'; and third, withdrawal, with what the report calls 'the entry of the bigger brethren', mainly foreign banks with much stronger capital ratios and with no family element anxious to maintain a significant degree of control. Many of these foreign banks had been brought to London by the rapid growth of the Euromarkets, and once their competition began to bite, especially by the 1970s in the Eurobond market, it is arguable that of the merchant banks only Warburgs really stayed the course.[20] Even so, and despite their reluctance to raise their capital base, the City's merchant banks did undoubtedly over this quarter of a century hugely increase the *scope* of their activities: one has only to read the relevant chapters in the histories of Kleinworts, Morgan Grenfell and Schroders to realize this.[21] They may have been only medium-sized players in a global sense, but the 'buzz' was quite different from the preceding four decades.

---

[19] T. Lupton and C.S. Wilson, 'The Social Background and Connections of "Top Decision Makers"', in *Manchester School*, Jan. 1959, pp. 30–51.

[20] Laing & Cruickshank, *Accepting Houses – 1984 Annual Report* (Sept. 1984), pp. 10–11.

[21] J. Wake, *Kleinwort Benson: the History of Two Families in Banking* (Oxford, 1997), chs 11 and 12; K. Burk, *Morgan Grenfell, 1838–1988: the Biography of a Merchant Bank*

Who sat in the parlours? The *Banker* in 1970 popped the question: 'Mr Hambro, you once spoke of "enlightened nepotism." Do you believe that the old banking families will continue to provide leadership as banks grow larger and more complex than in the past?' Jocelyn Hambro replied: 'Some banking families continue to produce hybrid vigour – others do not. There is competition within the family; they undergo rigorous selection and training, and not all members make the grade. But let us hope there will always be some that do'.[22] Through the 1970s and into the 1980s, the Hambros, the Barings and the Rothschilds continued to make that grade in their respective family banks, though in each case there was more scope for non-family promotion than there had been in the past. Overall, there was only patchy progress towards a non-Etonian meritocracy, with by the early 1980s that school still providing seven chairmen of the sixteen members of the Accepting Houses Committee.[23] The case of Schroders is particularly interesting. Back in 1957 it had brilliantly recruited Gordon Richardson, a thoroughgoing middle-class meritocrat with an unglamorous provincial background who through the 1960s gave the bank very professional leadership before in 1973 becoming one of the Bank of England's best governors this century. A clear guideline, one might have thought, when in 1977 Schroders had to choose a new chairman. The two candidates were the Earl of Airlie and James Wolfensohn, the former (to quote the bank's historian) an '"Establishment" figure' who 'personified integrity and prudence, and stood for continuity', the latter an Australian and a 'multifariously talented, intellectually brilliant internationalist', in short 'the embodiment of dynamism'. Schroders – in the year of punk, of Thatcher poised for power, of the City about to change for ever – plumped for the Scottish earl.[24]

How rare was that failure to pick up on the *Zeitgeist*? In the 1960s, arguably, the merchant banks had not done too badly, despite their relative lack of social mobility and proletarian appeal. Big was beautiful, the merchant banking structure itself was going through a fairly intense phase of rationalization, and houses like Warburgs, Schroders and Hill Samuel were well plugged into one of the decade's defining economic themes, the restructuring of British industry. In 1965 that invaluable guide to the *Zeitgeist*, *Queen* magazine, published its survey of English society: who and what were in, who and what were out. Recommended City jobs included a discount house, a jobbing firm, and a 'partnership in a merchant bank'; but to be a stockbroker or an underwriter at Lloyd's was to risk being a social outcast. Three merchant banks were listed as 'in' – Rothschilds, Lazards and Warburgs – and three as 'out' – Morgan Grenfell, Kleinwort Benson and Hill Samuel.[25] The 1970s were rather different. During the early, frenetic years, culminating in the ill-fated Barber boom, there was a sense of the traditional City

---

(Oxford, 1989), chs 7 and 8; Roberts, *Schroders*, chs 13, 14 and 15.

[22]   *Banker*, Aug. 1970, p. 819.

[23]   A. Sampson, *The Changing Anatomy of Britain* (New York, 1982), p. 315.

[24]   Roberts, *Schroders*, p. 484.

[25]   J. Stevens (ed.), 'The Sixties', in *Queen Magazine*, 1987, p. 126.

being by-passed by Slater Walker and its ilk; while later, one's impression is of the merchant banks mainly keeping their heads down, concentrating on their largely international business, and hoping that the eventual fall of Labour would lead to something better. Then in 1979 came Thatcher, the abolition of exchange controls, and in due course, of particular importance to merchant banks, the privatization phenomenon and a wave of ferociously contested takeovers. By the mid-1980s, that time of 'Big Bang' and *Serious Money*, the City seemed to lie at the centre of the national discourse, in a way that it had perhaps not done since the South Sea Bubble. And undoubtedly, in the eyes of most people, the flagships of that City were the merchant banks. Neither they nor those observing them could have imagined the traumas that lay ahead.

Let me finish briefly with some thoughts arising out of reading another recently published merchant banker's autobiography, Peter Spira's *Ladders and Snakes*.[26] The author, a doctor's son, spent the best years of his working life, 1957 to 1974, as a corporate financier at Warburgs. It was a bank that demanded total commitment – at one point Spira describes a dramatic office encounter with Siegmund Warburg at 7 p.m. on Christmas Eve 1962, a Friday to boot – and there is barely a whiff of the gentlemanly capitalist in these memoirs. Spira brings out very evocatively the compelling, powerful but in some ways strangely twisted world of Warburgs in its prime, and one acquires a sense of what made him and his colleagues run as hard as they did. Yet in the end, Spira's account is but one fragment of a much larger mosaic that as yet no historian has come close to assembling. We are fortunate to have had in the last ten years such a fruitful run of house histories, but we still await a Chapman and a Cassis to give us the big but detailed picture of merchant banks and merchant bankers since 1914. As most of those banks now fade from the scene, or at best are reconstituted into something barely recognizable, the right time for that task is surely at hand.

---

[26] P. Spira, *Ladders and Snakes* (privately published by the author, 63 Bedford Gardens, London W8 7EF, 1997).

Bibliography

M. Ackrill and L. Hannah, *Barclays: the Business of Banking 1690–1996* (Cambridge, 2001).

C. Adler, *Jacob Schiff: His Life and Letters* (Garden City, NY, 1928).

S. Adler-Rudel, 'Moritz Baron Hirsch: Profile of a Great Philanthropist', *Leo Baeck Yearbook*, 1971.

B.L. Anderson and P.L. Cottrell, 'Another Victorian Capital Market: a Study of Banking and Bank Investors on Merseyside', in *Economic History Review*, 2nd ser., vol. 28, 1975.

S. Angeli, *Proprietari, commercianti e filandieri a Milano nel primo Ottocento: Il mercato delle sete* (Milan, 1982).

[Anon.], *The Hebrew Talisman* (London, 1840).

[Anon.], *The Story of the Lancashire & Yorkshire Bank Limited 1872–1922* (Manchester, n.d. [1922]).

B. Armani, 'Banchieri e imprenditori ebrei nella Firenze dell'Ottocento: due storie di famiglia tra identità a integrazione', in *Archivi e Imprese*, vol. 16, 1997, pp. 333–64.

J. Armstrong and S. Jones, *Business Documents: Their Origins, Sources and Use in Historical Research* (London/New York, 1987).

M. Aspey, *The Rothschild Archive: a Guide to the Collection* (London, 2000).

A. Aspinall (ed.), *The Letters of King George IV, 1812–30* (Cambridge, 1938).

Associazione Bancaria Italiana, *Annuario delle aziende di credito e finanziarie 1941–49* (Rome, 1949).

Associazione Bancaria Italiana, *Uomini e denaro. Banche e banchieri italiani dal 1222 ad oggi* (Roma, 1952).

P. Assouline, *Le dernier des Camondo* (Paris, 1997).

J. Attali, *Sir Siegmund G. Warburg 1902–1982: Un homme d'influence* (Paris, 1985).

C. Aubert, *Les De la Rüe: Marchands, magistrats et banquiers, Genève, Gênes 1556–1905* (Lausanne, 1984).

D.A. Augustine, *Patricians and Parvenus: Wealth and High Society in Wilhelmine Germany* (Oxford, 1994).

——, 'The Banker in German Society, 1890–1930', in Y. Cassis (ed.), *Finance and Financiers in European History 1880–1960* (London and Paris, 1992).

J. Autin, *Les frères Pereire: Le bonheur d'entreprendre* (Paris, 1984).

J. Ayer, *A century of finance, 1804 to 1904: the London House of Rothschild* (London, 1904).

The Banker, Aug. 1970.

W. Bagehot, *Lombard Street: a Description of the Money Market* (London, 1873).

I. Balbo, *Banche e banchieri a Torino: identità e strategie (1883–1896)*, in *Archivi e imprese*, vol. 21, 1, 2000, pp. 79–85.

B. Balduino, *Un banchiere privato al lavoro: Ritratto di Domenico Balduino*, Tesi di laurea, Università degli Studi di Firenze, Facoltà di Scienze Politiche, anno accademico 1998–99.

F. Balfour, *The Life of George, 4th Earl of Aberdeen* (Paris, 1922).

Banca Commerciale Italiana, Archivio storico, collana inventari, Serie I, vol. I, *Presidenza e consiglio d'amministrazione (1894–1934)* (Milano, 1990).

Bank of England, *Bank of England Liabilities and Assets: 1696 to 1966* (London, 1967).

Bank of England Quarterly Bulletin (Jun. 1967).

Bankers' Magazine (1858, 1860, 1863, 1864, 1866).

A M Banti, *Storia della borghesia italiana: L'età liberale* (Rome, 1996).

B. Barth, 'Deutsch-jüdisch-europäische Privatbankengruppen vor und nach dem Ersten Weltkrieg', Arbeitskreis für Bankgeschichte der GUG, Arbeitspapier no. 5 (1997, unpublished).

A.S.J. Baster, *The Imperial Banks* (London 1929).

——, *The International Banks* (London, 1935).

——, 'The Origins of British Banking Expansion in the Near East', in *Economic History Review*, vol. 5, 1934/5.

R.A. Batchelor, 'The Avoidance of Catastrophe: Two Nineteenth-Century Banking Crises', in F. Capie and G.E. Wood (eds), *Financial Crises and the World Banking System* (London, 1986).

S. Battilossi, 'The History of Banking in Italy: the Debate from the Gerschenkronian Mixed Banks to the Financial Road to Development', in G.D. Feldman et al. (eds), *The Evolution of Modern Financial Institutions in the Twentieth Century*, B 12, Proceedings, Eleventh International Economic History Congress (Milan, 1994).

H. Bauer, *Société de Banque Suisse, 1872–1972* (Basel, 1972).

F. Baudequin, 'Clavière', in *Marchés et Techniques Financières*, vol. 12, 1989, pp. 42–3.

E.D. Becattini, *Firenze bancaria* (Florence, 1913).

——, *Milano bancaria* (Milan, 1907).

J.-F. Belhoste and H. Rouquette, *La Maison Seillière et Demachy, banque de l'industrie et du commerce depuis le XVIIIe siècle* (Paris, 1977).

L. Bergeron, *Banquiers, négociants et manufacturiers parisiens du Directoire à l'Empire* (Paris, 1978).

——, *Les capitalistes en France (1780–1914)* (Paris, 1978).

——, *Les Rothschild et les autres...La gloire des banqiers* (Paris, 1991).

——, 'Pourtalès & Cie (1753–1801): apogée et déclin d'un capitalisme', in *Annales. Economies, Sociétés, Civilisations*, vol. 25, 1970, pp. 498–517.

C.W. Berghoeffer, *Meyer Amschel Rothschild: Der Gründer des Rothschildschen Bankhauses* (Frankfurt am Main, 1924).

J.-F. Bergier, 'Le dynamisme de la banque privée (VIIe–XIXe siècles)', in A. Vannini Marx (ed.), *Credito, banche e investimenti, secoli XIII–XX* (Florence, 1985).

——, *Wirtschaftsgeschichte der Schweiz von den Anfängen bis zur Gegenwart* (Zurich, 1983, 1990).

M. Bergner, *Das württembergische Bankwesen: Entstehung, Ausbau und struktureller Wandel des regionalen Bankwesens bis 1923* (St. Katharinen, 1993).

G. Berta, *Capitali in gioco: Cultura economica e vita finanziaria nella City di fine Ottocento* (Venice, 1990).

A.M. Biscaini Cotula and P.L. Ciocca, 'Le struttura finanziarie: aspetti quantitativi di lungo periodo (1870–1979)', in F. Vicarelli (ed.), *Capitale industriale e capitale finanziario: il caso italiano* (Bologna, 1979).

W. Bodmer, *Der Einfluss der Refugianteneinwanderung von 1550–1700 auf die schweizerische Wirtschaft: Ein Beitrag zur Geschichte des Frühkapitalismus und der Textilindustrie* (Zurich, 1946).

H. Bolitho and D. Peel, *The Drummonds of Charing Cross* (London, 1967).

F. Bonelli, *La crisi del 1907: Una tappa dello sviluppo industriale in Italia* (Turin, 1971).

——, 'Il capitalismo italiano: Linee generali di interpretazione', in *Storia d'Italia, Annali 1* (Turin, 1978).

——, *Lo sviluppo di una grande impresa in Italia: La Terni dal 1884 al 1962* (Turin, 1965).

H. Bonin, *Histoire de banques: Crédit du Nord 1848–1998* (Paris, 1998).

——, *La Banque de l'union parisienne (1874/1904–1974): Histoire de la deuxième grande banque d'affaires française* (Paris, 2001).

——, *Société Générale in the United Kingdom* (Paris, 1996).

——, 'The Case of the French Banks', in R. Cameron and V.I. Bovykin (eds), *International Banking, 1870–1914* (Oxford, 1991).

——, 'The Political Influence of Bankers and Financiers in France in the Years 1850–1960', in Y. Cassis (ed.) *Finance and Financiers in European History 1880–1960* (London and Paris, 1992).

R. Bonney, *The King's Debts: Finance and Politics in France, 1589–1661* (Oxford, 1981).

K. Borchardt, 'Zur Frage des Kapitalmangels in der ersten Hälfte des 19. Jahrhunderts in Deutschland', *Jahrbücher für Nationalökonomie und Statistik*, vol. 173, 1961, pp. 401–21.

K.E. Born, *Geld und Banken im 19. und 20. Jahrhundert* (Stuttgart, 1977).

J. Bouvier, 'Activités bancaires et groupes bancaires', in P. Léon (ed.), *Histoire économique et sociale de la France*, vol. II (Paris, 1978).

——, *Le Crédit Lyonnais de 1863 à 1882: Les années de formation d'une banque de dépôt* (Paris, 1961).

——, *Les Rothschild* (Paris, 1967).

——, *Un siècle de banque française* (Paris, 1973).

S. Bradley and N. Pevsner, *The Buildings of England, London* I: *The City of London* (London, 1997).

B. Bramsen and K. Wain, *The Hambros 1779–1979* (London, 1979).

F. Braudel and E. Labrousse, *Histoire économique et sociale de la France*, vol. III: *L'avènement de l'ère industrielle, 1789–1880* (Paris, 1976).

J.M. Brophy, *Capitalism, Politics, and Railroads in Prussia 1830–1970* (Columbus, 1998).

H. Büchi, 'Solothurnische Finanzzustände im ausgehenden Ancien Régime (ca. 1750–98)', in *Basler Zeitschrift für Geschichte und Altertumskunde*, vol. 15, 1916, pp. 56–116.

C. Burhop, *Die Kreditbanken in der Gründerzeit* (Stuttgart, 2004).

K. Burk, *Morgan Grenfell, 1838–1988: the Biography of a Merchant Bank* (Oxford, 1989).

E. Bussière, *Horace Finaly, banquier 1871–1945* (Paris, 1996).

——, 'La politique financière de la Banque de l'Union Parisienne de 1919 à 1931', Mémoire de maîtrise (University of Paris IV, 1977).

——, *Paribas 1872–1972, l'Europe et le monde* (Antwerp, 1992).

P. Cafaro, 'Finanziamento e ruolo della banca', in S. Zaninelli (ed.), *Storia dell'industria lombarda*, vol. II.1, *Dall'Unità politica alla Grande Guerra* (Milan, 1990).

D.L. Cagliotti, 'Imprenditori evangelici nel Mezzogiorno dell'Ottocento', in *Archivi e imprese*, vol. 8, 16, 1997, pp. 245–81.

R. Cameron, *Banking in the Early Stages of Industrialization* (Oxford, 1967).

——, *La France et le développement économique de l'Europe, 1800–1914* (Paris, 1971).

F. Capie and A. Webber, *A Monetary History of the United Kingdom, 1870–1982*, 2 vols (London, 1985).

F. Capie, 'Structure and Performance in British Banking, 1870–1939', in P.L. Cottrell and D.E. Moggridge (eds), *Money and Power: Essays in Honour of L.S. Pressnell* (Houndmills/London, 1988).

G. Capodaglio, *Fondazione e rendimento della Società Italiana per le Strade Ferrate Meridionali* (Bologna, 1962).

V. Carosso, *The Morgans: Private International Bankers, 1854–1913* (Cambridge, Mass., 1987).

——, *Investment Banking in America* (Harvard Studies in Business History, 1970).

Y. Cassis, *Big Business: the European Experience in the Twentieth Century* (Oxford, 1997).

——, *Capitals of Capital: a History of International Financial Centres, 1780–2005* (Cambridge, 2006).

——, *City Bankers, 1890–1914* (Cambridge, 1994).

—— and J. Tanner, 'Finance and Financiers in Switzerland, 1880–1960', in Y. Cassis (ed.), *Finance and Financiers in European History, 1880–1960* (Cambridge, 1992).

——, 'Financial Elites in Three European Centres: London, Paris, Berlin, 1880s–1930s', in *Business History*, vol. 33, 3, 1991, pp. 53–71.

——, *La City de Londres, 1870–1914* (Paris, 1987).

——, *Les Banquiers de la City à l'époque Edouardienne* (Geneva, 1984).

——, 'London Banks and International Finance, 1890–1914', in Y. Cassis and E. Bussière (eds), *London and Paris as International Financial Centres in the Twentieth Century* (Oxford, 2005).

V. Castronovo, *Economia e società in Piemonte dall'Unità al 1914* (Milan, 1969).

P. Cayez, 'Les capitaux suisses à Lyon sous le Premier Empire', in *Colloque franco-suisse d'histoire économique et sociale*, Geneva, 5–6 May 1967 (Geneva, 1969).

A.D. Chandler jr, *Stati Uniti: L'evoluzione dell'impresa*, in *Storia economica Cambridge*, vol. 7, *L'età del capitale*, II, *Stati Uniti. Giappone. Russia*, ed. by M.M. Postan and P. Mathias (Turin, 1980).

G. Chandler, *Four Centuries of Banking*, II, *The Northern Constituent Banks* (London, 1968).

S. Chapman, *The Foundation of the English Rothschilds: N.M. Rothschild as a Textile Merchant, 1799–1811* (London, 1977).

——, *The Rise of Merchant Banking* (London, 1984).

F.R. Chateaubriand, *Correspondance générale de Chateaubriand* (Paris, 1913).

R. Chernow, *Die Warburgs: Odyssee einer Familie* (Berlin, 1994).

——, *The House of Morgan: an American Banking Dynasty and the Rise of Modern Finance* (New York, 1990).

——, *The Warburgs: the Twentieth-Century Odyssey of a Remarkable Jewish Family* (New York, 1994).

P. Clarke, *Child & Co. 1673–1973: the First House in the City* (London, 1973).

M. Collins, 'English Banks and Business Cycles, 1848–80', in P.L. Cottrell and D.E. Moggridge (eds), *Money and Power: Essays in Honour of L.S. Pressnell* (Houndmills/London, 1988).

——, 'Long-term Growth of the English Banking Sector and Money Stock, 1844–80', in *Economic History Review*, 2nd ser., vol. 36, 1983, pp. 383–5.

——, 'The Banking Crisis of 1878', in *Economic History Review*, 2nd ser., vol. 42, 1989.

[Count] E. Corti, *The Rise of the House of Rothschild* (London, 1928).

A. Confalonieri, *Banca e industria in Italia* (Milan, 1975), 3 vols.

——, *Banca e industria in Italia: Dalla crisi del 1907 all'agosto 1914* (Milan, 1982), vol. I.

L. Conte, *La Banca nazionale: Formazione e attività di una banca di emissione (1843–1861)* (Naples, 1990).

P.L. Cottrell, 'A Cluster of Corporate International Banks, 1855–75', in *Business History*, vol. 33, 3, 1991.

——, 'Albert Grant', in D. Jeremy (ed.), *Dictionary of Business Biography*, vol. II (London, 1984).

——, *British Overseas Investment in the Nineteenth Century, 1870–1914* (London, 1975).

——, 'Credit, Morals and Sunspots: the Financial Boom of the 1860s and Trade Cycle Theory', in P.L. Cottrell and D.E. Moggridge (eds), *Money and Power: Essays in Honour of L.S. Pressnell* (Houndmills/London, 1988).

——, 'David Chadwick', in D. Jeremy (ed.), *Dictionary of Business Biography*, I (London, 1984).

——, *Industrial Finance 1830–1914: the Finance and Organization of English Manufacturing Industry* (London/New York, 1980).

——, *Investment Banking in England 1856–1881: a Case Study of the International Financial Society* (New York/London, 1985).

——, 'London Financiers and Austria 1863–1875: the Anglo-Austrian Bank', in *Business History*, vol. 11, 1969.

——, 'Railway Finance and the Crisis of 1866: Contractors' Bills of Exchange and the Finance Companies', in *Journal of Transport History*, n.s., vol. 3, 1975.

——, 'The Business Man and Financier', in S. and V.D. Lipman (eds), *The Century of Moses Montefiore* (Oxford, 1985).

——, 'The Coalescence of a Cluster of Corporate International banks, 1855–75', in G. Jones (ed.), *Banks and Money: International and Comparative Finance in History* (London, 1991).

——, 'The Domestic Commercial Banks and the City of London, 1870–1939', in Y. Cassis (ed.), *Finance and Financiers in European History 1880–1960* (Cambridge, 1992).

C. Courtney and P. Thompson, *City Lives: the Changing Voices of British Finance* (London, 1996).

V. Cowles, *The Rothschilds: a family of fortune* (London, 1973).

W.F. Crick and J.E. Wadsworth, *A Hundred Years of Joint Stock Banking* (London, 3rd edn, 1958).

M. Da Pozzo and G. Felloni, *La borsa valori di Genova nel XIX secolo* (Turin, 1964).

M.J. Daunton, 'Financial Elites and British Society 1880–1950', in Y. Cassis (ed.), *Finance and Financiers in European History 1880–1960*, London and Paris (Cambridge, 1992).

N. Davenport, *Memoirs of a City Radical* (London, 1974).

J.A. Davis, *Società e imprenditori nel Regno borbonico, 1815–1860* (Bari, 1979).

R. Davis, *The English Rothschilds* (London, 1983).

F.G. Dawson, *The First Latin American Debt Crisis* (London, 1990).

A. De Benedetti, 'Il sistema industriale (1880–1940)', in P. Macry and P. Villani (eds), *Storia d'Italia. Le regioni dall'Unità a oggi: La Campania* (Turin, 1990).

M. De Cecco (ed.), *L'Italia e il sistema finanziario internazionale 1861–1914* (Rome Bari, 1990).

R. De Mattia (ed.), Banca d'Italia, *I bilanci degli istituti di emissione italiani 1845–1936* (Rome, 1967), 2 vols.

—— (ed.), *Gli istituti di emissione in Italia: I tentativi di unificazione (1843–1892)* (Rome Bari, 1990).

De Neuflize, Schlumberger et Cie, 1800–1950 (Paris, 1950).

M.A. Denzel, *Der Preiskurant des Handelshauses Pelloutier & Cie aus Nantes (1763–1793), Beiträge zur Wirtschafts- und Sozialgeschichte*, vol. 73 (Stuttgart, 1997).

——, 'Die Integration Deutschlands in das internationale Zahlungsverkehrssystem im 17. und 18. Jahrhundert', in E. Schremmer (ed.), *Wirtschaftliche und soziale Integration in historischer Sicht, Vierteljahrschrift für Sozial- und Wirtschaftsgeschichte*, vol. 128 (Stuttgart, 1996).

——, *'La Practica della Cambiatura': Europäischer Zahlungsverkehr vom 14. bis zum 17. Jahrhundert* (Stuttgart, 1994).

—— (ed.), *Währungen der Welt, vol. IX: Europäische Wechselkurse von 1383 bis 1620* (Stuttgart, 1995).

L. De Rosa, *Emigranti, capitali e banche (1896–1906)* (Naples, 1980).

——, 'La formazione del sistema bancario italiano', in *Società Italiana degli Storici dell'Economia, Credito e sviluppo economico in Italia dal Medio Evo all'Età contemporanea*, Atti del primo convegno nazionale, 4–6 June 1987 (Verona, 1988).

——, *L'industria metalmeccanica nel Mezzogiorno, 1840–1904* (Naples, 1968),

E.de Rothschild, *A Gilt-edged Life* (London, 1998).

P.F.H. de Serre, *Correspondance du comte de Serre 1796–1824, annotée et publiée par son fils* (Paris, 1876).

J. Dick, 'Banking Statistics of the U.K. in 1896', in *Journal of the Institute of Bankers*, vol. 17, 1897.

——, 'Business in the United Kingdom – Its Progress and Prospects', *Bankers' Magazine* (1894).

P.G.M. Dickson, *Finance and Government under Maria Theresia 1740–1780*, 2 vols (Oxford, 1987).

K. Donaubauer, *Privatbankiers und Bankenkonzentration in Deutschland von der Mitte des 19. Jahrhunderts bis 1932* (Frankfurt/Main, 1988).

G. Doria, *Investimenti e sviluppo economico a Genova alla vigilia della prima guerra mondiale*, vol. I, *Le premesse* (Milan, 1969).

H.T. Easton, *History of a Banking House* (London, 1903).

The Economist (1860, 1865, 1867).

L. Einaudi, 'Prefazione' to M. Segre, *Le banche nell'ultimo decennio con particolare riguardo al loro sviluppo patologico nel dopoguerra* (Milan, 1926).

P. Emden, *Jews of Britain* (London, 1944).

V. Fagiuolo, *I banchieri privati napoletani dall'Unità nazionale alla Prima Guerra Mondiale*, Tesi di laurea, Università degli Studi di Firenze, Facoltà di Scienze Politiche, anno accademico 1999–2000.

G. Federico, *Il filo d'oro: L'industria mondiale della seta dalla restaurazione alla grande crisi* (Venice, 1994).

W. Feldenkirchen, 'Kölner Banken und die Entwicklung des Ruhrgebietes', in *Zeitschrift für Unternehmensgeschichte*, vol. 27, 1982, pp. 81–106.

D. Feldman, *Englishmen and Jews: Social Relations and Political Culture, 1840–1914* (Yale, 1994).

D. Felisini, *Le finanze pontificie e i Rothschild* (Naples, 1990).

S. Fenoaltea, 'Decollo, ciclo e intervento dello stato', in A. Caracciolo (ed.), *La formazione dell'Italia industriale* (Bari, 1969).

——, 'Riflessioni sull'esperienza italiana dal Risorgimento alla prima guerra mondiale', in G. Toniolo (ed.), *Lo sviluppo economico italiano 1861–1940* (Bari, 1973).

N. Ferguson, *Die Geschichte der Rothschilds: Propheten des Geldes*, 2 vols (Stuttgart, 2002).

——, 'The Rothschilds: Finance, Society and Politics in the Nineteenth Century', paper delivered at the conference *Finance and the Making of Modern Capitalism*, Berkeley, University of California, Center for German and European Studies, 1997.

——, *The World's Banker: the History of the House of Rothschild* (London, 1998).

P. Ferris, *The City* (London, 1960).

P. Fierz, *Eine Basler Handelsfirma im ausgehenden 18. und zu Beginn des 19. Jahrhunderts: Christoph Burckhardt & Co. und verwandte Firmen* (Zurich, 1994).

G. Fiocca, 'Credito e conoscenze: le condizioni dell'ascesa imprenditoriale', in G. Fiocca (ed.), *Borghesi e imprenditori a Milano dall'Unità alla prima guerra mondiale* (Rome Bari, 1984).

A. Fischer, 'Jüdische Privatbanken im "Dritten Reich"', in *Scripta Mercaturae*, vol. 28, 1994.

N. Foà, 'Giulio Belinzaghi', in *Dizionario biografico degli italiani*, vol. V (Rome, 1965).

J. Fontana, *La revolucion liberal* (Madrid, 1977).

M. Fournier-Verneuil, *Paris: Tableau moral et philosophique* (Paris, 1826).

R. Fulford, *Glyn's 1753–1953: Six Generations in Lombard Street* (London, 1953).

L. Gall et al., *The Deutsche Bank 1870–1995* (London, 1995).

——, 'The Deutsche Bank from its Founding to the Great War 1870–1914', in L. Gall et al, *The Deutsche Bank* (London, 1995).

A.M. Galli, 'Credito e finanza. La Cassa di Risparmio e la crescita economica e sociale', in G. Rumi et al. (eds), *Milano nell'Unità nazionale 1860–1898* (Milan, 1991).

L.P. Gartner, *The Jewish Immigrant in England, 1870–1914* (London, 1960).

N. Gash, *Mr Secretary Peel* (London, 1961).

A. Gerschenkron, *Economic Backwardness in Historical Perspective* (Cambridge/ Mass., 1962).

——, *Il problema storico dell'arretratezza economica* (Turin, 1965).

B. Gille, *Histoire de la Maison Rothschild, vol. I: Des origines à 1848* (Geneva, 1965) and *Histoire de la Maison Rothschild, vol. II: 1848–70* (Geneva, 1967).

——, *Les investissements français en Italie (1815–1914)* (Turin, 1968).

——, *Lettres adressées à la maison Rothschild de Paris par son correspondant à Bruxelles*, 2 vols (Louvain, 1961, 1963).

A. Giuntini, *Leopoldo e il treno: Le ferrovie nel Granducato di Toscana 1824– 1861* (Naples, 1991).

R. Glanz, 'The Rothschild Legend in America', in *Jewish Social Studies* (1957).

C.A.E. Goodhart, *The Business of Banking 1891–1914* (London, 1972).

R.W. Goldsmith, *Financial Structure and Development* (New Haven, 1969).

[Viscount] Goschen, 'Seven Per Cent', in *Edinburgh Review* (Jan. 1865), reprinted in *Essays and Addresses on Economic Questions* (London, 1905).

——, 'Two Per Cent', in *Edinburgh Review* (Jan. 1868), reprinted in *Essays and Addresses on Economic Questions* (London, 1905).

P. Graham, *Private Banking in the East Midlands: a Study of Samuel Smith Esquire and Co.*, paper delivered at Nottingham University, May 1998.

A. Grant, *Twycross v. Grant and Others: Speech of Albert Grant* (London, 1876).

V. Gray, 'The Return of the Austrian Rothschild Archive', in The Rothschild Archive's *Review of the Year 2001–2000* (2002).

T.E. Gregory, *The Westminster Bank Through a Century*, 2 vols (London, 1936).

L.H. Grindon, *Manchester Banks and Bankers; Historical, Biographical, and Anecdotal* (Manchester, 2nd edn, 1878).

H. Großkreuz, *Privatkapital und Kanalbau in Frankreich 1814–1848: Eine Fallstudie zur Rolle der Banken in der französischen Industrialisierung, Schriften zur Wirtschafts- und Sozialgeschichte*, vol. 28 (Berlin, 1977).

B. Gruber-Meuricroffe, *Die Familie Meuricroffe in Neapel*, s. l., 1970.

G. Guderzo, *Vie e mezzi di comunicazione in Piemonte dal 1831 al 1861* (Turin, 1961).

Guide to The Baring Archive from the Eighteenth to the Early Twentieth Century, 3rd edn (London, ING Bank, 2006).

A.R. Hall, *The London Capital Market and Australia 1870–1914* (Canberra, 1963).

Hansard, 3 Feb. 1958.

J. Harris and P. Thane, 'British and European Bankers, 1880–1914: an "Aristocratic Bourgeoisie"?', in P. Thane, G. Crossick and R. Floud (eds), *The Power of the PastE Essays for Eric Hobsbawm* (Cambridge, 1984).

E. Healey, *Coutts & Co., 1692–1992: the Portrait of a Private Bank* (London/ Sydney/Auckland, 1992).

R. Heilbrunn, *Das Bankhaus J. Dreyfus & Co. 1868–1939* (Frankfurt/Main, 1962, unpublished).

——, 'Das Haus Rothschild: Wahrheit und Dichtung', Vortrag gehalten am 6. März 1963 im Frankfurter Verein für Geschichte und Landeskunde (1963).

W.O. Henderson, *The Zollverein* (London, 1939).

P. Hertner, 'German Banks Abroad Before 1914', in G. Jones (ed.), *Banks as Multinationals* (London, 1990).

——, *Il capitale tedesco in Italia dall'Unità alla prima guerra mondiale. Banche miste e sviluppo economico italiano* (Bologna, 1984).

G. Heuberger (ed.), *The Rothschilds: Essays on the History of a European Family* (Sigmaringen, 1994).

U. Heyn, *Private Banking and Industrialization: the Case of Frankfurt am Main 1825–1875* (New York, 1981).

M.E. Hidy, *George Peabody: Merchant and Financier* (New York, 1978).

R. Hidy, *The House of Baring in American Trade and Finance: English Merchant Bankers at Work, 1763–1861* (Cambridge, Mass., 1949).

[C. Hoare & Co.], *Hoare's Bank: a Record 1673 –1932* (London, 1932).

A.R. Holmes and E. Green, *Midland: 150 Years of Banking Business* (London, 1986).

C.-L. Holtfrerich, *Finanzplatz Frankfurt* (Munich, 1999).

W. Hoth, 'Zur Finanzierung des Eisenbahnstreckenbaus im 19. Jahrhundert', in *Scripta Mercaturae*, vol. 12, 1978, pp. 1–19.

http://www.historikerkommission.gv.at/

http://www.rothschildarchive.org/ib/?doc=/ib/articles/project1

http://www.rothschildarchive.org/ta/

Hundert Jahre Commerzbank, 1870–1970 (Frankfurt/Main, 1970).

H. Iliowzi, *'In the Pale': Stories and Legends of the Russian Jews* (Philadelphia, 1897).

Institut für Bankhistorische Forschung (ed.), *Deutsche Bankengeschichte* (Frankfurt am Main, 1982–1983).

H. James, *Verbandspolitik im Nationalsozialismus. Von der Interessenvertretung zur Wirtschaftsgruppe: Der Centralverband des deutschen Bank- und Bankiergewerbes 1932–1945* (Munich, 2001).

Jewish Chronicle, 24 Apr. 1896, 7 Apr. 1899, 13 Mar. 1908.

G. Jones, *British Multinational Banking 1830–1990* (Oxford, 1993).

J. Jonker, *Mees Pierson. The Link Between Past and Future: 275 Years of Tradition and Innovation in Dutch Banking* (Amsterdam, 1997).

——, 'Spoilt for Choice? Banking Concentration and the Structure of the Dutch Capital Market, 1900–1940', in Y. Cassis, G.D. Feldman and U. Olsson (eds), *The Evolution of Financial Institutions and Markets in Twentieth Century Europe* (Aldershot, 1995).

D. Joslin, *A Century of Banking in Latin America* (Oxford, 1963).

F. Jungmann-Stadler, 'Die Gründung der Bayerischen Hypotheken- und Wechselbank 1834/35', in *Zeitschrift für Bayerische Landesgeschichte*, vol. 60, 1997, pp. 889–924.

M. Jurk, 'The Other Rothschilds: Frankfurt Private Bankers in the 18th and 19th Centuries', in G. Heuberger (ed.), *The Rothschilds: Essays on the History of a European Family* (Sigmaringen, 1994).

J. Kaskel, 'Vom Hoffaktor zur Dresdner Bank: Die Unternehmerfamilie Kaskel im 18. und 19. Jahrhundert', in *Zeitschrift für Unternehmensgeschichte*, vol. 28, 1983, pp. 159–87.

I. Katz, *August Belmont: a Political Biography* (New York, 1968.)

E. Kaufmann, *La banque en France* (Paris, 1914).

C.P. Kindleberger, *A Financial History of Western Europe* (London, 1984).

W.T.C. King, *History of the London Discount Market* (London, 1936).

B. Kirchgässner, 'Zur Geschichte der Deutschen Bank Mannheim und ihrer Vorgänger (1785–1929)', in *Beiträge zu Wirtschafts– und Währungsfragen und zur Bankgeschichte*, vol. 23, 1988, pp. 59–92.

N. Klarmann, 'Unternehmerische Gestaltungsmöglichkeiten des Privatbankiers im 19. Jahrhundert – dargestellt am Beispiel des Hauses Erlanger & Söhne', in H. H. Hofmann (ed.), *Bankherren und Bankiers* (Limburg, 1978).

E. Klein, *Deutsche Bankengeschichte*, vol. 1, *Von den Anfängen bis zum Ende des alten Reiches (1806)* (Frankfurt a.M., 1992).

E. Kleßmann, *M.M. Warburg & Co.: Die Geschichte eines Bankhauses* (Hamburg, 1999).

I. Köhler, *Die 'Arisierung' der Privatbanken im Dritten Reich: Verdrängung, Ausschaltung und die Frage der Wiedergutmachung* (Munich, 2005).

M. Körner, 'Banques publiques et banquiers privés dans la Suisse préindustrielle: Administration, fonctionnement et rôle économique', in *Banchi pubblici, banchi privati e monti di pietà nell'Europa preindustrale*, Atti del Convegno, Genoa, 1–6 October, 1990 (Genoa 1991).

——, 'Banquiers et financiers suisses en France', in *Marchés et Techniques Financières*, vol. 12, 1989, pp. 40–41.

——, 'Expenditure', in R. Bonney (ed.), *Economic Systems and State Finance* (Oxford, 1995).

——, 'Public Credit', in R. Bonney (ed.), *Economic Systems and State Finance* (Oxford, 1995).

——, *Solidarités financières suisses au XVIe siècle: Contribution à l'histoire monétaire, bancaire et financière des Cantons suisses et des Etats voisins* (Lausanne, 1980).

C. Kopper, *Zwischen Marktwirtschaft und Dirigismus: Bankenpolitik im 'Dritten Reich' 1933–1939* (Bonn, 1995), pp. 254–91.

D. Krause, *Garn, Geld und Wechsel: 250 Jahre von der Heydt-Kersten & Söhne* (Wuppertal, 2004).

C. Kreutzmüller, *Händler und Handlungsgehilfen: Der Finanzplatz Amsterdam und die deutschen Großbanken (1918–1945)* (Stuttgart, 2005).

G. Kurgan-van Hentenryk, 'Entre tradition et modernité: le patronat bancaire en Belgique de 1850 à 1950', in *Les entreprises et leurs réseaux : hommes, capitaux, techniques et pouvoirs XIXe–XXe siècles. Mélanges en l'honneur de F. Caron* (Paris, 1998), pp. 457–70.

——, 'Finance and Financiers in Belgium 1880–1940', in Y. Cassis (ed.), *Finance and Financiers in European History* (Cambridge, Paris, 1992).

——, *Gouverner la Générale de Belgique: Essai de biographie collectiv.* (Bruxelles, 1996).

——, 'La formation d'un capitalisme national en Belgique', in *Tijdschrift voor Geschiedenis*, vol. 95, 4, 1982, pp. 488–506.

——, 'La Société Générale 1850–1934', in *La Générale de Banque 1822–1997* (Bruxelles, 1997).

——, 'Les banques européennes aux XIXe et XXe siècles', in H. van der Wee, R. Bogaert and G.Kurgan-van Hentenryk, *La Banque en Occident* (Anvers, 1991).

——, S. Jaumain and V. Montens, *Dictionnaire des patrons en Belgique: Les hommes, les entreprises, les réseaux* (Bruxelles, 1996).

D. Kynaston, *Cazenove & Co.: a History* (London, 1991).

——, *The City of London*, 2 vols (London, 1994, 1995).

E. Labrousse (ed.), *Histoire économique et sociale de la France*, vol. II: Des derniers temps de l'âge seigneurial aux préludes de l'âge industriel (1663–1789) (Paris, 1970).

J. Laffitte, *Mémoires de Laffitte* (Paris, 1932).

Laing & Cruickshank, *Accepting Houses – 1984 Annual Report* (Sept. 1984).

S. Lanaro, 'Genealogia di un modello', in S. Lanaro (ed.), *Storia d'Italia: Le regioni dall'Unità a oggi, Il Veneto* (Turin, 1984).

D.S. Landes, *Bankers and Pashas* (London, 1958).

——, 'Vieille Banque et Banque Nouvelle: la révolution bancaire du XIXe siècle', in *Revue d'Histoire moderne et contemporaine*, vol. 3, 1956, pp. 204ff.

J. Landmann, 'Der schweizerische Kapitalexport', in *Zeitschrift für schweizerische Statistik und Volkswirtschaft*, vol. 52, 1916, pp. 389–415.

——, *Die auswärtigen Kapitalanlagen aus dem Berner Staatsschatz im XVIII. Jahrhundert: Eine finanzhistorische Studie* (Zurich, 1903).

——, *Leu & Co. 1755–1905: Ein Beitrag zur Geschichte der öffentlichen und privaten Kreditorganisation* (Zurich, 1905).

H. Lefevre, *Le Change et la Banque* (Paris, 1880).

J.A.S.L. Leighton-Boyce, *Smiths the Bankers 1658–1958* (London, 1958).

S. Levati, *La nobiltà del lavoro: negozianti e banchieri a Milano tra Ancien Régime e restaurazione* (Milan, 1997).

P. Léon (ed.), *Histoire économique et sociale du monde*, vols I–IV (Paris, 1977–8).

——, 'Prestige du monde de la finance', in P. Léon (ed.), *Histoire économique et sociale du monde*, vol. II (Paris, 1978).

Le Refuge huguenot en Suisse (Lausanne, 1985).

M. Lévy-Leboyer, 'Le crédit et la monnaie', in *Histoire économique et sociale de la France*, vol. 3: 1789-années 1880 (Paris, 1976).

——, *Les banques européennes et l'industrialisation internationale dans la première moitié du XIXe siècle* (Paris, 1964).

——, *Les banques européennes et l'industrialisation internationale dans la première moitié du XIXe siècle*, in: P. Léon (ed.), *Histoire économique et sociale du monde*, vol. III, L'avènement de l'ère industrielle (1789-années 1850), vol. 1 (Paris, 1976).

——, 'Préface', *Les banques en Europe de l'Ouest de 1920 à nos jours* (Paris, 1995).

S. Licini, 'Banca e credito a Milano nella prima fase dell'industrializzazione (1840–1880)', in E. Decleva (ed.), *Antonio Allievi: dalle 'scienze civili' alla pratica del credito* (Milan Rome Bari, 1997).

A. Liesse, *Evolution of Credit and Banking in France* (Washington, 1909).

D. Lieven, *The Private Letters of Princess Lieven to Prince Metternich, 1820–1826* (London, 1948).

V.D. Lipman, *A Century of Social Service, 1859–1959: the Jewish Board of Guardians* (London, 1959).

M. Lisle-Williams, 'Merchant Banking Dynasties in the English Class Structure: Ownership, Solidarity and Kinship in the City of London, 1850–1960', in *British Journal of Sociology*, vol. 35, 1984, pp. 333–62.

G. Livet, 'Les guerres de réligion', *Que sais-je?*, 1016 (Paris, 1962).

T. Lupton and C.S. Wilson, 'The Social Background and Connections of "Top Decision Makers"', in *Manchester School*, Jan. 1959, pp. 30–51.

H. Lüthy, *La Banque Protestante en France de la Révocation de l'Édit de Nantes à la Révolution*, 2 vols (Paris 1959–1961).

G. Luzzatto, *L'economia italiana dal 1861 al 1894* (Turin, 1968).

S. Mace, 'The Archives of the London Merchant Bank of N.M. Rothschild & Sons', in *Business Archives: Sources and History*, vol. 64, 1992, pp. 1–14.

P. Macry, *Ottocento: Famiglia, élites e patrimoni a Napoli* (Turin, 1988).

G. Maifreda, 'Banchieri e patrimoni ebraici nella Milano ottocentesca', in D. Bigazzi (ed.), *Storie di imprenditori* (Bologna, 1996).

——, 'La costruzione di un rapporto fiduciario: Francesco Crispi e la banca Weill-Schott', in *Archivi e imprese*, vol. 16, 1997, pp. 285–6.

M. Marmo, 'Speculazione e credito mobiliare a Napoli nella congiuntura degli anni '80', in *Quaderni storici*, vol. 2, 1976.

K. Martin, *Editor: a Second Volume of Autobiography, 1931–1945* (London, 1968).

V.M. Martin, *Los Rothschild y las Minas de Almadén* (Madrid, 1980).

M. Mazbouri, *L'émergence de la place financière Suisse (1890–1913): Itinéraire d'un grand banquier* (Lausanne, 2005).

J.P. McKay, 'The House of Rothschild (Paris) as a Multinational Industrial Enterprise, 1875–1914', Conference on *Multinational Enterprise in Historical Perspective* (University of East Anglia, 1985).

C. Meier, *Die Entstehung des Börsengesetzes vom 22. Juni 1896* (St. Katharinen, 1993).

M. Meriggi, *Milano borghese: Circoli ed élites nell'Ottocento* (Venice, 1992).

B. Michel, *Banques et banquiers en Autriche au début du vingtième siècle* (Paris, 1976).

R.C. Michie, 'Income, Expenditure and Investment of a Victorian Millionaire: Lord Overstone, 1823–1883', in *Bulletin of the Institute for Historical Research*, vol. 58, 137, May 1985.

——, *The City of London: Continuity and Change, 1850–1990* (Basingstoke and London, 1992).

——, *The London and New York Stock Exchanges, 1850–1914* (London, 1987).

D.E. Moggridge, 'Keynes as a Monetary Historian', in P.L. Cottrell and D.E. Moggridge (eds), *Money and Power: Essays in Honour of L.S. Pressnell* (Houndmills/London, 1988).

A. Moioli, *Il commercio serico lombardo*, in *La seta in Europa (secc. XIII–XX)*, Atti della XXIV Settimana di studio dell'Istituto internazionale di storia economica 'F. Datini' (Florence 1993).

G. Mori, 'Dall'unità alla guerra: aggregazione e disgregazione di un'area regionale', in G. Mori (ed.), *Storia d'Italia. Le regioni dall'Unità a oggi: La Toscana* (Turin, 1986).

——, *L'industria del ferro in Toscana dalla Restaurazione alla fine del Granducato (1815–1859)* (Turin, 1966).

W.E. Mosse, *Jews in the German Economy: the German-Jewish Economic Elite 1820–1935* (Oxford, 1987).

E.V. Morgan and W.A. Thomas, *The Stock Exchange* (London, 1962).

E.W. Monter, 'Swiss Investment in England, 1697–1720', in *International Review of the History of Banking*, vol. 2, 1969, pp. 285–98.

L.H. Mottet, *Geschichte der Schweizer Banken: Bankier-Persönlichkeiten aus fünf Jahrhunderten* (Zurich, 1987).

L. Mottu-Weber, *Genève au siècle de la Réforme: Economie et refuge* (Geneva Paris, 1987).

——, 'Vie économique et refuge à Genève à la fin du XVIIe siècle', in *Genève au temps de la Révocation de l'édit de Nantes 1680–1705* (Geneva, 1985).

R. Muir and C. White, *Over the Long Haul: the Story of J. & W. Seligman & Company* (New York: privately printed, 1964).

L. Neal, *The Rise of Financial Capitalism: International Capital Markets in the Age of Reason* (Cambridge, 1990).

W. Newmarch, 'The Increase in the Number of Banks and Branches... 1858–1878', in *Bankers' Magazine* (1879), pp. 849–61.

D. Newsome, *A History of Wellington College, 1859–1959* (London, 1959).

S. Nishimura, 'The French Provincial Banks, the Banque de France and Bill Finance, 1890–1913', in *Economic History Review*, vol. 48, 3, 1995.

——, *The Decline of Inland Bills of Exchange in the London Money Market 1855–1913* (Cambridge, 1971).

H. Obenaus, 'Finanzkrise und Verfassungsgebung zu den sozialen Bedingungen des frühen deutschen Konstitutionalismus', in G.A. Ritter (ed.), *Gesellschaft, Parlament und Regierung* (Düsseldorf, 1984).

D.P. O'Brien (ed.), *The Correspondence of Lord Overstone*, vols 1–3 (London, 1971).

J. Orbell, *Asset Management and Barings: a Note on the Origins* (privately published by ING Barings plc, 1966).

——, *Baring Brothers & Co., Limited: a History to 1939* (privately published by Baring Brothers, 1985).

—— and A. Turton, *British Banking: a Guide to Historical Records* (Aldershot, 2001).

R. Palin, *Rothschild Relish* (London, 1970).

P. Palumbo, *Banchieri privati* (Turin, 1921).

S. Paquier, 'Swiss Holding Companies from the Mid-nineteenth Century to the Early 1930s: the Forerunners and Subsequent Waves of Creation', in *Financial History Review*, vol. 8, 2, 2001, pp. 163–82.

C. Pavese, 'Le origini della Società Edison e il suo sviluppo fino alla costituzione del "gruppo" (1881–1919)', in B. Bezza (ed.), *Energia e sviluppo: L'industria elettrica italiana e la Società Edison* (Turin, 1986).

E.J. Perkins, 'Conflicting Views on Fiat Currency: Britain and Its North American Colonies in the Eighteenth Century', in *Business History*, vol. 33, 1991, pp. 8–30.

——, *Financing Anglo-American Trade: the House of Brown, 1800–1880* (Cambridge, Mass., 1975).

R. Petri, *La frontiera industriale: Territorio, grande industria e leggi speciali prima della Cassa per il Mezzogiorno* (Milan, 1990).

H.C. Peyer, *Von Handel und Bank im alten Zürich* (Zurich, 1968).

Pictet & Cie, 1805–1955 (Geneva, 1955).

G. Piluso, *Dalla seta alla banca: Moneta e credito a Milano nell'Ottocento (1802–1860)*, Università Bocconi, dottorato di ricerca in Storia economica e sociale, VIII ciclo, anni accademici 1994–96.

——, *Il mercato del credito a Milano dopo l'Unità: strutture e dinamiche evolutive*, in *Banche e reti di banche nell'Italia postunitaria*, ed. by G. Conti and S.

La Francesca, vol. II, *Formazione e sviluppo di mercati locali del credito* (Bologna, 2000), pp. 503–56.

——, *L'arte dei banchieri: Moneta e credito a Milano da Napoleone all'Unità* (Milano, 1999).

——, 'Sulla struttura dell'offerta di credito in Italia: mercati e squilibri regionali (1860–1936)', in *Storia e problemi contemporanei*, vol. VIII (Roma, 1995).

E. Piscitelli, 'Figure di grandi banchieri italiani: Domenico Balduino', in *Bancaria*, vol. 41, 1958, p. 1292.

G.B. Pittaluga, *La monetizzazione del Regno d'Italia*, in *Il progresso economico dell'Italia: Permanenze, discontinuità, limiti*, ed. by P.L. Ciocca (Bologna, 1994).

A.-M. Piuz et al. (eds), *L'Economie genevoise de la Réforme à la fin de l'Ancien Régime, XVIe–XVIIIe siècles* (Geneva, 1990).

A. Plessis, 'Bankers in French Society, 1860s–1960s', in Y. Cassis (ed.) *Finance and Financiers in European History 1880–1960* (London and Paris, 1992).

——, 'Le "retard" français: la faute à la banque? Banques locales, succursales de la Banque de France et financement de l'économie sous le Second Empire', in P. Fridenson and A. Straus (eds), *Le capitalisme français, 19ᵉ–20ᵉ siècles: Blocages et dynamisme d'une croissance* (Paris, 1987).

——, 'Les banques locales, de l'essor du Second Empire à la "crise" de la Belle Epoque', in M. Lescure and A. Plessis (eds), *Banques locales et banques régionales en France au XIXᵉ siècle* (Paris, 1999).

——, *Régents et gouverneurs de la Banque de France sous le Second Empire* (Geneva, 1985).

V. Poggiali, *Storia della Banca Morgan Vonwiller* (Milano, 1969).

H. Pohl, 'Das deutsche Bankwesen (1806–1848)', *Deutsche Bankengeschichte*, ed. im Auftrag des Instituts für bankhistorische Forschung, vol. 2 (Frankfurt am Main, 1982).

H. Pohl (ed.), *Europäische Bankengeschichte* (Frankfurt/Main, 1993).

M. Pohl, T. Tortella and H. Van der Wee (eds), *A Century of Banking Consolidation in Europe* (Aldershot, 2001).

—— et al., *Deutsche Bankengeschichte*, 3 vols (Frankfurt/Main, 1982).

——, 'Die Entwicklung des deutschen Bankwesens zwischen 1848 und 1870', in Institut für Bankhistorische Forschung (ed.), *Deutsche Bankengeschichte* (Frankfurt/ Main, 1982–83).

——, 'Festigung und Ausdehnung des deutschen Bankwesens zwischen 1870 und 1914', in Institut für bankhistorische Forschung e.V. (ed.), *Deutsche Bankengeschichte*, vol. 2 (Frankfurt, 1982).

——, *Hamburger Bankengeschichte* (Mainz, 1986).

—— (ed.), *Handbook on the History of European Banks* (Aldershot and Brookfield, 1994).

——, *Konzentration im deutschen Bankwesen (1848–1980)* (Frankfurt/Main, 1982).

M. Pohle, 'Risk, Information and Noise: Risk Perception and Risk Management of French and German Banks During the Nineteenth Century', in *Financial History Review*, vol. 2, 1, 1995, pp. 25–39.

D. Pollen, *I Remember, I Remember* (privately published, 1983).

A. Polsi, *Alle origini del capitalismo italiano: Stato, banche e banchieri dopo l'Unità* (Torino, 1993).

——, *Stato e banca centrale in Italia: Il governo della moneta e del sistema bancario dall'Ottocento a oggi* (Roma Bari, 2001).

S.S. Prawer, *Heine's Jewish Comedy: a Study of His Portraits of Jews and Judaism* (Oxford, 1983).

L.S. Pressnell, 'Gold Reserves, Banking Reserves, and the Baring Crisis of 1890', in C.R. Whittlesey and J.S.G. Wilson (eds), *Essays in Money and Banking in Honour of R.S. Sayers* (Oxford, 1968).

——, and J. Orbell, *A Guide to the Historical Records of British Banking* (Aldershot, 1985).

F. Prochaska, 'Philanthropy', in F.M.L. Thompson (ed.), *The Cambridge Social History of Britain, 1750–1950*, vol. 3 (Cambridge, 1990).

F. Prochaska, *Philanthropy and the Hospitals of London: the King's Fund 1897–1990* (Oxford,1992).

——, *Royal Bounty: the Making of a Welfare Monarchy* (Yale, 1995).

——, *The Voluntary Impulse: Philanthropy in Modern Britain* (London, 1988).

——, *Women and Philanthropy in 19th Century England* (Oxford, 1980).

F. Redlich, *The Molding of American Banking: Men and Ideas* (New York, 1968).

J. Reeves, *The Rothschilds: the Financial Rulers of Nations* (London, 1887).

A.M. Regalsky, *Marchés financiers, groupes d'investissement et élites locales: Les investissements français en Argentine, 1880–1914* (thesis, University de Paris I, 1997).

M. Reitmayer, *Bankiers im Kaiserreich: Sozialprofil und Habitus der deutschen Hochfinanz* (Göttingen, 1999).

——, 'Der Strukturwandel im Bankwesen und seine Folgen für die Geschäftstätigkeit der Privatbankiers im Deutschen Reich bis 1914', in idem, *Der Privatbankier: Nischenstrategien in Geschichte und Gegenwart* (Stuttgart, 2003).

R. Roberts, *Schroders: Merchants & Bankers* (Basingstoke, 1992).

——, 'What's in a Name? Merchants, Merchant Bankers, Accepting Houses, Issuing Houses, Industrial Bankers and Investment Bankers', in *Business History*, vol. 35, 3, 1993.

M. Romani, *Storia economica d'Italia nel secolo XIX* (Bologna, 1982).

R. Romano, *L'industria cotoniera lombarda dall'Unità al 1914* (Milano, 1992).

R.R. Rosenbaum and A.J. Sherman, *M.M. Warburg & Co. 1798–1938: Merchant Bankers of Hamburg* (London, 1979).

N. Röthlin, 'Ein Blick auf die Bezugs- und Absatzgebiete des schweizerischen Grosshandels anhand einiger Bilanzen aus dem 18. Jahrhundert', in P. Bairoch et al. (eds), *Die Schweiz in der Weltwirtschaft / La Suisse dans l'économie mondiale* (Zurich, 1990).

[Lord Victor] Rothschild, *The Shadow of a Great Man* (London, 1982).

A. Sablon du Corail, J. Comble and M. Aspey, 'Rothschild Reunited: the Records of de Rothschild Frères', in The Rothschild Archive's *Review of the Year 2004–2005* (2005).

A. Sabouret, *MM. Lazard Frères et Cie: Une saga de la fortune* (Paris, 1987).

A. Sampson, *The Changing Anatomy of Britain* (New York, 1982).

V. Sannucci, 'Molteplicità delle banche di emissione: ragioni economiche ed effetti sull'efficacia del controllo monetario (1860–1890)', in *Ricerche per la storia della Banca d'Italia*, vol. I (Rome Bari, 1990).

R.S. Sayers, *Gilletts in the London Money Market 1867–1967* (Oxford, 1968).

——, *Lloyds Bank in the History of English Banking* (Oxford, 1957).

F. Schaum, *Das Französische Bankwesen* (Stuttgart, 1931).

R. Schofield, *Along Rothschild Lines: the Story of Rothschild and Railways across the World* (London, 2002).

[Sir] W. Schooling, *Alliance Assurance, 1824–1924* (London, 1924).

L. Segreto, 'La formazione del patrimonio dei Feltrinelli', in Società Italiana degli Storici dell'economia, *Tra rendita e investimenti: Formazione e gestione dei grandi patrimoni in Italia in età moderna e contemporanea*, atti del Terzo Convegno nazionale, Torino, 22–23 novembre 1996 (Bari, 1998).

——, Monte Amiata. *Il mercurio italiano: Strategie internazionali e vincoli extraeconomici* (Milan, 1991), pp. 30f.

L.A.M. Sencicle, *Banking on Dover* (London, 1993).

H. A. Shannon, 'The Limited Companies of 1866–1883', in *Economic History Review*, vol. 7, 1933.

C. Shaw, *The Necessary Security: an Illustrated History of Rothschild Bonds* (London, 2006).

M. Simon, 'The Pattern of New British Portfolio Foreign Investment, 1865–1914', reprinted in A.R. Hall (ed.), *The Export of Capital from Britain 1870–1914* (London, 1968).

S. Snell, *Stuckey's Bank: the Importance of a Family Banking Concern on the Economy of Langport and Somerset, 1770–1909*, paper delivered at the Langport and District Historical Society, Feb. 1998.

C.P. Snow, *The Conscience of the Rich* (New York, 1958).

[Messrs.] Spackman, *The Commercial History and Review of 1863* [supplement to *The Economist* (20 Feb. 1864)].

——, *The Commercial History and Review of 1866* [supplement to *The Economist* (9 Mar. 1867)].

P. Spira, *Ladders and Snakes* (privately published by the author, 63 Bedford Gardens, London W8 7EF, 1997).

H. Steffen, *Die Kompanien Kaspar Jodok Stockalpers: Beispiel eines Soldunternehmers im 17. Jahrhundert* (Brig, 1975).

F. Stern, *Gold and Iron: Bismarck, Bleichröder and the Building of the German Empire* (London, 1977).

J. Stevens (ed.), 'The Sixties', in *Queen Magazine*, 1987.

Storia di Milano, vol. 15, *Nell'Unità italiana 1859–1900*, Fondazione Treccani degli Alfieri per la storia di Milano (Milano, 1962).

M. Stürmer, G. Teichmann and W. Treue, *Striking the Balance: Sal. Oppenheim jr. & Cie., a Family and a Bank* (London, 1994).

——, *Wägen und Wagen: Sal. Oppenheim jr. & Cie.: Geschichte einer Bank und einer Familie* (Munich, Zürich, 1989, 3rd edn 1994).

[Sir John] N. Summerson, *The Architecture of Victorian London* (Charlottesville VA, 1976).

B.E. Supple, 'A Business Elite: German-Jewish Financiers in Nineteenth Century New York', in *Business History Review*, vol. 31, 2, 1957, pp. 143–78.

J. Sykes, *The Amalgamation Movement in English Banking 1825–1924* (London, 1929).

R. Sylla, 'The Role of Banks', in R. Sylla and G. Toniolo (eds), *Patterns of European Industrialization: the Nineteenth Century* (London, 1991).

G. Teichmann, 'Archive Survey: Sal. Oppenheim jr. & Cie., Cologne', in *Financial History Review*, vol. 1, 1994, pp. 69–78.

——, 'Das Bankhaus Oppenheim und die industrielle Entwicklung im Aachener Revier von 1836–1855', in M. Köhler and K. Ulrich (eds), *Banken, Konjunktur und Politik* (Essen, 1995).

P. Thane, 'Cassel, Sir Ernest Joseph', in D.J. Jeremy (ed.), *Dictionary of Business Biography*, vol. 1 (London, 1984).

P.G. Thielen, *Karl August von Hardenberg, 1750–1822* (Cologne/Berlin, 1967).

The Times, 4 Aug. 1836, 22 Apr. 1896, 5 Jan. 1996.

F.M.L. Thompson, *English Landed Society in the 19th Century* (London, 1971).

H. Thring, *Joint Stock Companies Acts 1857* (London, 1858).

R. Tilly, 'An Overview of the Role of the Large German Banks up to 1914', in Y. Cassis (ed.), *Finance and Financiers in European History, 1880–1960* (Cambridge, 1992).

——, *Financial Institutions and Industrialization in the Rhineland 1815–1870* (Madison, 1966).

——, 'German Banking, 1850–1914: Development Assistance for the Strong', in *Journal of European Economic History*, vol. 15, 1986, pp. 113–52.

——, 'International Aspects of the Development of German Banking', in R. Cameron and V. Bovykin (eds), *International Banking 1870–1914* (Oxford, 1991).

S. Tilman, *Les grands banquiers belges (1830–1935): Portrait collectif d'une élite* (Bruxelles, 2006).

K.S. Toft, 'A Mid-Nineteenth Century Attempt at Banking Control', in *Revue Internationale d'Histoire de la Banque*, vol. 3, 1970.

G. Toniolo, *Storia economica dell'Italia liberale 1850–1918* (Bologna, 1988).

W. Treue, 'Das Bankhaus Mendelssohn als Beispiel einer Privatbank im 19. und
20. Jahrhundert', in *Mendelssohn Studien*, vol. 1, 1972, pp. 29–80.

——, 'Das Privatbankwesen im 19. Jahrhundert', in H. Coing (ed.), *Wissenschaft
und Kodifikation des Privatrechts im 19. Jahrhundert*, vol. 5 (Frankfurt/Main,
1980).

——, 'Der Privatbankier am Wende der 19. zum 20. Jahrhundert', in *Tradition*,
vol. 5, 1970.

——, 'Die Gründung der Internationalen Bank von Luxemburg vor 125 Jahren',
in *Bankhistorisches Archiv*, vol. 7, 1981, pp. 3–15.

H.P. Ullmann, 'Der Frankfurter Kapitalmarkt um 1800: Entstehung, Struktur
und Wirkung einer modernen Finanzinstitution', in *Vierteljahrschrift für
Wirtschafts- und Sozialgeschichte*, vol. 77, 1990, pp. 75–92.

K. Ulrich, *Aufstieg und Fall der Privatbankiers: Die wirtschaftliche Entwicklung
von 1918 bis 1938* (Frankfurt/Main, 1998).

——, 'Von Simon Hirschland zu Burkhardt & Co.: Die Geschichte des
traditionsreichsten Bankhauses des Ruhrgebietes', in J.-P. Barbian and L. Heid
(eds), *Die Entstehung des Ruhrgebietes* (Düsseldorf, 1996).

H. Van der Wee (ed.), *La banque en occident* (Gent, 1991).

—— (ed.), *The Generale Bank 1822–1897* (Tielt, 1997).

B. Veyrassat, *Négociants et fabricants dans l'industrie cotonnière suisse 1760–
1840: Aux origines financières de l'industrialisation* (Lausanne, 1982).

F. Vittinghoff et al. (eds), *Handbuch der europäischen Wirtschafts- und
Sozialgeschichte*, vol. 3–4 (Frankfurt, 1986, 1993).

A. Volpi, *Banchieri e mercato finanziario in Toscana (1801–1860)* (Firenze,
1997).

F. von Gentz, *Briefe von Friedrich von Gentz an Pilat: Ein Beitrag zur Geschichte
Deutschlands im XIX. Jahrhundert*, ed. by K. von Mendelssohn-Bartholdy
(Leipzig, 1868).

J. Wake, *Kleinwort Benson: the History of Two Families in Banking* (Oxford, 1997).

B. Wehrli, *Das Finanzsystem Zürichs gegen Ende des 18. Jahrhunderts* (Aarau,
1944).

C. Wetzel, *Die Auswirkungen des Reichsbörsengesetzes von 1896 auf die
Effektenbörsen im Deutschen Reich* (Münster, 1996).

J. White, *Rothschild Buildings: Life in an East End Tenement Block, 1887–1920*
(London,1980).

K. Williams, *From Pauperism to Poverty* (London, 1981).

H. Winkel, 'Kapitalquellen und Kapitalverwendung am Vorabend des industriellen
Aufschwungs in Deutschland', in *Schmollers Jahrbuch*, vol. 90, 1970, pp.
275–301.

W. Winterstein, 'Privatbanken', in H. Pohl (ed.), *Das Bankwesen in Deutschland
und Spanien 1860–1960* (Frankfurt, 1997).

H. Wixforth, *Banken und Schwerindustrie in der Weimarer Republik* (Cologne, 1995).

—— and D. Ziegler, '"Bankenmacht": Universal Banking and German Industry in Historical Perspective', in Y. Cassis et al. (eds), *The Evolution of Financial Institutions and Markets in Twentieth-Century Europe* (Aldershot, 1995).

—— and D. Ziegler, 'Deutsche Privatbanken und Privatbankiers im 20. Jahrhundert', in *Geschichte und Gesellschaft*, vol. 23, 1997, pp. 205–35.

—— and D. Ziegler, 'The Niche in the Universal Banking System: the Role and Significance of Private Bankers within German Industry, 1900–1933', in *Financial History Review*, vol. 1, pp. 99–119.

L. Wolf, 'Rothschildiana', in idem, *Essays in Jewish History*, ed. by C. Roth (London, 1934).

S. Xenos, *Depredations, or Overend, Gurney & Co., and the Greek & Oriental Steam Navigation Company* (London, 1869).

K. Yamamura, 'L'industrializzazione del Giappone. Impresa, proprietà e gestione', in A. Chandler et al., *Evoluzone della Grande Impresa e Management* (Turin, 1986).

V. Zamagni, *Dalla periferia al centro: La seconda rinascita economica dell'Italia 1861–1981* (Bologna, 1990).

D. Ziegler, 'Banking and the Rise and Expansion of Industrial Capitalism in Germany', in A. Teichova et al. (eds), *Banking Trade and Industry: Europe, America and Asia from the Thirteenth to the Twentieth Century* (Cambridge, 1997).

——, *Eisenbahnen und Staat im Zeitalter der Industrialisierung* (Stuttgart, 1996).

——, 'Eugen Gutmann – Unternehmer und Großbürger', in *Eugen-Gutmann-Gesellschaft – Gründungsversammlung* (Frankfurt/Main, 2003b, unpublished).

——, 'Geschäftliche Spezialisierungen deutscher Privatbankiers in der Zwischenkriegszeit: Ein vergeblicher Überlebenskampf?', in idem *Der Privatbankier: Nischenstrategien in Geschichte und Gegenwart* (Stuttgart, 2003a).

—— and H. Wixforth, 'The Niche in the Universal Banking System: the Role and Significance of Private Bankers within German Industry, 1900–1933', in *Financial History Review*, vol. 1, 2, 1994, pp. 99–119.

P. Ziegler, *The Sixth Great Power: Barings, 1762–1929* (London, 1988).

Index